LINUX
COOKBOOK™

Other Linux resources from O'Reilly

Related titles
Linux Device Drivers
Linux in a Nutshell
Running Linux
Building Embedded Linux Systems
Linux Security Cookbook

Exploring the JDS Linux Desktop
Learning Red Hat Enterprise Linux and Fedora
Linux Pocket Guide
Understanding the Linux Kernel

Linux Books Resource Center
linux.oreilly.com is a complete catalog of O'Reilly's books on Linux and Unix and related technologies, including sample chapters and code examples.

ONLamp.com is the premier site for the open source web platform: Linux, Apache, MySQL, and either Perl, Python, or PHP.

Conferences
O'Reilly brings diverse innovators together to nurture the ideas that spark revolutionary industries. We specialize in documenting the latest tools and systems, translating the innovator's knowledge into useful skills for those in the trenches. Visit *conferences.oreilly.com* for our upcoming events.

Safari Bookshelf (*safari.oreilly.com*) is the premier online reference library for programmers and IT professionals. Conduct searches across more than 1,000 books. Subscribers can zero in on answers to time-critical questions in a matter of seconds. Read the books on your Bookshelf from cover to cover or simply flip to the page you need. Try it today with a free trial.

LINUX
COOKBOOK™

Carla Schroder

O'REILLY®

Beijing · Cambridge · Farnham · Köln · Paris · Sebastopol · Taipei · Tokyo

Linux Cookbook™
by Carla Schroder

Copyright © 2005 O'Reilly Media, Inc. All rights reserved.
Printed in the United States of America.

Published by O'Reilly Media, Inc., 1005 Gravenstein Highway North, Sebastopol, CA 95472.

O'Reilly books may be purchased for educational, business, or sales promotional use. Online editions are also available for most titles (*safari.oreilly.com*). For more information, contact our corporate/institutional sales department: (800) 998-9938 or *corporate@oreilly.com*.

Editor:	Mike Loukides
Production Editor:	Colleen Gorman
Cover Designer:	Emma Colby
Interior Designer:	David Futato

Printing History:

December 2004:	First Edition.

 This book uses RepKover™, a durable and flexible lay-flat binding.

ISBN: 0-596-00640-3
[M]

To Dawn Marie.

*During the writing of this book, she tilled the
fields, trained the horses, cooked the meals,
cleaned the ditches, and graciously fended off
generous neighbors bearing large zucchinis.
No author could ask for more. Thank you
for 14 great years; may we have many more.*

Table of Contents

Preface

So: you're a relatively new Linux user. You've got Linux installed, you've managed to log in, do some web browsing, send and receive email, and—now what? Although you can handle some of the basics, you feel like you're flying blind: you know you've got lots of really powerful stuff at your fingertips, or at least so your Linux guru friend told you, but how do you make it do tricks? What's there, and how does it work? What's this thing called grep that they're always talking about? How do you Samba? And where's the #$%^ documentation?

The Linux-Unix world is abundantly documented. No, really! You can always find an answer, if you know where to look. The problem, of course, is knowing where to look. There are man pages, info pages, READMEs, HTML manuals, and the code itself. You don't have to be a programmer to unearth useful bits in source code, because the comments often tell you what you need to know.

There are thousands upon thousands of online communities, one (or more) surrounding nearly every bit of software in the Linux universe. Nearly every program, no matter how small, has its own user mailing list. Every Linux distribution has its own mailing lists and user forums. There are forums and lists and Usenet groups for every computing subject under the sun.

And of course there are books and magazines of every description. So the real problem with Linux documentation is not the lack of it, but finding the bits you need without having to embark on a lengthy, heroic quest.

Audience

This book is aimed at folks who want to know what button to push. Understanding the underlying theory is useful, but if you can't make the darn thing work, not very helpful. So it's light on theory and heavy on how-to-make-this-go, with detailed, step-by-step instructions. I've included many references to additional resources.

Readers should have a bit of Linux experience. You don't need to be a guru, but you should have some familiarity with the basics of booting up and shutting down, starting applications, Web surfing, and poking around the filesystem. You should know how to find and use the command line, as well as work in a graphical environment. You should understand that Linux is a true multi-user system, and that you use an ordinary unprivileged user account as much as possible, and that you only invoke root when you really need to.

This book assumes that you are in charge of a PC or LAN, and can acquire rootly powers when the occasion calls for them. You might be a power user who wants complete control of your Linux box, or a home user who wants to run a personal web or mail server, or set up a small LAN. Perhaps you are a Windows system admininstrator who has suddenly been ordered to "do Linux," and you need to know how to set up Linux servers for Windows clients. Maybe you want to add Linux servers to an existing network. You might need to integrate Linux and Windows desktop users on a LAN.

Or you have no need for Windows at all, and just want to learn Linux system administration.

What Is Included/Omitted

Given that there are thousands of software packages to choose from, almost all of which do something useful, it was a foregone conclusion that I couldn't cover everything. Or even most of everything. I decided what to include, and what to leave out, based on my opinion of what a fundamental Linux skill set should include. (You may have different ideas.) I included programs that I consider to be the best-of-breed, such djbdns, GRUB, Apache 2, vim, and Postfix. And I didn't neglect old standbys like LILO and BIND.

You'll find some excellent, innovative scripts for:

- Adding users in batches
- Changing passwords in batches
- Finding all the installed documentation for a program
- Finding orphaned libraries on RPM-based systems, and adding them to the RPM database

I decided not to include productivity and desktop applications, like Open Office, KMail, Firefox, Konqueror, the Gimp, GnuCash, and so forth. This book is about building infrastructure. Once you master the fundamentals of running and maintaining a Linux system, it will take you anywhere you want to go.

Platforms

There are more Linux distributions than can be counted; there are literally thousands of distributions, many of which are peculiar to a company, a campus, or even a circle of friends who like to roll their own. However, the world of distributions breaks (not very cleanly) into two large camps: RPM-based systems, represented in this book by Red Hat and Fedora, and apt-based systems, represented by Debian. Debian-based distributions are spreading like weeds, such as Knoppix, Xandros, Libranet, Unbuntu, and Linspire.

Even if you are using a distribution that does not fall into one of these two categories, such as Slackware or Gentoo, the fundamentals are pretty much the same. The kernel is the same; the programs and utilities available are the same; the window managers are the same; the only substantial difference is the way you install software.

That's not to say there aren't other differences between Linux distributions. A chronic bugaboo with Linux is differing file locations on different distributions. Get used to it; it's not going to go away. This book provides several excellent methods for finding out where your particular distribution puts configuration files, executables, and program documentation.

Conventions

The following typographical conventions are used in this book:

Italic
> Used for filenames and pathnames, hostnames, domain names, commands, URLs, and email addresses. *Italic* is also used for new terms where they are defined.

`Constant width`
> Used for code examples and fragments.

`Constant width bold`
> Used for user input.

`Constant width italic`
> Used to indicate text that is replaceable.

 Indicates a tip, suggestion, or general note.

 Indicates a warning or caution.

One particularly important convention in this book involves the use of command line prompts. I can't say it too often: don't get into the habit of su'ing to root whenever you have to do anything remotely administrative. Even worse, don't say "It's my machine, I can do anything as root." Use root privileges only when you really need them. You'll be safer that way; you'll have some protection against your own mistakes, and against attacks made by outsiders.

To show you when you need root privileges, commands requiring root privileges are preceded by the root prompt, #. Commands that don't require root privileges are preceded by the default bash shell prompt, $.

Don't be confused—there are many file listings in the book, and in many of these files, comments are preceded by #. Yes, it can be confusing, but you'll get used to it.

Downloads and Feedback

Doubtless this book, despite the heroic efforts of me and the fabulous O'Reilly team, contains flaws, errors, and omissions. Please email your feedback and suggestions to *cookbook@bratgrrl.com*, so we can make the second edition even better. Be sure to visit *http://tuxcomputing.com* for errata, updates, and to download the scripts and configuration files used in the book.

This book was authored entirely in Open Office Writer, on Libranet Debian 2.8.

Comments and Questions

Please address comments and questions concerning this book to the publisher:

O'Reilly Media, Inc.
1005 Gravenstein Highway North
Sebastopol, CA 95472
(800) 998-9938 (in the United States or Canada)
(707) 829-0515 (international or local)
(707) 829-0104 (fax)

There is a web page for this book, which lists errata, examples, and any additional information. You can access this page at:

http://www.oreilly.com/catalog/linuxckbk/

To comment on or ask technical questions about this book, send email to:

bookquestions@oreilly.com

For more information about books, conferences, software, Resource Centers, and the O'Reilly Network, see the O'Reilly web site at:

http://www.oreilly.com

Acknowledgments

Thank you to ace O'Reilly editor Michael Loukides, whose good taste, eagle editorial eye, patient endurance, and implacable insistence made this a much better book.

Thank you to ace technical reviewer Jenn Vesperman, and her attention to detail. Silly computers are completely literal, and must be fed precise input—thanks Jenn!

Many thanks to Akkana Peck, Jenn Vesperman, Paul Heinlein, and Peter Samuelson, whose contributions appear in this book. Heartfelt thanks to the gang at Linuxchix, including Jenn Vesperman (benevolent dictator of Linuxchix), Dancer Vesperman, Danamania (the camera does not lie), Colby, Evilpig, Almut Behrens, Andrew (Mandrake Guru), Hamster, Piglet, Val Henson (uppity rabble rouser), H. Peter Anvin (kernel guru and rabbit rouser), Rik Rose, Devdas Bhagat, David North (for comic relief), Telsa Gwynne, Maria Blackmore, Meredydd Luff, Kai Mac-Tane, and Erinn Clark (for more uppity rabble-rousing). Linuxchix rawks!

I'm sure I missed some folks who patiently endured my endless pestering. Tell me who you are, and I'll fix it in the second edition.

## CHAPTER 1

Finding Documentation

1.1   Introduction

Documentation for Linux programs is abundant. Finding it can be a bit challenging, though. You're not going to find lots of sleek, glossy printed manuals, because most Linux software is distributed online, rather than in shiny boxed sets.

There's another difficulty, too: Linux follows the grand Unix tradition of small, specialized programs working cooperatively, so any Linux distribution contains a large number of individual programs. For example, Tom's Root Boot, "The most GNU/Linux on one floppy disk," contains over 230 separate, individual programs on a single 3.5" diskette. A general-purpose distribution such as Mandrake or SuSE contains several thousand programs and there are over 12,000 packages in the Debian repositories. While organizing and maintaining a printed library presents some difficulties, the good news is that all of these things are documented. Whatever you want to know, there is a way to find it.

man and info: The Universal Linux Manuals

Almost every program written for Linux has a *man* page. They're usually not the best teaching tool for newbies. Their purpose is to document the command syntax and every command option, and to be universally available. No matter what kind of strange desert-island scenario you may find yourself in, there will always be man pages. And because man pages are incorporated into the programs to which they belong, you'll find that only installed programs have man pages and that the versions of those pages are pertinent to your system.

info pages tend to be more verbose than man pages and are hyperlinked. The hyperlinks navigate to the various *nodes*, or chapters, inside the document and to cross-references in other info pages. Many info pages are simply reformatted man pages. But in some instances—primarily the GNU project programs—the info pages are more detailed, containing tutorials and extensive examples.

Other Documentation

A large number of README, CHANGELOGS, RELEASE NOTES, COPYRIGHT, INSTALL, integrated Help systems, and HTML docs are going to be squirreled away in various locations on your system. Yes, it's a jumble. Don't worry, you'll learn easy ways to find all these things in this chapter, including a nice Python script to do the finding for you.

There are many web sites that host complete archives of man and info pages, which comes in handy if your system is missing the ones you want, or you want to read them without having to download and install new programs. A Google search will find them quickly.

The commercial Linux distributions—for example, Red Hat, SuSE, Mandrake, Xandros, and Linspire—supply excellent user manuals. Every major Linux distribution provides a feast of online resources. Search engines, user mailing lists, Usenet, and all sorts of Linux web sites also supply a wealth of help and information.

Graphical Viewers

There are several good graphical man and info page viewers:

Konqueror
> The web and file browser in KDE also contains an excellent man and info page viewer. Simply type *man:foo* or *info:/foo* in the address bar. It is easy to print from Konqueror, and easy to select individual man or info pages for printing.

Yelp
> The Gnome viewer. Displays man and info pages, and Gnome's help documents. It is indexed and searchable.

Pinfo
> A nice ncurses-based info and man viewer for the console. Users can add new documents to it, and it supports regexp searches.

1.2   Understanding man Pages

Problem

You're trying to use some programs (for example, everyone's favorite, *grep*; the name tells you so much) and you can't make them them do what you want. So, heeding the standard "RTFM" (read the fine man page) advice, you dig up the relevant man pages. But they don't make a lot of sense—now what?

Solution

Learn how man pages are organized, and familiarize yourself with their conventions for teaching command syntax and options, and you'll find that man pages really are helpful.

Discussion

Linux sees all the man pages on a system as part of a single manual. This manual is divided into sections:

1   Executable programs or shell commands
2   System calls
3   Library calls
4   Special files (usually found in */dev*)
5   File formats and conventions
6   Games
7   Miscellaneous
8   System administration commands
9   Nonstandard kernel routines
n   New documentation, which may be moved later
l   Local documentation, specific to your system

Each individual program, utility, or function has its own page in this manual, like a page in a book. Finding the man page for a program or command is usually as easy as typing *man foo*, where *foo* is the name of the program.

You've probably seen references to numbered man pages, like *grep(1)*. This is referring to *man grep* in section 1. Call it up this way:

```
$ man 1 grep
```

Some man pages are in more than one section. *man foo* will only display the first one. You can list all of them with the *-f* switch:

```
$ man -f man
man (1)   an interface to the online reference manuals
man (7)   macros to format man pages
```

Each man page is divided into sections. The section names vary, but you'll usually see these: NAME, SYNOPSIS, DESCRIPTION, OPTIONS, FILES, EXAMPLES, SEE ALSO, BUGS, and AUTHOR.

Here's the notation used to show command syntax, found in the Synopsis of the man pages:

```
command-name [optional flags] any-other-required-elements
```

Command flags are shown this way:

bold text
Type this exactly as it is shown.

italic text
> Italic text indicates an argument, which means you replace it with your desired value. Depending on the viewer you are using, you may not see italics, but rather underlines or bold text.

[-abc]
> Everything inside square brackets is optional and can be combined.

[-a|-b|-c]
> Options separated by the pipe | (Shift-backslash) cannot be combined.

argument...
> The ellipsis indicates that several arguments can be listed. Watch out for delimiters—usually they are spaces, but sometimes commas are used.

[expression] ...
> The ellipsis indicates that several expressions can be listed.

Short options can be typed two ways:

```
-abc
```

or:

```
-a -b -c
```

Long options must be individually hyphenated, and they use double hyphens:

```
--option1 --option2 --option3
```

Long options are especially useful in scripts, so you can remember what the script does.

The bulk of most man pages is a list of the options available.

See Also

- *man(1)*

1.3   Finding Appropriate man Pages

Problem

You need a program or utility to perform a specific function—for example, counting the words in a file—but you don't know what to look for. If you knew what you were looking for, you wouldn't need to look for it, right? How do you get out of this dilemma?

Solution

Do keyword searches with *apropos* or *man -k*. For example, if you want a command to count the words in a file, use:

```
$ apropos count words
```

or:

```
$ man -k count words
american-english (5) - a list of english words
grpconv (8)          - convert to and from shadow passwords and groups.
grpunconv (8)        - convert to and from shadow passwords and groups.
kmessedwords (1)     - a letter order game for KDE
lppasswd (1)         - add, change, or delete digest passwords.
pwconv (8)           - convert to and from shadow passwords and groups.
pwunconv (8)         - convert to and from shadow passwords and groups.
shadowconfig (8)     - toggle shadow passwords on and off
wc (1)               - print the number of newlines, words, and bytes in files
```

It doesn't matter which you use; *apropos* and *man -k* are the same. There are a lot of options, but *wc* looks like the program you want.

Remember the *-f* switch, to find all versions of a man page:

```
$ man -f manpath
manpath (1)      - determine search path for manual pages
manpath (5)      - format of the /etc/manpath.config file
```

Discussion

These commands perform keyword searches in the Description sections of the man pages. You can use any number of search terms, but the more you use, the more results you'll get, because they search each keyword in sequence.

Because these are literal keyword searches, broad concepts like "bandwidth shaping" or "user management" do not carry the same meaning for *apropos* and *man -k*; they see "bandwidth shaping" as two unrelated search terms, so single-word searches usually work best.

See Also

- *apropos(1), man(1)*

1.4   Finding Lost man Pages

Problem

You can't find a *man* page for an installed program, and you're certain it should be on the system.

Solution

Sometimes the man database gets corrupted, users make strange modifications, or programs install man pages incorrectly. First try searching with *whereis -m*:

```
$ whereis -m cat
cat:/usr/man/man1/cat.1.gz /usr/share/man/man1/cat.1.gz
```

Now you've found the page. Read it with *man*:

```
$ man /usr/man/man1/cat.1.gz
```

If that doesn't work, try rebuilding the man database with *mandb*:

```
# mandb
```

If that doesn't work, try a system-wide search with *locate* and *egrep*:

```
$ locate / cat. | egrep -w 'cat\.[1-9][a-zA-Z]*[.gz]?'
```

This works for any man page—simply replace *cat* with whatever you're looking for.

If none of these approaches turn up the man page you are looking for, try the *finddoc* script in Recipe 1.11. If this doesn't find it, it's not on your system.

Discussion

There are all kinds of man page repositories on the Web, so you can always try a Google search. However, some programs simply don't have man pages, so don't ruin your health searching for one that may not exist.

See Also

- *whereis(1), mandb(8)*
- *grep* comes in several flavors; see *grep(1)* for details

1.5   Reading man Pages Without a man Viewer

Problem

You're working on a system that is seriously messed up, and you can't read man pages because the man viewer doesn't work.

Solution

Try reading the raw man page with *zcat* and *nroff*:

```
$ zcat /usr/man/man1/cat.1.gz | nroff -man | less
```

As a last resort, read the raw page code with *zless*:

```
$ zless /usr/man/man1/cat.1.gz
.\" DO NOT MODIFY THIS FILE!  It was generated by help2man 1.32.
.TH CAT "1" "July 2003" "cat (coreutils) 5.0" "User Commands"
.SH NAME
cat \- concatenate files and print on the standard output
.SH SYNOPSIS
.B cat
[\fIOPTION\fR] [\fIFILE\fR]...
```

It's not pretty, but it works.

Discussion

nroff is a wrapper for *groff*, for formatting man pages. *groff* is a document-formatting, or typesetting, program. It enables you to create many differently formatted documents from a single source file: HTML, *.pdf*, printed hard copies, info pages, and many more. See Chapter 9 of *Running Linux* for a good introduction.

See Also

- *mandb(8)*, *locate(1)*, *grep(1)*, *nroff(1)*, *groff(1)*, *zless(1)*, *zcat(1)*
- Recipe 1.6, "Configuring Your manpath"
- Chapter 9 of *Running Linux*, by Matt Walsh, Matthias Dalheimer, Terry Dawson, and Lar Kaufman (O'Reilly)

1.6 Configuring Your manpath

Problem

You're repeatedly having trouble finding man pages; using tools from Recipe 1.4, you find that most of the missing pages are in a directory that *man* doesn't seem to know about. Perhaps a newly-installed program put its man pages in a strange place, like */opt/man*. Or perhaps you want to put some man pages in a nonstandard location. How do you configure *man* to find them?

Solution

Edit */etc/manpath.config*.

Suppose the directory you want to add is */opt/man*. Add */opt/man* to */etc/manpath.config*:

```
# every automatically generated MANPATH includes
# these fields

MANDATORY_MANPATH                       /usr/man
MANDATORY_MANPATH                       /usr/share/man
MANDATORY_MANPATH                       /usr/X11R6/man
MANDATORY_MANPATH                       /usr/local/man
MANDATORY_MANPATH                       /opt/man
```

And you're done. Now *man* will find the man pages in the new directory.

When you create a custom man page directory, be sure to include the section directories:

```
$ ls /opt/man/local
man1  man2  man3  man4  man5  man6  man7  man8  man9
```

It's not necessary to include all the numbered sections, just the ones pertinent to the man pages you'll be storing there.

If you're going to have subdirectories—for example, */opt/man* and */opt/man/local*—be sure to list them in this order:

```
MANDATORY_MANPATH                    /opt/man/local
MANDATORY_MANPATH                    /opt/man
```

Subdirectories must be listed before parent directories, or they will be overlooked by the man viewer.

Discussion

You can run *manpath* with no options to see your current manpaths:

```
$ manpath
/usr/local/man:/usr/share/man:/usr/X11R6/man:/usr/man
```

See Also

- *manpath(1)*, *manpath(5)*

1.7   Using info Pages

Problem

You decide to give info pages a try, so you call up *info tar* (or any other info page of your choice). But you find that navigating *info tar* is confusing and difficult. What is the best way to learn your way around?

Solution

Use *info*'s built-in tutorial. Type *info* at any command line, hit the letter *h*, then do what it says. It should take 15–30 minutes, and it is time well-spent.

Discussion

Even though some folks think that info pages are unnecessarily complicated to navigate, it is worth getting acquainted with them. Even though they are more difficult to navigate than man pages, they are (usually) easier to understand. Once you get the hang of moving around in them, you can go very fast and find information quickly. Info pages often contain more information than man pages, and they sometimes include tutorials and extensive examples.

There are also a number of nice info viewers, such as pinfo, Konqueror, and Yelp. Pinfo runs in the console, and Konqueror and Yelp need X. Konqueror is especially easy to navigate and to use for printing selected pages.

See Also

- *info info*

1.8   Printing man Pages

Problem

You want to print a man page, nicely formatted and readable. You have tried *man foo | lpr*, but it doesn't look very good. The margins are too small, and all the formatting is lost.

Solution

One way to print a nicely formatted man page is to use the *-t* flag, which formats it especially for printing. *man finger* is good for practice, because it's only two pages long:

```
$ man -t finger | lpr
```

To use a networked printer:

```
$ man -t finger | lpr -P printername
```

To see your available printers:

```
$ lpstat -p -d
```

Another option is to use the following command, which formats the page in HTML and sends it to the web browser of your choice:

```
$ man -Hmozilla finger
```

Then use the browser's print command. Be sure there is no space between *-H* and the browser name.

Discussion

All of the major Linux distributions ship with CUPS, the Common Unix Printing System. CUPS supports both the System V (*lp*) and Berkeley (*lpr*) commands. This recipe uses the Berkeley commands. Here is the System V equivalent.

```
$ man -t finger | lp
```

To use a networked printer:

```
$ man -t finger | lp -d printername
```

See Also

- *man(1), lpr(1), lp(1)*
- Chapter 14, *Printing with CUPS*
- CUPS Software Users Manual (*http://localhost:631/documentation.html*)

1.9 Printing info Pages

Problem

You want to print some info pages, but there doesn't seem to be a built-in print command for *info*.

Solution

You can use *lpr*:

```
$ info finger | lpr
```

However, this may result in too-small margins and odd line breaks, depending on your printer defaults. Use *lpr* options to format it:

```
$ info finger | lpr -o cpi=12 -o page-left=54 -o page-right=54 -o page-top=54 \
 -o page-bottom=54
```

The numbered values are points, or 1/72". This example creates 3/4" margins all the way around. *cpi=12* sets the number of characters to 12 per inch. All of these options are documented in the *CUPS Software Users Manual*, at *http://localhost:631/documentation.html*.

Discussion

All of the major Linux distributions ship with CUPS, the Common Unix Printing System. CUPS supports both the System V (*lp*) and Berkeley (*lpr*) commands. This recipe uses the Berkeley commands. Here are the System V equivalents.

To print an info page use:

```
$ info finger | lp
```

To print the info page using *lp*'s formatting options use:

```
$ info finger | lp -o cpi=12 -o page-left=54 -o page-right=54 -o page-top=54 \
 -o page-bottom=54
```

See Also

- *info info*, *lpr(1)*, *lp(1)*
- Chapter 14, *Printing with CUPS*
- CUPS Software Users Manual (*http://localhost:631/documentation.html*)

1.10 Printing Selected man or info Pages

Problem

You would like to print selected man and info pages, because most man and info documents are quite long. For example, *man bash* consumes 33 printed pages. How can you print pages selectively?

Solution

Export the man or info page to a plain text file, using the *col* command. Then you can easily select the pages to print. To do this with *man bash* or *info bash* use:

```
$ man bash | col -b > bash.txt
$ info bash | col -b > bash.txt
```

Discussion

If you just type *man bash > bash.txt*, the results will be unpleasant. *col -b* cleans things up considerably by removing reverse line feeds, or backspaces. This is especially suited for converting man pages to plain text, because man pages are full of reverse line feeds, which then appear in text files as either empty boxes or repeated characters.

See Also

- *col(1)*

1.11 Finding All of the Documentation for a Program

Problem

You want to find all the relevant readmes, changelogs, howtos, guides, examples, samples, and other documentation that accompanies your installed programs.

Solution

Use *finddoc*, that wonderful Python script that comes to you courtesy of the excellent Akkana Peck.

You can call it anything you like. Remember to make it executable:

```
$ chmod +x finddoc
```

Using it requires only the script name and the name of the program for which you need the documentation. For example:

```
$ ./finddoc grep
/usr/share/doc/grep
```

```
/usr/share/doc/grep-dctrl
/usr/share/doc/grep-dctrl/changelog.gz
...
```

The output can be filtered through other commands, or redirected to a file:

```
$ ./finddoc | grep -i examples | lpr
$ ./finddoc | grep -i faq
$ ./finddoc | grep -i examples > python-examples.txt
```

Program: finddoc

```python
#!/usr/bin/env python

# Finddoc: A Script For Finding Linux Program Documentation
# When making your own copy of this script, be sure to
# preserve the leading spaces exactly as they are written
# here, because Python needs them.

# Search for documentation related to the given strings;
# case-insensitive, and whole-word only.
# Relies on "locate" and assumes that the locate
# database is current.
#
# Copyright 2003 by Akkana Peck.
# You may use, distribute or modify this program
# under the terms of the GPL.

import sys, os, string, re

# This is the list of document-related filenames
# to search for. You may edit this list as needed.
# Be sure to add only lowercase names.
docfilenames = [
  "changelog",
  "readme",
  "install",
  "howto",
  "authors",
  "news",
  "todo",
  "config",
  "sample",
  "samples",
  "example",
  "examples",
  "ref",
  "guide",
  "manual",
  "quickstart",
  "thanks",
  "notes",
  "features",
  "faq",
  "acknowledgement",
```

```python
    "bugs",
    "problems"
]

def system_out (cmdstr) :
 retlist = [ ]
 fp = os.popen(cmdstr)
 while 1:
  s = fp.readline( )
  if not s : break
  retlist.append(s)
 fp.close( )
 return retlist

# main( )
for arg in sys.argv :
 #print string.split(arg, " \t./")

 files = system_out("locate " + arg + " | grep -w " + arg);

 for path in files :
  #print path

  # Special case for anything with "man", "doc", or "info" in the path:
  if (string.find(path, "/man") >= 0) \
   or (string.find(path, "/doc") >= 0) \
   or (string.find(path, "/info") >= 0) :
   print path,
)
   continue

  # Now see if it matches any of the docfilenames:
  base = os.path.basename(path)
  for nam in docfilenames :
   if base == "" : continue

   # Non full word search would use this:
:

   # Full-word-search:
   # Make a regexp to search for nam as full-word only
   pat = "^" + nam + "$"
   if (re.compile(nam).search(base, 1)) :
    print path,
    base = ""
    continue
```

See Also

- *locate(1)*, *grep(1)*
- Chapter 9 of *Python in a Nutshell*

## CHAPTER 2

Installing and Managing Software on RPM-Based Systems

2.1   Introduction

Installing a Linux distribution is quite easy these days. Pop in a CD-ROM, make a few configuration choices, then go enjoy a cup of tea while it finishes. Modern Linuxes have excellent hardware detection, install quickly (typically in 30 minutes or less), and require no more than a single reboot.

Source-Built Systems: The Olde Way

Maintaining a Linux system has also evolved tremendously. Packages and intelligent dependency resolvers mean that keeping a system updated and patched is now easier and less error-prone. Today's youngsters have it so easy. We didn't have CD-ROMs in the primitive olden days of computing—instead of broadband, we had a station wagon full of floppy disks. To get new programs, us old-timers had to unpack laboriously downloaded tarballs, or copy them off floppy disks, then compile the programs from source code. Dependency problems? Why, us old geeks handled all those things without help from any fancy-pants dependency resolvers. It went something like this:

```
# tar -xvf someprogram.tar
# ./configure
# make
```

The *make* failed, because of unresolved dependencies. So the next step was to download a tarball containing the program with the required libraries, which took six hours over a 300-baud modem. You know, the kind with the rubber cup that fits over the phone. I passed the time by going outside and planting a garden. I came back inside when the download was finished, unpacked the new tarball, and tried again:

```
# ./configure
# make
```

Boy howdy, another long string of error messages indicating more unresolved dependencies. Download yet another tarball, do more garden work. By the time everything was installed and working, I had tomatoes the size of melons. It's a good thing we were so smart we hardly even needed computers.

Why was there all this dependency drama? Because Linux uses shared libraries that are dynamically linked at runtime. Many separate, unrelated programs can use the same libraries. This makes for a fast, efficient system. Less memory and storage resources are consumed, and programs are smaller and easier to distribute. But as Linux evolved and became more complex, managing source-built systems became more difficult. So programs were put into *packages*. Packages include compiled binaries, pre- and post-installation scripts, file indexes, uninstallation scripts, and other goodies. Each package knows what it needs to resolve its own dependencies. Package databases track all the installed-from-package files on a system.

Dependency Resolvers

However, not all was bliss in Whoville. *RPM*, the Red Hat Package Manager, is the most widely used Linux package manager. RPM is quite powerful. It runs dependency and version checks, and it tracks all installed packages in the RPM database. But it cannot fetch additional packages to resolve dependencies, nor can it manage the relationships between packages. When it gets stuck because of dependency problems, it tells you what additional packages to install, which means you have to find these packages and install them. This can lead to more dependency conflicts, and a simple installation can go haywire in a hurry. This is known as "RPM hell."

Many dependency resolvers have been developed for RPM-based systems, including *apt-rpm*, *urpmi*, Yum, and Ximian's Red Carpet. There are excellent distribution-specific installers/resolvers, such as Red Hat's *up2date* and SuSE's YaST and Maintenance Web. In this chapter we'll cover RPM basics and Yum, which was developed natively for RPM systems. For many users, Yum strikes the right balance of features and ease of use.

2.2   Installing RPMs

Problem

You need to know how to install software packages on Red Hat and Red Hat–type systems.

Solution

Use RPM, the Package Manager. Red Hat installation command syntax looks like this:

```
# rpm -i packagename
```

For example, the following command installs the drawing program Tuxpaint. *-v* adds verbose feedback, and *-h* draws progress hashmarks:

```
# rpm -ivh tuxpaint-9.13-1.i386.rpm
Preparing...########################### [100%]
   1. tuxpaint ####################### [100%]
```

To test the installation first, without installing anything, use:

```
# rpm -ivh --test tuxpaint-9.13-1.i386.rpm
Preparing...########################### [100%]
#
```

Discussion

RPM hell, or getting caught in an endless chain of unresolved dependencies, is the most common RPM problem. Here are some ways to prevent it:

- Do not let any dependencies remain unresolved. They don't fix themselves; they lurk and grow larger over time.
- The quality of RPMs varies wildly. Anyone can throw one together and post it for distribution. As much as possible, stick with RPMs built for your distribution and architecture. Polished Linux Distribution (PLD) builds good-quality RPMs for all x86 systems.
- Use CheckInstall when you need a source-built program. CheckInstall creates Red Hat, Debian, and Slackware packages, so you get the benefits of both a custom compilation and your package manager (see Recipe 4.5, "Using CheckInstall to Create Packages from Sources).

See Also

- *rpm(8)*
- RPM.org *(http://www.rpm.org/)*
- Maximum RPM *(http://www.rpm.org/max-rpm/index.html)*

2.3   Upgrading RPMs

Problem

You need to upgrade an installed RPM package: there's a new version of some program you like, with new features and important bug fixes.

Solution

Use the *-U* flag:

```
# rpm -Uvh tuxpaint-9.13-1.i386.rpm
```

To test the command first, use:

```
# rpm -Uvh --test tuxpaint-9.13-1.i386.rpm
```

Discussion

-*U* can be used in place of -*i*, install. It doesn't matter if you're upgrading a package or installing a new one, it works in both cases. -*U* replaces the old package. If you want to have multiple versions of the same package, such as *gcc*, or install several different kernels, don't use -*U*, use -*i*.

See Also

- *rpm(8)*
- RPM.org (*http://rpm.org/*)
- Maximum RPM (*http://www.rpm.org/max-rpm/index.html*)

2.4   Removing RPMs

Problem

You've gotten tired of some program and want to get rid of it. Or you've just installed something you don't want. So, you want to remove an RPM package.

Solution

rpm -e does the job:

```
# rpm -ev tuxpaint
```

You don't need the entire package name (e.g., *tuxpaint-9.13-1.i386.rpm*), just the label.

To uninstall several programs at once, use a space-delimited list:

```
# rpm -ev tuxpaint SDL_ttf  SDL_ttf-devel SDL_images
```

If you don't want to check dependencies:

```
# rpm -ev --nodeps tuxpaint
```

To test your command first, before executing it, use:

```
# rpm -ev --test tuxpaint SDL_ttf  SDL_ttf-devel SDL_images
```

Discussion

If RPM reports that it cannot remove a package because other packages depend on it, you either need to remove the other packages, or leave it alone. There are times when you need to break dependencies; for example, when replacing Sendmail. Your new MTA—Postfix, Exim, or qmail—will resolve Sendmail's dependencies, but you have to remove Sendmail first, which you can't do without breaking all kinds of dependencies.

See Also

- *rpm(8)*
- Maximum RPM (*http://www.rpm.org/max-rpm/index.html*)

2.5   Collecting Information on Installed RPMs

Problem

You want to know what packages are installed on your system, what files belong to a package, or what package a file belongs to. There are lots of reasons for wanting this information; you might want to know exactly what version of some program is on your system, or you may be asking, "what does this thingy belong to?" You might even change some file accidentally, and want to know what you've broken.

Solution

Use RPM's querying features. All queries start with *rpm -q*.

To query the RPM database to see if a program is already installed, use:

```
$ rpm -q tuxpaint
tuxpaint-9.13-1
```

To do a case-insensitive search for an installed RPM, using a partial package name, use:

```
$ rpm -qa | grep -i kde
lockdev-1.0.1-1.3
kdebase-3.1.4-6
kdeutils-3.1.4-1
kdegames-3.1.4-4
```

To list files in an installed package, use:

```
$ rpm -ql kdegames
/usr/bin/atlantik
/usr/bin/kasteroids
/usr/bin/katomic
...
```

To list the documentation for an application, use:

```
$ rpm -qd kdegames | grep katomic
/usr/share/doc/HTML/en/katomic/common
/usr/share/doc/HTML/en/katomic/index.docbook
...
```

To list the configuration files for a package, use:

```
$ rpm -qc openssh
/etc/ssh/moduli
```

To list the configuration files for a command, use:

```
$ rpm -qcf /usr/bin/ssh
/etc/ssh/ssh_config
```

To list all installed packages, use:

```
$ rpm -qa
setup-2.5.27-1.1
tzdata-2003d-1
bzip2-libs-1.0.2-10
...
```

To save the list to a file, while viewing the output on the screen, use:

```
$ rpm -qa | tee rpmlist.txt
```

To see what package a file belongs to, use:

```
$ rpm -qf /usr/bin/tuxkart
tuxkart-0.2.0-3
```

RPM queries will not follow symlinks, and will report that the file is "not owned by any package." To find the file that a symlink points to, use:

```
$ namei ~/tuxkart
f: tuxkart
 l tuxkart -> /usr/games/tuxkart
   d /
   d usr
   d games
   - tuxkart
```

To display package information, use:

```
$ rpm -qi kdegames
Name        :kdegames        Relocations/usr
Version     :3.1.4              Vendor:Red Hat, Inc.
Release     :2              Build date: Mon 13 Oct 2003
Install date:Tue Nov 5 2003 Build host:daffy.perf.redhat.com
Group       : Amusements/Games   Source RPM:kdegames-3.1.4-2.src.rpm
Size        :16167441       License: GPL
Signature   :DSA/SHA1, Tue 28 Oct 2003 Key ID b446d04f2a6fd2
Packager    :Red Hat, Inc.
<http://bugzilla.redhat.com/bugzilla>
Summary     :K Desktop Environment - Games
Description :
Games and gaming libraries for the K Desktop Environment
Included with this package are: kenolaba, kasteroids, kblackbox, kmhajongg, kmines,
konquest, kpat, kpoker, kreversi, ksame, kshisen, ksokoban, ksmiletris, ksnake,
ksirtet, katomic, kjumpingcube, ktuberling
```

Discussion

Another way to find documentation for a particular application is with the *finddoc* script in Recipe 1.11.

See Also

- *rpm(8)*
- Recipe 1.11, "Finding All of the Documentation for a Program"

- Maximum RPM (*http://www.rpm.org/max-rpm/index.html*)
- Chapter 16 of *Linux in a Nutshell* by Ellen Siever, Stephen Figgins, and Aaron Weber (O'Reilly)

2.6 Collecting Information from RPMs That Are Not Installed

Problem

You want to know what dependencies a new RPM requires, what files are in it, or if a particular file is in it.

Solution

Add the *-p* switch to run queries on uninstalled RPMs.

To list the documentation files, use:

```
$ rpm -qpd tuxpaint-9.13-1.i386.rpm
/usr/share/doc/tuxpaint-9.13-1/AUTHORS.txt
/usr/share/doc/tuxpaint-9.13-1/CHANGES.txt
/usr/share/doc/tuxpaint-9.13-1/COPYING.txt
...
```

To list all the files, use:

```
$ rpm -qpl tuxpaint-9.13-1.i386.rpm
/etc/tuxpaint/tuxpaint.conf
/usr/bin/tuxpaint
...
```

To see what dependencies this package requires, use:

```
$ rpm -qpR tuxpaint-9.13-1.i386.rpm
/bin/sh
SDL >= 1.2.4
SDL_image
...
```

To see what this package provides, use:

```
$ rpm -qp --provides tuxpaint-9.13-1.i386.rpm
config (tuxpaint) = 9.13-1
tuxpaint-9.13-1
tuxpaint = 9.13-1
```

Discussion

You can also get all this information on individual packages, before downloading them, from RPM repositories such as *http://freshrpms.net*, *http://rpmfind.net*, and *http://rpm.pbone.net*.

See Also

- *rpm(8)*
- Maximum RPM (*http://www.rpm.org/max-rpm/index.html*)
- FreshRPMS (*http://freshrpms.net/*)
- rpmfind (*http://rpmfind.net*)
- rpm.pbone (*http://rpm.pbone.net*)

2.7   Finding Recently Installed RPMs

Problem

You installed some new packages a few days ago, and you've forgotten what they are.

Solution

Use the *--last* option:

```
# rpm -qa --last
```

This command lists all installed RPMs, with the newest first.

Discussion

If the list is too long, pipe it into *less* or *head*: rpm -qa --last|head.

See Also

- *rpm(8)*
- Maximum RPM (*http://www.rpm.org/max-rpm/index.html*)

2.8   Rebuilding the RPM Database

Problem

You think your RPM database may be corrupted, or out-of-date, because it does not answer queries for RPMs you know are installed; or you've given your system a major overhaul and want to be sure the RPM database is up-to-date.

Solution

Try rebuilding the RPM database, as root:

```
# rpm --rebuilddb
```

or completely re-create it:

```
# rpm --initdb
```

Discussion

It is uncommon for the RPM database to need rebuilding, but it doesn't hurt anything to try. Any time you make major changes to your system is a good time to rebuild the RPM database. If you compare the size of */var/lib/rpm/packages* before and after running *rpm --rebuilddb*, you may notice some shrinkage, because it has removed unused portions of the database.

See Also

- *rpm(8)*
- Maximum RPM (*http://www.rpm.org/max-rpm/index.html*)
- Chapter 16 of *Linux in a Nutshell*

2.9   Tracking Source-Built Libraries on an RPM-Based System

Problem

You want to run both source-built programs and RPMs on the same system. But RPM does not know about the source-built libraries, so it incorrectly reports dependency errors.

Solution

Use the *rpm-orphan-find* script. This script searches for all the libraries on your system, then compares the results with the contents of the RPM database. Any orphaned libraries are then rolled into a new, virtual *.rpm*. There are no files in this *.rpm*, just a list of provides. Run this like any Bash script:

```
# chmod +x rpm-orphan-find
# ./rpm-orphan-find
```

When the script is finished, install the shiny new *.rpm,* and your formerly orphaned libraries will be included in your RPM database.

Program: rpm-orphan-find

Thank you to Paul Heinlein and Peter Samuelson for this great script.

```
#!/bin/bash
## rpm-orphan-find, a script that finds
## orphaned libs on an RPM-based system
## and rolls them into a virtual .rpm
## written by Paul Heinlein and Peter Samuelson
## Copyright 2003
## You may use, distribute or modify this
## program under the terms of the GPL.
```

```
OS=$(uname -s)
LIBS="/lib /usr/lib $(cat /etc/ld.so.conf)"
NAME=$(echo ${OS}-base-libs | tr '[A-Z]' '[a-z]')
VER=1.0; REL=1
TMPSPEC=$(mktemp /tmp/${NAME}.spec.XXXXXX)

exec 9>$TMPSPEC

cat <<__eof__ >&9
Summary: $OS Base Virtual Package
Name: $NAME
Version: $VER
Release: $REL
Group: System Environment/Base
License: None
__eof__

found=0; orphan=0;
echo "Scanning system libraries $NAME version $VER-$REL..."
find $LIBS -type f \( -name '*.so.*' -o -name '*.so' \) |
while read f
do
  ((found++))
  if ! rpm -qf $f >/dev/null 2>&1
  then
    ((orphan++))
    echo "Provides: $(basename $f)" >&9
  fi
  echo -ne "Orphans found: $orphan/$found...\r"
done
echo ''; echo ''

cat <<__eof__ >&9

%description
This is a virtual RPM package.  It contains no
actual files.  It uses the 'Provides' token from RPM 3.x and later to list many of
the shared libraries that are part of the base operating system and associated
subsets for this $OS environment.

%prep
# nothing to do

%build
# nothing to do

%install
# nothing to do

%clean
# nothing to do

%post
# nothing to do
```

```
%files

__eof__

exec 9>&-
rpmbuild -ba $TMPSPEC; rm $TMPSPEC
```

Note that *rpmbuild* has replaced *rpm*. Since when, you ask? Since the turn of the century. It first appeared in Red Hat 8, RPM Version 4.1. The old RPM commands often still work, though, because they are aliased in */etc/popt*. Run *rpm --version* to see what version you have.

If you have an older version of RPM, edit the last line of the script as follows:

```
rpm -bb $TMPSPEC; rm $TMPSPEC
```

See Also

- *rpm(8), rpmbuild(8)*
- Maximum RPM (*http://www.rpm.org/max-rpm/index.html*)

2.10   Fixing RPM Installation Problems

Problem

You are trying to install an RPM, but the installation fails with "Error: Failed dependencies." Welcome to dependency hell.

Solution

Collect all of the RPMs needed to satisfy the dependencies, then install them all at once. For example:

```
# rpm -ivh tuxpaint-0.9.13-1.i386.rpm
error: Failed dependencies
        SDL_image is needed by tuxpaint-0.9.13-1
        SDL_ttf is needed by tuxpaint-0.9.13-1
        libSDL_image-1.2.so.0 is needed by tuxpaint-0.9.13-1
        libSDL_ttf-2.0.so.0 is needed by tuxpaint-0.9.13-1
# rpm -ivh tuxpaint-0.9.13-1.i386.rpm  SDL_image-1.2.3-4.i386.rpm  SDL_ttf-2.0.6-
1.i386.rpm
```

The installer will sort them out and install them in the correct order.

What if RPM complains about a missing file or package, and you are certain it is installed? Sometimes the RPM database contains errors, so try rebuilding it:

```
# rpm -rebuilddb
```

If that doesn't help, reinstall the allegedly missing package with *--replacepkgs*:

```
# rpm -ivh --replacepkgs SDL_ttf-2.0.6-1.i386.rpm
```

If you are certain the necessary libraries exist on your system, try either forcing the installation, ignoring errors:

```
# rpm -ivh --force  tuxpaint-2002.10.20-1.i386.rpm
```

or don't check dependencies:

```
# rpm -ivh --nodeps tuxpaint-2002.10.20-1.i386.rpm
```

If you find yourself stuck with unresolvable dependency conflicts, try installing your new program and all of its dependent packages from source RPMs (see Recipe 2.11).

Discussion

Where do you find the packages you need? Your first stop should be the home page of the program you're trying to install. Be sure to read any available documentation.

RPM-based distributions are quite diverse these days, so be sure to get RPMs built for your system. These are some of largest public RPM archives:

FreshRPMs
    http://freshrpms.net
rpmfind
    http://rpmfind.net
rpm.pbone
    http://rpm.pbone.net

See Also

- *rpm(8)*
- RPM.org (*http://www.rpm.org/*)
- Maximum RPM (*http://www.rpm.org/max-rpm/index.html*)

2.11   Installing Source RPMs

Problem

You can't install an RPM because of binary incompatibilities with your system, or you just prefer to compile applications on your system, or you want to edit the source code then build the package.

Solution

Build your new program from source RPMs.

Download the SRPM—in this example, *tuxpaint-2002.10.20-1.src.rpm*—into your directory of choice. Be sure to get the SRPM for your Linux distribution.

Then run the package installer:

```
# rpm -ivh tuxpaint-2002.10.20-1.src.rpm
```

This will place sources in */usr/src/SOURCES* and the *spec* file in */usr/src/SPECS*:

```
$ ls /usr/src/SOURCES
tuxpaint-2002.09.29.tar.gz ruxpaint-Makefile.patch tuxpaint-stamps-2002.09.29.tar.gz
tuxpaint.desktop tuxpaint-opt.patch
$ ls /usr/src/SPECS
tuxpaint.spec
```

Build the *spec* file:

```
# rpmbuild -bb tuxpaint.spec
```

This creates a new RPM in */usr/src/RPMS/i386*:

```
# ls /usr/src/RPMS/i386
tuxpaint-2002.10.20-1.i386.rpm
```

You now have a nice, new Tuxpaint RPM, compiled for your system.

Discussion

The source directory on your particular distribution may be different. Fedora 1 uses */usr/src/redhat/RPMS/,* as did some early versions of Mandrake. Other distributions use */usr/src/RPM/RPMS*. Poke around and you'll find the right one.

This is not an escape from RPM hell. It simply lets you build an RPM from sources compiled on your system, so you have binary compatibility with system libraries and the RPM is optimized for your architecture. You still need to manually satisfy dependencies, which is not as much fun as it sounds.

Note that *rpmbuild* is a separate package from *rpm*.

See Also

- *rpmbuild(8), rpm(8)*
- RPM.org (*http://rpm.org/*)
- Maximum RPM (*http://www.rpm.org/max-rpm/index.html*)

2.12   Customizing Build Options in a Source RPM

Problem

Your site has some unique requirements requiring special non-default features to be built into some applications. Therefore, you want to control the compile-time options in a source RPM and make sure the features you need are built into the application.

Solution

First, download and install the source RPM:

```
# rpm -ivh samba-3.0.0-15.src.rpm
```

Then change to the *SPECS* directory, and open the *spec* file:

```
# cd /usr/src/redhat/SPECS
# vim samba.spec
```

Look for the section containing the *%configure* options:

```
%configure \
        --with-acl-support \
        --with-automount \
        --with-fhs \
...
```

Add or remove your desired configuration options, save and close the *spec* file, then build your RPM just like in Recipe 2.11:

```
# cd /usr/src/redhat/SPECS
# rpmbuild -bb tuxpaint.spec
```

Discussion

Where do you find a list of options? Change to the *SOURCES* directory, and unpack the source tarball:

```
# cd /usr/src/redhat/SOURCES
# tar xzvf samba-3.0.0.tar.bz2
```

As mentioned in Recipe 2.11, the source directory on your distribution may be different.

Poke around the unpacked tarball to find the *configure* script, and run its built-in *help* command:

```
# cd /usr/src/redhat/SOURCES/samba-3.0.0/source
# ./configure --help
'configure' configure this package to adapt to many kinds of systems
...
Optional Packages:
  with-PACKAGE[=ARG]    use PACKAGE [ARG=yes]
  without-PACKAGE       do not use PACKAGE
  with-fhs              Use FHS-compliant paths
  with-privated=DIR     Where to put smbpasswd
...
```

You'll also find the usual jumble of READMEs and howtos. When the *%configure* directive is customized to your satisfaction, save and close it.

Package maintainers cannot possibly meet the needs of every user. Customizing your source RPMs is a simple way to make sure you get what you want.

The most common reason to customize the build of a source RPM, in these modern times, is to add to or customize your authentication support. There are many different kinds of authentication backends (LDAP, MySQL, BerkeleyDB, PostgreSQL) and many different authentication protocols. It's a good security practice to enable only the options you need.

See Also

- *rpmbuild(8), rpm(8)*
- RPM.org (*http://www.rpm.org*)
- Maximum RPM (*http://www.rpm.org/max-rpm/index.html*)

2.13 Installing Yum

Problem

You're rather tired of getting sucked into RPM-dependency hell, and you're ready to let the computer do the work.

Solution

Use Yum, the Yellow Dog Updater, Modified.

Yum is standard on Fedora; on other systems you may need to install it:

```
# rpm -ivh yum-2.0.4-1.noarch.rpm
```

Next, download the appropriate GPG keys. This key is for downloads from the Fedora project:

```
# rpm --import http://www.fedora.us/FEDORA-GPG-KEY
```

You'll find more keys in the download directories, such as *http://download.fedora.redhat.com/pub/fedora/linux/core/2/i386/os/*. You'll need keys from all the repositories you configure Yum to use. Add this line to */etc/yum.conf* to make Yum automatically check the keys:

```
gpgcheck=1
```

Now you can install a new program:

```
# yum install tuxpaint
```

Your first Yum download will take as long as 30 minutes, because it will download package lists:

```
Gathering header information file(s) from server(s)
Server: Fedora Linux / stable for Red Hat Linux 9 (i386)
Server: Red Hat Linux 9 (i386)
Server: Red Hat Linux 9 (i386) updates
Finding updated packages
Downloading needed headers
getting /var/cache/yum/fedora-stable/headers/leafnode-0-1.9.43-0.fdr.1.rh90.i386.hdr
```

```
getting /var/cache/yum/fedora-stable/headers/libzvt-devel-0-2.0.1-
0.fdr.5.rh90.i386.hdr
...
Dependencies resolved
I will do the following:
[install: tuxpaint-2002.10.20-1.i386.rpm]
Is this ok [y/N]:
```

Say yes, and you're finished.

Discussion

FreshRPMs is a good source of quality packages. Yum mirrors are at *http://ayo.freshrpms.net*. Your Yum RPM from FreshRPMs will already be configured to use the FreshRPMs repositories. Be sure to install the GPG key:

```
# rpm --import http://freshrpms.net/packages/RPM-GPG-KEY.txt
```

Putting *gpgcheck=1* in *yum.conf*, and importing the keys, ensures that Yum will automatically check package signatures. It's an easy, painless method for checking that you are installing packages that have not been maliciously altered or messed up in transit.

See Also

- *yum(8), yum.conf(5)*
- Yum home page (*http://linux.duke.edu/projects/yum/*)
- Yum mirrors at FreshRPMs (*http://ayo.freshrpms.net*)

2.14   Configuring Yum

Problem

You want to change the download source from which Yum gets software.

Solution

Edit your download sources in */etc/yum.conf*. For example, say you want to use some Fedora mirrors at *http://www.fedora.us/wiki/FedoraMirrorList*:

```
University of Southern California, USA
    ftp://mirrors.usc.edu/pub/linux/fedora/
    http://mirrors.usc.edu/pub/linux/fedora/
```

Now edit */etc/yum.conf*, using the default entries as a template:

```
[base]
name=Fedora Core $releasever - $basearch - Base
baseurl=http://mirrors.kernel.org/fedora/core/$releasever/$basearch/os

baseurl=http://mirrors.usc.edu/pub/linux/fedora/$releasever/$basearch/os
```

Discussion

It's good netiquette to use mirrors whenever possible, as the primary site at *http://fedora.redhat.com* gets hammered.

See Also

- *yum(8), yum.conf(5)*
- Yum home page (*http://linux.duke.edu/projects/yum*)
- Yum mirrors at FreshRPMs (*http://ayo.freshrpms.net*)
- Fedora Mirror List (*http://www.fedora.us/wiki/FedoraMirrorList*)

2.15 Installing and Upgrading Packages with Yum

Problem

You need to know how to install packages, how to upgrade packages, and how to do system upgrades.

Solution

First, update your package list:

```
# yum check-update
```

To install a new package, use:

```
# yum -y install tuxkart
```

The *-y* flag allows unattended installation, by answering yes to all questions.

To update a single package, use:

```
# yum update gltron
```

To update several packages, use:

```
# yum update gltron ktron tuxracer
```

To update all installed packages, use:

```
# yum update
```

To search for a package to install, use:

```
# yum search quake
```

Now say you need a particular library, but you don't know what package provides it. Yum will find it:

```
# yum provides libc6.1-1.so.2
```

Discussion

One of the nicest features of Yum is that you can add it to an existing system. It reads the existing RPM database and creates a new package list, so you can use it right away without missing anything.

See Also

- *yum(8)*, *yum.conf(5)*
- Yum home page (*http://linux.duke.edu/projects/yum/*)
- Yum mirrors at FreshRPMs (*http://ayo.freshrpms.net*)
- Fedora mirror list (*http://www.fedora.us/wiki/FedoraMirrorList*)

2.16   Removing Packages with Yum

Problem

You want to delete some packages.

Solution

Yum can do this, too:

```
# yum remove gltron
```

You can also remove several packages at once:

```
# yum remove gltron ktron tuxkart xpoker
```

Discussion

Yum also removes dependent packages that are no longer needed by the system.

See Also

- *yum(8)*, *yum.conf(5)*
- Yum home page (*http://linux.duke.edu/projects/yum/*)

2.17   Getting Information on Installed Packages with Yum

Problem

You want to know what packages are installed on your system, or get information about specific packages.

Solution

Use Yum's querying commands. To list all installed packages, use:

```
# yum list installed
```

To search for specific packages, use:

```
# yum list installed | grep -i tux
tuxracer    i386        0.61-23
tuxkart     i386        0.2.0-3
```

To show information on a package, use:

```
# yum info tuxracer
```

To show packages with available updates, use:

```
# yum list updates
```

Discussion

You can get all the same information using RPM queries, but Yum does it a little more easily.

See Also

- *yum(8), yum.conf(5)*
- Yum home page (*http://linux.duke.edu/projects/yum/*)

2.18 Maintaining Yum

Problem

You want to keep downloaded RPMs from piling up on your system, or you want to ensure that Yum has fresh packages to work with.

Solution

Use the *clean* options. To delete all cached packages, use:

```
# yum clean packages
```

To force a fresh download of package headers, use:

```
# yum clean headers
```

To remove old headers that the system no longer needs, use:

```
# yum clean oldheaders
```

To remove cached packages and old headers, preserving the current headers, use:

```
# yum clean all
```

Discussion

It's a good idea to refresh your local package and header cache periodically, to help prevent odd errors, and to make sure installations and updates are getting current packages.

See Also

- *yum(8), yum.conf(5)*
- Yum home page (*http://linux.duke.edu/projects/yum/*)

## CHAPTER 3

Installing and Managing Software on Debian-Based Systems

3.1   Introduction

Debian is known for being extremely stable and reliable, and for its excellent package manager/dependency resolver, *apt*. Installing a new application is this simple:

```
# apt-get programname
```

All dependencies will be automatically fetched and installed. Not only is *apt* a sophisticated, intelligent tool, but the official Debian software repositories maintain strict packaging standards. The official Debian repositories contain over 12,000 programs, more than any other platform.

dpkg is RPM's Debian cousin, with an extra ability: *dpkg* also performs basic configurations. For example, when you install Postfix, *dpkg* will ask you for some basic system information, install startup files and configuration files, and fire it up.

Debian has three different releases: Stable, Testing, and Unstable. (There is also a fourth release for the adventurous, Experimental.) These are also known as Woody, Sarge, and Sid. Woody is extremely conservative. Packages are accepted into Woody only after extensive dependency testing and security patching. Sarge and Sid contain newer, less-tested releases. Security patches are swift for Woody and erratic for Sarge and Sid.

Which release should you use? The obvious choice is Woody (Stable). It's rock-solid. However, this stability comes at a price: programs in Woody are months, sometimes years behind the latest releases. Woody is great for servers. For desktops and workstations, Sarge (Testing) and Sid (Unstable) are more up-to-date. And despite the scary names—"Testing" and "Unstable"—they perform just fine.

As cute as the code names are, they shouldn't be used in configuration files. Unstable will always be Sid, but Woody and Sarge will not always be associated with Stable and Testing—someday the current Testing release, Sarge, will be promoted to Stable, and the current Woody will be retired. A well-maintained Debian system can be continuously upgraded forever and ever, without ever needing to be completely reinstalled, so you don't want to goober it up by using release codenames that will change.

These are the release codenames, all taken from the movie *Toy Story*:

"Buzz"—Buzz Lightyear, the spaceman (1.1)
"Rex"—Rex the tyrannosaurus (1.2)
"Bo"—Bo Peep (1.3.x)
"Hamm"—Hamm, the piggy bank (2.0)
"Slink"—Slinky Dog (2.1)
"Potato"—Mr. Potato Head (2.2)

And for the 3.x releases:

"Woody"—the cowboy (Stable)

"Sarge"—the leader of the Green Plastic Army Men (Testing)

"Sid"— the rotten kid who destroys toys (Unstable)

3.2   Getting Software for a Debian System

Problem

You need some software for your Debian system. There are gigabytes of software out there, waiting for you—but where do you find software that's packaged for Debian? How do you decide which software archives to use?

Solution

Debian packages come from official Debian package repositories, unofficial repositories, and CD-ROMs. You must specify these sources in */etc/apt/sources.list,* then use Debian's packaging tools to install software from these sources.

Visit these sites to find the addresses for download sites:

Official Debian mirror
http://www.debian.org/mirror/

Unofficial APT repositories
http://www.apt-get.org

Visit this site for a worldwide list of CD vendors:

Vendors of Debian CDs
http://www.debian.org/CD/vendors/

Use the Debian package search page to find individual packages:

Debian packages search page and information
http://www.debian.org/distrib/packages/

The next step is to edit */etc/apt/sources.list* with your selected sources. See the Discussion for some sample configurations.

Discussion

Here are three *sources.list* examples. Run *apt-get update* every time you change *sources.list*, and run it periodically to keep your package lists up-to-date.

sources.list for Woody:

```
# See sources.list(5) for more information
# Remember that you can only use http, ftp, or file URIs
# CD-ROMs are managed through the apt-cdrom tool.
deb http://http.us.debian.org/debian stable main contrib non-free
deb http://non-us.debian.org/debian-non-US stable/non-US main contrib non-free
deb http://security.debian.org stable/updates main contrib non-free
# Uncomment if you want the apt-get source function to work
#deb-src http://http.us.debian.org/debian stable main contrib non-free
#deb-src http://non-us.debian.org/debian-non-US stable/non-US main contrib non-free
```

sources.list for Sarge:

```
deb http://http.us.debian.org/debian testing main contrib non-free
deb http://non-us.debian.org/debian-non-US testing/non-US main contrib non-free
deb http://security.debian.org testing/updates main contrib non-free
# Uncomment if you want the apt-get source function to work
#deb-src http://http.us.debian.org/debian testing main contrib non-free
#deb-src http://non-us.debian.org/debian-non-US testing/non-US main contrib non-free
```

sources.list for Sid:

```
deb ftp://ftp.us.debian.org/debian unstable main contrib non-free
deb ftp://non-us.debian.org/debian-non-US unstable/non-US main contrib non-free
# Sources
deb-src ftp://ftp.us.debian.org/debian unstable main contrib non-free
deb-src ftp://non-us.debian.org/debian-non-US unstable/non-US main contrib non-free
```

apt-get always takes the newest package version, if it finds multiple sources. List your sources in order of preference, because *apt-get* starts at the top and works its way down.

Editing your *sources.list* a lot is perfectly acceptable, and it's a simple way to control installations. Put in all the lines you think you might ever want to use, and comment out the lines that are unneeded for specific installations.

A nice thing to do is to select official Debian mirrors for your *sources.list*, to take the load off the servers at Debian.org. A complete list of the official mirrors is at *http://www.debian.org/mirror/*.

Security updates are available only from *http://www.debian.org/ security/*. Security updates are not mirrored. See the appropiate *sources.list* above to get the correct lines for Stable and Testing. And remember while that Stable receives swift, timely security updates, they are issued much more slowly for Testing and Unstable.

See Also

- *sources.list(5)*
- Official Debian mirrors (*http://www.debian.org/mirror/*)
- Debian packages search page and information (*http://www.debian.org/distrib/ packages*)

3.3   Installing Debian Packages from CD-ROM

Problem

You want to install packages from a CD-ROM. The process we've just described assumes you want to download software from an archive. How do you add a CD to *sources.list*?

Solution

Modify */etc/apt/sources.list* with the *apt-cdrom* command. This is the only way to add CD archives to *sources.list*. There must be a disk in the drive, but it does not need to be mounted. Then type:

```
# apt-cdrom add
Using CD-ROM mount point /cdrom/
Unmounting CD-ROM
Please insert a Disc in the drive and press enter
Mounting CD-ROM
Identifying.. [0eabc03d10414e59dfa1622326e20da7-2]
Scanning Disc for index files..  Found 1 package indexes and 0 source indexes.
This Disc is called:
 'Libranet GNU/Linux 2.8.1 CD2'
Reading Package Indexes... Done
Wrote 1271 records.
Writing new source list
Source List entries for this Disc are:
deb cdrom:[Libranet GNU/Linux 2.8.1 CD2]/ archive/
Repeat this process for the rest of the CDs in your set.
```

Use the *-d* switch to add a CD in a different CD drive:

```
# apt-cdrom -d /cdrom1 add
```

To identify a disk, use:

```
$ apt-cdrom ident
Using CD-ROM mount point /cdrom/
```

```
Mounting CD-ROM
Identifying.. [0eabc03d10414e59dfa1622326e20da7-2]
Stored Label: 'Libranet GNU/Linux 2.8.1 CD2'
$
```

Discussion

apt-get selects the newest versions of packages to install from the available sources. As the Linux world advances swiftly, your online sources will always be the newest. To make sure a program gets installed from a CD, comment out the other lines in your *sources.list*.

 Remember to run *apt-get update* every time you change your *sources.list*.

See Also

- *apt-cdrom(8), apt-get(8)*
- Debian on CD, the ISO archives (*http://www.debian.org/CD/http-ftp/*)

3.4   Installing Packages on Debian-Based Systems

Problem

All these software archives, CDs, and so on are meaningless if you can't install the software. So: you need to know how to install packages on Debian.

Solution

Use *apt-get install*:

```
# apt-get install tuxkart
```

To reinstall a package, overwriting the files, use:

```
# apt-get install --reinstall tuxkart
```

To install several packages at once, use a space-delimited list:

```
# apt-get install tuxkart gltron frozen-bubble
tuxracer nethack galaga
```

To download only, without installing or unpacking, use:

```
# apt-get -d install tuxkart
```

Append *--dry-run* to test the command before executing it:

```
# apt-get install tuxkart gltron frozen-bubble tuxracer nethack galaga --dry-run
```

Discussion

To find package names, use Debian's package search page at *http://www.debian.org/distrib/packages/*. Debian's package names are often very different from their RPM cousins. For example, CyrusSASL is packaged as *sasl-2.x.rpm*, but on Debian it's split into several packages named *libsasl-**.

Remember to run *apt-get update* after changing */etc/apt/sources.list*, and run it periodically to stay current with the package repositories.

apt-get fetches and installs (and when necessary, deletes) all packages necessary to resolve all dependencies.

See Also

- *apt-get(8)*
- Local documentation (*/usr/share/doc/Debian/apt-howto*)

3.5   Removing Packages from a Debian System

Problem

You want to remove a package, or several packages, from your Debian system.

Solution

Use *apt-get remove*:

```
# apt-get remove tuxpaint
Reading Package Lists... Done
Building Dependency Tree... Done
The following packages will be REMOVED:
  tuxkart
0 upgraded, 0 newly installed, 1 to remove and 79 not upgraded.
Need to get 0B of archives.
After unpacking 188kB disk space will be freed.
Do you want to continue? [Y/n] y
(Reading database ... 141283 files and directories currently installed.)
Removing tuxkart ...
#
```

To test the *remove* command first, use:

```
# apt-get remove tuxpaint --dry-run
```

To remove all traces of a package, including configuration files, use:

```
# apt-get --purge remove tuxpaint
```

To remove several packages, use a space-delimited list:

```
# apt-get remove tuxkart gltron frozen-bubble tuxracer nethack galaga
```

- *apt-get(8)*
- Local documentation (*/usr/share/doc/Debian/apt-howto*)

3.6 Installing from Sources on a Debian System

Problem

You want to compile a program on your system, rather than installing the Debian binaries. Perhaps you want to edit the source code, or you want to run a package from Testing or Unstable on Stable, and recompiling it will ensure that the correct dependencies will be built.

Solution

Use *apt-get source*, with an assist from *dpkg*.

First, download the dependent headers and libraries into the directory in which you want to build the package:

```
# cd /usr/src
# apt-get build-dep tuxkart
```

To download and build the package:

```
# apt-get -b source tuxkart
```

and install the package:

```
# dpkg -i tuxkart.deb
```

Discussion

A common reason for building *.debs* from sources is to use packages from Testing or Unstable on Stable. Recompiling them adjusts the dependencies for Stable.

An alternative to building *.debs* from sources is to use *backports*. These are nice compiled Debian binaries, all ready to use. See *http://www.backports.org*.

If you want to install a program that is not in the Debian repositories, you can build a *.deb* using CheckInstall, a utility that creates RPM, *.deb*, and Slackware packages (see Recipe 4.5).

See Also

- *apt-get(8)*, *dpkg-source(1)*
- Local documentation (*/usr/share/doc/Debian/apt-howto*)
- Recipe 4.5, "Using CheckInstall to Create Packages from Sources"

3.7   Upgrading Packages on Debian

Problem

You want to upgrade a Debian package, because the new version has new features or bug fixes.

Solution

Use *apt-get install*:

```
# apt-get install gltron
Reading Package Lists... Done
Building Dependency Tree... Done
The following packages will be upgraded:
  gltron
1 upgraded, 0 newly installed, 0 to remove and 78 not upgraded.
Need to get 89.5kB of archives.
After unpacking 266kB of additional disk space will be used.
Get:1 ftp://ftp.debian.org sid/main gltron 3.53 [89.5kB]
Fetched 89.5kB in 5s (16.8kB/s)
Preconfiguring packages ...
(Reading database ... 141286 files and directories currently installed.)
Preparing to replace adduser 3.52 (using .../archives/adduser_3.53_all.deb) ...
Unpacking replacement gltron ...
Setting up adduser (3.53) ...
#
```

To upgrade several packages, use:

```
# apt-get install tuxkart gltron frozen-bubble tuxracer nethack galaga
```

Discussion

There is no separate command for upgrading a package. *apt-get install* always looks for the newest version.

See Also

- *apt-get(8)*
- Local documentation (*/usr/share/doc/Debian/apt-howto*)

3.8   Upgrading a Debian System

Problem

You want to upgrade all the packages on your system to the latest versions.

Solution

Make sure your */etc/apt/sources.list* is pointing to your desired sources, then run *apt-get upgrade*.

Always update your package lists first:

```
# apt-get update
```

This command upgrades all installed packages, but does not remove any packages to resolve dependencies:

```
# apt-get -u upgrade
```

This upgrades all installed packages, and removes or installs packages as needed to satisfy all dependencies:

```
# apt-get -u dist-upgrade
```

The *-u* flag gives you a chance to review all changes first. The upgrade can take several hours, depending on the speed of your Internet connection, and how many packages need to be downloaded.

Discussion

To make *-u* the default action, edit (or create) */etc/apt/apt.conf*:

```
// Always list packages to be upgraded
// and prompt user
APT::Get::Show-Upgraded "true";
```

Every time you want to run *apt-get dist-upgrade*, run *apt-get upgrade* first to reduce the chances of *dist-upgrade* encountering errors.

See Also

- *apt-get(8)*
- Local Documentation (*/usr/share/doc/Debian/apt-howto*)

3.9 Upgrading to a Newer Debian Release

Problem

You want to upgrade to a newer release; for example, from Woody to Sarge.

Solution

First, edit */etc/apt/sources.list* so that it has only Sarge entries. Then do the following:

```
# apt-get update
# apt-get -u upgrade
# apt-get -u dist-upgrade
```

The *-u* flag lets you review the changes first. Depending on the speed of your Internet connection and how many packages are required, this can take up to several hours.

If *apt-get -u dist-upgrade* shows any held packages, this indicates dependency conflicts that *apt* cannot resolve. See Recipe 3.13 for how to resolve these conflicts.

Discussion

At some point Sarge will be promoted to Stable, and Woody will be "retired." When that happens, this is how to "promote" your system as well.

See Also

- *apt-get(8)*
- Local Documentation (*/usr/share/doc/Debian/apt-howto*)

3.10   Running a Mixed Debian System

Problem

You want Stable for a base system, plus some programs from Testing. That is, you want a rock-solid base system, but for a few programs you need the most recent versions to get necessary features.

Solution

Edit */etc/apt/sources.list* to point to both Stable and Testing sources, then edit */etc/apt/apt.conf* to set the default release. In this example, Stable is the default. Then when you install or upgrade packages, select the version you want with the *-t* flag.

First, edit */etc/apt/sources.list* to point to both Stable and Testing. (See Recipe 3.2 for more information on *sources.list*.)

Now edit (or create) */etc/apt/apt.conf*:

```
// This is the default system release-
// version can be: woody, sarge, sid
// or stable, testing, unstable
APT::Default-Release "stable";
```

and update your package lists:

```
# apt-get update
```

Stable is now the default release, so it's not necessary to specify it when installing packages. This command installs Tuxkart from Stable:

```
# apt-get install tuxkart
```

To install a package from Sarge (Testing), use the *-t* switch:

```
# apt-get -t testing install tuxkart
```

Specifying the package number will ensure that you get exactly the version you want:

```
# apt-get install tuxkart=0.2.0-3
```

Discussion

You want to be careful running a mixed system, especially when Woody is the base system. As Woody ages, binary compatibility with Sarge/Sid becomes an issue. Key system files, such as *libc* and *gcc*, can diverge to the point that Sarge/Sid packages won't install on Woody. If that happens, try building the packages from sources, or using backports (Recipe 3.6).

See Also

- *apt.conf(5)*, *sources.list(5)*
- Debian package search page (*http://www.debian.org/distrib/packages*)

3.11   Finding Out What Is Installed on a Debian System

Problem

You want to know what packages are on your system, what packages files belong to, and what's in individual packages.

Solution

Use the querying features of *dpkg*.

To list all installed packages and pipe the list to a file, use:

```
$ dpkg -l | tee dpkglist
```

To find all packages related to your search term and show their installation status, use:

```
$ dpkg -l '*gnome*'
Desired=Unknown/Install/Remove/Purge/Hold
| Status=Not/Installed/Config-files/Unpacked/Failed-config/Half-installed
|/ Err?=(none)/Hold/Reinst-required/X=both-problems (Status,Err: uppercase=bad)
||/ Name            Version         Description
+++-===================================================
pn  gnome    <none>    (no description available)
un  gnome-about   <none>     (no description available))
ii  gnome-applets  2.4.2-1    Various applets for GNOME 2 panel
rc  gnome-bin     1.4.2-18     Miscellaneous binaries used by GNOME
```

To find only installed packages related to your search term, use:

```
$ dpkg -l | grep gnome
```

To list files belonging to a package, use:

```
$ dpkg -L gnome-applets
.
/usr
/usr/share
/usr/share/lintian
/usr/share/lintian/overrides
/usr/share/lintian/overrides/gnome-applets
...
```

To see what package a file belongs to, use:

```
$ dpkg -S boing.wav
tuxkart-data: /usr/share/games/tuxkart/wavs/boing.wav
```

To show complete package information, use:

```
$ dpkg -s kpoker
Package: kpoker
Status: install ok installed
Priority: optional
Section: games
Installed-Size: 428
Maintainer: Daniel Schepler <schepler@debian.org>
Source: kdegames
Version: 4:3.1.5-1
....
```

Discussion

The table displayed by *dpkg -l* is a bit cryptic, so here's a translation. Believe it or not, it's ASCII art.

```
$ dpkg -l gnome*
Desired=Unknown/Install/Remove/Purge/Hold
| Status=Not/Installed/Config-files/Unpacked/Failed-config/Half-installed
|/ Err?=(none)/Hold/Reinst-required/X=both-problems (Status,Err: uppercase=bad)
||/ Name            Version          Description
+++-=================================================
pn  gnome    <none>    (no description available)
un  gnome-about   <none>    (no description available))
ii  gnome-applets   2.4.2-1   Various applets for GNOME 2 panel
rc  gnome-bin    1.4.2-18    Miscellaneous binaries used by GNOME
```

On the *pn gnome* line, follow the *p* upward; there are three "arrows" pointing to *Desired=Unknown/Install/Remove/Purge/Hold*. This represents the state you wish the package to have (in this case, "purge").

The next column, *n*, points to the *Status* line, where we are informed that it is "Not/Installed."

The third column points to the error and is empty (a good thing). As the end of this line indicates, anything in the *Status* or *Err* columns in uppercase is really bad.

So, package *gnome* was installed once upon a time, but I desired it purged, and so it was.

un means a package has never been installed.

ii means a package is desired and installed.

rc means a package was once installed but then was removed, leaving the configuration files behind. This is easy to check:

```
$ dpkg -L gnome-bin
/etc/logcheck/ignore.d.server/gnome-bin
/etc/logcheck/ignore.d.workstation/gnome-bin
```

See Also

- *dpkg(8)*

3.12   Maintaining the Debian Package Cache

Problem

You want to keep your package cache and package lists tidy and up-to-date, so that *apt* will work correctly and not encounter bogus dependency problems.

Solution

Use *apt* and *dpkg*.

Remember to run *apt-get update* after making changes to */etc/apt/sources.list*, and run it periodically to keep package lists current.

To look for downloaded, uninstalled packages, use:

```
$ dpkg --yet-to-unpack
```

To check for broken dependencies, use:

```
# apt-get check
```

To remove cached packages that are no longer needed, use:

```
# apt-cache autoclean
```

To remove all cached packages, use:

```
# apt-cache clean
```

To show partially installed packages, use:

```
$ dpkg --audit
```

If *dpkg --audit* returns any results, as in the following case:

```
$ dpkg --audit
vpw    (no information available)
```

first check that the returned package exists:

```
$ dpkg -l vpw
Package `vpw' is not installed and no info is available.
```

If it exists, either complete the installation or remove it. If it is not installed, search both */var/lib/dpkg/available* and */var/lib/dpkg/status* for the offending entry, and remove it.

Discussion

Your package cache can easily consume tens, or even hundreds, of megabytes. See for yourself in */var/cache/apt/archives*. To conserve storage space, set up a local package cache for your network (Recipe 3.14).

See Also

- *dpkg(8), apt-cache(8), apt-get(8)*
- Local documentation (*/usr/share/doc/Debian/apt-howto*)
- The Debian Reference Manual (*http://qref.sourceforge.net/*)

3.13   Resolving Debian Dependency Conflicts

Problem

A program will not install because of dependency problems, or *apt-get dist-upgrade* leaves held packages behind and you need to clean them up.

Solution

There are several different commands to try; this recipe lists them in the order you should try them.

Suppose *libpam-modules* is the problem package, and it won't upgrade:

```
# apt-get install libpam-modules
...
The following packages have unmet dependencies:
  libpam-modules: Depends: libdb3 (>= 3.2.9-19.1) but 3.2.9-19 is to be installed
E: Broken packages
```

If you are running a mixed system, first try specifying the version:

```
# apt-get install -t stable libpam-modules
```

If that doesn't help, or you are not running a mixed system, try Debian's conflict resolver:

```
# apt-get -f install
```

Then run:

```
# dpkg --configure -a
```

Then run this one again:

```
# apt-get -f install
```

If it reports:

```
Reading Package Lists... Done
Building Dependency Tree... Done
0 upgraded, 0 newly installed, 0 to remove and 1 not upgraded.
```

That means it failed. Next, test what happens if you delete the existing *libpam-modules*:

```
# apt-get remove --dry-run libpam-modules
Reading Package Lists... Done
Building Dependency Tree... Done
The following packages will be REMOVED:
  adduser adminmenu apache at base-config courier-imap courier-imap-ssl courier-pop
courier-pop-ssl cron cupsys cupsys-driver-gimpprint dict-elements dict-foldoc dict-
gcide dict-jargon dict-vera dict-wn dictd gdm2...
....
WARNING: The following essential packages will be removed
This should NOT be done unless you know exactly what you are doing!
  login libpam-modules (due to login)
```

In this instance, it's going to take almost a system rebuild to correct the dependency conflict. Most times, there are only a few packages involved. In that case, delete the least important ones first, until all dependency conflicts are resolved, and then reinstall any that are needed.

If *apt-get -u dist-upgrade* shows any held packages, it is best to eliminate them. Packages are held because of dependency conflicts that *apt* cannot resolve. Try this command to find and repair the conflicts:

```
# apt-get -o Debug::pkgProblemResolver=yes dist-upgrade
```

If it cannot fix the conflicts, it will exit with:

```
0 upgraded, 0 newly installed, 0 to remove and 6 not upgraded.
```

Delete the *held* packages one by one, running *dist-upgrade* each time, until there are no more held packages. Then reinstall any needed packages. Be sure to use the *--dry-run* option, so that you are fully informed of consquences:

```
# apt-get remove --dry-run libsdl-perl
```

Discussion

These sorts of dependency conflicts are rare on single-release systems. Users of mixed systems run into them more often. The best prevention is to be very selective about what you install—when you first install Debian, take the time to select all the packages you want individually.

See Also

- *dpkg(8)*, *apt-get(8)*
- Debian User's List, with searchable archives (*http://lists.debian.org/debian-user/*)

3.14   Building a Local Debian Repository

Problem

You want to build a local package repository for your LAN to share. A local repository is useful if you have many users sharing a low-bandwidth Internet connection; your Debian systems can grab packages from the local repository, rather than going out over the network.

Solution

Use *apt-proxy:*

```
# apt-get install apt-proxy
```

apt-proxy starts up automatically after installation.

Next, edit the *add_backend/debian/* section of */etc/apt-proxy/apt-proxy.conf* so that it points to geographically close package mirrors. (See *http://www.debian.org/mirror/list* for a list of package mirrors.)

Now edit */etc/apt/sources.list* on the client machines to point to the *apt-proxy* server. The default port is 9999:

```
deb http://ip-or-hostname:9999/main stable main contrib non-free
deb http://ip-or-hostname:9999/non-US stable/non-US main contrib non-free
deb http://ip-or-hostname:9999/security stable/updates main contrib non-free
```

Run *apt-get update* on the client machines, and you're in business. Every time a client machine on your LAN installs a new program, it will be cached on the *apt-proxy* server. Subsequent requests for the same package will be served by the local cache.

Discussion

Most of the default settings in */etc/apt-proxy/apt-proxy.conf,* other than the package sources, are just fine, except for one thing: the "updates" frequency, which specifies how often to download the latest packages list. This is the default:

```
# Maximum frequency of Packages/etc. updates from back end (minutes)
# Keep high to speed things up.
BACKEND_FREQ=240
```

I set mine to 1440; once a day is plenty. There's really not so much happening that more frequent updates are necessary. The main reason to check as often as once a day is to stay on top of security updates.

See Also

- *apt-proxy(8), apt-proxy.conf(5)*
- The official Debian mirrors list (*http://www.debian.org/mirror/*)
- Apt-proxy home page (*http://apt-proxy.sourceforge.net/*)

3.15 Selecting Package Mirrors for apt-proxy.conf

Problem

The default package mirrors in *apt-proxy.conf* are all over the globe, how do you select which mirrors to use? Ideally, you'd like to use mirror sites that are close to you.

Solution

The default sources in */etc/apt-proxy/apt-proxy.conf* look like this:

```
add_backend /debian/                                   \
        $APT_PROXY_CACHE/debian/                        \
        http://ftp.us.debian.org/debian/               \
        http://ftp.de.debian.org/debian/               \
        http://ftp.uk.debian.org/debian/               \
        +ftp.us.debian.org::debian/
```

Visit *http://www.debian.org/mirror/list* for the current list of Debian mirrors. For example, here are some of the German mirrors on *mirror/list*:

```
DE Germany
----------
ftp.de.debian.org      /debian/            /debian/
ftp2.de.debian.org     /debian/            /debian/
ftp.tu-clausthal.de    /pub/linux/debian/  /pub/linux/debian/
debian.uni-essen.de    /debian/            /debian/
...
```

Replace the defaults with your selections, prefixing each entry with *http://*:

```
add_backend /debian/                                   \
        $APT_PROXY_CACHE/debian/                        \
        http://ftp.de.debian.org/debian/               \
        http://ftp2.de.debian.org/debian/              \
        http://ftp.tu-clausthal.de/pub/linux/debian    \
```

The */etc/apt/sources.list* files on the client machines do not need to be changed.

Discussion

You can use *ping* and *traceroute* to find out which mirrors have the fastest response times, because geographic proximity doesn't always mean faster responses.

Having three separate sources gives redundancy. *apt-proxy* queries them in order, so if the first one does not respond, it tries the next one.

See Also

- *apt-proxy(8)*, *apt-proxy.conf(5)*, *apt-proxy-import(8)*
- The official Debian mirrors list (*http://www.debian.org/mirror/*)
- *apt-proxy* home page (*http://apt-proxy.sourceforge.net/*)

3.16 Adding Your Existing Package Cache to apt-proxy.conf

Problem

You already have a sizeable *.deb* cache on your *apt-proxy* server, and you would like *apt-proxy* to use it instead of downloading everything all over again.

Solution

First run *apt-get update* on at least one client machine to initialize the cache. Then, on the server, run:

```
# apt-proxy-import -d /var/cache/apt/archives
```

And you're done.

See Also

- *apt-proxy(8)*, *apt-proxy.conf(5)*, *apt-proxy-import(8)*
- The official Debian mirrors list (*http://www.debian.org/mirror/*)
- *apt-proxy* home page (*http://apt-proxy.sourceforge.net*)

CHAPTER 4

Installing Programs from Source Code

4.1   Introduction

Even with all the package managers and dependency resolvers out there, there are times when building from sources is preferable. For example, a program you want may not be available in a packaged version, or you may need to control exactly what options and features are built into it, or you may want to optimize it for your architecture. Many experienced administrators recommend building programs critical to security (*ssh* and all servers, for example) from sources.

When building from sources, be sure to read all the instructions. While the *configure-make-make install* procedure is fairly standard, there are many exceptions, according to the quirks of the program authors. And there are often many configuration options, which only the documention for the program can tell you.

If you prefer using packages, all the tools are freely available for building your own RPMs and *.deb*s. However, it's a fair learning curve to learn to use RPM or to build your own *.deb*s. There is a third option: CheckInstall. CheckInstall is a great utility for easily building your own RPM, Debian, or Slackware packages from source code.

4.2   Preparing Your System for Compiling Programs from Sources

Problem

You know you need a compiler and maybe some other utilities to be able to compile programs from sources, but you're not sure exactly what.

Solution

There are two categories of programs that you will need:

- Essential development tools common to all Linux systems
- Specific libraries or utilities for whatever program you are compiling

Here is a list of the common Linux development tools:

GNU coreutils
> This is a large collection of essential system utilities: *shellutils*, *fileutils*, and *textutils*. See *http://www.gnu.org/software/cororeutils/* for a complete listing, or *info coreutils*.

GNU binutils
> Utilities for doing things to binary files (*http://www.gnu.org/software/binutils/*).

gcc
> GNU compiler collection, containing C, C++, Objective-C, Fortran, Java, and Ada, and libraries for these languages.

GNU tar
> Archiving utility for source tarballs; these end in *.tar*.

gunzip
> Compression utility often paired with tar. These end in *.tar.gz*.

bunzip2
> A super-compression format for packing and unpacking tarballs; these end in *.bz2*.

make
> This does the work of reading your configuration options and building the actual program files.

The documentation for the application you are building will tell you everything that it needs to build successfully.

Discussion

Most Linux distributions have an installation option for "Core Development Tools," or some such, so you don't have to hunt down and install them individually.

You'll need to read the documentation for the application you are building to find out any requirements specific to the program. Look for README, INSTALL, and other documentation in the source tarball. Read everything. When you run the configure script, it will check your system to see if all the required elements are present. If anything is missing, it will exit with errors, and tell what you need.

See Also

- Chapter 14 of *LPI Linux Certification in a Nutshell* by Jeff Dean (O'Reilly)

4.3 Generating a List of Files from a Source Install for Easy Uninstalls

Problem

You need to know what files are installed on your system when you install a program from source code, so that you can find and remove all of them if you decide you don't want them anymore. Some program authors thoughtfully include a "make uninstall" target to perform a clean uninstall, but many do not.

Solution

You can use standard Linux utilities to generate a pre-installation list of all files on your system. Then generate a post-installation list, and *diff* the two lists to make a list of newly-installed files. This example uses JOE: Joe's Own Editor:

```
# find / | grep -v -e ^/proc/ -e ^/tmp/ -e ^/dev/ > joe-preinstall.list
```

Compile and install your new program, then generate the post-installation list:

```
# find / | grep -v -e ^/proc/ -e ^/tmp/ -e ^/dev/ > joe-postinstall.list
```

Then create a list of files installed by Joe by *diff*ing the two lists:

```
$ diff joe-preinstall.list joe-postinstall.list > joe-installed.list
```

Discussion

Using *find* and *grep* together makes it easy to exclude directories that don't matter for your final list. The *-v* option for *grep* turns on verbosity. *-e ^* means "exclude the following directory."

You don't need to bother with */proc* or */tmp* files, because these are transient and constantly changing. */dev* files are managed by the system, so you can ignore these as well. And it's a also an important safety measure—when you remove a program manually, using your nice *diff* list, */proc*, */tmp*, and */dev* are all directories you shouldn't touch in any case.

See Also

- *grep(1)*, *find(1)*, *diff(1)*

4.4   Installing Programs from Source Code

Problem

You want to install a program from source code, but you're having trouble navigating the thickets of tarballs, makefiles, and bunzips.

Solution

Unpack the tarball (compressed archive), then *configure*, *make*, and *install* the program.

Start in the directory where you store your tarballs and source trees. This example uses JOE (Joe's Own Editor):

```
# cd /usr/src/downloads
# tar zxvf joe-2.9.8.tar.gz
# cd joe-2.9.8
# ls
# less README
# less INFO
# ./configure --help
# ./configure <options, if needed>
# make
# make install | tee joe-makeinstall
```

The last command stores the installation output in the text file *joe-makeinstall*.

Some programs are archived with the *bunzip2* utility, rather than the more traditional *gzip*. This is how to unpack a *.bz2* archive:

```
# tar jxvf joe-2.9.8.tar.bz2
```

To uninstall a source-built program, use:

```
# make uninstall
```

Uninstalling works only if the program author included a *make uninstall* option. Piping the output of *make install* to a text file gives you a reference if you have to remove all the files manually. Or generate a list using Recipe 4.3.

Discussion

The steps described in this section are the standard way of installing programs from source code. However, not all program authors follow the same procedures. Be sure to review all the program documentation first.

Studying your *configure* options is the most important part. Some programs, like Apache, have dozens of compile-time options. For prudent basic security, you only want to compile in support for things you really need. This is most important on servers that are exposed to untrusted networks, such as web and mail servers.

Good reasons to compile programs from source are:

- You can configure exactly the options you need.
- You can optimize the program for your architecture.
- You have ultimate control over what is installed.

The bad part:

- Upgrades and removals can be messy.
- Dependency hell is only a short step away.
- Compiling a large program can take hours.

Some servers should be built from sources. For example, an Apache web server really needs to be source-built to get full customization and optimization.

For a desktop system, forget it. They're too big and complex. Use the nice package-based Linux distributions for these.

See Also

- *info tar, make(1), bzip2(1)*

4.5   Using CheckInstall to Create Packages from Sources

Problem

You want to create Slackware, Red Hat, or Debian packages from source code, because an application that you want to install does not come in the package you want. You have read up on building packages, and it's very complicated. Isn't there an easier way?

Solution

Use CheckInstall. Again using Joe's Own Editor in this example, on Debian, do the following:

```
# mkdir /doc-pak
# tar zxvf joe-2.9.8.tar.gz
# cd joe-2.9.8
# ./configure
# make
# checkinstall -D
```

CheckInstall replaces *make install*, so it must run from the root of the source tree. Follow the prompts and do what they say. It will build and install a *.deb*, as we can verify:

```
$ dpkg -l | grep joe
ii  joe           2.9.8-1      joe's own editor, my fave
```

And that's it. It's installed and ready to go to work. A copy of the package will remain in the source directory.

To build a Slackware package, use:

```
# checkinstall -S
```

To build an RPM package, use:

```
# checkinstall -R
```

Discussion

The *doc-pak* directory is where CheckInstall places READMEs and other program documentation. If you don't create the *doc-pak* directory, CheckInstall asks if you want to build a default documentation directory. If you say no, your package will have no documentation.

CheckInstall uses the native installation program's package manager: RPM on Red Hat, *installpkg* on Slackware, *.apt* on Debian. To remove a CheckInstall package, simply use your system's package manager.

CheckInstall supports any install scripts. For example:

```
# checkinstall -D make install_packages
# checkinstall -R make modules_install
# checkinstall -S install.sh
# checkinstall -D setup
```

Remember to study the README of the program you're installing, and any other included documentation. Not all source packages use the traditional *configure-make-make install* dance. Some use other installation scripts, as in the example above.

CheckInstall does not yet allow creating a package without automatically installing it, though this may change in future releases.

See Also

- CheckInstall home page (*http://asic-linux.com.mx/~izto/checkinstall/news.php*)

CHAPTER 5

Discovering Hardware from Outside the Box

5.1　Introduction

Linux comes with several good utilities for getting detailed information on what's inside the box. You can sit down at a machine and in minutes have an inventory of all its components.

Not only do these utilities save you the hassle of opening the box and poking around, but they are invaluable for finding the correct drivers for a device, or finding out if it is supported in Linux at all. In a foolishly Windows-centric world, determining if a modem, NIC, or video card has Linux drivers usually requires that you know the chipset used in the device. There are a few chipsets that go into many brands and models. Some manufacturers change chipsets without changing model numbers, so don't count on model numbers. Once you know the chipset, you can find drivers.

Hardware Compatibility Lists

Linux support for most PC hardware is quite good, as valiant Linux programmers continue to churn out drivers, often with little or no support from hardware manufacturers. But you still need to shop carefully. And even if a device has Linux drivers, it may not come with the nice management utilities, or complete feature set, that Windows users get.

Your first and best stop is the web site of your Linux distribution. Most of them have hardware compatibility lists (HCLs). If your particular flavor of Linux has no HCL, borrow one from another distribution. Whatever works on one Linux distribution should work on all of them. What differentiates them are the levels of out-of-the-box support. For example, Mandrake and Linspire are configured for advanced sound and video support. Other distributions are capable of running the same devices, but you may have to find and install the drivers yourself. Sometimes it may even be necessary to compile some kernel modules (which is no big deal for us ace Linux users, just inconvenient). So be sure to first research any distribution-specific issues.

A fast way to get information on a particular device is to search Google Groups, like this:

```
debian linux riva tnt2
```

Most of the time this zeros right in on useful links.

My final choice is the device manufacturer's web site. Sometimes you get pleasantly surprised and find actual Linux information on these sites.

Why Binary-Only Drivers Are Bad

Some hardware vendors limit their Linux support to providing binary drivers. Avoid these, if that's at all possible. Binaries are compiled against a single architecture and kernel version. This means you are dependent on the vendor to supply upgrades and alternate versions. It is so easy to recompile a program so that it works correctly on your system that it's just plain silly to deny users this option. We end-users are sheltered from these issues when we use package-based systems, such as Red Hat, SuSE, and Debian, because the package maintainers do the work for us. But again, they need the source code. Linus Torvalds said,

> I allow binary-only modules, but I want people to know that they are *only* ever expected to work on the one version of the kernel that they were compiled for. Anything else is just a very nice unexpected bonus if it happens to work.

(See *http://lwn.net/1999/0211/a/lt-binary.html* for the whole message.)

5.2   Detecting Hardware with lspci

Problem

You're looking at new systems, or installing Linux on a box that used to run a different OS, and you're wondering if all the components—video, modem, Ethernet, sound—will work on Linux. The vendors can't, or won't, tell you if their products will work on Linux. You need to know what the chipsets are, to find out if there are Linux drivers.

Alternatively, you want to know what components are installed inside a computer, and you don't feel like hauling the thing out, popping the case open, and tearing it apart.

Solution

Use *lspci:*

```
# /sbin/lscpi
# /sbin/lspci -v
# /sbin/lspci -vv
```

To show a summary of all devices connected to the PCI bus, use:

```
$ /sbin/lspci
00:00.0 Host bridge: VIA Technologies, Inc. VT8363/8365 [KT133/KM133] (rev 02)
```

```
00:01.0 PCI bridge: VIA Technologies, Inc. VT8363/8365 [KT133/KM133 AGP]
00:06.0 Ethernet controller: Linksys Network Everywhere Fast Ethernet 10/100 model
NC100 (rev 11)
...
```

Use the *-v* or *-vv* flags to display more information:

```
# /sbin/lspci -v
0000:01:00.0 VGA compatible controller: 3Dfx Interactive, Inc. Voodoo 3 (rev 01)
(prog-if 00 [VGA])
        Subsystem: 3Dfx Interactive, Inc.: Unknown device 1252
        Flags: 66MHz, fast devsel, IRQ 10
        Memory at d4000000 (32-bit, non-prefetchable) [size=32M]
        Memory at d8000000 (32-bit, prefetchable) [size=32M]
        I/O ports at c000 [size=256]
        Expansion ROM at <unassigned> [disabled] [size=64K]
        Capabilities: [54] AGP version 1.0
        Capabilities: [60] Power Management version 1
```

If you're looking for drivers, you can now take this output (e.g., *VT8363/8365* or *3Dfx Interactive, Inc. Voodoo 3 (rev 01)*) to run a Google search.

Discussion

lspci reads some information from the PCI bus, then displays additional information from its own database of hardware IDs—vendors, devices, classes and subclasses—at */usr/share/misc/pci.ids*. There is even a command to update this file:

```
# update-pciids
```

The *lspci* maintainers welcome submissions of new data; please read */usr/share/misc/pci.ids* for how to make submissions.

If there is a device attached to the system that the *lspci* simply does not recognize, such as a very old, odd ISA device, you'll have to open the case to see what it is. Or try running *dmesg* (Recipe 5.3).

See Also

- *lspci(8)*

5.3   Using dmesg to Collect Hardware Information

Problem

PCI is fine, but it's yesterday's news; you need an inventory of all the devices on the system, not just PCI devices. You're interested in USB devices, SCSI devices, memory configuration, even the CPU.

Solution

Use *dmesg*. *dmesg* is a record of everything detected by the kernel.

To view all *dmesg* output, use:

```
$ dmesg | less
```

You can also filter the output of *dmesg* to find specific devices. For example, to list all USB devices, use:

```
$ dmesg | grep -i usb
```

To list ISA devices, use:

```
$ dmesg | grep -i isa
isapnp: Scanning for PnP cards...
isapnp: SB audio device quirk - increasing port range
isapnp: Card 'SupraExpress 56i Voice'
```

To see how much physical memory is on the system, use:

```
$ dmesg | grep -i memory
Memory: 256492k/262080k available (1467k kernel code, 5204k reserved, 516k data, 96k
init, 0k highmem)
```

This shows IDE devices using the SCSI emulation subsystem, which is used on 2.4 and older kernels:

```
$ dmesg | grep -i scsi
Kernel command line: root=/dev/hda6 ro hdb=scsi hdc=scsi
ide_setup: hdb=scsi
ide_setup: hdc=scsi
SCSI subsystem driver Revision: 1.00
hdb: attached ide-scsi driver.
hdc: attached ide-scsi driver.
scsi0 : SCSI host adapter emulation for IDE ATAPI devices
...
```

Here are what "real," not emulated, SCSI devices look like:

```
$ dmesg | grep -i scsi
SCSI subsystem driver Revision: 1.00
scsi0 : Adaptec AIC7XXX EISA/VLB/PCI SCSI HBA DRIVER, Rev 6.2.8
    <Adaptec aic7892 Ultra160 SCSI adapter>
    aic7892: Ultra160 Wide Channel A, SCSI Id=7, 32/253 SCBs
...Vendor: IBM-PSG   Model: DPSS-336950M M   Rev: S9HA
Attached scsi disk sda at scsi0, channel 0, id 0, lun 0
(scsi0:A:0): 160.000MB/s transfers (80.000MHz DT, offset 63, 16bit)
SCSI device sda: 71096640 512-byte hdwr sectors (36401 MB)
Partition check:
 sda: sda1 sda2 sda3 sda4 < sda5 sda6 >
```

Shown here is information about a USB camera that is connected to the system, including its location in the filesystem. Typically, USB output runs to a dozen lines or more:

```
$ dmesg | grep -i usb
...
```

```
usb.c: registered new driver ibmcam
ibmcam.c: IBM PC Camera USB camera found (model 2, rev. 0x030a)
usbvideo.c: ibmcam on /dev/video0: canvas=352x240 videosize=352x240
```

To show serial ports, use:

```
$ dmesg | grep -i tty
ttyS00 at 0x03f8 (irq = 4) is a 16550A
```

To show CPU or CPUs, use:

```
$ dmesg | grep -i cpu
Initializing CPU#0
CPU: L1 I Cache: 64K (64 bytes/line), D cache 64K (64 bytes/line)
CPU: L2 Cache: 64K (64 bytes/line)
Intel machine check reporting enabled on CPU#0.
CPU:     After generic, caps: 0183f9ff c1c7f9ff 00000000 00000000
CPU:     Common caps: 0183f9ff c1c7f9ff 00000000 00000000
CPU: AMD Duron(tm) Processor stepping 01
```

Note that these searches only return lines containing your search string. There is often more information adjacent to these lines, which you'll find by eyeballing the whole file:

```
Initializing CPU#0
Detected 801.446 MHz processor.
```

Discussion

dmesg always provides up-to-date information, even if you're changing hardware frequently (for example, plugging in and detaching hotplug USB devices).

See Also

- *dmesg(8)*

5.4   Getting Live Hardware Snapshots with /proc

Problem

You want to monitor a running system in real time, and view things like physical memory and CPU information, or identify drives.

Solution

Read the */proc* virtual filesystem. Use only *cat* to read */proc*, or utilities designed expressly for it, such as *sysctl*, *lspci*, *ps*, and *top*. The syntax is the same as for reading any file:

```
$ cat /proc/filename
```

You can explore */proc* just like any filesystem and easily find the information you want. Look to the named folders for hardware information:

```
$ ls /proc
bus cmdline cpuinfo devices dma driver filesystems ide kcore kmsg ksyms
loadavg meminfo misc modules mounts mtrr partitions pci scsi swaps sys tty
```

For example, to show CPU information, use:

```
$ cat /proc/cpuinfo
processor       : 0
vendor_id       : AuthenticAMD
cpu family      : 6
model           : 3
model name      : AMD Duron(tm) Processor
stepping        : 1
cpu MHz         : 801.442
...
```

To show physical memory and swap usage, use:

```
$ cat /proc/meminfo
total:    used:     free: shared: buffers:  cached:
Mem:  262746112 237740032 25006080       0 11575296 150138880
Swap: 534601728 81661952 452939776
MemTotal:        256588 kB
MemFree:          24420 kB
...
```

To tell all about an IDE hard drive, use:

```
$ cat /proc/ide/via
-------VIA BusMastering IDE Configuration---------
Driver Version:                 3.37
South Bridge:                   VIA vt82c686a
Revision:                       ISA 0x22 IDE 0x10
Highest DMA rate:               UDMA66
BM-DMA base:                    0xd400
PCI clock:                      33.3MHz
...
```

To see disk geometry, both real and logical, use:

```
$ cat /proc/ide/ide0/hda/geometry
physical    39870/16/63
logical     2501/255/63
```

To identify a drive, use:

```
$ cat /proc/ide/ide0/hda/model
IBM-DTLA-305020
```

To show driver versions for all IDE drivers, use:

```
$ cat /proc/ide/drivers
de-scsi version 0.93
ide-cdrom version 4.59-ac1
ide-floppy version 0.99.newide
```

```
ide-disk version 1.17
ide-default version 0.9.newide
```

To show capabilities of CD drives, use:

```
$ cat /proc/sys/dev/cdrom/info
CD-ROM information, Id: cdrom.c 3.12 2000/10/18
drive name:             sr1     sr0
drive speed:            40      32
...
Can read multisession: 1       1
Can read MCN:          1       1
Reports media changed: 1       1
Can play audio:        1       1
Can write CD-R:        1       0
Can write CD-RW:       1       0
Can read DVD:          0       1
Can write DVD-R:       0       0
Can write DVD-RAM:     0       0
```

To show SCSI devices, using the following command. Note that it does not differentiate between devices attached to the SCSI bus and IDE devices using the SCSI-emulation subsystem. These are IDE CD drives:

```
$ cat /proc/scsi/scsi
Attached devices:
Host: scsi0 Channel: 00 Id: 00 Lun: 00
  Vendor: TOSHIBA  Model: DVD-ROM SD-M1202 Rev: 1020
  Type:    CD-ROM                     ANSI SCSI revision: 02
Host: scsi0 Channel: 00 Id: 01 Lun: 00
  Vendor: LITE-ON  Model: LTR-24102B     Rev: 5S54
  Type:    CD-ROM                     ANSI SCSI revision: 02
```

This following command is just plain fun and has absolutely no practical value. It requires a functioning sound system. Warning: it's noisy—this is the sound of your CPU in action. Ctrl-C stops it:

```
# cat /proc/kcore > /dev/dsp
```

For AMD Users

Since AMD went to "performance ratings," instead of plain ole gigahertz, CPU ratings can be confusing. Your shiny new Athlon 3200 won't appear in */proc/cpuinfo* as "cpu MHz 3200"—instead, it will be something like 2800. You're not being ripped off; that's a result of how AMD chooses to rate the performance of their processors. In a nutshell, they claim that clock speed alone is not an accurate measure of performance, so they devised a different scale that more accurately reflects the CPU's true abilities. Visit *http://www.amd.com* for details.

On the other hand if your Pentium 3200 shows up in */proc/cpuinfo* as a number other than 3200, there is a problem, because Intel uses the literal clock speeds.

Discussion

Disk geometry, as expressed by */proc* or any other utility, is largely a fiction. Modern drives are far more complex than the old "heads × sectors × cylinders" model.

As mentioned earlier, to read */proc* use only *cat* or utilities designed expressly for it, such as *sysctl*, *lspci*, *ps*, and *top*. Pagers like *less* and *more* give a different picture, because they re-read */proc* with each page. And you don't want to use a text editor, or any utility with write powers, because you can mess up your system in a heart-beat.

See Also

- *proc(5)*

5.5   Viewing Drive Partitions with fdisk

Problem

You need to see all the partitions on a hard drive or drives. You may need to see exactly how space is allocated on the disk drives; you may want to "reclaim" some old Windows partitions, convert an unused partition to swap space, or find the */dev* number for a partition. *fdisk* also tells you the filesystem on the partition, and shows any free space on a drive.

Solution

Use *fdisk*. To display all partitions on all hard drives, use:

```
# /sbin/fdisk -l
Disk /dev/hda: 20.5 GB, 20576747520 bytes
255 heads, 63 sectors/track, 2501 cylinders
Units = cylinders of 16065 * 512 = 8225280 bytes
 Device Boot    Start      End    Blocks   Id  System
/dev/hda1   *    1        893    7172991    7  HPFS/NTFS
/dev/hda2       894      1033    1124550    c  W95 FAT32 (LBA)
/dev/hda4      1034      2501   11791710    f  W95 Ext'd (LBA)
/dev/hda5      2437      2501     522081   82  Linux swap
/dev/hda6      1034      1670   5116639+   83  Linux
/dev/hda7      1671      2436   6152863+   83  Linux
Disk /dev/hdb: 40.0 GB, 40020664320 bytes
16 heads, 63 sectors/track, 77545 cylinders
Units = cylinders of 1008 * 512 = 516096 bytes
 Device Boot    Start      End     Blocks   Id  System
/dev/hdb1   *    1       4162    2097616+  82  Linux swap
/dev/hdb2      4163     77545   36985032   83  Linux
Partition table entries are not in disk order
```

To display the partition table on a selected drive, use:

```
# /sbin/fdisk -l /dev/hda
Disk /dev/hda: 20.5 GB, 20576747520 bytesDisk /dev/hda: 20.5 GB, 20576747520 bytes
255 heads, 63 sectors/track, 2501 cylinders
Units = cylinders of 16065 * 512 = 8225280 bytes
...
```

Discussion

You can also see what type of filesystem is located on any partition. In this example, you see two different types of Windows filesystems (HPFS/NTFS, FAT32) and a Windows extended partition on which some Linux filesystems and a swap partition have been built.

See Also

- *fdisk(8)*

5.6   Calculating Hard Drive Capacity

Problem

You want to measure precisely the capacity of a hard drive, but you can't seem to get a straight answer because of confusion over measurement values. How much is a megabyte—is it 1 million bytes, or 2^{20} bytes? Which measurement is used for the rated size of your drive?

Solution

Use *fdisk* to get the total disk size in bytes:

```
# /sbin/fdisk -l /dev/hda
Disk /dev/hda: 20.5 GB, 20576747520 bytes
```

Then do a little math to get the value in *gibibytes*, which is a power of 2:

```
20576747520 / 1,073,741,824 = 19.16 gibibytes
```

Gigabytes, which are most often used as powers of 10, are easy to figure:

```
20576747520 / 10 = 20.58 gigabytes
```

Table 5-1 shows a comparison of binary and decimal multiples.

Table 5-1. Comparison of binary and decimal multiples

Base-2 values			Base-10 values		
Kibibyte	1,024 bytes	2^{10}	Kilobyte	1,000 bytes	10^3
Mibibyte	1,048,576 bytes	2^{20}	Megabyte	1,000,000 bytes	10^6
Gibibyte	1,073,741,824 bytes	2^{30}	Gigabyte	1,000,000,000 bytes	10^9

Discussion

In 1998, the International Electrotechnical Commission (IEC) decided that we needed new terminology and ratified some nice new words for us to use. So now we have *kibibyte*, *mibibyte*, *gibibyte*, *tebibyte*, and so forth. Even though they are weird to pronounce, it's good to have precise terminology.

There are times when it is important to know the precise size of a drive, such as when you're selecting drives for a RAID array, or calculating the number of disks needed for a system backup. The debate over how much a gigabyte or megabyte is will probably continue for as long as computer users have breath, and drive manufacturers use whatever math gives the most inflated numbers. In the example above, it appears that using gigabytes inflates the drive capacity by well over one gigabyte (or gibibyte—take your pick). As the base unit of measurement is a byte, I say stick with base 2.

To get an unambiguous, absolute value, you're probably stuck with bytes—unless someone starts messing with them, too.

See Also

- Prefixes for binary multiples (*http://physics.nist.gov/cuu/Units/binary.html*)

## CHAPTER 6

Editing Text Files with JOE and Vim

6.1   Introduction

Mastering a text editor is an important skill for anyone who wants to be a happy, proficient Linux user. Choosing one can get interesting, as the Linux world is over-full of ASCII text editors. There are two reasons for the proliferation of text editors: creating a text editor is a good, and common, project for newbie programmers; and a text editor is a rather personal tool. Linux gurus often write or alter them to suit their own personal whims...er, requirements.

Linux users love to engage in flamewars over text editors (especially Emacs versus Vim), which are fun, but pointless. The idea is to find one that suits your needs and temperament. The beauty of Linux, and free/open source software in general, is the wealth of choices for users. There is something for everybody, including entertaining flamewars.

In this chapter we'll look at using JOE, Joe's Own Editor, and Vim, which is a descendant of vi. Why not Emacs? Emacs is a wonderful program; it's big, complex, and endlessly customizable and extensible. It is not a mere text editor; it's more of a complete integrated environment. With Emacs, users can read mail and Usenet posts, write programs, play games, fuss endlessly over custom macros and key bindings, cobble up windowed environments when X Windows is not available, and consult their psychiatrists (*M-x doctor*). Emacs will do nearly anything you want it to, if you can figure out how. For someone who simply wants to edit text files, it's a bit much. Emacs weighs in at over 22 megabytes, while JOE and Vim both fit on a floppy disk, with room left over.

JOE and Vim are both well suited to the everyday task of editing configuration files. Of course, they can also be used for writing any kind of text file—articles, web pages, coding, whatever you like.

Which brings me to something that may be a bit of an unpleasant reality for some: typing skills matter. The better you can type, the more productive you'll be. For sheer speed and satisfaction, it's hard to beat never having to take your hands off the keyboard, or your eyes off the screen.

Typing Tutor

There is an excellent, free Linux typing tutor called Gtypist (*http://www.gnu.org/ software/gtypist/gtypst.html*), for anyone who wants a little help. It teaches both QWERTY and Dvorak, and it has typing tutorials in English, Czech, Russian, Spanish, German, French, and Norwegian. Like most ncurses-based programs, it looks better in a text console than in X.

JOE is a "modeless" editor, which means that entering commands and editing text happens on the same screen. Vim has two modes: Normal/Command mode, and Insert/Edit mode. When you're in Normal mode, everything you type is treated as a command. In Insert mode, it's all treated as typed text. This vexes some folks who try Vim for the first time, because there is no helpful animated assistant to tell them that it is necessary to switch between the two modes to get anything done. Vim is a serious power tool, and as you'll see in this chapter, it's not that difficult to learn.

vi/Vim, the Universal Editor

vi (officially pronounced "vee eye," though I like to say "vi," rhyming with "fie," just to be annoying) is the universally available text editor. No matter what sort of Linux system you may find yourself working on, you can count on vi, or one of its many offspring, being present.

vi has inspired a host of cleverly named clones: Vim, elvis, vile, calvin, Vigor, viper, and virus, to name a few. These sorts of projects come and go, but Vim, elvis, and vile are popular and actively maintained. Vigor is noteworthy for its snide animated paperclip, the intentionally annoying Vigor Assistant. The Vigor Assistant continually interrupts your work with "helpful" comments, like "Are you sure you want to move left?" and "Don't cry—it won't help." Vigor is fun, and useful too, because it is an extension of nvi, which is yet another vi clone. Yes, you can do real work with Vigor, though the author himself finds this questionable: "One user actually found Vigor to be useful! After all that time and effort I put into making a totally useless app, somebody has to go and get some benefit out of it."

Moving back to the serious side of the vi ledger, Vim is the most popular vi descendant. When you fire up vi on most Linux distributions, such as Red Hat, Debian, and Mandrake, you get Vim. Vim does windows and color syntax highlighting, and it has extensive online help and documentation. This is handy, because even if you find yourself stuck on a desert island with only the ancestral vi, your Vim skills will serve you well.

JOE, the Five-in-One Editor

JOE has a number of nice features. It has multiple personalities, and onscreen help. You can fire up JOE and start muddling around and editing files without bothering to read any documentation. Of course, this is not the the optimum method, but in a pinch it works.

JOE has three emulation modes:

> *jstar* (WordStar)
> *jpico* (Pico)
> *jmacs* (Emacs)

and two native modes, JOE and RJOE. RJOE is "Restricted JOE"; it can only open files specified on the command line. After RJOE is up and running, you cannot open new files from inside RJOE, or open any command shells. This makes RJOE a good option for your *sudo* users, preventing them from escaping to a command shell with their rootly powers. All five modes run from the same 200-kilobyte executable.

See Also

- *joe(1), vi(1)*
- Gtypist (*http://www.gnu.org/software/gtypist/gtypist.html*)
- Vigor (*http://vigor.sourceforge.net/index.shtml*)

6.2   Finding JOE Commands

Problem

How do you make JOE do anything useful? You want a complete command reference for JOE, in all of its personalities. And you want it online, so you can use it while you type.

Solution

Turn on the online help, which is present in every one of JOE's personalities.

To start up JOE with the Help screen turned on, use:

```
$ joe -help
```

Do the same for *rjoe, jpico, jmacs*, and *jstar*.

Discussion

JOE uses a lot of three-key commands. The caret (^) is the Ctrl key. Hit the first two keys (e.g., ^*K*) together, then release them and strike the third key. Here are some of the basic Help screen commands:

JOE and RJOE

> ^K H toggles the Help screen on and off.
>
> *Esc .* moves forward in the Help screens, *Esc ,* moves backward.

Jpico

> ^G toggles the Help screen on and off.
>
> *Esc .* moves forward, *Esc ,* moves backward.

Jmacs

> ^X H toggles the Help screen on and off.
>
> ^X . moves forward, ^X , moves backward.

Jstar

> ^J toggles the Help screen on and off.
>
> *Esc .* moves forward, *Esc ,* moves backward.

See Also

- *joe(1)*

6.3   Customizing JOE

Problem

JOE has many personalities and command-line options. You want it to have customized defaults, so at startup everything is just the way you want it.

Solution

Create a personalized *.joerc* file containing your preferences, and put it in your home directory.

First take a peek in */etc/joe*, because that's where JOE's default initialization files are:

```
$ ls /etc/joe
jmacsrc joerc jpicorc jstarrc rjoerc terminfo
```

This example uses *joerc*—just plain ole JOE, not pretending to be anyone else. Copy it to your home directory, make it a hidden file, and keep the filename:

```
$ joe -linums -help /etc/joe/joerc
^K D
Name of file to save (^C to abort): ~/.joerc
Could not make backup file.  Save anyway (y,n,^C)? Y
File ~/.joerc saved
```

^ means the Ctrl key. Don't worry about case; *K D* is the same as *k d.*

While *.joerc* lets you micromanage every last little thing, the first two sections contain the most useful options. For example:

```
-marking        Text between ^K B and cursor is highlighted
                (use with -lightoff)
```

```
-force          Force final newline when files are saved
-lightoff       Turn off highlighting after block copy or
                move
-exask          ^K X always confirms filename
-beep           Beep on errors and when cursor goes past
                extremes
-keepup         %k and %c status-line escape sequences
                updated frequently
-help           Start with help on
-linums         Enable line numbers on each line
```

Inactive options have a leading space or tab. To activate an option, simply delete the leading space, and make sure the line is all the way flush left.

Discussion

A nice feature of JOE is that your work is done in a copy of the original file. The original file is saved as a backup file. (This is a configurable option that can be turned off in *.joerc*.)

See Also

- *joe(1)*
- Recipe 6.4, "Organizing JOE's Preferences in a Separate File"

6.4 Organizing JOE's Preferences in a Separate File

Problem

JOE's *rc* files are large, so it's not easy to keep track of your changes. How do you keep your changes separate from the things that have stayed the same?

Solution

Put your changes in a separate file, which in this example is called *.joercprefs*. Call this file by adding the following line near the top of *.joerc*; anywhere before the "First Section" is good. Be sure to include the leading colon, and make it flush left:

```
:include .joercprefs
```

Discussion

Here's an example of *.joercprefs:*

```
my JOE preferences---active options only---
created 2/15/2004

-marking        Text between ^K B and cursor is highlighted (use with -lightoff)
-force          Force final newline when files are saved
```

```
-lightoff       Turn off highlighting after block copy or move
-exask          ^K X always confirms filename
-beep           Beep on errors and when cursor goes past extremes
-keepup         %k and %c status-line escape sequences updated frequently
-help           Start with help on
-linums         Enable line numbers on each line
```

Keeping all of your changes in a separate file will save your sanity, guaranteed. Note that *.joercprefs* does not overwrite *.joerc*—any options that are explicitly enabled or disabled in *.joerc* will remain that way, regardless of what *.joerc* says. However, options in *.joerc* that begin with leading whitespace are ignored, so these can be enabled or disabled in *.joercprefs*.

See Also

- *joe(1)*

6.5   Copying Between Two Files in JOE

Problem

All right, you're sold. You want to have your own *~/.joercprefs*. But how do you create this file without having duplicate entries or entries that conflict with the original *~/.joerc*?

Solution

Open two windows inside of JOE, one containing *~/.joerc* and the second containing the new file, *~/.joercprefs*. Copy your desired preferences from *~/.joerc* into *~/.joercprefs*.

First, make a backup copy of the original *~./joerc*.

```
$ cp ~/.joerc ~/.joerc.bak
```

Open *~/.joerc*, then open a second window and name the new file:

```
$ joe -linums -help ~/.joerc
^K O
^K E
Name of file to edit (^C to abort): ~/.joercprefs
```

Navigate between the two windows with ^K P and ^K N. Sometimes the windows play tricks on you; toggle ^K I to show all windows/hide inactive windows.

Mark a block of text to copy with ^K B and ^K K. Position the cursor at your insertion point, and copy with ^K C.

Discussion

Because *~/.joerc* is so large, it can be helpful to display only the inactive options. In the *~/.joerc* window, use JOE's filter command to *grep* the inactive options:

```
^K /
$ grep '^[[:space:]]'
```

Now you can easily see which commands are inactive and copy the ones you wish to activate into ~/.joercprefs.

You can also show only the active options:

```
$ grep '^[^[:space:]]'
```

Hit ^K X to save ~/.joercprefs and exit.

Now your changes are nicely separated for easy tracking and editing.

See Also

- *joe(1)*

6.6   Searching and Replacing in JOE

Problem

You're editing some document and finding a particularly annoying misspelling all over the place. What tools does JOE offer for finding and replacing words, text strings, and punctuation in a document?

Solution

Use the *^K F* command for all of your find-and-replace needs. Use special search sequences, which are JOE's regular expressions, for fine-grained, precise searches.

Begin a search with *^K F*. Use the up and down arrows to scroll through your previous search and replace terms. *^L* continues a search without the replace function.

For example, say you find yourself typing "nucular," even though you know better, because you hear it all day from your annoying coworker. You need to go back through your work and change it to "nuclear." Here's how:

```
^K F
Find (^C to abort): \<nucular\>
(I)gnore (R)eplace (B)ackwards Bloc(K) NNN (^C to abort): r
Replace with (^C to abort): nuclear
Replace (Y)es (N)o (R)est (B)ackup (^C to abort)? r
```

Note the use of \<\>. This tells JOE to perform a whole-word search. Otherwise, JOE will conduct a literal search for your search string, even if it's inside another word.

Rather than correcting the spelling, you may wish to draw attention to this annoying habit of your coworker by putting quotation marks around the word:

```
Replace with (^C to abort): "\&"
```

The result is:

```
"nucular"
```

Or you can really go nuts, using:

```
Replace with (^C to abort): "It's nuclear, not "\&" dammit!!"
```

which creates:

```
"It's nuclear, not "nucular" dammit!!"
```

To find a match only at the beginning of a line, use:

```
\^nucular
```

To find a match only at the end of a line, use:

```
nucular\$
```

To find empty lines, use:

```
\^\$
```

To find whitespace, press the spacebar and tab key inside the square brackets:

```
\[    ]
```

To match any character in the square brackets (for doing a case-insensitive search), use:

```
\[Nn]ucular
```

To match any number of characters, use:

```
nu\*r
```

To match exactly one character, use:

```
nuc\?l
```

See Also

- *joe(1)*
- The "Special search sequences" in JOE's online help

6.7   Selecting Text Vertically in JOE

Problem

You've laboriously created a table and want to move the columns around. That is, you want to select a section of text vertically—for example, the first word on several lines, or chunks of text in the middle of several lines, or a column.

Solution

Use JOE's *rectangle mode*.

The command ^T X turns on rectangle mode. Use ^K B and ^K K to select a block of text, then do with it as you will.

Discussion

These are some useful commands to use on blocks of text:

^K B, ^K K

Mark/unmark the beginning and end of a block of text.

^K M

Move the block to where the cursor is.

^K C

Copy the block to where the cursor is.

^K Y

Delete the block of text.

^K .

Move the block right.

^K ,

Move the block left.

^K A

Center text.

^K /

Open a command line for your favorite text-manipulating command.

See Also

- *joe(1)*
- JOE's online help

6.8   Finding and Opening Files in JOE

Problem

You have lots of work to do. Lots of files to edit, lots of tasks to accomplish. You don't want to be starting and stopping JOE all the time. You want to search for files and open them without leaving JOE.

Solution

To search for files from inside JOE, use ^K R or ^K E. This either opens an existing file, or creates a new file:

```
^K E
Name of file to edit (^C to abort):
```

Use tab completion to expand existing filenames. In this example, type *ga*, then hit Tab twice. JOE inserts the asterisk when you hit the Tab key, so don't type it yourself:

```
^K E
Name of file to edit (^C to abort):.ga*
.gaby/   .gaim/   .gaimrc  .galeon/
```

To navigate up and down the file tree, use Enter/Return to go "down" the tree; Backspace to go "up," or toward the root directory (but aren't roots down in the earth?); and Tab to select.

To insert an existing file at the cursor, use:

```
^K R
Name of file to edit (^C to abort):
```

Remember the window navigation commands:

^K O

 Opens a new window.

^K I

 Shows all/ hides inactive windows.

^K P and ^K N

 Navigates up and down between windows.

Discussion

Even though JOE does not have mouse support, you can copy and paste from other applications with the mouse, in an X session. This is a terminal function, not a JOE function. You'll need to use the classic Unix method: highlight text with the mouse, then click the middle mouse button to paste. Don't use ^V or ^C, because those mean other things in JOE.

See Also

- *joe(1)*

6.9   Learning Vim Quickly

Problem

You have done a bit of homework, including reading the "Introduction" to this chapter, and you have decided to use Vim. So you want to get up to speed on Vim as quickly as possible, and learn it right the first time.

Solution

Run the Vim tutor. Simply type *vimtutor* at any command line. Within 30–60 minutes, you'll be cruising like an old pro. This is the #1 best way to get proficient quickly.

Discussion

Vim rewards good typing skills. If you're a not-so-good typist, consider brushing up your skills with Gtypist, the free typing tutor.

It may be that the tutorial teaches all the commands you'll ever need to know. For additional study and a reference for Vim's nine zillion and four abilities, make use of the excellent user and reference manual by Bram Moolenaar, the author of Vim. This comes in Vim's own internal help system, and in several versions online at *http:// vimdoc.sourceforge.net* (searchable HTML, *.pdf*, and printable HTML).

To access the user manual inside Vim, type:

```
:help
```

Use arrow keys to scroll through the table of contents, and hit ^] to open a chapter.

Or you can go directly to a topic:

```
:help quickref
:help tutor
:help usr_06.txt
```

To search for a particular term and bring up a list of choices, type:

```
:help vimrc
```

Do not hit Return, but hit ^D. The output looks like this:

```
:help vimrc
vimrc       vimrc-intro        system-vimrc    _gvimrc
vimrc       vimrc-filetype     gvimrc          :mkvimrc
_vimrc      vimrc_example.vim  .gvimrc
```

Then choose the one you want:

```
:help  vimrc_example.vim
```

There are two very good actual printed books on VIM:

- *Vi IMproved—Vim*, by Steve Oualline, available at *http://iccf-holland.org/ click5.html*. Not only is this an excellent book, but a percentage of the proceeds goes to helping orphans in Uganda.
- *Learning the vi Editor*, by Linda Lamb and Arnold Robbins (O'Reilly).

If you're new to Vim, be sure to practice with the Vim tutor first. The following recipes show how to customize your work environment and navigate Vim.

See Also

- *vimtutor(1)*
- Vim.org documentation page (*http://www.vim.org/docs.php*)
- The Vimdoc page at SourceForge (*http://vimdoc.sourceforge.net/*)
- Gtypist (*http://www.gnu.org/software/gtypist/gtypist.html*)

6.10 Creating Autotext with Vim's Abbreviations

Problem

You do a lot of repetitious typing, such as copyright statements, code comments, signatures, and so forth, and you would like some kind of auto-text feature.

Solution

Use Vim's abbreviations feature. Abbreviations are created in Normal mode:

```
:ab th This is an example of a Vim abbreviation.
```

To use the abbreviation, switch to Insert mode and type *th*, followed by any whitespace above (space, tab, or carriage return).

To see all of your abbreviations, type:

```
:ab
```

To remove an abbreviation, use:

```
:unabbreviate th
```

To delete all abbreviations, use:

```
:abclear
```

Like everything else in Vim, abbreviations can be preserved forever in *~/.vimrc*.

Discussion

You can use the abbreviation as an automatic spelling-fixer (like Recipe 6.6). Just define your common misspellings as abbrevations. This trick works best for typos (teh for the, for instance).

See Also

- Vim's online help (*:help map.txt*)
- Recipe 6.12, "Customizing Vim"
- Chapter 24 of *Vi IMproved—Vim*
- Chapter 7 of *Learning the vi Editor*

6.11 Mapping Commands to Keystrokes

Problem

Some of Vim's commands are long and complex, and you are amassing your own collection of custom commands, so you would like to create keyboard shortcuts for your most-used commands.

Solution

Use the *map* command to assign custom keystrokes to any command or text string. *map* creates keymappings for Normal mode; *map!* creates keymappings for Insert mode. To see your current set of mappings, type:

```
:map
```

or:

```
:map!
```

 Be careful when creating your own maps—don't map to keys that already have commands assigned to them by Vim, as *map* will happily, and without comment, overwrite them. (This is a good reason to wait until you're proficient before going crazy with maps.)

Creating a new keymapping is done like this:

```
:map <F3> :runtime! syntax/2html.vim
```

This command adds HTML tags to the current document, in a new window. Now hitting F3 activates it.

You can delete a map like this:

```
:unmap <F3>
```

You have to spell out the names of the *Esc*, *<CR>* (carriage return) and *<F2>–<F12>* keys, because if you simply press the keys they will execute whatever command is assigned to them.

This example maps a command to F3 that goes into Insert mode, inserts an HTML tag around a word, and leaves off in Insert mode so you can continue typing:

```
:map <F3> i<B><Esc>ea</B><Esc>a
```

These are examples of Insert mode mappings for quickly adding HTML tags. They're fast, because you never leave Insert mode, and it's unlikely that such comma-letter combinations will come up in ordinary typing.

```
:map! ,ah <A href="">
:map! ,a </A>
:map! ,b <B><Esc>ea</B><Esc>a
:map! ,i <I><Esc>ea</I><Esc>a
:map! ,l <LI><Esc>ea</LI><Esc>a
```

Discussion

The safest keys to use are F2–F12 and Shift-F2–F12. (F1 is mapped to Vim's help pages.) However, you'll use those up pretty quickly, so using combinations like comma-letter that usually do not occur in normal usage gives you the ability to create as many keymappings as you like.

See *:help map-which-keys* for complete information on Vim's built-in keymappings. You can also query Vim's help for a specific key or combination:

```
:help CTRL-V
:help F5
:help /b
```

Remember to spell out CTRL and F5; don't press the Ctrl and F5 keys.

See Also

- Vim's online help (*:help 2html.vim*, *:help key-mapping*)
- Chapter 8 of *Vi IMproved—Vim*
- Chapter 7 of *Learning the vi Editor*

6.12   Customizing Vim

Problem

All this customization is great, but it goes away when you quit. You don't want to re-type all your abbreviations and mappings each time you start. How do you customize your Vim environment, and preserve your abbreviations and custom keymappings?

Solution

Create a *~/.vimrc* file with your desired options. You can create one from scratch, or copy and modify the global */etc/vim/vimrc* file.

What can you put in your *~/.vimrc*? Any Vim option that you want. And what might those options be? You can list all option names by typing:

```
:set all
    aleph=224
noarabic
    arabicshape
noallowrevins
noaltkeymap
...
```

Then look up what they mean:

```
:help noaltkeymap
```

This opens the hyperlinked options help page:

```
:help options
```

As you can see, a person could happily spend a lifetime fine-tuning Vim (and, with luck, completely avoid doing any real work).

Discussion

When you read the Vim documentation, it's easy to become overwhelmed by its flexibility, and the sheer number of possible options. Start with the basics, as illustrated here, and don't worry about the super-duper geeky stuff until you're sure you actually need it. There comes a point where plain old typing does the job just fine.

This sample *~/.vimrc* demonstrates three fundamental Vim features: customizing startup options, abbreviations, and keymaps. Quotation marks are used to comment out lines.

```
"""""""""""""""""""""""""""""""""""""""""""""""""
"   Carla's  vimrc, created 4/22/2004   "
"              Vim options              "
"""""""""""""""""""""""""""""""""""""""""""""""""
" Turn off vi compatibility, to get all of Vim's features
set nocompatible
" Tabs use 4 spaces
set tabstop=4
" more powerful backspacing
set backspace=indent,eol,start
" Syntax highlighting on by default
syntax on
" auto-detect filetypes for syntax highlighting
filetype plugin indent on
"""""""""""""""""""""""""""""""""""""""""""""""""
"             Abbreviations             "
"""""""""""""""""""""""""""""""""""""""""""""""""
:ab Qu Carla Has Gone Fishing, Back Much Later
:ab Co Copyright (c) 2004 Carla Schroder all rights reserved
:ab Em carla@bratgrrl.com
:ab Wb http://tuxcomputing.com
"""""""""""""""""""""""""""""""""""""""""""""""""
"   HTML tag mappings, for Insert mode    "
"""""""""""""""""""""""""""""""""""""""""""""""""
:map! ,ah <A href="">
:map! ,a </A>
:map! ,b <B><Esc>ea</B><Esc>a
:map! ,i <I><Esc>ea</I><Esc>a
:map! ,l <LI><Esc>ea</LI><Esc>a
```

Any changes made to *~/.vimrc* take effect the next time you open Vim.

See Also

- *vim(1)*
- Vim's online help (*:help vimrc, :help usr_05.txt, :help ab*)
- Chapter 11 of *Learning the vi Editor*
- Chapter 8 of *Vi IMproved—Vim*

6.13 Navigating Quickly in Vim with Marks

Problem

You are editing a large document, or you are editing several files at once, and you need to jump back and forth between different sections. But it takes time, and you keep losing your place.

Solution

Use Vim's *marks* to mark cursor positions, like bookmarks.

There are 52 available marks: *a–z* and *A–Z*. In Command mode, position the cursor, then type:

```
ma
```

to mark the spot. To return to this mark, type:

```
`a
```

That is a backtick, not an apostrophe.

Lowercase marks work only inside a single file. Use uppercase marks to navigate between files. Suppose you mark a location in the file *configstuff.txt*:

```
mA
```

Now when you hit `A from any other open file, or any Vim window, it will go to that location in *configstuff.txt,* opening it if necessary. Uppercase marks are stored in *~/.viminfo*, so they survive between sessions.

Numbered marks are a cool thing that Vim does for you. Every time you exit Vim, it stores your last cursor position. Next time you fire up Vim, you can return to where you left off by typing:

```
`0
```

Vim stores these marks in *~/.viminfo* and rotates through numbers 0–9. So, if you want to go back to where you exited three sessions ago, type:

```
`2
```

To see all of your marks, type:

```
:marks
```

See Also

- Vim's online help (*:help mark-motions, :help viminfo*)

6.14 Picking Up Where You Left Off: Using Vim's Sessions

Problem

You get all involved in a project, then have to shut down for the night before you're finished. Wouldn't it be nice to save everything—options, mappings, open files, open windows, window positions and sizes—that normally goes away when you close out?

Solution

No problem—create *sessions*. A Vim session saves everything, and restores it exactly the way you left it the next time you start the session. When you reach a point where you would like to preserve the work environment, save all open files, then name the session:

```
:wall
:mksession myarticle.vim
```

If more than one file is open, use *:wqall* to save and close all of them at once. This example creates a file called *myarticle.vim*. To start up the same session, enter:

```
$ vim -S myarticle.vim
```

After working in this session, you have two choices. You can save all your changes under the same filename:

```
:mksession! myarticle.vim
```

or do your own quick-and-easy version control by changing the session name:

```
:mksession myarticle_rev2.vim
```

You can also go directly to another session without shutting down:

```
:wall
:mksession! myarticle_rev2.vim
:source myarticle.vim
```

Another cool thing you can do with sessions is create your perfect working environment, then save it for posterity:

```
$ vim
:help
^W w
:vertical split /~
```

Figure 6-1 shows what this looks like.

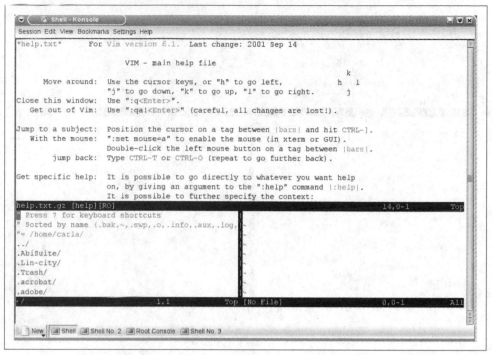

Figure 6-1. Create an ideal working environment

Enlarge the file tree window and shrink the help window until they're just right. Use ^W w to navigate between the windows and ^W + or - to adjust the window sizes. When it's all perfect, save it as *:mksession 3pane.vim* (Figure 6-2).

Discussion

Using sessions gives you a fast, powerful way to create custom working environments. It's a good idea to organize your session files in their own directory, so you can find them quickly.

See Also

- Vim's online help (*:help session, :help usr_08.txt*)
- Chapter 21 of *Vi IMproved—Vim*

Figure 6-2. Make your adjustments and save the session

6.15   Setting Your Default Editor

Problem

By now, you're totally sold on Vim and JOE. But some programs, such as *crontab* and *quota*, require use of the default editor, and the editor you get by default is some creaky old monster. How do you set the default editor to something you like?

Solution

Edit your environment variables, in *~/.bashrc* or *~/.bash_profile*. *~/.bashrc* is preferable, because it applies to all shells opened during a session. *~/.bash_profile* is read only at login.

Add these lines to *~/.bashrc*, or modify any existing entry:

```
EDITOR=vim
VISUAL=$EDITOR
export EDITOR VISUAL
```

Obviously, you'll enter the editor of your choice. Usually it is better to use a console text editor like JOE, Pico, Vim, or Emacs. You may select an X editor like Kwrite or GEdit, but keep in mind there may be times when X is not available, so these won't always work. It is important to use both the VISUAL and EDITOR variables. VISUAL is an older term, leftover from ancient times, but some programes still look for it.

Make sure your *~/.bash_profile* calls *~/.bashrc*:

```
# include .bashrc if it exists
if [ -f ~/.bashrc ]; then
        source ~/.bashrc
fi
```

See Also

- *bash(1)*
- Chapter 17 of *LPI Linux Certification in a Nutshell*

6.16   Discovering Vim's Compile-Time Options

Problem

You are having some troubles with Vim, and you think some features you need were not compiled in. How do you find out what options Vim was compiled with?

Solution

Open Vim and run:

```
:version
```

This shows all of Vim's compile-time options and initialization file locations on your system.

Discussion

Here is a simplified example of what *:version* output looks like. + means a feature is included; - means excluded. Now you can easily find out if you need to recompile Vim to enable a feature you want.

```
:version
VIM - Vi IMproved 6.2 (2003 Jun 1, compiled Apr  1 2004 23:39:33)
Included patches: 1-298, 300-426
Compiled by Norbert Tretkowski <nobse@debian.org>
Big version with GTK2 GUI.  Features included (+) or not (-):
+arabic +autocmd +balloon_eval +browse ++builtin_terms +byte_offset +cindent
+clientserver
 -hangul_input +iconv +insert_expand +jumplist

   system vimrc file: "$VIM/vimrc"
     user vimrc file: "$HOME/.vimrc"
      user exrc file: "$HOME/.exrc"
  system gvimrc file: "$VIM/gvimrc"
```

```
      user gvimrc file: "$HOME/.gvimrc"
    system menu file: "$VIMRUNTIME/menu.vim"
  fall-back for $VIM: "/usr/share/vim"

Compilation: gcc -c -I. -Iproto -DHAVE_CONFIG_H -DFEAT_GUI_GTK  -I/usr/include/gtk-
2.0 -I/usr/lib/gt
k-2.0/include -I/usr/include/atk-1.0 -I/usr/include/pango-     -O2 -DFEAT_LANGMAP -
DFEAT_KEYMAP -DF
EAT_SIGNS -DFEAT_RIGHTLEFT  -I/usr/X11R6/include
Linking: gcc  -L/usr/X11R6/lib  -L/usr/local/lib -o vim   -Wl,--export-dynamic -lgtk-
x11-2.0 -lgdk-x
```

See Also

- Vim online help (*:help version*) for a description of every available feature

## CHAPTER 7

Starting and Stopping Linux

7.1   Introduction

There are a lot of ways to start and stop a Linux system. Plus, there are initialization scripts for controlling how various services start up, and there are different system runlevels, each of which can run a different set of services. Run this command:

```
$ ps axfl
```

Take a look at the top, at process number 1 (this is slimmed-down; yours will show more columns and lines):

```
UID  PID  PPID  STAT  TTY   TIME   COMMAND
0    1    0     S     ?     0:03   init
```

That's *init*, the grandmother of all processes on a Linux system. Notice that the *ppid*, or parent process ID, is zero, because *init* is the first process started after the kernel runs.

But why doesn't *ps afxl* show *init* as the root of the process tree? The *ppid*s tell the story:

```
UID  PID  PPID  STAT  TTY   TIME  COMMAND
0    1    0     S     ?     0:03  init
0    2    1     SW    ?     0:00  [keventd]
0    0    1     SWN   ?     0:00  [ksoftirqd_CPU0]
0    0    1     SW    ?     0:00  [kswapd]
0    10   1     SW    ?     0:00  [kreiserfsd]
0    101  1     SW    ?     0:00  [kapmd]
1    274  1     S     ?     0:00  /sbin/portmap
0    360  1     S     ?     0:00  /sbin/syslogd
0    376  1     S     ?     0:00  /usr/sbin/slapd
0    387  376   S     ?     0:00  \_ /usr/sbin/slapd
0    388  387   S     ?     0:00     \_ /usr/sbin/slapd
0    389  1     S     ?     0:00  /usr/sbin/cupsd
```

The Linux boot process goes something like this:

1. The system BIOS initializes hardware, then loads the boot sector.

2. The master boot record (MBR) loads the bootloader, which points the way to the kernel.

3. The kernel initializes peripheral devices, loads drivers, and mounts the root filesystem, then calls */sbin/init*.

4. */sbin/init* is the master startup program that spawns all user-level processes. It reads */etc/inittab*, then it moves on to activate yet more scripts, which are named in */etc/inittab*.

5. Now it gets distribution-specific. On Debian, the next script in line is */etc/init.d/ rcS*, which then hands off to whatever */etc/rc*.d* directory is specified in */etc/ inittab*. The Debian default is runlevel 2, so */etc/rc2.d* is used, and all the scripts in */etc/rc2.d* are executed. This is the SysV style of startup.

   On Red Hat, */etc/rc.d/rc.sysinit* comes next, then the scripts in the default runlevel directory (usually */etc/rc3.d* or */etc/rc5.d*).

   Slackware does it a little differently. It's more akin to the BSD style of system startup, which has a single */etc/rc.d/* directory with an *init* script for each runlevel, though it incorporates some SysV features as well.

On Red Hat and Debian systems, the */etc/rc*.d* directories do not contain the actual startup scripts, but rather symlinks to scripts in */etc/init.d*. By linking to a master script directory, */etc/init.d*, unnecessary duplication is avoided. And, in a master stroke of sheer ingenuity, the way the symlinks are named determines how the services will run. For example, consider:

```
$ ls -go S20cupsys
lrwxrwxrwx  1 16 Sep  9 17:51 S20cupsys -> ../init.d/cupsys
```

S20 means the service *cupsys* is to be started with a priority level of 20. Lower numbers equal higher priority. If it were *K20cupsys*, that would mean the service is to be killed. (The Linux world is harsh.) This is a simple way to ensure that services are stopped and started the way you want, and in the right order.

Runlevels

This is the common Linux runlevel scheme:

0 Halt

1 Single user

2–5 Multiuser

6 Reboot

These are the runlevels in Debian distributions:

0   Halt the system

1   Single user

2–5 Multiuser mode (the defaults are all the same)

6   Reboot

The runlevels in Red Hat distributions are:

0   Halt the system

1   Single-user text mode

2   Not used (user-definable)

3   Multiuser text mode

4   Not used (user-definable)

5   Multi-user graphical mode

6   Reboot

The runlevels in Slackware distributions are:

0   Halt the system

1   Single-user mode

2   Unused, same as 3

3   Multiuser text mode

4   Multiuser graphical mode

5   Unused, same as 3

6   Reboot

There may be even more variations in other distributions, and theoretically runlevels 7–9 exist, though they are not used. It's easy enough to see what each runlevel does—simply read the *rc*.d* directories.

7.2   Changing Runlevels After Bootup

Problem

Somewhere during the installation of your Linux system, you selected either "boot to text mode" or "boot to graphical mode." Maybe you didn't quite understand what these options meant—or maybe you did, but now you want a nice graphical interface instead of a boring text-only console. Or you're having problems with the graphical interface, and want to drop to a runlevel with minimal services for troubleshooting.

Solution

Use *init*. First, check what runlevel you are in:

```
# /sbin/runlevel
N 5
```

The *N* means you have not previously booted to a different runlevel. If you had, the number of the runlevel would be displayed. You must be root to change the runlevel:

```
# /sbin/init 3
```

This will stop all runlevel 5 services, then start up the runlevel 3 services. It's like doing a partial reboot. All users will be logged out.

Sometimes you need to change to runlevel 1 to get out of trouble:

```
# /sbin/init 1
```

This stops X and drops you to a root shell, with limited services and no X. On Red Hat, you don't need to supply the root password after dropping to runlevel 1, so don't give any *sudo* users *init* access.

Discussion

In Red Hat, Fedora, Mandrake, and Slackware, changing runlevels is one way to kill an X session, because runlevel 3 boots to a text console. However, it's rather drastic, as it stops and restarts all services and boots out all logged-in users.

Why change runlevels with *init*? Here are some good reasons:

- To drop to runlevel 1 for troubleshooting and repairs.
- To stop or reboot the system when normal methods don't work.
- To restart all services, or to switch to a different set of services.

Bad reasons include:

- To change from a text console session to an X session, because *init* must be run as root, and running an X session as root is a very bad idea. It's insecure, and it's too easy to inadvertently make mistakes and mess up your system.
- To exit an X session.

There are other, better ways to manage switching between X sessions and console sessions, as you'll see in Recipe 7.4, "Starting and Stopping X."

telinit works too, as it's simply a hard link to *init* ("tell init"—more clever geek wordplay):

```
$ ls -al /sbin/telinit
lrwxrwxrwx    1 root    root    4 Oct 31 07:51 /sbin/telinit -> init
```

See Also

- *init(8)*
- Recipe 7.4, "Starting and Stopping X"
- Chapter 5 of *Running Linux*, by Matt Welsh, Mattias Dalheimer, Terry Dawson, and Lar Kaufman (O'Reilly)
- Chapter 10 of *LPI Linux Certification in a Nutshell*

7.3   Changing the Default Runlevel

Problem

You don't like the runlevel your system boots to, and you want to change it. For example, you might boot into text-mode rather than a nice window system. Or perhaps you have customized different runlevels to run different sets of services, and after a suitable amount of testing and tweaking, you're ready to choose one for a default.

Solution

Easy as pie. Edit */etc/inittab*, and look for this line:

```
# The default runlevel.
id:2:initdefault:
```

Simply change *id:2* to whatever number you desire (except 0 or 6).

If you're commitment-shy and want the most flexibility at boot time, comment out the *id:X:initdefault* line. Then *init* will ask you during bootup which runlevel you want.

Discussion

Debian's default 2–5 runlevels are all the same and will boot either to a text console or a graphical login manager, depending on what was selected at installation. Runlevel 2 is the Debian default. Recipe 7.5 tells how to customize Debian's runlevels.

See Also

- *inittab(5)*
- Recipe 7.5, "Managing Debian's Runlevels"
- Chapter 5 of *Running Linux*
- Chapter 10 of *LPI Linux Certification in a Nutshell*

7.4   Starting and Stopping X

Problem

You don't like the idea of changing runlevels just to kill an X session. After all, it means restarting all services, and it will mess up any users who are logged in. What's a better way to stop an X session?

Solution

There are several choices. The best way is to configure one runlevel to boot to a text console. Then start X when you want it with the *startx* command:

```
$ startx
```

Then you can exit X simply by logging out of the X session. You won't be logged out of Linux, just X.

On most distributions, runlevel 3 boots to a text console. On Red Hat, Fedora, Mandrake, and SuSE, runlevel 5 is a graphical login manager. On Slackware, this is runlevel 4.

Debian users may have to take some extra steps, as Debian's default 2–5 runlevels are all the same. See Recipe 7.6 to learn how to customize Debian's runlevels.

Discussion

There are other ways to stop an X session. These are better suited for when X locks up.

Any user can use "xkill", by typing Ctrl-Alt-Backspace.

If you're running a graphical login manager (*xdm*, *kdm*, or *gdm*), root can stop the login manager. This also logs out users:

```
# /etc/init.d/gdm stop
```

See Also

- The "Introduction" to this chapter
- Recipe 7.3, "Changing the Default Runlevel"
- Recipe 7.6, "Creating Both Text and Graphical Login Runlevels on Debian"

7.5   Managing Debian's Runlevels

Problem

You need to manage what services start up at boot on a Debian system, on each runlevel, because when you install new services, such as Apache, Exim, or OpenSSH,

Debian configures them to start at boot. You're still testing things, so you want to start/stop them manually. Or you want different services to start on different runlevels during testing.

Solution

Use the *update-rc.d* command. This example adds a new service, the KDE Display Manager, to runlevel 5. *kdm* is the name of a startup file in */etc/init.d*. There must be a trailing dot ending the runlevels list:

```
# update-rc.d kdm  start 99 5 . stop 01 0 1 2 3 4 6 .
```

This command removes a service from all runlevels. Removal is all or nothing; you cannot be selective:

```
# update-rc.d -f kdm remove
```

Changing the runlevels for an existing service is a two-step process: first remove it, then add it back to the levels in which you want it to run. Be sure to make an entry for every service on every runlevel, either stop or start.

Discussion

Remember, *update-rc.d* operates on the script names in */etc/init.d*. You can test-drive the *update-rc.d* commands with the *-n* option, which means "not really":

```
# update-rc.d -f -n kdm remove
```

You can delete *init.d* scripts if you really really want to, with the *remove* option:

```
# update-rc.d --purge kdm remove
```

But it's usually better to leave them in place, because you may want them again.

See Also

- *update-rc.d(8)*

7.6   Creating Both Text and Graphical Login Runlevels on Debian

Problem

Your Debian system boots to a graphical login manager. You want to change this so that your Debian system's runlevel 3 is a text console, and runlevel 5 boots to a graphical login.

Solution

First you need to know which display manager the system is using. Then you can add it to or remove it from the appropriate levels. To see which one is running, use:

```
$ ps ax | grep dm
  537 ?          S       0:00 /usr/bin/kdm
  544 ?          S<      0:10 /usr/X11R6/bin/X :0 -dpi 100 -nolisten tcp vt7 -auth /var/
lib/kdm/A:0-PbCLdj
```

kdm, the K display manager, is running. First remove it from all runlevels:

```
# update-rc.d -f kdm remove
update-rc.d: /etc/init.d/kdm exists during rc.d purge (continuing)
 Removing any system startup links for /etc/init.d/kdm ...
   /etc/rc0.d/K01kdm
   /etc/rc1.d/K01kdm
   /etc/rc2.d/S99kdm
   /etc/rc3.d/S99kdm
   /etc/rc4.d/S99kdm
   /etc/rc5.d/S99kdm
   /etc/rc6.d/K01kdm
```

Now have *kdm* start on runlevel 5, and stop on all the others:

```
# update-rc.d kdm  start 99 5 . stop 01 0 1 2 3 4 6 .
 Adding system startup for /etc/init.d/kdm ...
   /etc/rc0.d/K01kdm -> ../init.d/kdm
   /etc/rc1.d/K01kdm -> ../init.d/kdm
   /etc/rc2.d/K01kdm -> ../init.d/kdm
   /etc/rc3.d/K01kdm -> ../init.d/kdm
   /etc/rc4.d/K01kdm -> ../init.d/kdm
   /etc/rc6.d/K01kdm -> ../init.d/kdm
   /etc/rc5.d/S99kdm -> ../init.d/kdm
```

Note that it's important to have an entry on every runlevel, explicitly starting or stopping each service. The priority number must always be two digits. 99 is the lowest priority. Last to live, first to die, that's the fate of *kdm*.

Finally, edit */etc/inittab* so that your chosen runlevel becomes the default:

```
# The default runlevel.
id:3:initdefault:
```

When you reboot, your new runlevel scheme will take effect. You can also comment out the line, and then you'll be asked during boot up to select a runlevel.

Discussion

gdm is the Gnome display manager, *xdm* is the X display manager, and *kdm* belongs to KDE. It's not uncommon to find all three installed. *xdm* is pretty barebones; it does nothing but provide a graphical login screen. Both *kdm* and *gdm* have several login and shutdown options, including a menu for selecting your window manager.

See Also

- *update-rc.d(8)*
- Recipe 7.3, "Changing the Default Runlevel"
- The Debian Reference manual (*http://qref.sourceforge.net*)
- This chapter's "Introduction"

7.7   Managing Red Hat's Runlevels

Problem

Unless you took the time to do a custom installation, Red Hat/Fedora typically starts all kinds of services when it boots. If you took the fast way, you probably have all sorts of services running that you'd like to shut off. Or you'd like to start different services on different runlevels, for testing and tinkering.

Solution

Use *chkconfig*. For example, configuring *ssh*:

```
# chkconfig --level 2345 ssh on
# chkconfig --level 016 ssh off
```

You need both steps—define which runlevels the service will run on, and define which runlevels it will not run on. "Off" means kill, and "on" means start.

To add a new service to all levels, use:

```
# chkconfig --add ssh
```

To delete a service from all runlevels, use:

```
# chkconfig --del ssh
```

xinetd services are slightly different, and are also managed with *chkconfig*:

```
# chkconfig ktalk on
# chkconfig rsync off
```

xinetd services are either on or off; you don't have to worry about different runlevels.

To display the status of all services, on all runlevels, and *xinetd* services, use:

```
# chkconfig --list
anacron  0:off  1:off  2:on  3:on  4:on  5:on  6:off
syslog   0:off  1:off  2:on  3:on  4:on  5:on  6:off
cups     0:off  1:off  2:on  3:on  4:on  5:on  6:off
apmd     0:off  1:off  2:on  3:on  4:on  5:on  6:off
xinetd based services:
     chargen-udp    off
     rsync:         off
     sgi-fam:       on
```

To query a single service, use:

```
# chkconfig --list syslog
syslog   0:off 1:off 2:on  3:on  4:on  5:on  6:off
```

Discussion

chkconfig gets its default priority and runlevel values from the program's startup script. For example, in */etc/rc.d/init.d/cups*:

```
#  Linux chkconfig stuff
#  chkconfig 2345 90 10
```

This tells *chkconfig* to start in runlevels 2, 3, 4, and 5, with a priority of 90 for starting and 10 for stopping. Of course, you can easily change these to suit yourself, by either editing the original *init.d* script or simply renaming the links:

```
# mv /etc/rc.d/rc3.d/S90cups /etc/rc.d/rc3.d/S45cups
```

See Also

- *chkconfig(8)*
- The Red Hat Customization Guide (*http://www.redhat.com/docs/manuals/linux/*)

7.8   Manually Configuring Startup Services

Problem

You need to manually configure your startup services, either because you think using these fancy-schmancy utilities like *update-rc.d* to manage your runlevels is sissy, you don't care for the utility that your Linux distribution provides, or you're stuck on some strange barebones system with no helpful utilities.

Solution

Create entries in the */rc*.d* directories with the *ln* command. Delete entries for services that are not going to be used at all.

As an example, let's create a nice soft link to start up CUPS in runlevel 3:

```
# ln -s /etc/rc.d/init.d/cups  /etc/rc.d/rc3.d/S90cups
```

Now repeat this for every runlevel. Don't forget the "kill" runlevels:

```
# ln -s /etc/rc.d/init.d/cups  /etc/rc.d/rc0.d/K01cups
```

Priority choices are 1–99. It doesn't matter if there are duplicates; priority 20 is the most common. Priorities usually aren't all that important, but some things, such as firewalls and logging, should be assigned an early priority between 1–10 (for starting up) and a late priority 80 or greater (for stopping). Also, pay attention to sequence. For example, networking needs to be started before services that depend on networking.

Discussion

Doing it this way is a little more work, but it's you're no big deal—you're just creating soft links. Remember, every service that you start must also be explicitly stopped in all runlevels in which it is not going to run. Also, some services in 0, 1, and 6 should not be killed, as these are important system services created by Linux. Make a record of these before changing anything:

```
$ ls /etc/rc0.d /etc/rc1.d /etc/rc6.d > original-runlevels.txt
```

Also include *rcS.d*, and any others that may be hanging around. You can do anything you want in runlevels 2–5, but take care not to mess up the others.

See Also

- *ln(1)*
- Chapter 5 of *Running Linux*

7.9   Manually Starting and Stopping Services

Problem

You need to start, stop, or restart a service, but you don't want to make it permanent. Maybe your network connection has wedged or your web server has died. Or you changed the configuration file for a service, and need to restart it to activate the changes. Or you are testing a new service, so you want to start it up only when you're testing it.

Solution

Run the program's startup script in */init.d*. Find the appropriate script in *init.d*, then read the script to see the available options. For example, restarting networking is a common need. Take a look in */etc/init.d/networking*:

```
echo "Usage: /etc/init.d/networking {start|stop|restart|force-reload}"
```

There's a line like this in every *init* script. Another way to get this information is to run the script with no arguments:

```
# /etc/init.d/networking
Usage: /etc/init.d/networking {start|stop|restart|force-reload}
```

So, to stop networking, use the command:

```
# /etc/init.d/networking stop
```

Discussion

For any program that has a startup script, it is preferable to use the script, rather than executing the program's binary, because the script includes include error and file checking, and any needed conditional tests.

7.10   Shutting Down or Rebooting Linux

Problem

Look at all these shutdown and reboot commands: *shutdown, halt, init 0, poweroff, Ctrl-Alt-Delete*, etc. What's the right one to use?

Solution

It doesn't matter all that much; use what suits you. Only root can use these commands to shut down:

```
# shutdown -h now
```

or:

```
# poweroff
```

or:

```
# halt
```

To shut down in six minutes:

```
# shutdown -h +6
```

shutdown sends a notification to all logged-in users. To make your own message, use:

```
# shutdown -h +6 "Time to stop working and start partying."
```

Console users will see:

```
Broadcast message from root (pts/6) Wed Aug 14 13:51:24 2003
Time to stop working and start partying.
The system is going DOWN for system halt in 6 minutes!
```

To cancel a shutdown as root, use:

```
# shutdown -c
```

To reboot, you can use:

```
# shutdown -r now
```

or:

```
# reboot
```

or press Ctrl-Alt-Delete. Any user can do this, unless you disable it in */etc/inittab*. (See Recipe 7.11 to learn to disable this, or how to grant permission to specific users.)

Discussion

The most important thing to remember is to always have a controlled shutdown. All computers, including Linux machines, have to do a lot of tidying up and putting away before they can be turned off. Services must be turned off, filesystems unmounted, and buffers written to disk.

shutdown, poweroff, and *halt* all must be executed by the root user. This seems rather silly, as all window managers and desktop environments have their own shutdown menus that any user can use, and anyone physically sitting at the machine can hit the power switch. However, there it is, and we must deal with it. One option is to grant limited privileges for *shutdown* commands with *sudo*. Another is to create a "shutdown" group.

See Also

- *shutdown(8), poweroff(8)*
- Recipe 8.20, "Using su to Be Root Temporarily"
- Recipe 8.21, "Granting Limited Rootly Powers with sudo"
- Chapter 25 of *Unix Power Tools*, by Shelley Powers, Jerry Peek, Tim O'Reilly, and Mike Loukides (O'Reilly)
- Chapter 8 of *Running Linux*

7.11   Disabling or Limiting Access to Ctrl-Alt-Delete

Problem

We all know that Ctrl-Alt-Delete reboots the machine. But is this what you want? From a security standpoint, a machine is vulnerable when booting; and anyone with access to the keyboard can force a reboot. Therefore, you want to disable Ctrl-Alt-Delete for rebooting the machine, or you want to limit it to some users.

Solution

To disable it completely, comment out this line in */etc/inittab*:

```
# ca:12345:ctrlaltdel:/sbin/shutdown -t1 -r now
```

To enable it for a specific set of users, add the *-a* switch:

```
ca:12345:ctrlaltdel:/sbin/shutdown -t1 -a -r now
```

Then add your list of allowed users to */etc/shutdown.allow*.

Discussion

You may need to create the */etc/shutdown.allow* file, if it does not already exist.

See Also

- *shutdown(8)*

7.12   Shutting Down Automatically

Problem

Your users are careless watt-wasters who refuse to develop the habit of shutting down their PCs at night, or maybe you think it would be nice to have your machine turn itself off at night, so you can just walk away and not worry about it.

Solution

It's easy as pie, thanks to *cron*. Add this line to */etc/crontab* to automatically shut down your machine every night at 11p.m.:

```
# m   h   dom mon dow  user    command
  00  23  *   *   *    root     /sbin/shutdown -h now
```

Discussion

/etc/crontab is perfect for simple *cron* setups. Note that it has a name field, so any user can have entries in this file. However, only root can edit */etc/crontab*.

Another way is to use the *crontab* command:

```
# crontab -u root -e
```

This opens the root user's *crontab*. Edit and save, and you're done. Don't try to name the file yourself—during editing, it's a */tmp* file, which is automatically renamed by *crontab* when you save it. It will end up in */var/spool/cron/crontabs*, or somewhere close by.

A Brief Word on Uptimes

You've probably noticed Linux users bragging and obsessing about their uptimes. There's even an *uptime* command. There is nothing sacred about uptimes. Yes, I too love that Linux is stable as a table, and that most software installations and system upgrades never require a reboot. But let's not go nuts. If a particular machine does not need to be running 24 × 7, turn it off. It saves electricity, reduces the risk of something bad happening, and extends the life of your hardware.

See Also

- *cron(8), crontab(1), crontab(5)*

## CHAPTER 8

Managing Users and Groups

8.1 Introduction

On a Linux system, both human users and system processes have user accounts. Some system processes need user accounts to control privileges and access rights, just like human users.

Remember the most fundamental Linux security principles:

1. Use the minimum necessary privileges to get the job done.
2. Strong passwords work.

Following these two principles will prevent all sorts of aggravation and mishaps.

Linux has a collection of utilities for managing users and groups: *useradd, groupadd, userdel, groupdel, usermod, groupmod, passwd, chfn*, and *chsh*. These are part of the "Shadow Suite."

The Shadow Suite was created by Julianne Frances Haugh to improve password security and to make user account management easier. In the olden days, all the relevant files had to be edited individually, and encrypted passwords were stored in */etc/passwd*. But because */etc/passwd* must remain world-readable, storing passwords in it, even if they're encrypted, is asking for trouble. Anyone who copies it can then crack the passwords at their leisure. Relocating the encrypted passwords to */etc/shadow*, which is accessible only by root, adds a useful layer of protection.

useradd behaves differently on different systems. Traditionally, it lumped all new users into the same login group, *users (100)*. This meant that all home directories were wide open by default, because users all belonged to the same group. Red Hat changed this with their "User Private Group" scheme. Red Hat's *useradd* creates a private group for each new user, with the same user ID (UID) and group ID (GID). Obviously, different users have different needs, and some prefer that their user's directories be open. A fundamental security principle is "deny all, allow as needed."

Newer arrivals on the scene are *adduser* and *addgroup*, which are Perl script wrappers for *useradd* and *groupadd*. These scripts walk you through a complete new user configuration. *adduser* and *addgroup* are very nice for making individual entries, but they're no good for batch operations (unless, of course, you modify the *adduser* or *addgroup* scripts yourself).

See Recipe 8.17 for a custom script for adding new users in batches and changing passwords en masse.

8.2 Sorting Human Users from System Users

Problem

Every Linux system has a bunch of system accounts (root, uucp, daemon, etc.) in addition to regular users. They're all lumped together in */etc/password*. How do you list your human users separately from system accounts?

Solution

Take advantage of Linux's user identification (UID) numbering scheme and *awk*'s ability to sort by fields or columns. This is for a Debian or Slackware system:

```
$ awk -F: '$3 > 999 { print $0}' /etc/passwd
nobody:x:65534:65534:nobody:/nonexistent:/bin/sh
carla:x:1000:1000::/home/carla:/bin/bash
foober:x:1001:1001::/home/test:/bin/false
bitchkat:x:1002:1002::/home/test2:/bin/bash
colby:x:1003:1003::/home/test3:/bin/bash
```

To show a subset use:

```
$ awk -F: '($3 >= 1000) &&($3 <=1005)  { print $0}' /etc/passwd
```

This is for a Red Hat or SuSE system:

```
$ awk -F: '$3 > 499 { print $0}' /etc/passwd
```

To sort them alphabetically use:

```
$ awk -F: '$3 > 499 { print $0}' /etc/passwd | sort
```

There's a neat trick you can do with UIDs, if you cannily plot out a numbering scheme in advance. For example:

- Trainers 1000–1100
- Coaches 1101–1200
- Players 1200–2000

Following a convention like this gives you a simple tool to sort your users and add them in batches to groups.

Discussion

Using a numbering scheme like the "Trainers, Coaches, Players" example works all right for smaller user bases that are fairly static. For large, busy establishments with a lot of change, it's more headache than help. In those circumstances, it's better to put your energy into keeping group assignments orderly and up-to-date.

As always, there are interesting little differences between distributions.

UIDs and GIDs on all Linuxes range from 0 to 65534.

For example, on Debian:

- IDs 0–99 are for system accounts.
- IDs 100–999 are for user-installed programs and daemons, such as Postfix, Fetchmail, *gdm*, *dictd*, and so on.
- IDs 1000–29999 are ordinary user accounts.
- IDs 30000–65533 are reserved, according to the Debian policy manual, but you may use them however you like.
- ID 65534 is user "nobody," an account with no rights or permissions.

And on Red Hat:

- IDs 0–499 are reserved for system use.
- IDs 500–60000 are for ordinary users.
- ID 65534 is user "nobody," an account with no rights or permissions.

Most Linuxes follow similar numbering schemes. Feel free to tinker with the number ranges reserved for ordinary user accounts, but don't mess with the system or UIDs.

See Also

- *awk(1)*
- Recipe 8.17, "Adding Batches of Users to Groups"
- Chapter 5 of *Running Linux*, by Matt Welsh, Matthias Dalheimer, Terry Dawson, and Lar Kaufman (O'Reilly)
- *sed & awk Pocket Reference*, by Arnold Robbins (O'Reilly)
- Debian Policy Manual, Chapter 9.2.2 (*http://www.debian.org/doc/debian-policy/*)
- Red Hat Linux Reference Guide(*http://www.redhat.com/docs/manuals/linux/*)

8.3   Finding a User's UID and GID

Problem

You want to know a quick way to check the UIDs of users and see what groups they belong to.

Solution

Use the *id* command:

```
$ id carla
uid=1000(carla) gid=1000(carla)
groups=1000(carla),20(dialout),24(cdrom),25(floppy),29(audio),30(dip),44(video),
105(windows),432(usb),1001(cdrecording)
```

Discussion

id has a few options:

-u

> Show the UID only.

-g

> Show the GID only.

-gn

> Show the user's primary group name, instead of the GID.

See Also

- *id(1)*

8.4   Adding Users with useradd

Problem

You need to add new users to a Linux system.

Solution

Use *useradd -m* to create a login name, home directory, and other environment variables, and use the *passwd -e* command to set the new password. The account is not active until you create a password.

This is the simplest invocation. The *-m* flag creates a home directory and copies in the files from */etc/skel*:

```
# useradd -m newusername
```

Under most circumstances, you should also specify the user's full name, using the *-c* (comments) flag. Put four commas after the user's name, to leave other parts of the comments field (office number, etc.) blank.

```
# useradd -m -c Grace Hopper,,,, ghopper
```

When adding a new user, *newusername* becomes the user's login name. This must be a unique name.

Next, run *passwd -e*. The *-e* flag expires the password at first login, forcing the user to change it:

```
# passwd -e ghopper
Enter new UNIX password:
Retype new UNIX password:
passwd: password updated successfully
```

The user's environment is created according to the defaults in */etc/default/useradd* and */etc/skel/*. You can display the *useradd* defaults:

```
# useradd -D
```

Any of the default values can be overridden at the command line—for example, the UID and shell:

```
# useradd -u 1500 -s tcsh ghopper
```

Or you can add to the default values—for example, adding additional group memberships:

```
# useradd -G users,cdrecord,dialout ghopper
```

Discussion

useradd, unlike its cousin *adduser*, performs splendidly in scripts (such as the *mass_useradd* script in Recipe 8.17).

The comments fields are also known as the *GECOS* data. GECOS has five comma-delimited subfields. If you're going to use the comments fields, it is best to include all four commas, even if you don't enter all the values. This pays off handsomely over the long run, especially for batch and search operations. The traditional values are full name, room number, work phone, home phone, and other (this field can be used for anything you like). Many external programs, such as mail servers, use the full name field. But you can use the other subfields any way you like. It provides a useful way to arbitrarily categorize and sort users (see Recipe 8.19).

GECOS is a dusty holdover from the very olden days; it stands for the "General Electric Comprehensive Operating System." Visit the Jargon File for the full story.

See Also

- *useradd(8)*
- The Jargon File (*http://www.catb.org/~esr/jargon/*)

8.5   Adding Users with adduser

Problem

You want to use *adduser* instead of *useradd*, because it walks you through a complete new user setup—password, GECOS fields, and all.

Solution

To add a user, simply run *adduser newusername* and follow the prompts:

```
# adduser anitab
Adding user anitab...
Adding new group anitab (1008).
Adding new user anitab (1008) with group anitab.
Creating home directory /home/anitab.
Copying files from /etc/skel
Enter new UNIX password:
Retype new UNIX password:
passwd: password updated successfully
Changing the user information for anitab
Enter the new value, or press ENTER for the default
        Full Name [ ]:
        Room Number [ ]:
        Work Phone [ ]:
        Home Phone [ ]:
        Other [ ]:
Is the information correct? [y/n] y
```

You can assign a UID, overriding the default:

```
# adduser --uid 1500 anitab
```

adduser's defaults are configured in */etc/adduser.conf*.

Discussion

The full name is the only important part of the user information. Any external pro-grams that use */etc/passwd*, such as mail servers, need the full user name. And, believe it or not, *finger* still lingers on most Linuxes:

```
$ finger anitab
Login: anitab                   Name:
Directory: /home/anitab         Shell: /bin/bash
On since Sun May 30 08:46 (PDT) on tty1   10 hours 55 minutes idle
    (messages off)
No mail.
No plan.
Phone 555-5555
Office Fooo
```

The other fields for the user data can contain anything you want. Using these fields is a quick and easy way to keep notes on users, or to categorize them.

Users can change their own room and phone numbers with *chfn*, but they can't change the full name or the "other" field.

See Also

- *adduser(8), adduser.conf(5), finger(1)*

8.6   Modifying User Accounts

Problem

You need to make changes to an existing user account, such as changing the login or UID, updating the GECOS data, or home directory.

Solution

Use *usermod* and *chfn*.

Anything and everything is modifiable, including the login name and UID. To change the login, list first the new login name, then the old one:

```
# usermod -l aborg anitab
```

The following command changes the UID—in this example, from the original 1050 to 1200—without changing the login name. Name the new UID first, then the login:

```
# usermod -u 1200 anitab
```

Group memberships are not changed. All files in the user's home directory will automatically be updated with the new UID. However, you must hunt down and change any files outside the user's home directory, such as *crontab*s, mail directories, */tmp* files, and files in shared directories. You can hunt them down with *find,* searching for the original UID, if you want to review them before making changes:

```
# find / -uid 1050
/usr/src/include/lber.h
/usr/src/include/ldap.h
/usr/src/include/ldbm.h
```

Use *chown* to update ownership of the files:

```
# chown 1200 /usr/src/include/lber.h
```

Doing this one file at a time can be rather tedious. *chown* and *find* can do the work for you:

```
# find / -uid 1050 -exec chown -v 1200 {} \;
changed owner of `/usr/src/include/lber.h' to 1200
changed owner of `/usr/src/include/ldap.h' to 1200
changed owner of `/usr/src/include/ldbm.h' to 1200
```

The following command moves the user's home directory, and its contents, to a different location. It will create the new directory if it does not already exist. Name the new directory first, then the login name. Be sure to use both the *-d* and *-m* flags:

```
# usermod -d /server1/home/aborg/ -m  aborg
```

To change a user's GECOS information use:

```
# chfn aborg
```

Users can change their own GECOS data with *chfn*, with the exception of the full name and "other" fields, which only the superuser can edit.

Discussion

It is better not to change the login and UID, as changing these has system-wide repercussions. If you do, remember to hunt down all the files belonging to the user, change the name on the user's home directory, and update group memberships.

You can make *find* verify each change by substituting the *-ok* flag for *-exec*, rather than letting it make all the changes automatically:

```
# find / -uid 1050 -ok chown -v 1200 { } \;
```

This will prompt you to approve each change.

This particular use of *find* is endlessly useful. The *-exec* or *-ok* options tell *find* to execute the command that follows. *{ }* is replaced by the current file being processed. The semicolon tells *find* where the *chown* command stops, and the backslash escapes the semicolon so it isn't gobbled by the shell.

See Also

- *usermod(8)*, *chfn(1)*
- The Jargon File (*http://www.catb.org/~esr/jargon/*)

8.7   Deleting a User

Problem

You need to delete a user, and you want to track down all the files that belong to the user.

Solution

Use *userdel* to delete the account, and use *find* to locate the files belonging to the user.

To delete a user:

```
# userdel aborg
```

The user cannot be logged in or running any processes for *userdel* to work.

userdel removes the user from all system account files (*/etc/passwd, etc/shadow, /etc/group*), but it does not touch files owned by the user. To remove the user's home directory and mail spool, add the *-r* flag:

```
# userdel -r aborg
```

Other files, such as *crontab*s and data files outside the home directory, will have to be hunted down separately:

```
# find / -uid 1200
```

Discussion

The politics and policies around terminating someone's account are sensitive. If this is a home system, do whatever you want. If it's a commercial system, make sure you understand your company's policies. It's always a good idea to remove or lock the account of any employee who is terminated. Then back up the employee's files.

See Also

- *userdel(8)*, *find(1)*
- Recipe 8.9, "Disabling Accounts"

8.8   Killing User Processes the Easy, Fun Way

Problem

You need to delete a user, but *userdel* reports that some of the user's processes are running. You sure would like single command to find and stop all of the user's processes.

Solution

Use the *slay* program:

```
# slay foober
slay: -KILL is kicking foober's butt!
slay: Whoa, I have the power supreme.
```

slay finds and kills all the user's processes at once, saving you the trouble of hunting them down and killing them yourself. *slay* has four modes: nice, normal, mean, and butthead. Mean mode kills any nonprivileged user who attempts to slay another user. Set your desired mode in */etc/slay_mode*.

Discussion

The traditional method of finding processes belonging to a user is to use *ps*, as in:

```
$ ps U 1007
```

or:

```
$ ps U foober
3936 ?         S         0:00 xchat
3987 ?         S         0:00 /usr/lib/galeon-bin
4209 ?         S         0:00 kdeinit: kio_file file /tmp/ksocket-carla/
klauncherkF21rc.slave-
```

You can then kill one by one:

```
# kill 3936
# kill 3987
# kill 4209
```

See Also

- *slay(1), kill(1)*

8.9   Disabling Accounts

Problem

You need to disable an account and temporarily prevent the user from logging in, but you don't want to delete the account.

Solution

To temporarily deactivate an account, disable the user's password with the *-l* (lock) flag:

```
# passwd -l aborg
Password changed.
```

To re-enable, or unlock, a user's password use:

```
# passwd -u aborg
Password changed.
```

Discussion

Another way to disable an account is to insert an exclamation point at the beginning of the password field in */etc/shadow*:

```
foobar:!$1$wiDlQr34$mitGZA76MSYCYO4AHIY1:12466:0:99999:7:::
```

Yet another way is replace the *x* in the password field in */etc/passwd* with an asterisk (*):

```
foober:*:1025:1025:Foober Smith,,,:/home/foober:/bin/bash
```

You can also take away the user's login shell:

```
# usermod -s /bin/false foober
```

But it's best to stick with *passwd -l* and *-u*.

See Also

- *passwd(1), passwd(5)*

8.10 Managing Passwords

Problem

You need to reset a password, or put an expiration date on it, or you want to set a limit on failed login attempts. Resetting a password is the solution to the perennial "I forgot my password" problem; many Linux administrators think it's a good idea to "expire" passwords, forcing users to change them periodically.

Solution

Use *passwd* to set and configure passwords.

To reset or change a password use:

```
# passwd aborg
```

Users can also change their own passwords:

```
aborg@server04:~$ passwd
```

This command sets aborg's password to expire after six months, with five days' warning:

```
# passwd -x 180 -w 5 -i 1 aborg
```

To view a user's password settings, use:

```
# passwd -S option
aborg P 02/18/2004 0 10 5 1
```

Discussion

Passwords can consist of numbers, letters, and punctuation marks, and they are case-sensitive. Don't use spaces or function keys. Strong passwords work best—this means no names, no dictionary words, no birthdays or addresses. The best way to keep track of passwords is write them down and keep them in a safe place. Most people, if they can't remember all of their passwords, end up choosing weak, easily guessable passwords, or leaving them in obvious, insecure places (such as on a note stuck to the monitor).

Linux passwords are not designed to be recoverable. If a password is lost, the user must depend on the benevolence of the superuser to create a new one.

See Also

- *passwd(1)*, *passwd(5)*

8.11 Adding Groups with groupadd

Problem

You need to create some new user or system groups. Any server programs that you install should have their own users and group.

Solution

Use *groupadd*.

This command creates a new group, using the system values configured in */etc/default/useradd* and */etc/skel/*:

```
# groupadd newgroup
```

You can create a system group with *-r* flag:

```
# groupadd -r newgroup
```

The *-r* flag is a Red Hat–specific option. If your version of *groupadd* does not have it, you'll have to specify the next available system group number:

```
# groupadd -g 127 newgroup
```

Look in */etc/group* to see the next available group number.

Discussion

It's a good idea to stick to a consistent group numbering scheme. Linux doesn't care, for the most part, but for your own sanity it's essential. Red Hat system groups are 0–499; Debian's are 100–999. See the "Discussion" section in Recipe 8.2 for more information on numbering schemes.

See Also

- *groupadd(8)*

8.12 Deleting Groups with groupdel

Problem

You need to delete a group or groups, and you want to be sure there are no orphaned files or users.

Solution

First reassign the group members, if necessary, by editing */etc/group*. Simply copy and paste them into another group. Then use *groupdel* to delete the group, and *find* and *chgrp* to locate and reassign the group's files to another group.

To delete a group use:

```
# groupdel groupname
```

Deleting a group tends to be messy, because there is no utility for automatically migrating or deleting any files or users belonging to the group. You'll need to hunt these down and change the GIDs manually:

```
# find / -gid 750
/usr/src/include/lber.h
/usr/src/include/ldap.h
/usr/src/include/ldbm.h
```

You can change these one at a time:

```
# chgrp 800 /usr/src/include/lber.h
```

Or you can let *find* and *chgrp* do the work:

```
# find / -gid 750 -exec chgrp -v  800 { } \;
```

See Also

- *groupdel(8)*, *find(1)*, *chgrp(1)*
- Recipe 8.6, "Modifying User Accounts," for an explanation of how the *find* command works in these examples

8.13   Creating a System User

Problem

You need to know how to create system users for programs like Postfix, Apache, or Squid. These programs should have their own unique user accounts and not just all pile into "nobody."

Solution

Both *adduser* and *useradd* can do this. *adduser* works like this:

```
# adduser --system  --no-create-home --group squid
Adding system user squid...
Adding new group squid (109).
Adding new user squid (109) with group squid
Not creating home directory
```

Check your work:

```
# cat /etc/passwd | grep squid
squid:x:109:109::/home/squid:/bin/false
```

Even though it lists */home/squid*, a home directory is not created.

Here's how *useradd* does it:

```
# useradd -d /dev/null -g squid -s /bin/false squid
```

Discussion

The *nobody* user is the default for a lot of daemons and processes that need a system account, but an increasing number of applications require their own unique users. Use a unique user whenever possible, because it's a good security practice. The *nobody* account is a common cracker target, and you don't want to expose all kinds of processes and daemons to a common point of attack.

See Also

- *adduser(8)*, *adduser.conf(5)*, *useradd(8)*

8.14 Creating System Groups with addgroup

Problem

You need to create some new system groups, and you want to use *addgroup*.

Solution

Here's how to create system groups with *addgroup*:

```
# addgroup --system  newsysgroup
```

You can assign the GID, overriding the default. Remember to stick with your distribution's (or your personal) numbering scheme:

```
# addgroup --system  --gid 300 newsysgroup
```

See Also

- *addgroup(8)*
- Recipe 8.11, "Adding Groups with groupadd"

8.15 Adding and Deleting Group Members

Problem

You need to give users some group memberships, or delete some users from groups.

Solution

Edit */etc/groups* manually. Just copy and paste; it's the fastest way.

Discussion

You may also use *adduser* and *usermod*, but beware of sneaky gotchas: *adduser* will only add a user to one group at a time, but *usermod*, which allows you to list several groups at once, will overwrite any existing group assignments.

See Also

- *adduser(8)*, *usermod(8)*

8.16   Checking Password File Integrity

Problem

There's a lot going on in all these files (*/etc/group*, */etc/passwd*, */etc/shadow*, and */etc/gshadow*), and you need some kind of password file syntax integrity checker. You don't want to find out that you've made some mistake—like forgetting to give someone a password—after an attacker has broken into your system!

Solution

Use *pwck* for checking */etc/passwd* and */etc/shadow*, and use *grpck* for */etc/group* and */etc/gshadow*:

```
# pwck
# grpck
```

If they exit silently, no errors were found. Otherwise, errors will be listed; you will have to correct the errors, or the program will exit. You can get around this, and simply view all errors, by running in read-only mode:

```
# pwck -r
# grpck -r
```

Discussion

pwck performs a consistency check on the */etc/passwd* and */etc/shadow* files. It checks each user account, and verifies that it has:

- The correct number of fields
- A unique user name
- A valid user and group identifier
- A valid primary group
- A valid home directory
- A valid login shell

pwck will report any account that has no password. I love the wording in the man page: "The checks for correct number of fields and unique user name are fatal."

That's hardly an inducement to utilize this useful program! However, rest assured—
you are perfectly safe and will not be harmed.

When *pwck* finds an error, your choices are to delete the account or to ignore the
account, in which case *pwck* shuts down and won't check any more lines (with one
exception: if it finds a duplicate name, it will continue checking even if you don't
delete the account)

grpck checks the */etc/group* and */etc/gshadow* files to verify that each group has:

- The correct number of fields
- A unique group name
- A valid list of members and administrators

See Also

- *pwck(8), grpck(8)*

8.17   Adding New Users in Batches

Problem

You want to be able to add several users at once, rather than having to enter each
one individually.

Solution

Use the *mass_useradd* script. It's a shell script, so it should run just about anywhere.
You'll also need *mass_passwd*. Store the two scripts in the same directory. You
should also install the *pwgen* utility, for generating passwords. You'll need a colon-
delimited text list of logins and usernames in this format:

```
login:firstname lastname
```

You may also include additional GECOS data, like this:

```
dawns:Dawn Marie Schroder,,123-4567,trainers
```

Then invoke the *mass_useradd* script. It creates entries in */etc/passwd, /etc/group,* and
/etc/shadow; home directories; personal login groups; and passwords that expire at
first use.

This tells *mass_useradd* to use the list of new users in *newusers* and to overwrite or
create the output file *newlogins.txt*:

```
# sh mass_useradd < newusers > newlogins.txt
```

This appends the new logins and passwords to *newlogins.txt*:

```
# sh mass_useradd < newusers >> newlogins.txt
```

In addition to the output file, which is a simple list, *mass_passwd* creates a separate file for each user, containing the new login name and instructions. This makes it easy to print them individually for distribution. These files, plus a log file, are stored in the home directory of the user who runs the scripts (usually root):

```
# ls /root/mass_passwds
dawns.passwd.txt  nikitah.passwd.txt  mass_passwd.log  rubst.passwd.txt
```

Discussion

Because the scripts use standard Shadow Suite utilities, they are easy to customize by adjusting the options for the various utilities used in the scripts.

The output file looks like this:

```
dawns     shabaefi    1002
nikitah   gohbinga    1003
rubst     ahtoohaa    1004
```

/etc/passwd looks like this:

```
dawns:x:1002:1002:Dawn Marie Schroder,,123-4567,trainers:/home/dawns:/bin/bash
nikitah:x:1003:1003:Nikita Horse,,123-4567,equine:/home/nikitah:/bin/bash
rubst:x:1004:1004:Rubs The Cat,101,,234-5678,,test:/home/rubst:/bin/bash
```

The individual files generated for each user look like this:

```
------------------------------------------------------------
          Login name: rubst
          Password:   eejahgue
     Please log in and change your password; the system should prompt you to do this
when you log in.  You can change your password at any time with the 'passwd' command.
          Choose a strong password - everyday words, birthdays, names of people or
animals, all these are too easy to guess.
     Also, DO NOT give your password to anyone, ever.  The IT
     staff will never ask you for your password, and neither
     should anyone else.  You will be held responsible for all
     activity done via your account.
------------------------------------------------------------
```

Program: mass_useradd

```
#!/bin/sh

## Mass Useradd For Linux
## This script extracts new user data from a delimited
## text file, and automatically generates new user accounts.
## It generates a random password for each login, and exports
## the new logins and passwords to a text file.
## Passwords automatically expire at first login. The
## input file format is "username: full name" (no quotes) for
## each line.
##
## Mass Useradd creates a "User Personal Group."
## The UID and the GID are the same. User's home directories
```

```
## are created with restrictive permissions, chmod 700.
## Mass Useradd uses standard Shadow Suite utilities.
## Values and behaviors are easily modifiable, according
## to the individual utility being called.  It calls
## a companion script, mass_passwd, to set each user password.
## You should have received mass_passwd from the same source
## as mass_useradd.
##
## This script was created by Aaron Malone, and modified by
## Meredydd Luff, Peter Samuelson, and Kathryn Hogg.
## Many thanks!
## Carla Schroder wrote the documentation and pestered
## the aforementioned persons to write the script.
## Copyright (C) 2003  Carla Schroder
## carla at bratgrrl dot com
## This program is free software; you can redistribute
## it and/or modify it under the terms of the GNU General
## Public License as published by the Free Software
## Foundation; either version 2 of the License, or (at your
## option) any later version.
##
## This program is distributed in the hope that it will
## be useful, but WITHOUT ANY WARRANTY; without even the
## implied warranty of MERCHANTABILITY or FITNESS FOR A
## PARTICULAR PURPOSE.  See the
## GNU General Public License for more details.
## http://www.fsf.org/licenses/gpl.html
##
##   Usage:
##     #  sh mass_useradd < inputfile >> new-passwords.txt
##


PATH=/usr/local/sbin:/usr/sbin:/sbin:/usr/local/bin:/usr/bin:/bin:$PATH


# Read a line of input.
# the format of the input file must be like this:
# userlogin : FirstName LastName
# to use a comma-delimited file, change IFS=":$IFS" to
# IFS=",$IFS"

while IFS=":$IFS" read username realname; do

# First, weed out blank lines and #comments
        case "$username" in
                '' | \#*) continue ;;
        esac

# this part reads /etc/passwd and /etc/group, and calculates
# the next available UID and GID.
# it starts at {id=1000}, change this to suit
        id=$({ getent passwd; getent group; } | cut -f3 -d: | sort -un |
            awk 'BEGIN { id=1000 }
                 $1 == id { id++ }
                 $1 > id { print id; exit }')
```

```
# Now users are added to /etc/group, /etc/passwd,
# and home directories with chmod 700 are created
# Any of the groupadd, useradd, and chmod options
# can be changed to suit
        groupadd -g $id $username
        useradd -m -c "$realname" -g $username -u $id $username
        chmod 700 /home/$username

# Set the password.  This calls another script from
# this toolkit, mass_passwd, which can be used independently.
# mass_passwd outputs the username, password and userid.
        $(dirname $0)/mass_passwd -M $username

done
```

Program: mass_passwd

```
#!/bin/sh

## Mass Password Change for Linux
## This requires the Shadow Suite utilities.
## Usage:
##    mass_passwd username username ...
##    mass_passwd -g groupname groupname ...
##    mass_passwd -a
##
## This program is free software; you can redistribute
## it and/or modify it under the terms of the GNU General
## Public License as published by the Free Software
## Foundation; either version 2 of the License, or (at your
## option) any later version.
##
## This program is distributed in the hope that it will
## be useful, but WITHOUT ANY WARRANTY; without even the
## implied warranty of MERCHANTABILITY or FITNESS FOR A
## PARTICULAR PURPOSE.  See the
## GNU General Public License for more details.
## http://www.fsf.org/licenses/gpl.html


############################################################

## This is where the "username.passwd.txt" files will
## be dumped. It will be created if it doesn't already exist
text_file_dir=$HOME/mass_passwds
log_file=mass_passwd.log

## Minimum userid considered a regular (human) user
min_uid=1000

## Length of generated passwords
pass_len=8

## Length of time, in days, before a password expires
pass_expire=90
```

```
###########.###############################################
## Few user-serviceable parts inside.
## You may wish to edit the text between the two ---------
## lines, below.

# Get the name of this program (probably "mass_passwd")
prog=${0##*/}

usage () {
        echo "usage: $prog [-v] [-n] username ..."
        echo "       $prog [-v] [-n] [-g] groupname ..."
        echo "       $prog [-v] [-n] [-a]"
        echo "  -g   change passwords of everyone in a group"
        echo "  -a   change everyone's password"
        echo "  -v   verbose"
        echo "  -n   don't do it, just simulate (implies -v)"
        exit 0
}
short_usage () {
        echo >&2 "usage: $prog [-v] [-g] [-a] name..."
        echo >&2 "       $prog -h    for help"
        exit 1
}

# echo something, but only if in verbose mode
vecho () {
        test -n "$verbose" && echo "$@"
}

# Generate a random password.
#
# If pwgen is available, use that - that's what it's for, and it works well.
#
# If not, read /dev/urandom and filter out all non-
#alphanumeric characters until we have enough for a password.
# The numbers in the "tr -d" are ASCII values, in octal
# notation, of ranges of character values to delete.
#
# Using /dev/urandom like this is very inefficient, but
# who cares?
randompass () {
        pwgen $pass_len 1 2>&- ||
        tr -d '[\000-\057][\072-\100][\133-\140][\173-\377]' < /dev/urandom |
           dd bs=$pass_len count=1 2>&-
}

# Interpret usernames / groupnames / "-a" mode, and return
# a list of usernames
get_users () {
        if [ -n "$all_mode" ]; then
                getent passwd | awk -F: '{if ($3 >= '$min_uid') {print $1}}'
                return
        fi
        if [ -z "$group_mode" ]; then
```

```
                echo "$@"
                return
        fi


# ok, we're in group mode, must look up the users who
# belong to a group
        while [ -n "$1" ]; do
                g_ent=$(getent group "$1" 2>&-)
                if [ -z "$g_ent" ]; then
                        echo >&2 "warning: $1: group not found"
                        continue
                fi
                members=${g_ent##*:}
                gid=${g_ent%:*}
                gid=${gid##*:}
                echo "$members" | tr ',' ' '
                getent passwd | awk -F: '{if ($4 == '$gid') { print $1 } }'
                shift
        done
}


############################################################
## main body

group_mode=; verbose=; all_mode=; simulate=; eol=;
while [ -z "$eol" ]; do
        case "$1" in
                -g) group_mode=1; shift ;;
                -v) verbose=1; shift ;;
                -a) all_mode=1; shift ;;
                -n) simulate=true; verbose=1; shift ;;
             # we're called from mass_useradd
                -M) mass_out=1; shift ;;
                -h | -? | --help) usage ;;
                --) eol=1; shift ;;
                -*) short_usage ;;
                *) eol=1 ;;
        esac
done

# Set up a secure environment and the directory for
# printable text files
PATH=/usr/sbin:/usr/bin:$PATH
umask 077
mkdir -p $text_file_dir
cd $text_file_dir

processed=0
for u in $(get_users "$@"); do
        vecho -n "generating password for $u..."
        pass=$(randompass)
        echo "$u:$pass" | eval $simulate chpasswd
        vecho -n "."
        eval $simulate chage -M $pass_expire -d 2003-01-01 $u
```

```
        vecho -n "."

        rm -f $u.passwd.txt
        echo > $u.passwd.txt "\
-------------------------------------------------------------
                    Login name: $u
                    Password:    $pass
        Please log in and change your password; the system should prompt you to do
this when you log in.  You can change your password at any time with the 'passwd'
command.
        Choose a strong password - everyday words, birthdays, names of people or
animals, all these are too easy to guess. Use combinations of letters and numbers.
Write down your password in a safe place.
    Also, DO NOT give your password to anyone, ever.  The IT
    staff will never ask you for your password, and neither
    should anyone else.  You will be held responsible for all
    activity done via your account.
-----------------------------------------------------------------"
        printf >> $log_file "$(date)   %-12s %s\\n" $u $pass
        vecho "$pass"
        if [ -n "$mass_out" ]; then
                uid=$(getent passwd $u | cut -f3 -d:)
                echo -e "$u\\t$pass\\t$uid"
        fi
        processed=$(expr $processed + 1)
done

if [ $processed -gt 0 ]; then
        test -z "$mass_out" &&
        echo >&2 "$processed password(s) reset - see $text_file_dir/$log_file"
else
        echo >&2 "no users specified - see '$prog -h' for help"
fi
```

See Also

- *bash(1)*, *pwgen(1)*
- Get *pwgen* from the usual package repositories or from its home page (*http:// sourceforge.net/projects/pwgen/*)

8.18   Changing Masses of Passwords

Problem

As part of your routine security policy, you would like to periodically be able to easily change batches of passwords. Or your network may have been compromised, so you want to change all the passwords yourself and not leave it up to your users.

Solution

Use the *mass_passwd* script in Recipe 8.17. It lets you select batches of users in three different ways:

```
# mass_passwd username1 username2...
# mass_passwd -g groupname groupname...
# mass_passwd -a
```

The first method uses a simple space-delimited list of logins.

The second method changes the passwords of users belonging to the named groups.

The third method changes every password in */etc/passwd*.

Then *mass_passwd* generates a separate file for each user, containing their new login names and passwords and whatever instructions or policies you choose to include. This is designed to make it easy to print a separate instruction sheet for each user.

Discussion

You may do a dry run with the *-n* flag:

```
# ./mass_passwd -v -g -n usergroup
generating password for dawns.....teivuphu
generating password for nikitah.....kohfahsh
2 password(s) reset - see /root/mass_passwds/mass_passwd.log
```

No passwords are changed; this just lets you test-drive your options before committing to any changes.

See Also

- Recipe 8.17, "Adding New Users in Batches"

8.19   Adding Batches of Users to Groups

Problem

You need to add a whole bunch of users to a group.

Solution

Paste your list of login names directly into */etc/group*.

Here's a quick way to generate a list of users to add to */etc/group*. This depends on having a UID numbering scheme already in place, so that you can easily sort out selected groups of users (as we discussed in Recipe 8.2 with our "Trainers, Coaches, Players" example). Let's add some Trainers to a group:

```
$ awk -F: '($3 >= 1050) && ($3 <=1060)  { print $1}' /etc/passwd | tr '\n' ','
bcool,bkind,frnow,kthxbye,oknodo,
```

Now copy and paste into */etc/group*.

What if you do not have a nice, tidy, organized UID scheme? This is where the GECOS fields come in handy. Go back and pick one for entering some kind of label. The "other" field is best, because users are blocked from changing it. Where is this "other" field? It's inside the "full name," or GECOS, field which contains five comma-delimited fields. It looks like this:

```
bcool:x:1300:1300:Bob Cool,,,,trainer:/home/bkind:/bin/bash
bkind:x:1055:1055:Bev Kind,,,,trainer:/home/bkind:/bin/bash
```

Once you've added the labels, *grep* and *awk* can easily fetch these users for you:

```
$ cat /etc/passwd | grep trainer | awk -F: '{ print $1}' | tr '\n' ','
bkind,bcool,
```

Discussion

Here is the complete */etc/passwd* fields scheme:

```
username:passwd:UID:GID:full name,room number,work phone,home phone,other:directory:shell
```

See Also

- *passwd(5)*, *awk(1)*
- *sed & awk Pocket Reference*, by Arnold Robbins (O'Reilly)

8.20   Using su to Be Root Temporarily

Problem

Like all good Linux users, you understand the importance of using the least necessary privileges to get a job done. You know that root is all-powerful, so you run as root only when absolutely necessary. How do you temporarily switch to root when you need to?

Solution

Use the *su*, or "switch user," command when you need to do system chores:

```
carla@windbag:~$ su
Password:
root@windbag:/home/carla#
```

Then go back to being yourself:

```
root@windbag:/home/carla# exit
exit
carla@windbag:~$
```

To change to root and invoke root's shell and environment settings use:

```
carla@windbag:~$ su -
Password:
root@windbag:~#
```

To change to a different shell use:

```
$ su - --shell=tcsh
Password:
```

Available shells are listed in */etc/shells*.

Discussion

You can change to any user, as long as you have the password.

The dash after *su* makes a world of difference. Without it, you're still in your own system environment, using your environment variables—shell, default editor, paths, and umask.

See Also

- *su(1)*

8.21 Granting Limited Rootly Powers with sudo

Problem

You would like to delegate some system administration chores to other users, or set up an extra layer of safety for your own root chores—but you want to do it in a way that uses only limited rootly powers, and does not give away root's password.

Solution

Use *sudo*. *sudo* grants limited root powers to specific users for specific tasks, logs activity, and does not give away root's password.

Let's say that you have a user, *jhaugh*, upon whom you wish to bestow full rootly powers. Because *sudo* users use their own passwords, root's password is protected. Edit */etc/sudoers* with *visudo*—it will open in your default text editor:

```
# visudo
# sudoers file.
#
# This file MUST be edited with the 'visudo'
# command as root.
# See the man page for details on how to write
# a sudoers file.
#
# Host alias specification

# User alias specification

# Cmnd alias specification

# User privilege specification
root    ALL=(ALL) ALL
```

First, set up a host alias:

```
Host_Alias LOCALHOST= localhost
```

Under the "User privilege specification" line, you can add individual users:

```
jhaugh    ALL=(ALL) ALL
```

This gives *jhaugh* root powers for everything on the system and on all connected machines. Now say you have another user, *tgwynne*, who needs root privileges only on the local machine. Add the following line for this user:

```
tgwynne    LOCALHOST = ALL
```

Adding to your delegation of minions is *msmith*, who is allowed only to shut down the local machine:

```
msmith    LOCALHOST = /sbin/shutdown, /sbin/halt
```

This grants groups of ordinary users shutdown privileges on their own machines:

```
# Host alias specification
Host_Alias LOCALHOST= localhost

# User alias specification
User_Alias    USERS = tgwynne, msmith, jhaugh, \
abyron, jwinters

# Cmnd alias specification
Cmnd_Alias  SHUTDOWN = /usr/sbin/shutdown, /usr/sbin/halt, \
/usr/sbin/reboot, /usr/sbin/poweroff

# User privilege specification
USERS    LOCALHOST = SHUTDOWN
```

To execute a *sudo* command, users do this:

```
$ sudo /usr/sbin/halt
```

They will be prompted for their passwords, then the command will execute. Users can check which commands they are authorized for with the following command:

```
$ sudo -l
User jhaugh may run the following commands on this host:
    (ALL) ALL
```

sudo logs all errors to the syslog, and tattles to root:

```
$ sudo /usr/sbin/halt
carla is not in the sudoers file.  This incident will be reported.
```

Groups of servers can be defined, and users can be given privileges to the groups:

```
# Host alias specification
Host_Alias    FILESERVERS = host1, host2, host3

# User alias specification
User_Alias    FILESERVADMINS = jhaugh, abyron, jwinters
```

```
# Cmnd alias specification
Cmnd_Alias   FILEUTILS = /bin/chgrp, /bin/chmod, \
  /bin/chown, /bin/cp, /bin/dd, /bin/df, \
  /bin/dir, /bin/dircolors, /bin/du, /bin/install, \
  /bin/ln, /bin/ls, /bin/mkdir, /bin/mkfifo, \
  /bin/mknod,bin/mv, /bin/rm, /bin/rmdir, \
  /bin/shred, /bin/touch, /bin/vdir sync

# User privilege specification
FILESERVADMIN    FILESERVERS = FILEUTILS
```

Discussion

sudo can also be used to let users execute scripts, such as backup scripts. Be very careful with scripts, or any command that gives shell access or invokes a text editor, because these may allow users to escalate their privileges. You can try to restrict *sudo* users to RJOE, which is a restricted editor that cannot invoke a shell, but it's better to be careful with how you delegate rootly chores in the first place.

See Also

- *su(1)*, *sudo(8)*, *sudoers(5)*
- Chapter 49 of *Unix Power Tools*
- *sudo* main page (*http://www.courtesan.com/sudo/*)

8.22   Using Disk Quotas

Problem

You want to limit the amount of disk storage any user can consume. Most sites have a few disk hogs around, who just love to fill the disk with their MP3 collections and downloaded sitcoms.

Solution

Use the Linux Disk Quota package. This contains several components, including *quota*, *edquota*, *quotacheck*, and *repquota*.

First, edit */etc/fstab* and select the partitions to enable quotas. Your choices are *usrquota*, for individual users, or *grpquota*, for putting quotas on groups. It's okay to have both:

```
/dev/hda6 /      ext3 defaults                    0  1
/dev/hda7 /home  ext3 defaults,usrquota,grpquota  0  2
```

Now remount the filesystem:

```
# mount -o remount /home
```

Quota's *init* script will run *quotacheck*, which will examine the installation, create a database of disk usage, and create quota files.

Next, assign a quota to a user. This opens a configuration file in your default editor:

```
# edquota -u vhenson
Disk quotas for user vhenson (uid 1550):
 Filesystem  blocks   soft hard   inodes   soft   hard
 /dev/hda7   550466   0    0      47466    0      0
```

Soft limits allow a grace period, with warnings to the user. *Hard limits* cut them off immediately. To set limits, simply edit the file:

```
# edquota -u vhenson
Disk quotas for user vhenson (uid 1550):
 Filesystem  blocks   soft    hard    inodes   soft   hard
 /dev/hda7   550466   650000  700000  47466    0      0
```

Blocks are always 1024 bytes, so 650,000 blocks is about 665 megabytes.

Save and close the file, and verify that the quota is in effect:

```
# quota vhenson
Disk quotas for user vhenson (uid 1550): 650000   700000
```

To assign a quota to a group use:

```
# edquota -g engineers
```

Note that if a single greedy user in a group uses up the group quota, it's too bad for the rest of the group—it's all gone.

This invokes the default editor, for setting the grace period for soft limits on the entire filesystem:

```
# edquota -t
Grace period before enforcing soft limits for users:
Time units may be: days, hours, minutes, or seconds
 Filesystem    Block grace period    Inode grace period
 /dev/hda3     7days                 7days
```

You can use one "prototype" user as the model for new users:

```
# edquota -p vhenson dnorth
```

or for a whole bale of users:

```
# edquota -p vhenson `awk -F: '$3 > 999 {print $1}' /etc/passwd`
```

Or you can list several at once:

```
# edquota -p vhenson dnorth jvesperman sanvin
```

You'll doubtless want to keep an eye on things. This *repquota* command gives a system-wide snapshot of current usage:

```
# repquota -a
```

For a specific filesystem, use:

```
# repquota /home
```

Discussion

Add this line to the *mass_useradd* script, after the *chmod* line, to automatically apply *vhenson*'s quota to all the new users:

```
/usr/sbin/edquota -p vhenson $username
```

The *adduser* command can be configured to apply quotas. Edit *adduser.conf*:

```
QUOTAUSER="vhenson"
```

And now, the bad news. Quota is in a transition phase. The Quota code in the 2.2 and 2.4 kernel trees is obsolete and doesn't work with the current versions of Quota. If your distribution has kindly patched the kernel for you, you're good to go. You probably won't know for sure until you install and configure it and try to set a quota on a user (although it's possible that your distribution's documentation tells the story). If your distribution does not come with a ready-to-go version of Quota, you'll probably have to install a raft of kernel patches. See the "Quota mini-HOWTO" for complete instructions.

SuSE supplies the only reliable ready-to-go Quota-enabled ReiserFS, as of this writing. ReiserFS patches for other distributions are available from the ReiserFS home page at *http://www.numesys.com*.

The good news is that the 2.6 kernel tree fully supports Quota, so we won't have to go through all this fol-de-rol forever.

After passing the kernel hurdle, the next step is to install the latest Quota. It's best to find the RPM for your system (Debian users, use *apt-get install quota*). That way the *init* scripts will be set up and ready to go. If you find handcrafting *init* scripts to be an enjoyable activity, you can download the tarball and have at it. Instructions are in the "Quota mini-HOWTO."

See Also

- *man(1) quota*, *man(8) edquota*, *man(8) quotacheck*, *man(8) repquota*
- The *mass_useradd* script (Recipe 8.17)
- "Quota mini-HOWTO" (*http://www.tldp.org/HOWTO/Quota.html*)
- Quota project home page (*http://sourceforge.net/projects/linuxquota/*)
- ReiserFS home page (*http://www.numesys.com*)

## CHAPTER 9

Managing Files and Partitions

9.1   Introduction

Understanding filesystem fundamentals is key to understanding how Linux works. Everything is a file—data files, partitions, pipes, sockets, and hardware devices. Directories are simply files that list other files.

The Filesystem Hierarchy Standard (FHS) was developed as a voluntary standard. Most Linuxes follow it. These are the required elements of the Linux root filesystem:

/
> Root directory, even though it is always represented at the top

/bin
> Essential system commands

/boot
> Static boot loader files

/dev
> Device files

/etc
> Host-specific system configuration files

/lib
> Shared libraries needed to run the local system

/mnt
> Temporary mount points

/opt
> Add-on software packages (not used much in Linux)

/proc
> Live kernel snapshot and configuration

/sbin
> System administration commands

/tmp
> Temporary files—a well-behaved system flushes them between startups

/usr
> Shareable, read-only data and binaries

/var
> Variably sized files, such as mail spools and logs

These are considered optional because they can be located anywhere on a network, whereas the required directories must be present to run the machine:

/home
> User's personal files

/root
> Superuser's personal files

The FHS goes into great detail on each directory, for those who are interested. Here are some things for the Linux user to keep in mind:

- */tmp* and */var* can go in their own individual partitions, as a security measure. If something goes awry and causes them to fill up uncontrollably, they will be isolated from the rest of the system.

- */home* can go in its own partition, or on its own dedicated server, for easier backups and to protect it from system upgrades. You can then completely wipe out and re-install a Linux system, or even install a different distribution, while leaving */home* untouched.

- Because all configuration files are in */etc* and */home*, backups are simplified. It is possible to get away with backing up only */etc* and */home* and to rely on your installation disks to take care of the rest. However, this means that program updates will not be preserved—be sure to consider this when plotting a disaster-recovery plan.

Linux File Types

Remember that "everything is a file." There are seven file types in Linux; everything that goes in the file tree must be one of the types in Table 9-1.

Table 9-1. File types

Type indicator	Type of file
-	Regular file
d	Directory
l	Link
c	Character device
s	Socket
p	Named pipe
b	Block device

The type indicators show up at the very front of the file listings:

```
# ls -l /dev/initctl
prw-------  1 root   root     0 Jan 12 00:00 /dev/initctl
# ls -l /tmp/.ICE-unix/551
srwx------  1 carla  carla    0 Jan 12 09:09 /tmp/.ICE-unix/551
```

You can specify which file types to look at with the *find* command:

```
# find / -type p
# find / -type s
```

Ctrl-C interrupts *find*, if it goes on for too long.

File Attributes

Take a look at the attributes of a file, such as this shell script, *sortusers*:

```
$ ls -l sortusers
-rwxr-xr-x 1 meredydd  programmers   3783 Jan  7 13:29 sortusers
```

-rwxr-xr-x 1 meredydd programmers tells us a lot of things:

- The - means that this is a regular file. This attribute is not changeable by the user. This is the bit that tells Linux what the file type is, so it does not need file extensions. File extensions are for humans and applications.
- *rwx* are the file owner's permissions.
- The first *r-x* is the group owner's permissions.
- The second *r-x* applies to anyone with access to the file, or "the world."
- *1* is the number of hard links to the file. All files have at least one, the link from the parent directory.
- *meredydd programmers* names the file owner and the group owner of the file. "Owner" and "user" are the same; remember this when using *chmod*'s symbolic notation u = user = owner.

Permissions and ownership are attributes that are configurable, with the *chmod*, *chgrp*, and *chown* commands; *chmod* changes the permissions, *chown* and *chgrp* change ownership.

All those *rwx* things look weird, but they are actually mnemonics: *rwx* = read, write, execute. These permissions are applied in order to user, group, and other.

So, in the *sortusers* example, *meredydd* can read, write, and execute the file. Group members and others may only read and execute. Even though only *meredydd* may edit the file itself, nothing is stopping group and other users from copying it.

Since this is a shell script, both read and execute permissions must be set, because the interpreter needs to read the file. Binary files are read by the kernel directly, without an interpreter, so they don't need read permissions.

File Type Definitions

Let's take a closer look at what the file types in Linux really are:

Regular files
> Plain ole text and data files, or binary executables.

Directories
> Lists of files.

Character and block devices
> Files that could be considered as meeting points between the kernel, and device drivers—for example, */dev/hda* (IDE hard drive), */dev/ttyS1* (serial modem), and so forth. These allow the kernel to correctly route requests for the various hardware devices on your system.

Local domain sockets
> Communications between local processes. They are visible as files but cannot be read from or written to, except by the processes directly involved.

Named pipes
> Also for local interprocess communications. It is highly unlikely that a Linux user will ever need to do anything with either *sockets* or *pipes*; they are strictly system functions. Programmers, however, need to know everything about them.

Links
> Links are of great interest to Linux users. There are two types: *hard links* and *soft links*. Links are pointers to files. A hard link is really just another name for a file, as it points to a specific *inode*. All the hard links that point to a file retain all of the file's attributes—permissions, ownership, and so on. *rm* will happily delete a hard link, but the file will remain on disk until all hard links are gone and all processes have released it. Hard links cannot cross filesystems, so you can't make hard links over a network share. Soft links point to a filename; they can point to any file, anywhere. You can even create "dead" soft links by deleting the files they point to, or changing the names of the files.

Filesystem Internals

Here are some more useful definitions relating to filesystems:

Logical block
> The smallest unit of storage, measured in bytes, that can be allocated by the filesystem. A single file may consume several blocks.

Logical volume
> A disk partition, a disk, or a volume that spans several disks or partitions—any unit of storage that is perceived as a single, discrete allocation of space.

Internal fragmentation

Empty spaces that occur when a file, or a portion of a file, does not a fill a block completely. For example, if the block is 4K, and the file is 1K, 3K are wasted space.

External fragmentation

Fragmentation occurs when the blocks that belong to a single file are not stored contiguously, but are scattered all over the disk.

Extent

A number of contiguous blocks that belong to a single file. The filesystem sees an extent as a single unit, which is more efficient for tracking large files.

B+trees

First there were *btrees* (balanced trees), which were improved and became b+trees. These are nifty concepts borrowed from indexed databases, which make searching and traversing a given data structure much faster. Filesystems that use this concept are able to quickly scan the directory tree, first selecting the appropriate directory, then scanning the contents. The Ext2 filesystem does a sequential scan, which is slower.

Metadata

Everything that describes or controls the internal data structures is lumped under *metadata*. This includes everything except the data itself: date and time stamps, owner, group, permissions, size, links, change time, access time, the location on disk, extended attributes, and so on.

Inode

Much of a file's metadata is contained in an *inode*, or index node. Every file has a unique inode number.

Journaling Filesystems

Our faithful old Ext2 filesystem is showing its age. It can't keep up with users who need terabytes to play with and who need fast recovery from service interruptions. For the majority of users, who still measure their storage needs in gigabytes or less, fast recovery and data integrity are the most important reasons to use a journaling filesystem.

Linux filesystems are *asynchronous*. They do not instantly write metadata to disk, but rather use a write cache in memory and then write to disk periodically, during slack CPU moments. This speeds up overall system performance, but if there is a power failure or system crash, there can be metadata loss. In this event, when the filesystem driver kicks in at restart and *fsck* (filesystem consistency check) runs, it finds inconsistencies. Because Ext2 stores multiple copies of metadata, it is usually able to return the system to health.

The downside to this is recovery time. *fsck* checks each and every bit of metadata. This can take from a few minutes to 30 minutes or more on a large filesystem. Journaling filesystems do not need to perform this minute, painstaking inspection, because they keep a journal of changes. They check only files that have changed, rather than the entire filesystem.

Linux users have a number of great choices for journaling filesystems, including Ext3, ReiserFS, XFS, and JFS. Ext3 is a journaling system added to Ext2. ReiserFS, XFS, and JFS are all capable of handling filesystems that measure in exabytes on 64-bit platforms. *ia32* users are limited to mere terabytes, I'm afraid.

Which one should you use? There's no definitive "best" one; they're all great. Here's a rundown on the high points:

Ext3
> This one is easy and comfortable. That's what it's designed to be. It fits right on top of Ext2, so you don't need to rebuild the system from scratch. All the other filesystems discussed here must be selected at system installation, or when you format a partition. You can even have "buyer's remorse"—you can remove Ext3 just as easily. Because it's an extension of Ext2, it uses the same file utilities package, *e2fsprogs*. One major difference between Ext3 and the others is that it uses a fixed number of inodes, while the others allocate them dynamically. Another difference is that Ext3 can do data journaling, not just metadata journaling. This comes at a cost, though, of slower performance and more disk space consumed. Ext3 runs on any Linux-supported architecture.

ReiserFS
> ReiserFS is especially suited for systems with lots of small files, such as a mail server using the *maildir* format, or a news server. It's very efficient at file storage; it stuffs leftover file bits into *btree* leaf nodes, instead of wasting block space. This is called "tail packing." It scales up nicely, and it handles large files just fine. ReiserFS runs on any Linux-supported architecture.

JFS
> This is IBM's entry in the Way Big Linux Filesystems contest, ported from AIX and OS/2 Warp. It supports multiple processors, access control lists (ACLs), and—get this—native resizing. That's right, simply remount a JFS filesystem with the new size you desire, and it's done. Note that you may only increase the volume size, not decrease it.

XFS
> This is SGI's brainchild, ported from IRIX. XFS thinks big—it claims it can handle filesystems of up to nine exabytes. Its strength is handling very large files, such as giant database files. There is one excellent feature unique to XFS, called *delayed allocation*. It procrastinates. It puts off actually writing to disk, delaying the decision on which blocks to write to, so that it can use the largest possible number of contiguous blocks. When there are a lot of short-term temp files in use, XFS might never allocate blocks to these at all, in effect ignoring them until they go away. XFS has its own native support for quotas, ACLs, and backups and restores.

On a 32-bit system, there's only so much addressing space available, so the theoretical upper filesystem size limit is 16 terabytes (as of the 2.5 kernel). Calculating the maximum possible filesystem size depends on hardware, operating system, and block sizes, so I shall leave that as an exercise to those who really need to figure out those sort of things.

Another way to while away the hours is to compare performance benchmarks, or run your own. About all they agree on is that Ext3 really isn't suited for high-performance, high-demand applications. It's fine for workstations and light-to-medium-duty servers, but the others are better choices for high-demand servers.

When Not to Use a Journaling Filesystem

Stick with plain ole Ext2 when you have a */boot* partition and are running LILO. LILO cannot read any filesytem but Ext2 or Ext3. The */boot* partition is so small, and so easily backed up and restored, that there's no advantage to be gained from journaling in any case. You can put a journaling filesystem on your other partitions; in fact, you can mix and match all you like, as long as your kernel supports them.

On small partitions or small disks, such as 100-MB Zip disks, the journal itself consumes a significant amount of disk space. The ReiserFS journal can take up to 32 MB. Ext3, JFS, and XFS use about 4 MB, but if data journaling is enabled in Ext3, it will eat up a lot more space.

See Also

- JFS (*http://www-124.ibm.com/jfs/*)
- XFS (*http://oss.sgi.com/projects/xfs/*)
- ReiserFS (*http://www.namesys.com*)
- Ext2/3 (*http://e2fsprogs.sourceforge.net/ext2.html*)
- Filesystem Hierarchy Standard (*http://www.pathname.com/fhs/*)

9.2 Setting File and Directory Permissions with chmod's Numeric Notation

Problem

You need to control who can access what file. Either you need to keep prying eyes away from the recipe for the secret sauce, or you have some other secure information that needs protection. Or (more likely) you want to make something executable. In any case, you need to set permissions on files, and you need to understand how to calculate the correct numeric permission values.

Solution

Use the *chmod* (change mode) command. Only root user (superuser) and the file's owner can change permissions.

For example, this command gives the file owner read and write access to */archive/ datafile,* with verbose output. No other user, except root, can access this file at all:

```
$ chmod -v 600 /archive/datafile
mode of `/archive/datafile' changed to 0600 (rw-------)
```

Here the owner of */shared/list* makes it world-readable, but only the file owner and root can make changes to it:

```
$ chmod -v 644 /shared/list
mode of `/shared/list' changed to 0644 (rw-r--r--)
```

Any script must have the *executable bit* set for it to work. This command makes a script editable only by the owner, and readable and executable by everyone:

```
$ chmod 755 /shared/somescript
```

Directories must always have the executable bit set, or they won't work:

```
$ chmod 755 /shared
```

Set permissions for a directory and its contents, including subdirectories, with the *-R* (recursive) flag. *-v* turns on verbosity, so you can see what it is doing:

```
$ chmod -R -v 755 /shared
```

Discussion

Use Table 9-2 to calculate file permissions. Simply add the values you need for each type of user, and list them in the order shown in the table: file owner, group owner, all other users. Special bits are explained in Recipe 9.7.

Table 9-2. Calculating file permissions

Special bits	Permission	Owner	Group	Other
setuid 4	Read	4	4	4
setgid 2	Write	2	2	2
sticky 1	Execute	1	1	1

See Also

- *info chmod*
- *Linux in a Nutshell,* by Ellen Siever, Stephen Figgins, and Aaron Weber (O'Reilly)
- Chapter 4 of *LPI Linux Certification in a Nutshell,* by Jeff Dean (O'Reilly), for exhaustive detail on permissions and ownership, right down to the binary level

9.3   Doing Batch Operations with chmod

Problem

You need to set permissions on all the files or a directory, or on batches of files.

Solution

chmod supports operating on lists of files. You can also use *find* or shell wildcards to generate a list.

To make several files read-only for everyone, you can use *chmod* as follows:

```
$ chmod 444 file.txt file2.txt file3.txt
```

To make all files in the current directory readable/writable, for the file owner and group, without changing the directory permissions, use:

```
$ find . -type f  -exec chmod -v 660 {} \;
```

You can also change all files belonging to a particular user. This example starts at the root of the filesystem:

```
$ find / -user terri -exec chmod -v 660 {} \;
```

You can set permissions for a directory and its contents, including subdirectories, with the *-R* (recursive) flag:

```
$ chmod -R -v 755 /shared
```

This example makes all the *.txt* files in the current directory readable/writable to the owner, and world-readable:

```
$ chmod -v 644 *.txt
```

To change all files in the current directory that begin with your chosen string, use:

```
$ chmod -v 644 apt*
```

See Also

- *info chmod*
- *Linux in a Nutshell*
- Chapter 4 of *LPI Linux Certification in a Nutshell* for exhaustive detail on permissions and ownership, right down to the binary level

9.4   Setting File and Directory Permissions with chmod's Symbolic Notation

Problem

You would like to change specific permission bits, rather than using the all-or-nothing approach of *chmod*'s numeric notation, such as marking a script as executable.

Solution

The most common use for symbolic notation is to add the executable bit to a file's permissions without changing any other permissions:

```
$ chmod +x scriptname
```

The default action is *a*, or *all*, so the example makes *scriptname* executable by everyone. This adds the executable bit to the file owner only:

```
$ chmod u+x scriptname
```

You can surgically remove a specific mode bit. In this example, the group and other users lose their executable bits:

```
$ chmod go-x scriptname
```

This is a quick way to set the *setgid* bit on a directory, for creating a shared directory. All files created in this directory will have the same group ownership as the directory:

```
$ chmod +s /shared-directory
```

You can remove all permissions for group and other users by doing the following:

```
$ chmod go= scriptname
```

To make group permissions the same as the file owner's, use:

```
$ chmod g=u scriptname
```

Discussion

Using *chmod*'s symbolic notation can get quite elaborate. This examples erases all existing permissions and starts over:

```
$ chmod -v a=,u=rwx,g=rx,o=r scriptname
```

You can do the same thing with *chmod 754*. Here's the key:

Symbolic notation is also called mnemonic notation:

r   Read

w   Write

x   Execute

X   File must already have execute permissions, or be a directory

s   Set user or group ID on execution—dangerous! do not use on executables, unless you really really know what you are doing!

t   Sticky bit

u   User, or file owner

g   Group file owner

o   Everyone else; others

+   Adds the new values to the existing values

=   Overwrites

-     Subtracts from existing values

See Also

- *info chmod*
- Recipe 9.7, "Setting Up a Shared Directory with setgid and the Sticky Bit," for an explanation of sticky bits
- Chapter 4 of *LPI Linux Certification in a Nutshell*, for exhaustive detail on permissions and ownership, right down to the binary level

9.5   Setting File Ownership with chown

Problem

You need to change ownership on a file or directory. Perhaps you've copied something to someone else's directory but she still can't edit it, because it's owned by you. Many Linux problems result from incorrect ownership or permission. You're seeing messages like "Permission denied" or "File is read-only" when it shouldn't be.

Solution

Use *chown* (change owner) to change the file owner, the file and group owner, or the group owner:

```
# chown user filename
# chown user:group filename
# chown :group filename
```

For example:

```
$ chown -v carlas:share index.txt
changed ownership of `index.txt' to carlas:share
$ chown -v :share toc.txt
changed ownership of `toc.txt' to :share
```

Discussion

Ordinary users can only make changes to files that they own, and they cannot transfer file ownership to another user. However, ordinary users can change group file ownership, provided that they belong to both the original group and the final group.

See Also

- *info chown*

9.6   Doing Batch Operations with chown

Problem

You want to change ownership of directories and their contents, or just the contents of directories, a list of files, or change ownership of files from one UID to another.

Solution

chown supports some batch operations, or you can use *find*, or you can use shell wildcards.

To change several files at once with *chown*, use a space-delimited list:

```
# chown carlas file.txt file2.txt file3.txt
```

Alternatively, you can use shell wildcards:

```
# chown carlas *.txt
```

To give all of a user's files to another user, use:

```
# chown -R -v --from valh  piglet  /shared/scripts
```

You can do the same thing with *find*:

```
# find / -user valh -exec chown -v piglet {} \;
```

find can also search by UID, which *chown* cannot:

```
# find / -uid 1050 -exec chown -v 1200 {} \;
```

To change the ownership of a directory, including subdirectories and files, with verbose output, use:

```
# chown -R -v  piglet  /shared/scripts
changed ownership of `scripts' to piglet
changed ownership of `scripts/backups.tgz' to piglet
changed ownership of `scripts/fake-spec-rpm' to piglet
```

Either the user's login name or UID can be used. If you've deleted a user and the user has left behind orphan files, you'll need the UID.

See Also

- *info chown*
- Recipe 8.6, "Modifying User Accounts," for how to hunt down and change all files on the system belonging to a particular user

9.7   Setting Up a Shared Directory with setgid and the Sticky Bit

Problem

Your users need a directory for sharing files, and you want all the shared files to belong to the same group.

Solution

Use the *setgid* bit to automatically set the shared group ownership on files.

This is how to set it with octal notation:

```
# chmod -v 2775 /shared-directory
```

You can also use symbolic notation:

```
# chmod -v +s /shared-directory
```

Keep in mind that *+s* sets both the *setgid* and *setuid* bits, which could be a security problem if executables or scripts are stored in this directory. *chmod 2775* sets only the *setgid* bit.

 setuid is a big fat security hole. Do not use it on executables. Programs that use it, such as */usr/bin/passwd*, have safeguards built in to prevent privilege escalation and other mischief. If there are scripts that you want users to run, create a group for that purpose.

Add the sticky bit to prevent anyone but the file owner from deleting the file, by using:

```
# chmod +t /shared-directory
```

or:

```
# chmod 3775 /shared-directory
```

Discussion

Any files created in the directory will have the same group owner as the directory. Any files copied into the directory will retain their original group ownership. Users must belong to a common group to access the directory. Files created in the directory will have permissions as determined by the *umask*s of the file owners.

A classic example of a directory making canny use of the sticky bit is */tmp*:

```
$ stat /tmp
...
Access: (1777/drwxrwxrwt) Uid: ( 0/ root) Gid: ( 0/    root)
```

/tmp needs to be world-readable and writable, but we do not want users or processes deleting temp files that do not belong to them. So the sticky bit takes care of that.

The *setuid* bit lets users run a command with the same permissions as the file owner. This is how ordinary users are able to change their own passwords, even though */etc/ passwd* can only be written to by root:

```
$ stat /usr/bin/passwd
  File: `/usr/bin/passwd'
  Size: 26584    Blocks: 56   IO Block: 4096   regular file
...
Access: (4755/-rwsr-xr-x) Uid: ( 0/ root) Gid: ( 0/  root)
```

Discussion

Sticky bits have one other use. A long time ago, setting the sticky bit on an executable kept it in memory after execution had finished. In the olde Unix days of less sophisticated memory management and feebler hardware, this made programs start faster. These days, don't bother—it won't do a thing.

See Also

- *info chmod*
- The mode tables in Recipes 9.2 ("Setting File and Directory Permissions with chmod's Numeric Notation") and 9.4 ("Setting File and Directory Permissions with chmod's Symbolic Notation")

9.8   Setting Permissions Defaults with umask

Problem

You want to understand why files are created with a certain set of default permissions, and how to configure them yourself.

Solution

The *umask* (user file-creation mode mask) controls this behavior. To see what yours is, use:

```
$ umask
0022
```

or:

```
$ umask -S
u=rwx,g=rx,o=rx
```

To change it temporarily, for the duration of your login session, use:

```
$ umask 0002
```

You can set the umask permanently by inserting the line *umask 0022* or whatever value you want in your *~/.bashrc* file. Table 9-3 shows common umask values.

Table 9-3. Common umask values

umask	User	Group	Other
0002	All	All	Read and Execute
0022	All	Read and Execute	Read and Execute
0007	All	All	None
0077	All	None	None

Discussion

Table 9-4 shows that you can come up with a *umask* for any occasion.

Table 9-4. All umask values

umask	File permissions	Directory permissions
7	None	None
6	None	Execute
5	Write	Write
4	Write	Write and execute
3	Read	Read
2	Read	Read and execute
1	Read and write	Read and write
0	Read and Write	Read-write-execute

*umask*s "subtract" permissions—though I warn you, do not say this to a programmer, because you will be subjected to a tedious lecture on how it's not subtraction, it's that "the umask is bitwise and-ed to whatever modes are specified when the file is created." However, I do not have a problem with calling it subtraction.

When a program, such as a text editor or a compiler, creates a file, it is hardcoded to set the file permissions at either 0666 or 0777. If it knows the file it is creating is executable, it sets the permissions to 0777. The most common value is 0666, which is why you have to *chmod +x* scripts. Neither 0666 nor 0777 are appropriate permissions most of the time, so *umask* screens out the bits you don't want. For example, a *umask* of 0002 means regular files will become 0664, and executable files will become 0775.

See Also

- Chapter 4 of *LPI Linux Certification in a Nutshell*, for exhaustive detail on *umask*, right down to the binary level

9.9 Mounting and Unmounting Removable Disks

Problem

You need to know how to insert and remove removable disks, such as floppies, CDs, or USB storage devices.

Solution

Use the *mount* and *umount* commands.

This example mounts a CD drive:

```
# mount -r -t iso9660 /dev/scd0 /cdrom
```

-r means read-only; *-t iso9660* is the filesystem type. */dev/scd0* is the name the kernel assigns to the device. */cdrom* is the directory in which it is mounted. The */cdrom* directory must already be present before you try to mount the disk.

To find the filesystem type, use the *file* command:

```
$ file - < /dev/scd0
/dev/stdin: ISO 9660 CD-ROM filesystem data 'Data1
```

You can omit the *-r* (read-only) flag when mounting a CD-ROM. It will complain, but it'll mount the disk anyway:

```
# mount -t iso9660 /dev/scd0 /cdrom
mount: block device /dev/scd0 is write-protected, mounting read-only
```

This mounts a floppy disk readable/writable:

```
# mount -w /dev/fd0 /floppy
```

The following command mounts a USB storage device. The *noatime* option should be used on rewritable media that have a limited number of rewrites, such as CD/DVD-RW and flash storage devices:

```
# mount -w -o noatime /dev/sda1 /memstick
```

To unmount the device, use:

```
# umount /memstick
```

You may get a response like:

```
# umount /memstick
umount: /memstick: device is busy
```

This means something (an application, a shell, or a file manager) is reading the filesystem. You can find out what with *lsof* (list open files):

```
$ lsof /memstick
COMMAND PID   USER    FD   TYPE DEVICE SIZE NODE NAME
gs      938 dawnm  128r   DIR  2,0  1024   12 /memstick/may-04.pdf
bash    938 dawnm  129r   DIR  2,0  1024   24 /memstick
```

Now you can either close out the applications, or kill the lot with a single command:

```
# kill -9 `lsof -t /memstick`
```

mount can only be run by root. To give non-root users permission to mount removeable disks, you'll need to edit */etc/fstab* (see the next recipe).

Discussion

The *umount* "device is busy" error most commonly comes from having a terminal window open with the mounted device as a current working directory, like this:

```
carla@windbag:/floppy$
```

It is important to unmount a disk before removing it. This gives the system a chance to complete any writes and to cleanly unmount the filesystem.

On newer Linux systems, you can get away without specifying the filesystem type, because *mount* autodetects the filesystem types.

See Also

- *mount(8)*
- Recipe 9.10, "Configuring Filesystem Mounts with /etc/fstab"

9.10 Configuring Filesystem Mounts with /etc/fstab

Problem

Users need to make their own backups on CDs, and use USB memory sticks and other types of removeable media. You don't want to give them root privileges just so they can mount these devices. But only root can use the *mount* command we discussed in Recipe 9.9. And you also want to control which filesystems are automatically mounted at boot.

Solution

Add entries to */etc/fstab*, defining mountpoints and access permissions.

This example shows a Linux partition, two Windows partitions, and removeable media:

```
#<device>   <mountpoint>  <type>     <options>                     <dump> <pass>
/dev/hda6   /rh-data      reiserfs   defaults,user,noauto          0      1
/dev/hda1   /win2k        ntfs       defaults,user,ro,gid=win2k    0      0
/dev/hda2   /win98        vfat       defaults,user,gid=win98       0      0
/dev/hdc0   /cdrom        auto       defaults,user,noauto,ro       0      0
/dev/fd0    /floppy       auto       defaults,user,noauto          0      0
/dev/sda1   /memstick     auto       defaults,user,noauto          0      0
```

Once a device has an entry in *etc/fstab*, it can be mounted by using the mountpoint:

```
$ mount /cdrom
$ mount /memstick
```

And unmounted the same way:

```
$ umount /cdrom
```

Discussion

These are the six fields that make up *etc/fstab*:

device
> The device name assigned by the kernel.

mountpoint
> The directory to which the filesystem is attached, which is user-defined.

type
> The filesystem type. It's okay to use "auto" in this field for most filesystems. See *mount(8)* for the supported filesystem types.

options
> Command options in a comma-delimited list. See *mount(8)* for a complete list

dump
> If you're using the *dump* command for backups, this tells *dump* the backup interval, in days. 1 means every day, 2 means every other day, and so on.

pass
> This tells *fsck* which filesystem to check first at boot up, if it ever needs to. Make your root filesystem 1, any other Linux filesystems 2, and non-Linux filesystems 0.

Let's take a closer look at what goes in the *options* field. All these values belong to the *defaults* option:

rw
> Read/write.

suid
> Allow *setuid* and *setgid* bits to operate.

dev
> Interpret block and character devices.

exec
> Allow execution of binaries.

auto
> This is used in boot scripts (Debian uses *etc/init.d/mountall.sh*; Red Hat uses *etc/rc.d/rc.sysinit*), indicating which filesystems are to be started at boot up.

nouser

Non-root users cannot mount or unmount the filesystem.

async

Asynchronous I/O, which is standard for Linux.

The *defaults* values are overridden by appending additional options, as on the win2k line in the */etc/fstab* example above (*defaults,user,ro,gid=win2k*). The options are:

user

Non-root users can mount and unmount the device, provided they were the ones who mounted it.

users

Any user can unmount the device.

noauto

The device must be explicitly mounted by a user and does not automatically mount at boot.

ro

The device is read-only. Be sure to use this for NTFS volumes.

noatime

Do not update the "time accessed" file attribute. This speeds up filesystem performance. It also extends the life of CD-RWs and DVD-RWs that use packet-writing, and of USB storage media, by reducing the number of writes.

gid=win2k

Assign group membership, if you are controlling access with groups.

Mounting filesystems, not devices

We tend to think of mounting devices and partitions, but strictly speaking, only filesystems are mounted. "Mount" and "attach" mean the same thing, if you want a different word to use. Some Linux distributions, such as Red Hat, use the */mnt* directory. Debian uses top-level directories, such as */floppy* or */cdrom*. There's no hard-and-fast rule; put them wherever it suits you. Just be careful not to mount two filesystems in the same directory. If you do, the existing files will disappear until the intruder filesystem is unmounted.

Usually it's not necessary to specify the filesystem type, because *mount* will figure it out. First, it will probe the superblock. Currently *adfs, bfs, cramfs, ext, ext2, ext3, hfs, hpfs, iso9660, jfs, minix, ntfs, qnx4, reiserfs, romfs, udf, ufs, vxfs, xfs*, and *xiafs* are supported. If that fails, it will try each filesystem listed in */proc/filesystems*, which shows all the filesystems supported by your kernel.

See Also

- *mount(8), fstab(5)*

9.11 Mounting and Unmounting Filesystems on Hard Drives

Problem

You have a multiboot system with several different Linux versions, or Linux and Windows, and you want to access the filesystems from whatever Linux you've booted into—or maybe you've created some new partitions, and you don't know how to access them.

Solution

Use *fdisk* to find all the partitions on local drives, *mount* to access them, and */etc/fstab* to automate mounting. First, identify all the local partitions:

```
# /sbin/fdisk -l
Disk /dev/hda: 20.5 GB, 20576747520 bytes
255 heads, 63 sectors/track, 2501 cylinders
Units = cylinders of 16065 * 512 = 8225280 bytes

   Device Boot  Start    End    Blocks  Id  System
/dev/hda1   *      1     893  7172991    7  HPFS/NTFS
/dev/hda2        894    1033  1124550    c  W95 FAT32 (LBA)
/dev/hda3       1034    2501 11791710    f  W95 Ext'd (LBA)
/dev/hda5       2437    2501   522081   82  Linux swap
/dev/hda6       1034    1670  5116639+  83  Linux
/dev/hda7       1671    2436  6152863+  83  Linux

Disk /dev/hdc: 255 heads, 63 sectors, 4865 cylinders
 Units = cylinders of 16065 * 512 bytes
   Device Boot  Start    End    Blocks  Id  System
/dev/hdc1   *      1       5    40131   83  Linux
/dev/hdc2          6    4865 39037950    5  Extended
/dev/hdc5          6      69   514048+  83  Linux
/dev/hdc6         70    2680 20972826   83  Linux

Partition table entries are not in disk order
```

How do you know which ones are already mounted, and what their mountpoints are? Use *df* (disk free) to show which partitions are mounted, and their mountpoints:

```
$ df
Filesystem   1K-blocks    Used  Available Use% Mounted on
/dev/hda6     5116472  1494584    3621888  30% /
/dev/hda7     6152668  4011652    2141016  66% /home
```

You can use *df* to show information on a single mounted partition. Use the *-h* flag to make "human-readable" numbers:

```
$ df -h /dev/hdc6
Filesystem    Size  Used  Avail  Use%  Mounted on
/dev/hdc6     4.9G  1.4G   3.5G   29%  /home
```

To mount */dev/hda1*, the Windows NTFS partition, follow these steps:

```
# mkdir -m  755 /win2k
# mount -t ntfs -r /dev/hda1 /win2k
```

 Write access for NTFS is still experimental. Don't enable write access unless you wish to risk your NTFS data. That's why we used the *-r* option in the *mount* command. If you need to share NTFS files, use Samba.

To unmount, use:

```
# umount /win2k
```

Discussion

Remember to adjust mount directory permissions to suit your own needs. If you're running a multiboot system, you can access all installed filesystems with the *mount* command.

See Also

- *mount(8)*
- The NTFS FAQ (*http://linux-ntfs.sourceforge.net/info/ntfs.html*)

9.12 Finding Device Names for mount and fstab

Problem

You want to mount a storage disk, such as an IDE or SCSI hard drive, CD, DVD, USB storage device, or Zip disk. You don't know what device name to use—where do you look?

Solution

Use *dmesg* and *fdisk*. *dmesg* finds device names, and *fdisk* shows the partition numbers on hard drives. Referring to *http://www.lanana.org/docs/device-list/devices.txt* can be helpful as well, as it is the list of official */dev* names. (If you have kernel sources installed, the *devices.txt* file may be present on your system in the */usr/src/** directory.)

This command searches *dmesg* for CD drives:

```
$ dmesg | grep -i cd
hdc: ATAPI CDROM, ATAPI CD/DVD-ROM DRIVE
hdc: ATAPI 40X CD-ROM DRIVE, 128K cache, UDMA (33)
```

A quick search in *devices.txt* reveals

```
Second IDE hard disk/CD-ROM interface
0 = /dev/hdc          Master: whole disk (or CD-ROM)
```

Ignore the *0 =* part; your device name is */dev/hdc*.

This is what CD drives using the IDE-SCSI subsystem look like:

```
$ dmesg | grep -i cd
hdb: TOSHIBA DVD-ROM SD-M1202, ATAPI CD/DVD-ROM drive
hdc: LITE-ON LTR-24102B, ATAPI CD/DVD-ROM drive
ide-cd: ignoring drive hdb
ide-cd: ignoring drive hdc
  Type:   CD-ROM              ANSI SCSI revision: 02
  Type:   CD-ROM              ANSI SCSI revision: 02
Attached scsi CD-ROM sr0 at scsi0, channel 0, id 0, lun 0
Attached scsi CD-ROM sr1 at scsi0, channel 0, id 1, lun 0
scd0: scsi3-mmc drive: 32x/32x cd/rw xa/form2 cdda tray
Uniform CD-ROM driver Revision: 3.12
scd1: scsi3-mmc drive: 131x/40x writer cd/rw xa/form2 cdda tray
```

So the drive names are */dev/scd0* and */dev/scd1*.

With hard drives, you must select specific partitions, since each partition is a separate block device. *fdisk -l* displays all partitions on all detected hard drives:

```
# /sbin/fdisk -l
Disk /dev/hda: 20.5 GB, 20576747520 bytes
255 heads, 63 sectors/track, 2501 cylinders
Units = cylinders of 16065 * 512 = 8225280 bytes

   Device   Boot  Start    End    Blocks   Id  System
/dev/hda1    *      1      893    7172991   7   HPFS/NTFS
/dev/hda2          894    1033    1124550   c   W95 FAT32 (LBA)
/dev/hda4         1034    2501   11791710   f   W95 Ext'd (LBA)
/dev/hda5         2437    2501     522081  82   Linux swap
/dev/hda6         1034    1670   5116639+  83   Linux
/dev/hda7         1671    2436   6152863+  83   Linux

Partition table entries are not in disk order
```

Copy the device name from the *Device* column exactly as it is shown.

This is what a USB pen drive looks like in *dmesg*:

```
hub.c: new USB device 00:1d.0-2.3, assigned address 5
usb.c: USB device 5 (vend/prod 0x1915/0x2220) is not claimed ...
SCSI device sda: 128000 512-byte hdwr sectors (66 MB)
sda: Write Protect is off
sda: sda1
```

Your device name is */dev/sda1*.

This how *fdisk* sees USB drives:

```
# fdisk -l
Disk /dev/sda: 65 MB, 65536000 bytes
8 heads, 32 sectors/track, 500 cylinders
Units = cylinders of 256 * 512 = 131072 bytes

   Device   Boot  Start    End    Blocks   Id  System
/dev/sda1    *      1      499     63856    6   FAT16
```

Discussion

All storage devices are block devices in *dev*. *dev* names them according to their physical connections. For example:

/dev/hda
> Primary device on IDE0 (whole disk)

/dev/hdb
> Secondary device on IDE0 (whole disk)

/dev/fd0
> Floppy drive on controller 0, drive 0

/dev/fd1
> Floppy drive on controller 0, drive 1

/dev/sda
> First SCSI disk (whole disk)

/dev/sdb
> Second SCSI disk (whole disk)

Storage devices on Linux follow this naming convention:

/dev/fd*
> Floppy disks

/dev/hd*
> IDE drives

/dev/sd*
> SCSI drives

/dev/sd*
> USB storage devices

/dev/hd*
> IDE/Atapi CD/DVD-ROM drives

/dev/sd*
> IDE/Atapi CD/DVD-R/RW drives

/dev/sd*, */dev/hd**, or */dev/XXXx4*
> Zip drives

IDE and USB devices that use the SCSI emulation subsystem are sometimes named */dev/sr**, which is symlinked to */dev/sd**.

If you have kernel sources installed, look for the *devices.txt* file to see the definitions of all those */dev* names.

See Also

- Chapter 5, *Discovering Hardware from Outside the Box*
- Official list of */dev* names (*http://www.lanana.org/docs/device-list/devices.txt*), or the *devices.txt* file in your system's */usr/src/** directory

---

9.13   Creating Files and Directories

Problem

You want to organize your files by placing them in directories. But where do directories come from? For that matter, how do you create a file?

Solution

Use *mkdir* and *touch*.

mkdir creates directories. Mind your filepaths! This comand creates a new subdirectory in the current directory:

```
$ mkdir photos
```

This creates a new top-level directory. Only the superuser can do this:

```
# mkdir /local_bins
```

You can set permissions when you create a directory:

```
# mkdir -m 755 /shared
```

To create a subdirectory and all of its parent directories at once, use the *-p* flag:

```
$ mkdir -p photos/scanned/jpgs/thumbs
```

Most files are created by a program, such as a word processor, image editor, or compiler. You can also create a new, empty file with *touch*:

```
$ touch newfile.txt
```

Discussion

touch is useful in scripting, when you need the script to create a new file. It's also useful for creating placeholders, or for populating a directory for testing things.

See Also

- *mkdir(1), touch(1)*

9.14   Deleting Files and Directories

Problem

You have files and directories all over the place. How do you get rid of the ones you don't want?

Solution

Use *rm* (remove)—with caution! *rm* will happily delete everything, with no warning.

To delete a single file, with verbose output, use:

```
$ rm -v games-stats.txt
removed 'game-stats.txt'
```

To prompt for confirmation first, use:

```
$ rm -vi dpkglist
rm: remove regular file `dpkglist'? y
removed `dpkglist'
```

Use the *-r* (recursive) flag to delete a directory, with all files and subdirectories:

```
$ rm -rvi /home/games/stats/baseball
```

That deletes the */baseball* directory, and everything in it. To delete */games* and every-thing in it, use:

```
$ rm -rvi /home/games
```

You can use shell wildcards to delete groups of files, as in:

```
$ rm -v *.txt
removed `file4.txt'
removed `file5.txt'
removed `file6.txt'
removed `file7.txt'
```

Or:

```
$ rm -v file*
```

 Use the *-f* (force) flag to make it work, no matter what. This is very dangerous! It will not prompt you, it will simply delete everything in its path:

```
$ rm -rf /home/games
```

Be very careful when you're using the *-rf* flags. *rm* will happily erase your entire drive.

Discussion

rm -rf / will erase your entire root filesystem. Some folks think it is a funny prank to tell newbies to do this.

Even though the common usage is "*rm* deletes files," it does not actually delete them, but rather unlinks them from their inodes. A file is not truly deleted until all hard links pointing to it are removed, and it is overwritten. Ordinary users can *rm* any files in any directories to which they have access, but they can *rm* only directories that they own.

touch is actually for changing the timestamps on files. Using it to create new empty files is an unintended bonus.

There's also a *rmdir* command for deleting directories. *rmdir* won't delete a directory that has something in it. This may make you feel safer, but over time, it will become annoying; lots of programs create files that don't show up in a normal listing (filenames starting with a . are ignored unless you use *ls -a*). So you'll try to use *rmdir* and it will tell you that there are still files in the directory. Eventually, you'll just use *rm -r*.

See Also

- *touch(1)*, *rm(1)*

9.15 Copying, Moving, and Renaming Files and Directories

Problem

You've got directories, you've got files. How do you get the files into the directories? How do you change a file's name? And how do you make a copy?

Solution

Use the *cp* and *mv* commands.

This command copies two files from the current working directory into the *~/images2* directory:

```
$ cp -v navbar.gif redheart.gif  ~/images2
`navbar.gif ' -> `/home/terri/images2/navbar.gif'
`redheart.gif ' -> `/home/terri/images2/redheart.gif'
```

If you're overwriting files, you might want to use the *-b* flag to create backups of the old files in the destination directory:

```
$ cp -bv icon-zip.gif  main.gif ~/data2
`icon-zip.gif' -> `/home/terri/data2/icon-zip.gif' (backup: `/home/terri/data2/icon-zip.gif~')
`main.gif' -> `/home/terri/data2/main.gif' (backup: `/home/terri/data2/main.gif~')
```

What if you need to preserve the full filepath? Use the *--parents* flag:

```
$ cp -v --parents  ~/homes/images/kitchen.jpg ~/data2
'/home/terri/homes/images/kitchen.jpg' ->
'/home/terri/data2/homes/images/kitchen.jpg'
```

Use the *-s* flag to create soft links to files, instead of copying the files:

```
$ cp -s navbar.gif  redheart.gif  ~/images2
```

Copy a directory and all of its contents with the *-r* flag:

```
$ cp -rv ~/homes/images/  /shared/archives
```

Moving and renaming files are done with the *mv* command. To move two files to another directory, use:

```
$ mv -v about.gif  arrow.gif  ~/data2
`about.gif' -> `/home/terri/data2/about.gif'
`arrow.gif' -> `/home/terri/data2/arrow.gif'
```

To rename a file, use:

```
$ mv -v downloads.gif email.gif
`downloads.gif' -> `email.gif'
```

Discussion

A graphical file manager, such as Nautilus, Konqueror, Midnight Commander, Gentoo file manager, *gmc*, or Rox Filer, often makes chores like these go faster and easier.

See Also

- *mv(1), cp(1)*
- *Linux in a Nutshell*

9.16   Creating Linux Disk Partitions with fdisk

Problem

You need to partition a new hard drive, or partition free space on an existing hard drive.

Solution

One way is to boot up a Knoppix disk and use QTParted, a great graphical application that creates, deletes, moves, and resizes partitions, without destroying the data. It even resizes NTFS partitions.

You can also use *fdisk*. This example shows how to create a primary partition:

```
# fdisk /dev/hda
The number of cylinders for this disk is set to 2501.
There is nothing wrong with that, but this is larger than 1024,
and could in certain setups cause problems with:
1) software that runs at boot time (e.g., old versions of LILO)
2) booting and partitioning software from other OSs
   (e.g., DOS FDISK, OS/2 FDISK)
Command (m for help): n
Command action
   l   logical (5 or over)
   p   primary partition (1-4)
p
Partition number (1-4): 3
First cylinder (511-1232, default 511): 511
Last cylinder or +size or+sizeM or +sizeK (511-1232, default1232): +3000M
Command (m for help): w
The partition table has been altered!

Calling ioctl( ) to re-read the partition table
Syncing disks
#
```

That's it. You can change your mind right up to the end, until you hit *w* to write the new partition table to disk. At any time, you can hit *m* to see a menu of commands. *q* always quits.

Before you can put any data on the new partition, you'll need to reboot, then put a filesystem on it (see the next recipe).

Discussion

Use Linux's *fdisk* only to create Linux volumes. For Windows volumes, use MS-DOS's *fdisk*.

Here is a list of the more commonly used Linux *fdisk* options:

m Display help.

p Show the current partition table.

d Delete a partition.

n Create a new partition.

w Write the partition table to disk.

l Display the list of filesystem types.

q Quit *fdisk* without changing anything.

See Also

- *fdisk(8)*

9.17   Creating a Filesystem on a New Partition

Problem

You have a brand-new disk partition all ready to go to work. But you can't use it yet. A partition by itself is just a chunk of disk. How do you put a filesystem on it?

Solution

Use the commands specific to the filesystem you want to use.

Ext2
```
# mke2fs   /dev/hda3
```
Ext3
```
# mke2fs -j /dev/hda3
```
ReiserFS
```
# mkreiserfs /dev/hda3
```

JFS

```
# mkfs.jfs   /dev/hda3
```

XFS

```
# mkfs.xfs   /dev/hda3
```

Discussion

mke2fs is for creating Ext2/3 filesystems. It is part of the *e2fsprogs* package, available from *http://e2fprogs.sourceforge.net*.

mkreiserfs comes with ReiserFS, as part of *reiserfsprogs*. Get it from *http://www.namesys.com*.

mkfs.jfs is part of *jfsutils*, from *http://www-124.ibm.com/jfs/*.

mkfs.xfs is part of *xfsprogs*, which can be downloaded from *http://oss.sgi.com/project/xfs*.

See Also

- This chapter's "Introduction," for more information on the four filesystems in this recipe
- JFS (*http://www-124.ibm.com/jfs/*)
- XFS (*http://oss.sgi.com/projects/xfs/*)
- ReiserFS (*http://www.namesys.com/*)
- Ext2/3 (*http://e2fsprogs.sourceforge.net/ext2.html*)

## CHAPTER 10

Patching, Customizing, and Upgrading Kernels

10.1 Introduction

Patching, customizing, and upgrading the Linux kernel are useful tasks to master, and they're really not all that scary. These are among the few system maintenence chores that require a reboot, which can be dismaying for those who glory in sustaining long uptimes. Other than that, it's no worse than patching or upgrading any other software.

You'll need kernel sources, and *gcc*, the GNU C compiler. There are two places to get kernel sources: from your own distribution, or from *http://kernel.org*. The different Linux distributions modify kernels to varying degrees. Red Hat, SuSE, and Mandrake ship heavily modified kernels. Debian and Slackware mess with them only a little bit. It's possible that installing a vanilla kernel from *http://kernel.org* will cause things to break on distributions that use modified kernels, so it's better to use kernel sources for your distribution. (See Chapters 2 and 3 for more information on obtaining and installing Linux software, and Recipe 4.2 to learn about build tools.)

As with most Linux software, when you patch a kernel, you're not patching your existing kernel; rather, you're patching the sources and building a new binary, so you'll end up with two kernels. This is a good thing, because then you'll have your original kernel to use in the event the new one doesn't boot. You can install as many different kernels as you like, and test the latest releases and different configurations.

When should you modify a kernel?

- To optimize it for your hardware
- To get new functionality
- To remove unneeded functions
- To test new features
- To upgrade

Configuring the New Kernel

Configuration is the most time-consuming part of building a new kernel. It's also the most important. This step is where you decide what hardware, filesystems, power-management features, and other features are going to be supported. There are over a hundred different items to choose from, and there are potentially three decisions to make for each feature: should it be enabled, and if so, as a loadable module or statically compiled into the kernel? As a general rule, if it can be made into a module, do it. This conserves memory, as memory is not allocated for modules until they are actually in use. Also, it's easier to update or add modules than it is to rebuild the whole kernel.

The kernel configurator contains help entries for almost every item. It tells you if a feature can be built as a module, or if it must be built into the base kernel. The help entries describe what each feature is for and advise you what to do with it if you're not sure it should be enabled. If there is no help entry and you don't know what to do, it's safe to enable it. At worst, you'll have a fatter kernel with features you don't use.

The kernel configuration program won't let you make something into a module if it needs to be part of the base kernel, with one important exception: the driver for the disk drive that contains the root filesystem. This must be built into the base kernel, so that the system can boot. Otherwise, you're in a chicken-and-egg situation: drivers are needed to load the root filesystem, but the filesystem cannot be loaded because the drivers are on the filesystem. If you don't build the drivers into the kernel, you'll need to create an *initrd* image. *initrd* creates an initial *ramdisk* that loads the disk drivers, so that the system can boot.

A common misconception is that using loadable modules is slower than building everything into a monolithic kernel. Either way, it simply involves calls to memory locations, so there is no speed difference at all.

Use *menuconfig* for configuring 2.4 kernels, and use either *menuconfig* or *xconfig* for 2.6 kernels. *menuconfig* is ncurses-based, so you don't need X. If you don't have ncurses, your options are to install it or to use *config*, which is a seriously dreadful choice. *config* is the original kernel configurator. It takes forever, and if you make a single mistake you have to start over.

xconfig was completely redesigned for the 2.6 kernel. It's efficient and extremely helpful, containing good help files for every option. You'll need Qt, *qt-devel*, gtt, and X to run it. Figure 10-1 shows you the xconfig user interface in all its glory. As you can tell, there are lots of optional features you can configure.

The kernel build tree contains reams of documentation. Look in *linux-$VERSION/Documentation/*. Also, see *linux-$VERSION/README* for important installation tips, and read *linux-$VERSION/Documentation/Changes* for important information on what versions of *gcc* and other utilities.

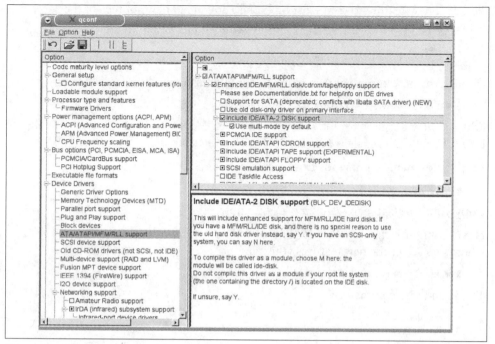

Figure 10-1. xconfig user interface

10.2   Adding New Features to the 2.4 Kernel

Problem

You want to add some new feature to your existing 2.4 kernel, such as support for new hardware, new filesystems, or additional networking capabilities. For example, you've just finally gotten around to buying a USB drive for backup, and you've never used USB before. How do you find out whether your system supports USB now? And how do you add it if it doesn't?

Solution

Download fresh kernel sources and compile a new kernel using your existing *.config* file, adding the new features you want.

The prerequisites are:

- First, make sure you have at least 500 MB of free disk space for the build process.
- Next, make hard copies of the outputs of *dmesg*, *lscpi*, *cat /proc/cpuinfo*, and *lsusb*. (See Chapter 5 for more information on these.)
- Back up all of your data, and have a bootable rescue disk at hand.
- You'll also need a kernel *.config* file.

To add a new feature to your existing kernel, download new sources of the same kernel version. To find your kernel version, use *uname*:

```
$ uname -r
2.4.22
```

Unpack the new kernel sources into a folder in your home directory, such as *~/src*:

```
$ tar xvjf linux-2.4.22.tar.bz2
```

Edit the new kernel makefile (*~/src/linux-2.4.22/Makefile*), giving a custom value to *EXTRAVERSION*, such as *EXTRAVERSION = -new-kernel*.

Run the following commands from *~/src/linux-2.4.22*:

```
$ make mrproper
```

Copy your *.config* file to *~/src/linux-2.4.22* now.

Next, configure the new kernel. The configurator will ask many questions. This is where you select the new features you want:

```
$ make oldconfig
```

Then run these commands:

```
$ make dep
$ make bzImage
$ make modules
$ su
# make modules_install
# cp ~/src/linux-2.4.22/arch/i386/boot/bzImage  /boot/vmlinuz-2.4.22-new-kernel
# cp ~/src/linux-2.4.22/System.map /boot/System.map-2.4.22-new-kernel
```

Finally, to use your new kernel, add it to your bootloader and reboot. A GRUB entry looks like this:

```
title    Kernel 2.4.22, new kernel
root     (hd0,0)
kernel   /boot/vmlinuz-2.4.22-new-kernel root=/dev/hda1 ro
```

LILO users do this:

```
image=boot/vmlinuz-2.4.22-new-kernel
    label=Kernel 2.4.22, new kernel
    root=/dev/hda1
    read-only
```

And remember to re-run LILO, to write the new configuration to the boot record:

```
# /sbin/lilo
```

Save a copy of your new *.config* file in a directory outside of the build tree, so that it does not get deleted or overwritten. Give it a unique, helpful name:

```
$ cp ~/src/linux-2.4.22/.config  ~/kernel-configs/.config-2.4.22-jan-04
```

You can also add coments to the *.config* file itself, to help you keep track:

```
# Automatically generated by make menuconfig: don't edit
#
# jan 2004 added udf r/w support, jfs, and xfs
```

When you're satisfied that the new kernel works correctly, you can delete the old kernel, its */lib/modules/$VERSION* directory, the build tree, and its bootloader entries (or you can hang on to them, if you prefer).

Discussion

A lot of documentation tells you to put your kernel sources and build tree in */usr/src/linux*. This is a bad idea. As the kernel Readme states: "Do NOT use the */usr/src/linux* area! This area has a (usually incomplete) set of kernel headers that are used by the library header files. They should match the library, and not get messed up by whatever the kernel-du-jour happens to be." And you don't want to abuse rootly powers by using a directory that requires root access. A kernel can be built anywhere, even on a completely separate PC.

Finding .config

If you've previously built a kernel on your system, you'll find the *.config* file in the top-level directory of the old build tree. If you have not built a kernel on the system, look in */boot* for *.config*, as most distributions put it there. If you find one in */usr/src/linux*, it's most likely a generic *.config*, and not useful to you.

If there is not a *.config* file for your system, skip ahead to Recipe 10.3, because you'll have to configure your new kernel from scratch. *make oldconfig* will still work, but it will use the defaults in the build tree, which will not suit your system at all. *make oldconfig* tells you which file it is using:

```
$ make oldconfig
...
# Using defaults found in arch/i386/defconfig
```

You don't want to use that one! It should say this:

```
# Using defaults found in .config
```

Hit Ctrl-C to interrupt and start over, if necessary.

Explanations of the build commands

You can have several kernels on your system, as long as you remember to give each one a unique *EXTRAVERSION* value and to use a unique name when copying the new kernel image to */boot*.

Documentation/Changes recommends using *gcc* 2.95.3. Most newer distributions ship with 3.x, which ought to work, but if you have problems you can install more than one version of *gcc* on your system, and select the one you want to use at compile-time:

```
$ make bzImage CC=gcc-2.95.3
```

make mrproper cleans the build tree to a pristine state, removing configuration files, dependency information, and object files. Do this even with freshly downloaded sources. (*mrproper*, according to Linux lore, is named for Mr. Proper. Mr. Proper is the European version of Mr. Clean, for those occasions when you need to make something cleaner than clean.) *mrproper* cleans the build tree more thoroughly than *make clean*, which removes object files but does not touch configuration or dependency files. Read the Makefile to see exactly what files are removed.

make oldconfig reuses your existing kernel configuration. When you're making a minor addition to your kernel, *make oldconfig* lets you whiz right through and only asks about new things. It will not let you change any existing settings. "y/n/m/?" means "yes, build this into the kernel / no, do not add this feature / yes, add this as a module / help, please."

If you don't know what to choose, hit ? for help.

make dep builds all the necessary dependencies.

make bzImage compiles the new kernel. This can take up to an hour, depending on the speed of your PC and how complex your new kernel is.

make modules compiles all of the necessary modules.

make modules_install is the first operation that requires superuser privileges. For this example, your new modules are installed into */lib/modules/2.4.22*.

cp ~/src/arch/i386/boot/bzImage /boot/vmlinuz-2.4.22-new-kernel copies your nice new kernel image to the */boot* directory, and renames it. It is important, when installing multiple kernels, to make sure each one has a unique name and to use the same kernel name in your bootloader.

cp ~/src/System.map /boot/System.map-2.4.22-new-kernel copies the new System.map to */boot*. Be sure that the System.map has the same version number as the kernel to which it belongs. The System.map is a symbol table that maps kernel addresses to human-readable names. For example:

```
c01001f8 t int_msg
c0100210 t ignore_int
c0100232 t idt_descr
```

The kernel is happier with numbers, while human coders do better with names. This map keeps everyone happy. If you are running multiple kernels on a system, each kernel needs its own System.map. If you have the wrong System.map, the consequences are not dire. You'll occasionally see the "System.map does not match actual kernel" error message, and you won't get accurate kernel debugging if you need to troubleshoot.

See Also

- This chapter's "Introduction," for where to get kernel sources and where to look for documentation
- The online help in the kernel configurator—almost every configuration item has an entry

10.3   Slimming a Stock 2.4 Kernel

Problem

You would like to overhaul the kernel that came with your distribution and weed out all the unnecessary drivers, getting rid of support for hardware and functions you don't need.

Solution

Download new sources of the same kernel version and compile the new kernel, configuring it from scratch. To find your kernel version, use *uname*:

```
$ uname -r
2.4.22
```

The prequisites are:

- First, make sure you have at least 500 MB of free disk space for the build process.
- Next, make hard copies of the outputs of *dmesg*, *lscpi*, *cat /proc/cpuinfo*, and *lsusb*. (See Chapter 5 for more information on these.)
- Back up all of your data, and have a bootable rescue disk at hand.

Unpack the new kernel sources into a folder in your home directory, such as *~/src*:

```
$ tar xvjf linux-2.4.22.tar.bz2
```

Edit the new kernel makefile (*~/src/linux-2.4.22/Makefile*), giving a custom value to *EXTRAVERSION*, such as *EXTRAVERSION = -slim-kernel*

All of the following commands are run from *~/src/linux-2.4.22*:

```
$ make mrproper
$ make menuconfig
$ make dep
$ make bzImage
$ make modules
$ su
# make modules_install
# cp ~/src/linux-2.4.22/arch/i386/boot/bzImage  /boot/vmlinuz-2.4.22-new-kernel
# cp ~/src/linux-2.4.22/System.map /boot/System.map-2.4.22-new-kernel
```

When you configure the kernel, keep in mind that you are starting from scratch, so you must explicitly enable every feature that you want. And you must make sure that features you do not want are not enabled. These are some core features that you definitely want:

- Loadable module support, built into the kernel.
- Under the "General Setup" menu, be sure that support is built in for a.out binaries, ELF binaries, and MISC binaries.
- Be sure to build support for all of your boot devices—IDE drives, CD-ROM, floppy disk, SCSI disk, or USB—into the kernel. If you leave them out, or build them as modules, your system will require a *ramdisk* (*initrd* image) to boot.

When you're finished, add the new kernel to the bootloader, reboot, and enjoy. Remember to copy your new *.config* file to a directory outside of the build tree to preserve it.

Discussion

This procedure configures the new kernel from scratch. *make oldconfig* doesn't work, because it does not let you change the old configuration; it only lets you add new things.

A typical base kernel runs around 1–3 MB (compressed), and the corresponding */lib/modules/$version* runs around 10–30 MB. Some folks like to strip their kernels to the absolute bare essentials. On a server, especially one that is exposed to the Internet, it's a good security practice to keep it as lean as possible. But having a bit of fat on a desktop system or workstation isn't all that significant, and it may be convenient for future changes.

The name *vmlinuz*, according to lore, came about because the kernel on old Unix systems was *vmunix*. The *vm* stands for "virtual memory," to distinguish it from older kernels that did not have this feature. In your build tree, you'll see a *vmlinux* file. *vmlinuz* is the compressed version of this file. There's no need to be dull and stick with naming your kernels *vmlinuz-$version*. You can name them anything you like—kernel-mustard, kernel-panic, kernel-of-truth, fred-and-ginger... anything at all.

See Also

- This chapter's "Introduction," for where to get kernel sources and where to look for documentation
- The online help in the kernel configurator—almost every configuration item has an entry
- Recipe 10.2, for explanations of build commands, managing *.config* files, and installing the new kernel

10.4   Upgrading to the Latest Stable Version of the 2.4 Kernel

Problem

You've heard there have been many updates and patches to the kernel. You would like to update your old kernel to the latest stable version (e.g., from 2.4.22 to 2.4.25), because this is the easiest way to get all the updates and patches.

Solution

Back up of all of your data, and have a bootable rescue disk at hand.

Make hard copies of the outputs of *dmesg*, *lscpi*, *cat /proc/cpuinfo*, and *lsusb*.

Unpack the new kernel sources into a folder in your home directory, such as ~/*src*:

```
$ tar xvjf linux-2.4.25.tar.bz2
```

Edit the new kernel makefile (~/*src/linux-2.4.25/Makefile*), giving a custom value to *EXTRAVERSION*, such as *EXTRAVERSION = -new-kernel*.

All of the following commands are run from ~/*src/linux-2.4.25*:

```
$ make mrproper
```

If want to use your existing *.config* file, copy it to ~/*src/linux-2.4.25* now and continue with this recipe. If not, go back to Recipe 10.3.

Run the following commands:.

```
$ make oldconfig
$ make dep
$ make bzImage
$ make modules
$ su
# make modules_install
# cp ~/src/linux-2.4.25/arch/i386/boot/bzImage  /boot/vmlinuz-2.4.25-new-kernel
# cp ~/src/linux-2.4.25/System.map /boot/System.map-2.4.25-new-kernel
```

Add the new kernel to your bootloader, reboot, and enjoy.

Discussion

http://lwn.net and *http://kerneltrap.org* are good sites for keeping on top of kernel news, changes, improvements, and problems.

See Also

- This chapter's "Introduction," for where to get kernel sources and where to look for documentation
- Recipe 10.2, "Adding New Features to the 2.4 Kernel," for complete details on building and installing a kernel
- The online help in the kernel configurator—almost every configuration item has an entry

10.5   Building the 2.6 Kernel

Problem

You would like to try the 2.6 kernel, and you need to know the new build commands, which are different from those for the 2.4 kernel.

Solution

In this example, our new kernel is version 2.6.3. Back up of all of your data, and have a rescue disk at hand.

Make hard copies of the outputs of *dmesg*, *lscpi*, *cat /proc/cpuinfo*, and *lsusb*.

Download and unpack new kernel sources into a folder in your home directory, such as *~/src*. Change to the top-level directory of your new source tree (*~/src/linux-2.6.3*).

Edit the new kernel makefile (*~/src/linux-2.6.3/Makefile*), giving a custom value to *EXTRAVERSION*, such as *EXTRAVERSION =-test*. Then run the following commands:

```
$ make mrproper
$ make xconfig
$ make
$ su
# make modules_install
# cp ~/src/linux-2.6.3/arch/i386/boot/bzImage  /boot/vmlinuz-2.6.3-test
# cp ~/src/linux-2.6.3/System.map  /boot/System.map-2.6.3-test
```

Save a copy of your new *.config* file in a directory outside of the build tree. Add the new kernel to your bootloader, reboot, and have fun.

Discussion

You need Qt, *qt-devel*, and X to run *xconfig*. *menuconfig* also works nicely.

The *make* command, all by itself, replaces *make dep*, *make bzImage*, and *make modules*.

See Also

- This chapter's "Introduction," for where to get kernel sources
- Recipe 10.2, "Adding New Features to the 2.4 Kernel," for explanations of the build commands and how to configure the bootloader
- The online help in the kernel configurator—almost every configuration item has an entry

10.6   Adding New Features to the 2.6 Kernel

Problem

You need to add features to your 2.6 kernel.

Solution

Follow Recipe 10.5, except you'll use *oldconfig* instead of *xconfig*:

```
$ make mrproper
```

Copy your existing *.config* file to *~/src/linux-2.6.3* now. Then run the following commands:

```
$ make oldconfig
$ make
$ su
# make modules_install
# cp ~/src/linux-2.6.3/arch/i386/boot/bzImage /boot/vmlinuz-2.6.3-test
# cp ~/src/linux-2.6.3/System.map  /boot/System.map-2.6.3-test
```

Add your new kernel to your bootloader, and you're ready to go.

Discussion

Do not try to use a 2.4 *.config* file—the two kernels are quite different, and it will cause many troubles.

The *make* command, all by itself, replaces *make dep, make bzImage,* and *make modules.*

See Also

- The documentation in the kernel build tree, starting with the Readme, which covers building, configuring, and compiling the kernel
- This chapter's "Introduction," for where to get kernel sources and where to look for documentation
- Recipe 10.2, "Adding New Features to the 2.4 Kernel," for explanations of the build commands and how to configure your bootloader

10.7   Adding a New Loadable Kernel Module

Problem

You have changed or added some hardware, such as a NIC card, sound card, or USB device, and you need to install a new kernel module (driver) for the device.

Solution

The steps are the same for 2.4 and 2.6 kernels. Change to the directory that contains the build tree (e.g., *~/src/linux-2.4.25*). You'll need a good, up-to-date *.config* file. Copy it to the top level of your build tree, then run:

```
$ make oldconfig
```

As you go through the configuration, find the driver you need and select it as a module (for example, the *tulip* module, which is a common driver for many Ethernet cards). Then:

```
$ make dep
$ make modules
# make modules_install
# depmod -av
```

Load the module with *modprobe*:

```
# modprobe tulip
```

This whole process doesn't need a reboot.

Discussion

make menuconfig also works, if you can't use *oldconfig*. It just takes longer, and you have to be careful to not leave out anything important.

If you're installing a third-party module that is not in the kernel tree, you must rely on the vendor's installation instructions. The usual method is to download sources, build the module, then load it with *modprobe*. Some vendors, like nVidia, provide a script that does everything for you.

Most distributions probe hardware at bootup, and automatically load the correct modules. If this does not happen, you'll need to configure some startup files. On Red Hat and SuSE, add the module to */etc/modules.conf*. On Debian, add it to */etc/modules*. Slackware uses *rc.modules*.

Even easier is to enable *kmod*, the automatic module loader, in your kernel. Most distributions enable it by default. In the kernel configurator, look for "Automatic kernel module loading" (2.6 kernel) or "Kernel module loader" (2.4) under "Loadable module support."

Don't use *kerneld*; *kmod* replaced it starting from the 2.2 kernel.

See Also

- This chapter's Introduction, for where to get kernel sources and where to look for documentation
- Recipe 10.2, "Adding New Features to the 2.4 Kernel," for explanations of the build commands, where to find a *.config* file, and how to preserve it for reuse

10.8   Patching a Kernel

Problem

You want to add a new feature or correct a problem by patching your kernel, test some new features, or update to the next point release.

Solution

Download and apply the patch to the kernel sources, then compile and build the new kernel. In this example, we are upgrading the 2.6.3 kernel to 2.6.4.

The patch must be in the next-highest directory upstream from your build tree, like this:

```
$ ls ~/src
linux-2.6.3  patch-2.6.4.bz2
```

Now change to the top level of your build tree, then unpack and apply the patch:

```
$ cd linux-2.6.3
$ bzip2 -dc ../patch-2.6.4.bz2 | patch -s -p1
```

Or, you can do a test drive with the *--dry-run* option:

```
$ bzip2 -dc ../patch-2.6.4.bz2 | patch -s -p1 --dry-run
```

Now configure and build your kernel, and away you go.

Your build tree thoughtfully includes a script to handle applying patches for you, in */scripts/patch-kernel*. This is a great little script, especially when you have several patches to apply, because it automatically applies them in the correct order. Usage is simple. From your top-level source directory, run:

```
$ scripts/patch-kernel
```

Patches must be applied in order, and you must have all of them. For example, to use *patch-2.6.5-rc6*, you also need the first five patches in the series (*rc1* through *rc5*). When you're upgrading to a newer point release, you can't skip any of them; all of them have to be applied in sequence.

Discussion

This is what the different *patch* options mean:

-d

Decompress.

-c

Send output to stdout.

../ patch-2.6.4.bz2

Specifies that the patch file is one directory level up.

-s

Silent output, except for errors.

-p

Strips directory prefixes from the filenames in the patch, also called the "patch level." *p1* strips the first prefix from the filepaths in the patch, because it's highly unlikely that you have the same directory structure as the author of the patch. *p0* would do a literal copy, and the operation would probably fail.

-s

Successful operation returns no output

Kernel patches come in several flavors. Release candidate (*rc*) patches are one step removed from being accepted into the stable kernel trees; pre-release (*pre*) candidates are two steps away. If you're dying to have a new feature and you don't want to wait for the final stable release, *rc* and *pre* patches are the way to go. Numbering is seemingly backward: *patch-2.6.5-rc3* will wind up in the 2.6.4 kernel.

The official kernel releases on Kernel.org are the "Linus" kernel trees. These are well tested and considered production-ready. Even-numbered kernels are stable releases; odd-numbered kernels are under development. The Linux kernel is actively maintained back to 2.0, and all kernels back to the beginning of Linux are available in the archives.

Each stable kernel has its own maintainer. Linus Torvalds, of course, is the Big Boss of everything. The maintainers of the individual kernels are.

- David Weinehall (2.0)
- Marc-Christian Petersen (2.2)
- Marcelo Tosatti (2.4)
- Andrew Morton (2.6)

Then there are the various kernel trees, run by different maintainers. These are where new designs and features are tested. If they survive, they will eventually be merged into the stable kernel tree. Patches from these have the maintainer's initials appended, as in *patch-2.6.5-rc3-mm4*. The abbreviations you'll see are:

-ac

> Maintainer: Alan Cox. Pending patches for sending to Marcelo (for 2.4 series), and extra add-ons, fixes, etc.

-ck

> Maintainer: Con Kolivas. 2.4-based patchset for performance tweaks to the scheduler and vm, and faster desktop performace.

-mm

> Maintainer: Andrew Morton. Primarily virtual memory improvements.

-rmap

> Maintainer: Rik van Riel. *rmap* relates to performance and design of virtual memory management.

-aa

> Maintainer: Andrea Arcangeli. Virtual memory updates, fixes, and improvements.

-dj

> Maintainer: Dave Jones. Forward ports of 2.4 bugfixes to 2.5 series.

-osdl

> For the enterprise; large, heavy-use machines and high-performance databases.

See Also

- *patch(1)*
- Kernel Newbies (*http://kernelnewbies.org*)
- Kernel.org (*http://kernel.org*)

10.9   Removing a Kernel Patch

Problem

You applied a patch, and now you want to get rid of it. It may be unstable or buggy, or maybe you simply made a mistake and want to start over.

Solution

Use the same command you used to unpack and apply it, adding the *-R* option:

```
$ bzip2 -dc ../patch-2.6.4.bz2 | patch -s -p1 -R
```

See Also

- *patch(1)*
- Kernel Newbies (*http://kernelnewbies.org*)
- Kernel.org (*http://kernel.org*)

10.10 Creating an initrd Image

Problem

You are using SCSI drives, and you like to load the drivers as modules, because there are so many different SCSI drivers. You want the flexibility to change drives or controllers without rebuilding the kernel every time, and you don't want to fatten your kernel by compiling in every possible driver. But how will the system boot without the SCSI driver built into the base kernel?

Solution

Build an *initrd* (initialize RAM disk) image with *mkinitrd* (make initial RAM disk) after you build the kernel. Then add an entry to your bootloader that loads the image.

On both 2.4 and 2.6 kernels, after running *make modules_install*, run *mkinitrd*:

```
# mkinitrd -o /boot/initrd-2.4.25-new-kernel.img
```

This builds the image and installs it into the */boot* directory. Then create your bootloader entries. In GRUB:

```
title    Kernel  2.4.25, new kernel
root     (hd0,0)
kernel   /boot/bzImage-2.4.25-new-kernel root=/dev/hda1 ro
initrd   /boot/initrd-2.4.25-new-kernel.img
```

LILO users do this:

```
image=/boot/bzImage-2.4.22-new-kernel
    initrd=/boot/initrd-2.4.25-new-kernel.img
    label=Kernel 2.4.22, new kernel
    root=/dev/hda1
    read-only
```

Remember to run */sbin/lilo* to activate the changes.

Discussion

Be sure to read the *mkinitrd* man page for your system, as the options differ slightly between the different distributions.

It's perfectly okay to build your SCSI driver into the base kernel; using *initrd* isn't required.

Most of the major Linux distributions use *initrd*, so that their stock kernels will boot on most systems without needing every driver in the world to be built in.

See Also

- *mkinitrd(8)*

10.11 Creating a Boot Disk on Debian

Problem

You forgot to create a boot diskette when you installed your Linux system, and now you want to make one. You know how to create a GRUB or LILO boot diskette, and you know that you can download and burn a nice Knoppix disk for free. But all you really want is a nice little generic boot diskette for your Debian system.

Solution

Use the *mkboot* utility and a new, blank diskette. The default is to create a bootdisk using *vmlinuz* and the current root partition:

```
$ mkboot
```

You may specify a kernel:

```
$ mkboot vmlinuz-2.4.21
```

Or a different root partition and kernel:

```
$ mkboot /dev/hda2 vmlinuz-2.4.21
```

If your floppy drive has a non-standard location, use the *-d* flag to tell *mkboot* where it is:

```
$ mkboot -d /dev/fd1
```

Discussion

mkboot is part of the *debianutils* package.

Remember to write-protect your diskette by moving the little slide up, so that the slide is open. Always test boot disks before putting them away, and be sure to keep it with the system it was created on.

See Also

- *mkboot(8)*

10.12 Creating a Boot Disk on Red Hat

Problem

You forgot to create a boot diskette when you installed your Linux system, and now you want to make one. You know how to create a GRUB or LILO boot diskette, and you know that you can download and burn a nice Knoppix disk for free. But all you really want is a nice little generic boot diskette for your Red Hat/Fedora system.

Solution

Use the *mkbootdisk* utility and a new, blank diskette. You must specify the kernel name:

```
$ mkbootdisk vmlinuz-2.6.5-1.358
```

mkbootdisk, by default, does not generate any output. You can turn on verbosity:

```
$ mkbootdisk --verbose vmlinuz-2.6.5-1.358
```

If your floppy drive is not */dev/fd0*, you must specify the device name:

```
$ mkbootdisk --device /dev/fd1 vmlinuz-2.6.5-1.358
```

Discussion

Remember to write-protect your diskette by moving the little slide up, so that the slide is open. Always test boot disks before putting them away, and be sure to keep it with the system it was created on.

See Also

- *mkbootdisk(8)*

## CHAPTER 11

CD and DVD Recording

11.1 Introduction

Linux offers a host of CD/DVD writing and authoring utilities. The entire field is evolving rapidly, and CD/DVD standards are in a chaotic state. There are several competing, incompatible standards, and more are looming on the horizon as commercial distributors toil to develop a magical disc that will permit playback but not copying. This chapter sidesteps all of this drama and introduces some basic techniques for writing data CDs and DVDs. You'll need the *cdrtools* and *dvd+rw-tools* packages.

To create discs the easy way, use K3b. It is a graphical frontend to *cdrtools*, *cdrdao*, *mkisofs*, *growisofs*, and other command-line editing tools. K3b makes it easy to set up your drives and to give users any necessary root privileges, such as those required by *cdrecord* and *cdrdao*. The layout is logical and simple to use; it gets my vote as the best CD/DVD writer on any platform. Of course, the Linux world offers many more choices, such as GCombust, X-CD-Roast, and Gnome Toaster. These are all simple to use, so this chapter will cover the command-line tools. Understanding these will also make the graphical tools more useful, as you'll understand the commands and weird terminology.

A major change in the 2.6 kernel is that you no longer need to use SCSI emulation for CD/DVD drives. Instead of running *cdrecord scanbus* to find the SCSI bus addresses, simply use the */dev* names of the devices:

```
# cdrecord dev=/dev/hdc <commands>
```

If you have upgraded from a 2.4 to a 2.6 kernel and you used IDE-SCSI for your CD/DVD drives, be sure that the IDE-SCSI entries are removed from your bootloader, or you'll get strange boot errors.

Glossary of Formats and Standards

Here are the hardware standards:

CD-R
  CD-Recordable, or WORM (Write Once, Read Many). CD-Rs are universal and should be readable in any CD-ROM drive.

CD-RW
  CD-Rewritable, or WMRM (Write Many, Read Many). A drive must be "multi-read" to be able to read CD-R and CD-RW discs. CD-RWs should be readable in all contemporary drives.

CD-ROM
  Compact Disc-Read-Only Memory. Commercially produced discs are pressed, not burned with a laser, and cannot be written to.

Mount Rainier ReWrite
  The circuitry needed by a drive to support UDF.

DVD-Video
  The standard used on commercially produced movie discs, playable on all DVD machines.

DVD-R and DVD+R
  WORM format. Playable on all DVD players. DVD-R has two different, incompatible disc types: DVD-R(A) and DVD-R(G). You can't use A discs in G writers, and vice versa.

DVD-RAM
  Rewritable, designed for data storage. Theoretically, it can take up to 100,000 rewrites per disc. You can also record and play movies on a PC, but a standalone DVD player probably won't be able to read DVD-RAMs.

DVD-R/RW
  Designed for recording movies. This DVD standard is supported by the DVD Forum (*http://www.dvdforum.com*).

DVD+R/RW
  A competing, incompatible standard to DVD-R/RW, supported by the DVD+RW Alliance (*http://www.dvdrw.com*). Only DVD+R/RW supports UDF.

The newest generation of DVD drives for computers support all formats. Standalone DVD recorders are still fighting standards wars between the DVD+ and DVD- formats.

Here are the CD and DVD filesystem standards:

El Torito
  Bootable format specification.

UDF
  Universal Disk Format, the industry-standard incremental packet-writing filesystem. This allows dropping files directly on to a disc, just like on a 3.5" diskette.

It was expected that Linux would fully support this in the 2.6 kernel, but it's not there yet.

ISO-9660

The old file layout standard, allowing only 8.3 filenames (from the ancient MS-DOS days, where filenames could have only up to 8 letters and had to have 3-letter file extensions).

Rock Ridge

Extensions to ISO-9660, allowing long filenames and Unix-style symlinks. It preserves all file attributes, such as ownership and permissions. Unix file attributes are not displayed when the disc is read on a Windows system.

Joliet

Microsoft extension to the ISO-9660 filesystem that allows Unicode characters to be used in filenames, as well as long filenames. It also creates truncated filenames for MS-DOS compatibility (these weird-looking things: *FILENA~1.TXT*). It allows filenames of up to 64 characters, including spaces, and is readable by Windows 95 or later and by Macintosh computers running the Joliet Volume Access extension. Macs will not read Joliet filenames that are longer than 31 characters.

Here are the CD standards books:

Yellow Book

Physical format for data CDs

Orange Book

Physical format for recordable CDs, with multisession capability:

> Part I: CD-MO (Magneto-Optical)
> Part II: CD-R (Write-once; includes "hybrid" spec for PhotoCD)
> Part III: CD-RW (Re-writable)

Red Book

CD Audio standard that describes the physical properties of the disc and the digital audio encoding

These books can be purchased from *http://www.licensing.philips.com*, if you really want to get into the gory details.

These are the write options:

Session

Any single recorded segment on a disc, which can contain data files or a number of music tracks. A disc can contain several sessions.

Track

The program area of a CD is divided into tracks; each track can contain data of only one type. A disc (even a DVD) holds a maximim of 99 tracks—the number is hardcoded.

Multisession

Allows adding files to a single disc over time, rather than having to record all of your files in a single session. For a disc to be readable, the session must be "closed," or fixated. However, this prevents adding more files to the disc. Multi-session links the individual sessions and updates the disc's table of contents so that it appears as a single directory.

SAO (session-at-once)

A single, complete session (lead-in, program, and lead-out areas) of a CD-R or CD-RW disc, written in one uninterrupted sequence.

DAO (disc-at-once)

Writes the entire CD in one pass, or session. The entire burn must complete without interruption, and no more sessions may be added. This is the most reliable way to record audio tracks.

TAO (track-at-once)

Allows the writes to be done in multiple passes. There is a maximum of 99 tracks per disc. Sometimes this causes audio CDs to not play correctly on audio disc players, though I've found it to be reliable.

For more information on DVDs, see the DVD FAQ at *http://www.dvddemystified.com/dvdfaq.html*.

For more information on CDs, see the CD Recordable FAQ at *http://www.cdrfaq.org*.

11.2   Finding the SCSI Address for CD and DVD Writers

Problem

You're using a 2.4 kernel and want to write a CD or DVD. You need to know the SCSI bus address, or *dev=* number, for your CD/DVD writer.

Solution

cdrecord -scanbus will find it for you. This is what a CD/DVD-ROM and a CD writer on a single system look like:

```
$ cdrecord -scanbus
Cdrecord 1.10 (i686-pc-linux-gnu) Copyright (C) 1995-2001 Jrg Schilling
Linux sg driver version: 3.1.24
Using libscg version 'schily-0.5'
scsibus0:
0,0,0 0) 'TOSHIBA ' 'DVD-ROM SD-M1202' '1020' Removable CD-ROM
0,1,0 1) 'LITE-ON ' 'LTR-24102B ' '5S54' Removable CD-ROM
0,2,0 2) *
0,3,0 3) *
0,4,0 4) *
```

```
0,5,0 5) *
0,6,0 6) *
0,7,0 7) *
```

DVD writers look like this:

```
1,2,0 2) 'PIONEER ' 'DVD-ROM DVD-303 ' '1.09' Removable CD-ROM
```

The first three numbers for each item refer to the SCSI bus, device ID, and LUN (Logical Unit Number), respectively. The fourth number is the device ID again. *cdrecord* wants the first three numbers, like this:

```
dev=0,1,0
```

Discussion

cdrecord requires root privileges. The most common convention for giving users permissions to use *cdrecord* is to create a *cdrecord* group.

Sometimes you'll see documentation where it looks like this:

```
dev=1,0
```

It's a common convention to leave off the leading 0 for devices on SCSI bus 0. However, it's not much trouble to type an extra digit and leave no room for doubt.

The 2.6 kernel needs no special steps to determine the device ID. Simply use the */dev* name:

```
$ cdrecord dev=/dev/hdc <commands>
```

See Also

- *cdrecord(1)*

11.3   Enabling SCSI Emulation for IDE/Atapi CD and DVD Writers

Problem

Your CD-writing program (whether it's *cdrecord* or one of the good graphical programs such as X-CD-Roast or K3b) reports that it cannot find any drives on your system, or it sees your CD-R/RW drive just fine but does not see your CD-ROM drive, so you can't copy discs.

Solution

Make sure the IDE-SCSI emulation system is enabled and your drives are configured to use it. This applies only to the 2.4 Linux kernel, because the 2.6 kernel supports IDE/ATAPI drives directly, using the standard */dev/hd** designations.

First, verify that the *ide-scsi pseudo-device driver* is available:

```
$ locate ide-scsi.o
/lib/modules/2.4.21/kernel/drivers/scsi/ide-scsi.o
```

Next, there are two text files to edit: */etc/modules.conf*, and the configuration file for your bootloader. (Debian users, please refer to the "Discussion" section of this recipe, as file locations are different.) First, find the device names for your drives:

```
$ dmesg | grep '^hd.:'
hda: IBM-DTLA-305020, ATA DISK drive
hdb: TOSHIBA DVD-ROM SD-M1202, ATAPI CD/DVD-ROM drive
hdc: LITE-ON LTR-24102B, ATAPI CD/DVD-ROM drive
```

The CD drives are *hdb* and *hdc*. Add the following to */etc/modules.conf*:

```
alias scsi_hostadapter ide-scsi
options ide-cd ignore="hdb hdc"
alias scd0 sr_mod
pre-install sg      modprobe ide-scsi
pre-install sr_mod modprobe ide-scsi
pre-install ide-scsi modprobe ide-cd
```

Next, LILO users, add the following to the end of *lilo.conf,* using the *hd** designations for your devices:

```
append="hdb=ide-scsi"
append="hdc=ide-scsi"
```

GRUB users, add the following to */etc/grub.conf* at the end of the kernel line, using the *hd** designations for your devices:

```
hdb=scsi hdc=scsi
```

It should look like this, all on one line:

```
kernel   /boot/vmlinuz-2.4.21 root=/dev/hda1 ro hdb=scsi hdc=scsi
```

Reboot, then verify that the *ide-scsi* module loaded:

```
$ lsmod | grep ide-scsi
ide-scsi          9456   1
scsi_mod          55124  2 [ide-scsi sr_mod]
```

Now when you run *cdrecord -scanbus* it should show SCSI device names for all the drives you configured to use IDE-SCSI, and you should be ready to start CD writing.

Note that the device names are changed now, so when you mount the discs the device names won't be */dev/hd** any more, but rather */dev/scd**. You'll probably want to update */etc/fstab* with the new */dev* names.

Discussion

Debian's module configuration files are in different locations. First, Debian uses */etc/modules* and */etc/modutils/idecd_opts*. Add:

```
ide-scsi
```

to *etc/modules.* Then add:

    options ide-cd ignore="hdb hdc

to */etc/modutils/idecd_opts.*

There is no downside to running all of your CD/DVD drives under the IDE-SCSI subsystem, except for having different device names.

The 2.6 kernel needs no special steps. Simply use the */dev* name:

    $ cdrecord dev=/dev/hdc <commands>

Remember, you can use a *cdrecord* group to grant permissions to users for *cdrecord*.

See Also

- *grub(8), lilo(8)*

11.4   Making a Data CD for General Distribution

Problem

You want to create a data CD that will be readable on Linux and Windows, with non-restrictive file permissions. The disk may contain text files, documents, programs, or graphical images.

Solution

Use *mkisofs, mount*, and *cdrecord.* First use *mkisofs* to package all of the files into a single *.iso* file, then mount the *.iso* to verify the filesystem is good. Then write to disk with *cdrecord.*

In this example, the *.iso* is called *data.iso*, the CD is named *data_disk*, and all the files will be copied from the */disk-data* directory. The mountpoint for the *.iso* is */test-iso*.

Here are the commands:

    # mkisofs -J -r -v -V data_disk -o data.iso /disk-data
    # mkdir /test-iso
    # mount -t iso9660 -o ro,loop data.iso /test-iso
    # ls /test-iso
    # umount /test-iso
    # cdrecord -v -eject dev=0,1,0 data.iso

Discussion

This recipe shows the root user running all commands, for simplicity, because *mount, mkisofs*, and *cdrecord* require root privileges. To allow users to run the *mount* command, use *sudo*. To allow users to run *mkisofs* and *cdrecord*, create a *cdrecord* group. Make it own *mkisofs* and *cdrecord*, and put users in the *cdrecord* group.

Remember that the 2.6 kernel doesn't need IDE-SCSI, so you can just use the */dev* name:

```
# cdrecord dev=/dev/hdc <commands>
```

There's a whole lot of doings packed into these few lines. Let's break them down one at a time. *mkisofs* takes all of your files and rolls them into one big *.iso* file. If you've ever downloaded a Linux distribution to burn to CD, it was packaged as an *.iso* file. This is a common source of confusion for Linux newbies, who don't understand why they have this giant single file, instead of a nice directory tree full of Linux files.

Let's look at the *mkisofs* line in more detail:

```
# mkisofs -J -r -v -V data_disk -o data.iso  /disk-data
```

Here are the options:

-J

Use Joliet naming conventions, for Windows compatibility.

-r

Use Rock Ridge naming conventions for Unix/Linux compatibility, and make all files publicly readable.

-v

Use verbose mode.

-V data_disk

Create a volume ID (*data_disk*); this is the disc name that shows up in Windows Explorer and with the *file - < /dev/scd** command (see Recipe 9.12 for how to find the */dev* names).

-o data.iso /disk-data

The name of the new *.iso* image, and the files selected for packaging into the *.iso*, which in this case is everything in */disk-data*. Note that the root directory */disk-data* is not copied, only the contents.

Mounting the *.iso* before burning the disc is cheap insurance to make sure you're not creating a coaster. If you see all of your files, it's good to go. If not, the *.iso* is no good, and it needs to be rebuilt. Here's how to test your *.iso*:

```
# mkdir /test-iso
# mount -t iso9660 -o ro,loop data.iso  /test-iso
```

Then look in the */test-iso* directory to verify your files.

Here are the parts of the *mount* command:

-t iso9660

The filesystem type. Data CDs are always *iso9660* (except when they are *udf*, but you would not need to create an *.iso* image for these).

-o ro,loop data.iso

> Mount options for the file *data.iso*: in this case read-only, using the loop device. The *loop device* lets you mount filesystems that are embedded in files, the classic use being *.iso* images.

/test-iso

> The directory created to be the mountpoint.

Now that the *.iso* is all ship-shape, we can burn it to disc.

```
# cdrecord -v -eject dev=0,1,0 data.iso
```

The options are:

-v

> Be verbose.

-eject

> Eject the disc when finished. This is optional.

dev=0,1,0

> The SCSI address of the CD writer.

data.iso

> The name of the *.iso* file that contains the files you want burned to disc.

cdrecord automatically writes at the highest speed the drive and disc support. If there are errrors, try specifiying a lower write speed:

```
# cdrecord -v -eject speed=4 dev=0,1,0 data.iso
```

Modern writers have fast write speeds (20X and higher). However, many CD-R/RW discs are limited to much slower speeds. Usually, *cdrecord* will auto-detect the appropriate write speed.

See Also

- *cdrecord(1), mount(8), mkisofs(8)*
- Recipe 9.12, "Finding Device Names for mount and fstab"
- Recipe 11.2, "Finding the SCSI Address for CD and DVD Writers"

11.5   Building File Trees on a Data CD

Problem

When you select directories for writing to CD, *mkisofs* discards the root directories and keeps only the files and subdirectories. But you'd like to preserve the file trees, or create new ones.

Solution

Use the *-graft-points* option in *mkisofs*. This example preserves the existing directory structure for the directories *scripts* and *finances*:

```
$ ls
finances  scripts
$ mkisofs -r -J -v  -o cdimg1.iso -graft-points scripts/=scripts  finance/=finances
...
```

Which is easily verified by mounting the image and viewing the file tree with the *tree -d* command:

```
$ sudo mount -t iso9660 -o ro,loop cdimg1.iso  /mnt/iso
$ tree -d /mnt/iso
mnt
|-- finances
`-- scripts
```

Suppose you want to move these two directories into */files/archive/june* on the CD. First, the directory */files/archive/june* must be present on the hard drive. Then run:

```
$ mkisofs -r -J -v  -o cdimg1.iso -graft-points \
files/archive/june/finances/=finances    files/archive/june/scripts/=scripts
```

Again, we can mount it and check:

```
$ tree -dL 4 /mnt/iso
mnt
`-- files
    `-- archive
        `-- june
            |-- finances
            `-- scripts
```

This works for both files and directories.

See Also

- *tree(1), mkisofs(8)*

11.6   Copying a CD or DVD

Problem

You need to make copies of CDs or DVDs—data, audio, video, or any format.

Solution

To directly copy from the source disc to the recordable disc, use this command:

```
$ cdrecord -v dev=0,1,0 -isosize /dev/scd0
```

This is fast, but risky, because any interruption to the data stream will spoil the entire copy. It's better to cache it to a hard drive first. This example makes a dummy run first:

```
$ dd if=/dev/scd0 of=/tmp/diskfile.iso
$ cdrecord dev=0,1,0 fs=8m -v -eject -dummy /tmp/diskfile.iso
```

Simply delete the *-dummy* flag to write to disc.

Discussion

Remember that the 2.6 kernel doesn't need IDE-SCSI—just use the */dev* name:

```
# cdrecord dev=/dev/hdc <commands>
```

Don't forget that you'll need a *tmp* file as large as the disc you're copying.

The *dd* command does a literal, byte-by byte copy. Its components are:

if

Input, or source, file.

/dev/scd0

/dev name for the drive. Be sure to use the correct */dev* name for your drive (see Recipe 11.3). The disc does not need to be mounted.

of

Output, or destination, file.

/tmp/diskfile.iso

Temporary copy of the source disc on the hard drive. Call it anything you want, as long as it has an *.iso* extension.

The *cdrecord* options are the same as in Recipe 11.4, with two new ones:

fs=8m

This defines the size of the ring buffer: the bigger the better, up to a point. Remember, interruptions are fatal; *fs=8m* creates a large enough buffer to keep the recorder working if something slows down the data transfer. If 8 MB isn't enough, you might need a better PC. On the other hand, more than 8 MB is not necessarily better, as the operating system can waste time reloading the Memory Management Unit (MMU) tables. The default is 4 MB.

-dummy

A marvelous option for doing a dry run before risking an actual disc. The recorder does everything with the laser turned off, giving the user a chance to catch errors before committing them to disc.

See Also

- *cdrecord(1), dd(1)*
- Recipe 11.4, "Making a Data CD for General Distribution"

11.7   Erasing a CD-RW

Problem

You want to erase a rewritable disk, to prepare it for recording new material, or you might want to erase single tracks.

Solution

Use the *blank* option for *cdrecord*. *blank=fast* erases only the table of contents (TOC), the program memory area (PMA), and the pregap:

```
$ cdrecord -v blank=fast dev=0,1,0
```

A more complete erasure is done with the *all* option:

```
$ cdrecord -v blank=all dev=0,1,0
```

Don't count on this for a secure erasure; data can still be recovered. *blank=fast* is perfectly fine for routine use, and it's a lot faster—plus, your CD-RW will last longer.

You can erase the last session on a multisession disc:

```
$ cdrecord blank=session
```

And on the off chance that your drive supports blanking at the track level, you can erase tracks just like sessions, starting with the last one:

```
$ cdrecord blank=track
```

Discussion

Blanking at track level is not supported by most drives. Erasing tracks or sessions in random order is not possible, either—you have to start at the end and work your way back. If you get error messages when using any of the *blank* options, try adding *-force*:

```
$ cdrecord blank=track -force
```

However, the disc is probably damaged or defective, so the wiser course is to discard it.

To see all the blanking options, use:

```
$ cdrecord blank=help
```

Keep in mind that CD-RWs have a limited lifespan and can take only so many erasures. The number varies, but you should get at least 100 rewrites before it becomes unreliable.

See Also

- *cdrecord(1)*

11.8 Recording a Multisession Data CD

Problem

You want to add data files to a disc over time, rather than all at once. *cdrecord* closes and fixates discs, so that no additional files can be added. How do you get around this?

Solution

This is a two-step process. Both *cdrecord* and *mkisofs* have special options for creating multisession discs. The first time you write files to a CD, create an *.iso* in the usual manner, then use the *-multi* switch in *cdrecord*:

```
$ cdrecord -v -eject dev=0,1,0 -multi first-image.iso
```

Then create additional *.iso* images using the *-C* and *-M* options:

```
$ mkisofs -o second-image.iso -J -r -V Session2 -C `cdrecord dev=0,1,0 -msinfo` \
-M 0,1,0 /path-to-new-files
```

Then write the new *.iso* to disc, using the *-multi* option again:

```
$ cdrecord -v -eject dev=0,1,0 -multi  second-image.iso
```

Do this as many times as you like. When you get to the last session, omit the *-multi* option. It's important to close and fixate the disc, or it won't be readable in most drives. Another way to close and fixate the disc, without recording an additional session, is with the *fix* option:

```
$ cdrecord -v -fix  -eject dev=0,1,0
```

Discussion

CDs are written in *sessions*. Each session covers a number of disc *sectors*. On a single-session disc, there is a lead-in, a single TOC, the data, and a lead-out, which finalizes the disc and prevents further recording on the disc. *mkisofs* links multiple sessions together on a multisession disc. To do this, it needs to know the starting and ending sector numbers of each session. Let's take it a piece at a time:

```
$ mkisofs -o second-image.iso -J -r  -C `cdrecord dev=0,1,0 -msinfo` \
-M 0,1,0 /path-to-new-files
```

-o second-image.iso
> Give the new *.iso* you are building a name; call it anything you want.

-J
> Use Joliet naming conventions, for Windows compatibility. This is optional.

-r

> Use Rock Ridge naming conventions for Unix/Linux compatibility, and make all files publicly readable. This is required for creating multisession discs.

-C `cdrecord dev=0,1,0 -msinfo`

The *-C* flag goes by several names: *CD+, CDExtra, last_sess_start, next_sess_start*. It tells *mkisofs* the ending point of the last session and the starting point of the next session. The backticks tell the shell to find and use the values automatically. You can generate these values manually, and see for yourself:

```
$ cdrecord dev=0,1,0 -msinfo
12968,20172
```

-M 0,1,0

The *-M* flag must be used when you use the *-C* flag. This is the SCSI bus address of the CD writer.

/path-to-new-files

List here the files, or directory, that are going into the new *.iso*.

See Also

- *cdrecord(1), mkisofs(8)*

11.9   Creating a Bootable CD

Problem

You need to burn a bootable CD. You already have the boot image and data files.

Solution

The boot image needs to be rolled into the *.iso* with *mkisofs*.

If the bootable image is on a floppy disk, first make a *boot/* directory in the file tree that is going on the CD, and copy it there:

```
$ dd if=/dev/fd0 of=~/cd-files/boot/boot.img bs=10k count=144
```

Or copy it from another location on the hard drive:

```
$ cp boot.img  ~/cd-files/boot/boot.img
```

Then package the *.iso*:

```
$ mkisofs -r -b boot/boot.img -c boot/boot.catalog -o bootable-cd.iso ~/cd-files
```

Now burn it to disc with *cdrecord*, in the usual fashion, and you have a bootable CD.

Discussion

mkisofs uses the El Torito specification to create a boot image that fools a PC into thinking it's seeing a boot floppy. All you need is the boot image, and *mkisofs* creates the boot catalog.

The options are:

-r

> Set the file ownership and modes so that anyone can read the files.

-b boot/boot.img

> Specify the path and filename of the boot image. The *boot/* directory is relative to the root filesystem of the CD.

-c boot/boot.catalog

> Create and name the boot catalog file.

-o bootable-cd.iso ~/cd-files

> Name the new *.iso*, and give the path to the files that go into it.

See Also

- *mkisofs(8)*

11.10 Spanning a Large File over Several CDs

Problem

You have a very large file, such as a *tar* archive or a large graphical image, that you wish to store on CD. However, it is larger than a single disc.

Solution

Use the *split* utility to divide the file, then convert the new files to *.iso* images and burn them to discs. Use *cat* to reassemble the original file.

For example, here is a 2-GB *tar* archive named *big-backup*. This example splits it into 650-MB chunks. The CD capacity is 700 MB, but there must be room for file overhead:

```
$ split -b 650m big-backup.tar.gz
creating file `xaa'
creating file `xab'
creating file `xac'
```

Each file is now about 682 MB. Now convert each one to an *.iso* image:

```
$ for i in xa*; do echo -e "$i"; mkisofs -o $i.iso $i; done
```

This generates a lot of output. When it's finished, the *ls* command will show this:

```
$ ls
xaa  xaa.iso  xab  xab.iso  xac  xac.iso
```

Now you can transfer each one of the *.iso* files to its own CD:

```
$ cdrecord -v -eject dev=0,1,0 xaa.iso
$ cdrecord -v -eject dev=0,1,0 xab.iso
$ cdrecord -v -eject dev=0,1,0 xac.iso
```

To reassemble the tarball, copy the *.iso* files from the CD to your hard drive, and use the *cat* command:

```
$ cat xaa xab xac > big-backup.tar.gz
```

Or, append the contents of each CD to the archive on your hard drive one at a time, without having to copy them over first:

```
$ cat /cdrom/xaa > big-backup.tar.gz
$ cat /cdrom/xab >> big-backup.tar.gz
$ cat /cdrom/xac >> big-backup.tar.gz
```

You can name the reassembled file anything you like—just be sure to preserve the *tar.gz* extension. And you can now extract the archive:

```
$ tar xvzf big-backup.tar.gz
```

Discussion

This is a good way to make a quick and dirty backup, or to move a large number of files, but don't count on it for regular backups. If any of the split files become corrupted, it is difficult to recover the data, especially from compressed files.

See Chapter 16 to learn how to do large backups.

See Also

- *split(1), tar(1), cat(1)*
- Chapter 16, *Backup and Recovery*

11.11 Recording Data DVDs

Problem

You want to record data files on DVD, such as backups, image galleries, or Linux installation discs from *.iso* images.

Solution

Use *growisofs*, from *dvd+rw-tools*. Before you touch anything, make sure you do not have automount or supermount enabled for your DVD writer. Supermount/automount will guarantee a coaster.

Copying files from a hard drive to DVD is done in one step:

```
# growisofs -Z <device name> <mkisofs commands> <files>
```

For example:

```
# growisofs -Z dev=1,2,0 -dvd-compat -udf -R -J -v /home/carla
```

It is easy to add more files to the DVD. Always use the -Z option for the first batch of files written to the DVD, then use the -M flag for all additional files:

```
# growisofs -Z dev=1,2,0 -dvd-compat -udf -R -J -v /etc
# growisofs -M dev=1,2,0 -dvd-compat -udf -R -J -v /shared/projectfiles
# growisofs -M dev=1,2,0 -dvd-compat -udf -R -J -v /var/www/public_site
```

There's no need to explicitly close and fixate the disc.

You may also write .iso images; for example, when you want to create a Linux installation disc on DVD:

```
# growisofs -Z dev=1,2,0=KNOPPIX_V3.4-2004-05-17-EN.iso
```

Discussion

An increasing number of Linux distributions are becoming available on DVD-sized .isos, and none too soon, as some take up eight or more CDs.

growisofs replaces cdrecord, and is a frontend to mkisofs, so you get to use the same, familiar mkisofs options, with these two exceptions:

- Don't use -o to specify an output file, because growisofs writes directly to the DVD.

- Don't use -C, because growisofs figures out the starting and ending points of tracks all by itself.

-dvd-compat helps to ensure compatibility with the majority of DVD drives.

-udf adds limited udf support. As this was written, packet writing was still not reliably implemented in the Linux kernel. This can be left out, though the price of including it "just-in-case" is just a few bits of extra metadata.

There are RPMs, Debian packages, and tarballs for dvd+rw-tools. The tarball also includes a spec file, if you want to roll your own RPM.

It's not necessary to format new DVD-RW discs, because from version 5.10 growisofs does it automatically as you add files to the DVD. To get your version number, run:

```
$ growisofs --version
```

supermount is supposed to enable inserting and removing disks, like floppies, without having to enter mount and unmount commands. It is starting to appear on Red Hat, SuSE, and other distributions, and is usually enabled by default.

To disable supermount temporarily:

```
# /usr/sbin/supermount -i disable
```

Use -i enable to reenable it. Unfortunately, supermount doesn't work very reliably yet, so you might be better off disabling it permanently. Remove supermount entries from /etc/fstab to do so. To get rid of it with extreme prejudice, remove the *magicdev* package:

```
# rpm -q magicdev
```

or in Debian:

```
# apt-get remove magic-dev
```

See Also

- The *dvd+rw-tools* home page (*http://fy.chalmers.se/~appro/linux/DVD+RW*)

11.12 Recording an Audio CD for Standard CD Players

Problem

You want to know how to record audio CDs for playback on a standard audio disk player, like in your car. You need to know how to convert different audio file formats, such as *ogg-vorbis*, *mp3*, *.wav*, and *.cdr*, because these do not play on standard audio CD players, only on computers.

Solution

Use *sox*, *normalize*, and *cdrecord*. And use CD blanks that are made for audio recording.

The first step is to use *sox* to convert your sound files to *.cdr* format, to convert them to the correct file structure; then convert the *.cdr* to *.wav* format.

Then, the *-audio* option for *cdrecord* converts *.wav* files to CD-DA (Compact Disk Digital Audio) format, which is what standard audio CD players need.

```
$ sox soundfile filename.cdr
$ sox filename.cdr filename.wav
$ cdrecord -v -nofix -eject dev=0,1,0 -audio -pad filename.wav
```

The *-pad* options ensures that disk sectors will be filled correctly, and *-nofix* leaves the disk open for adding additional music tracks. To fix and close the disk:

```
$ cdrecord -v -fix  -eject dev=0,1,0
```

Converting files one at a time is tedious. This Bash command converts a batch of *.ogg* files to *.cdr* format:

```
$ for i in *.ogg ; do echo $i ; sox $i ${i%%.ogg}.cdr ; echo ${i%%.ogg}.cdr;done
```

Simply substitute whatever file extensions you need to convert.

If you're compiling a collection of tracks from diverse sources, use the *normalize* utility to equalize sound volumes, with the *-m* (mixed-mode) option:

```
$ normalize -m /soundfiles/*.wav
```

There are many ways to select tracks to record. This command records all the *.wav*-formatted songs in the */home/songs* directory, in sorted order: numbers first, then alphabetic capitals, then alphabetic lowercase.

```
$ cdrecord -v -nofix -eject dev=0,1,0 -audio -pad /home/songs/*.wav
```

Or, you can change to the */songs* directory, then list individual songs:

```
$ cdrecord -v -nofix -eject dev=0,1,0 -audio -pad song1.wav song3.wav song7.wav
```

Be sure to use an audio CD-R made for playback in standard audio players.

Discussion

Newer versions of *sox* are supposed to support *.mp3*, but this isn't always the case. Run *sox -h* to see what formats it supports. If your particular version of *sox* will not convert *.mp3*s, use *mpg123* and *sox*:

```
$ mpg123 -b 10000 -s  filename.mp3  | sox -t raw -r 44100 -s -w -c 2 -filename.wav
```

-b 10000
> This sets the buffer size, in bytes.

-s

> The *-s* flag redirects to stdout, instead of trying to play the file.

sox -t raw -r 44100 -s -w -c 2
> This is the same as *.cdr* format, only all the specs are spelled out.

There is a limit of 99 songs per disk. They would have to be very short songs to actually stuff that many on to a CD. You could record about 30 Ramones songs, or a single Beethoven symphony, so it just depends.

If your music files are already in the *.wav* format, like the files you get from online music services, you probably don't need to convert them. However, not all *.wav* files have the correct structure for making CDRs; *cdrecord* will halt and give an error message if this is the case. Use *sox* to convert the errant *.wav* to *.cdr*, then *.cdr* to *.wav*.

.wav and *.flac* formats are the highest-quality digital audio formats. Always start with these, if you can. Then convert them to other formats as needed. The primary reason to convert is to save disk space, as *.wav* and *.flac* files are very large. An *.ogg* file is typically one-tenth the size of a *.wav* file.

Ogg Vorbis is an open, patent-free, audio encoding and streaming technology. It has no licensing fees or other restrictions that accompany patented, proprietary formats like MP3. It delivers decent sound quality in a compressed, lossy format. "Lossy" means bits are stripped away to reduce file sizes.

MP3 is also a compressed, lossy format of good quality. It's a patented, proprietary format, so there are restrictions on its use, the code is closed, and there are licensing fees for artists and distributors. Thomson and Fraunhofer, who control the MP3 format, are adding DRM (Digital Rights Management, or copy restriction) technology to the MP3 format.

See Also

- *cdrecord(1)*, *sox(1)*, *normalize(1)*

## CHAPTER 12

Managing the Bootloader and Multi-Booting

12.1 Introduction

Linux has two excellent bootloaders: GRUB (the Grand Unified Bootloader) and LILO (Linux Loader). GRUB is newer and more capable than the elder LILO. Both are flexible, configurable, and capable of managing complex boot scenarios, such as multibooting several different operating systems or different Linux kernels, and passing in boot-time kernel options.

If you're still running LILO, it might be worth considering migrating to GRUB. While they work similarly, there are four major differences that set GRUB apart:

- You can discover boot images, kernels, and root filesystems from the GRUB command shell.

- GRUB stores boot information in a filesystem, rather than in the master boot record (MBR).

- GRUB reads filesystems and kernel executables, rather than inflexibly restricting the user to disk geometry.

- And best of all, GRUB is completely operating system–independent. If you install GRUB into a separate boot partition, you can remove and reinstall operating systems to your heart's content, without having to reinstall the bootloader every time.

Both GRUB and LILO can boot non-Linux operating systems, such as Windows, OS/2, the BSD Unixes, and so forth. For operating systems that they cannot boot directly, such as Windows, GRUB and LILO employ *chain loading*. That is, they point the way to Windows's own bootloader.

The MBR is the first 512 bytes of the first sector of the first partition on the drive. It contains the partition table and the first-stage bootloader. The first-stage loader is a wee bit of code stored in the first 446 bytes of the MBR, which points the way to the second-stage loader, which is stored in the */boot* directory. The remaining 66 bytes are for the partition table.

Linux partitioning is limited to 63 total partitions per IDE drive: 3 primary partitions, with the 4th containing up to 60 logical partitions in a single extended partition.

SCSI drives are limited to 15 partitions per drive: 3 usable primary partitions, and 12 logical partitions in a single extended partition.

12.2   Migrating from LILO to GRUB

Problem

You've read the advantages of GRUB in the previous section. You are using LILO and would like to replace it with GRUB, preferably without needing to overhaul your entire system.

Solution

GRUB can be installed without disrupting anything.

First, install GRUB, or upgrade to the latest version. To get the version number, use:

```
$ grub --version
grub (GNU GRUB 0.94)
```

Then, take a few preparatory steps:

1. Make a hard copy of your partition table (*fdisk -l | lpr*).
2. Make a hard copy of *lilo.conf*.
3. Back up your data and have a rescue disk, like a LILO boot diskette or Knoppix, at hand.
4. Leave your LILO installation intact, in case you want it back.

Next, follow these steps, in order:

1. Create a GRUB boot diskette.
2. Install GRUB to the MBR.
3. Boot the system.
4. Edit GRUB's configuration file, *menu.lst*.

To create a boot floppy, find the */grub/i386* directory. The official location is */usr/lib/grub/i386-pc*. Red Hat uses */usr/share/grub/i386-pc*, and other distributions may vary as well. Copy the *stage1* and *stage2* files to the diskette with *dd*:

```
$ dd if=stage1 of=/dev/fd0 bs=512 count=1
1+0 records in
1+0 records out
512 bytes transferred in 0.550740 seconds (930 bytes/sec)
$ dd if=stage2 of=/dev/fd0 bs=512 seek=1
209+1 records in
```

```
209+1 records out
107250 bytes transferred in 6.889581 seconds (15567 bytes/sec)
$
```

Now reboot to the diskette. You will be greeted by the nice blue GRUB screen:

```
GRUB version 0.93 (640K lower / 3072K upper memory)

[ Minimal BASH-like line editing is supported. For the first word, TAB lists possible
command completions. Anywhere else TAB lists the possible completions of a device/
filename. ]

grub>
```

Next, you need to find the *root device,* which is the partition that contains GRUB's first- and second-stage boot files:

```
grub> find /boot/grub/stage1
  (hd0,0)
```

This value is our root device. Set the root device:

```
grub> root (hd0,0)
```

Note that GRUB has its own partition numbering scheme. *hd0,0* is the same as */dev/ hda1.* (See the "Discussion" section of this recipe for details.)

Now install GRUB to the MBR, which is the first sector of the first drive:

```
grub> setup (hd0)
```

Now it is time to finish booting. Again, set the root device:

```
grub> root (hd0,0)
```

Next, enter the path to the kernel and the path to the root filesystem. These are in *lilo.conf.* Be sure to append *ro,* to mount the kernel and root filesystem read-only:

```
grub> kernel /boot/vmlinuz-2.4.21 root=/dev/hda1 ro
```

Don't confuse "root" on the kernel line with the root device. "Root" on the kernel line identifies the root filesystem. The root device is the partition containing the */boot* directory.

This step applies only to systems that require a *ramdisk* to boot. Enter the path to the *initrd* image, which should also be in *lilo.conf*:

```
grub> initrd /boot/initrd-2.4.21.img
```

Finally, enter the *boot* command, and the system should start normally:

```
grub> boot
```

If your root and kernel parameters do not work, see Recipe 12.7 for how to find them from the GRUB command shell.

Now you'll probably want to create the GRUB boot menu. See Recipe 12.9 for details.

Discussion

Always test your rescue disks before you need them.

GRUB uses its own partition numbering scheme; it starts from 0, instead of 1. Both SCSI and IDE drives are represented by *hd*. Floppy drives are *fd*.

This is the Linux partition table:

1–4	Primary partitions
5 and up	Extended partitions

In GRUB, it's like this:

0–3	Primary partitions
4 and up	Extended partitions

Additional drives are *hd1*, *hd2*, and so on. So *hd0,3* is the same as */dev/hda4*; *hd1,5* is */dev/hdb6*.

Note that the root device uses GRUB's numbering system:

```
grub> root (hd0,0)
```

and the root filesystem, which is specified on the kernel line, does not:

```
grub> kernel /boot/vmlinuz-2.4.21 ro root=/dev/hda1
```

See Also

- This chapter's "Introduction" for a comparison of GRUB and LILO
- Recipe 12.7, "Discovering Boot Parameters from the GRUB Command Shell"
- Recipe 12.9, "Creating the GRUB Boot Menu"
- The GRUB Manual (*http://www.gnu.org/software/grub/manual/grub.html*)
- *info grub*

12.3   Installing GRUB Without a Floppy Disk

Problem

You would like to install GRUB, but your system does not have a floppy drive. Or you have a floppy drive but can't find a usable floppy disk.

Solution

Use GRUB's own command shell to set it up.

First, install GRUB, or upgrade to the latest version. To get the version number, use:

```
$ grub --version
grub (GNU GRUB 0.94)
```

Next, take a few preparatory steps:

1. Make a hard copy of your partition table (*fdisk -l | lpr*).
2. Make a hard copy of *lilo.conf*.
3. Back up your data and have a rescue disk, like Knoppix, at hand.
4. Leave your LILO installation intact, in case you want it back.

Then open a root shell on your Linux system, and start up a GRUB shell:

```
# grub
Probing devices to guess BIOS drives. This may take a long time.

GNU GRUB  version 0.94  (640K lower / 3072K upper memory)
[ Minimal BASH-like line editing is supported.  For the first word, TAB lists
possible command completions. Anywhere else TAB lists the possible completions of a
device/filename. ]

grub>
```

Find the *stage1* loader:

```
grub> find /boot/grub/stage1
 (hd0,0)
```

Now run these three commands:

```
grub> root (hd0,0)
grub> setup (hd0)
grub> quit
```

Reboot, and you will be greeted by the GRUB command shell.

You'll probably want to boot into Linux and create a GRUB boot menu. See Recipes 12.7 and 12.9 to learn how to do this.

Discussion

This is what happened with those three little commands:

grub> root (hd0,0)	Set the root device.
grub> setup (hd0)	Install GRUB to the MBR.
grub> quit	Exit GRUB.

You will see output similar to this:

```
grub> root (hd0,0)
 Filesystem type is reiserfs, partition type 0x83

grub> setup (hd0)
 checking if "/boot/grub/stage1" exists...yes
 checking if "/boot/grub/stage2" exists...yes
 checking if "/boot/grub/e2fs_stage1_5" exists...yes
 Running "embed /boot/grub/e2fs_stage1_5 (hd0)"... 15
 sectors are embedded.
 Succeeded.
```

```
Running "install /boot/grub/stage1 (hd0) (hd0)1+15 p
(hd0,0)/boot/grub/stage2 /boot/grub/menu.lst"...Succeeded

grub> quit
```

See Also

- Recipe 12.7, "Discovering Boot Parameters from the GRUB Command Shell"
- Recipe 12.9, "Creating the GRUB Boot Menu"
- The GRUB Manual (*http://www.gnu.org/software/grub/manual/grub.html*)
- *info grub*

12.4   Installing GRUB with grub-install

Problem

Recipe 12.3 does not work on your Debian, Gentoo, or other Linux system, because the GRUB files are installed into */usr/lib/grub*. Or maybe you just want a simpler method for installing GRUB without a floppy disk.

Solution

Use GRUB's built-in installation script, *grub-install*.

First, install GRUB, or upgrade to the latest version. To get the version number, use:

```
$ grub --version
grub (GNU GRUB 0.94)
```

Then run *grub-install*. When you have a separate */boot* partition, you must specify it:

```
# grub-install --root-directory=/boot   /dev/hda
```

Otherwise, all you need is the device name for the drive:

```
# grub-install   /dev/hda
```

Then run:

```
# update-grub
```

This creates a new *menu.lst*. When you reboot, the GRUB menu will appear and your system will boot normally.

Discussion

update-grub probably won't create a complete *menu.lst* on a multiboot system, but it will enable you to boot into Linux. Then you can add your other operating systems to *menu.lst*.

See Also

- *grub-install(8)*
- *info grub*
- The GRUB Manual (*http://www.gnu.org/software/grub/manual/grub.html*)

12.5 Preparing a System for Multibooting Linux

Problem

You plan to multiboot several different Linux distributions, and you want to prepare your system. You want a standalone */boot* partition and shared */home* and */swap* partitions.

Solution

Most Linux distributions let you customize the partitioning during installation. Create new partitions only as you need them during each installation, and leave free space for additional installations.

Let's walk through a clean Fedora installation on a 20-GB IDE drive, using this partitioning scheme:

/dev/hda1	Primary	100 MB	*/boot*
/dev/hda2	Primary	2,500 MB	*/*
/dev/hda3	Primary	3,000 MB	*/home*
/dev/hda4	Extended		
/dev/hda5		256 MB	*/swap*
Free space		14,144 MB	

Here are the steps:

1. Boot up the first installation CD. Select your keyboard, mouse, and display. When you get to the Disk Partitioning Setup window, select "Manually partition with Disk Druid." A nice graphical display shows your hard drive.

2. Delete any existing partitions. Highlight them one at a time, then click the "delete" button.

3. Next, highlight "Free Space," and click "New." The mountpoint is */boot*. Select Ext2 for the filesystem, and enter the partition size. One hundred megabytes is the minimum Fedora will accept for */boot*. Click OK. That is now */dev/hda1*.

4. Highlight "Free Space" again and click "New." The mountpoint is /. Select Ext3, 2500 MB. Click OK. That's */dev/hda2*.

5. Highlight "Free Space" again and click "New." The mountpoint is */home*. Select Ext3, 3000 MB. Click OK. That's */dev/hda3*.

6. Highlight "Free Space" again and click "New." Scroll down "filesystem options" until you find "swap." There is no mountpoint; make it 256 MB. Click OK. This is */dev/hda5*.

7. At this point you may go back and make changes, because the new partition table has not yet been written to disk. When you're finished, write the changes to disk by clicking OK in the main Disk Druid menu.

Now you can continue with the installation. Make sure that you install GRUB, not LILO. When you install additional Linuxes, they will share */home* and */swap*. You can install any number of Linuxes, until your disk is full or you have used all available partitions.

Discussion

Most modern Linux distributions install GRUB by default. Make sure you don't install LILO.

QTParted is an excellent graphical utility for creating, deleting, moving, and resizing disk partitions. QTParted is included on Knoppix, so you can set up your partitioning before installing a new Linux, if you prefer. You can also make changes after installation, even to partitions with data on them. Of course, you must have good backups first. QTParted does a good job, but messing with partitions can backfire.

Putting */swap* on its own partition improves performance, and it can be shared on a multiboot system. Giving */home* its own partition lets you share it between the different Linux systems you're running, and it allows you to do all sorts of system installations and removals without forcing you to restore your data from backup every time.

Linux partitioning is limited to 63 partitions per IDE drive: 3 usable primary partitions, with the 4th containing up to 60 logical partitions in a single extended partition.

SCSI drives are limited to 15 partitions per drive: 3 usable primary partitions, and 12 logical partitions in a single extended partition.

See Also

- *fdisk(8)*
- Chapter 13, *System Rescue and Recovery with Knoppix*
- QTParted home page (*http://qtparted.sourceforge.net*)

12.6   Adding More Linuxes to a Multiboot System

Problem

You have your nice new boot partition all set up, and your first Linux installed. Now you're ready to add more Linuxes.

Solution

Install additional Linuxes into logical partitions. Then you'll need to create GRUB boot menu entries for each one.

First, prepare the system according to Recipe 12.5.

Next, boot the installation CD of the second Linux. This example uses Libranet Debian for the second Linux. When you get to the disk partitioning menu, select "Partition & layout drives." You will then see a menu showing the existing disk partitions. Highlight "Free" and select "New." Enter 2500 MB for the partition size. The mountpoint is /. Choose your filesystem type, and make sure "Initialize?" is checked. This is now */dev/hda6*.

Select */dev/hda3* to "Modify." Select */home* and Ext3, and do *not* check "Initialize?"

You may now go back and make changes to the partitioning, or select "Write" to write your new partition table to disk. After you select "Write," a warning will appear: "ALL EXISTING DATA ON THESE PARTITIONS WILL BE DESTROYED," with a list of partitions that are going to be formatted, or "initialized." Only / should be listed here.

Continue with the installation. When you get to the bootloader installation menu, do not overwrite the MBR. The installer will ask, "Do you want Linux to handle booting your system?" Say no. You want the boot files installed to the first sector of the root partition, which is */dev/hda6*.

When Libranet requires a reboot, bring up the GRUB command shell at boot, and boot Libranet manually:

```
grub> root (hd0,0)
grub> kernel /boot/vmlinuz-2.4.21 root=/dev/hda6 ro
grub> boot
```

(See Recipe 12.7 to learn how to discover the boot parameters from GRUB.)

When everything is working satisfactorily, edit *menu.lst* to add the new system to the GRUB boot menu. (See Recipe 12.9.)

Write down the partitions you create during installation; it will help when you edit *menu.lst*.

Discussion

The Libranet installer will automatically find any existing swap partitions; you don't need to select them during installation.

You can edit *menu.lst* from any of your new Linuxes. Simply mount the boot partition, and there it is:

```
# mkdir /bootpartition
# mount /dev/hda1  /bootpartition
# vim /bootpartition/boot/grub/menu.lst
```

This highlights some of the benefits of using a boot partition—you always know where it is, and it is safely isolated from your root filesystems.

Partitioning is probably the most complicated part of building a multiboot system. Use logical partitions as much as possible. With only four primary partitions available per physical hard disk, you'll run out pretty quickly if you don't.

See Also

- The GRUB Manual (*http://www.gnu.org/software/grub/manual/grub.html*)
- *info grub*

12.7   Discovering Boot Parameters from the GRUB Command Shell

Problem

You don't know the locations of Linux kernels and root devices on your system, and you need to find them so you can boot the system.

Solution

Use GRUB's tab completion to find root devices and kernel images.

First, boot to the GRUB command shell by hitting *c* when GRUB starts up.

To find the root device (partition containing */boot*), type *root (hd0* and hit the Tab key until you see some partitions displayed:

```
grub> root (hd0,<tab>
  Possible partitions are:
     Partition num: 0, Filesystem type is ext2fs, partition type 0x83
     Partition num: 1, Filesystem type is ext2fs, partition type 0x83
```

When there are several partitions displayed, and you are not sure which one you want, it does not hurt to try them all. First, try *(hd0,0)*:

```
grub> root (hd0,0)
  Filesystem type is ext2fs, partition type 0x83
```

Then search for the kernel image. Type *kernel /boot/vmlinuz*, and hit Tab. If there is no */boot/vmlinuz*, GRUB will tell you:

```
grub> kernel /boot/vmlinuz<tab>
  Error 15: File not found
```

If this happens, reset the root device to the other partition, and look for a kernel image there:

```
grub> root (hd0,1)
  Filesystem type is ext2fs, partition type 0x83
```

```
grub> kernel /boot/vmlinuz<tab>
  possible files are: vmlinuz vmlinuz-2.4.21
```

Okay, you've found a kernel. Type the path to the kernel and the root filesystem:

```
grub> kernel /boot/vmlinuz-2.4.21 ro root=/dev/hda2
```

Remember, GRUB's partition numbering starts from zero, so *hd0,1* = */dev/hda2*.

These next two steps apply only to systems that require a *ramdisk* to boot. Find *initrd*:

```
grub> find /boot/init<tab>
grub> find /boot/initrd-2.4.22-1.img
```

Load the *initrd* image:

```
grub> initrd /boot/initrd-2.4.22-1.img
```

Now you can boot up:

```
grub> boot
```

And the system should start normally.

Discussion

If you are not sure that the usual kernel naming conventions were followed, have GRUB display the entire contents of */boot*. Type *kernel /boot/*, and hit tab:

```
grub> kernel /boot/<tab>
  System.map  System.map-2.4.21  System.map-2.6.3  boot  grub  config-2.4.21  config-
  2.6.3  splash.xpm.gz  vmlinuz  vmlinuz-2.4.21  kernel-of-truth-2.6.3
```

Well, it looks like we have a wackily-named 2.6 kernel, "kernel-of-truth-2.6.3." Regardless of the silly name, it should work just like its more soberly named cousins.

With tab completion, you can easily search entire filesystems. This is useful for exploring unfamiliar systems, as you can start from the root:

```
grub> root (hd0,6)
grub> find /<tab>
  Possible files are bin dev etc lib mnt opt tmp sys var usr boot home proc sbin root
  cdrom floppy initrd
```

However, this is a big security hole, as anyone with access to the GRUB command shell can read any file on the system with *cat*:

```
grub> cat /root/secretpersonalstuff.txt
grub> cat /etc/shadow
```

To close this hole, see Recipe 12.14 to learn how to password-protect GRUB.

GRUB will find root devices and kernels anywhere they may be. Suppose, for example, you have two IDE hard drives. The second drive has a Linux root filesystem installed on */dev/hdb5*. Boot it this way:

```
grub> root (hd1,4)
grub> kernel /boot/vmlinuz-2.4.21 ro root=/dev/hdb5
grub> boot
```

On an unfamiliar system, you can have GRUB detect all installed hard drives:

```
grub> root (hd <tab>
   Possible disks are:   hd0  hd1
```

See Also

- The GRUB Manual (*http://www.gnu.org/software/grub/manual/grub.html*)
- *info grub*

12.8   Configuring the Boot Partition

Problem

Because you are using a boot partition, instead of a */boot* directory on the root file-system, you're not sure that the filepaths are correct.

Solution

Use *df* to see what partitions your filesystems are on. You'll need to make sure any partitions you want to check are mounted.

First, you can verify that your filesystems are installed to the correct partitions with *df*:

```
$ df -h
Filesystem    Size    Used    Available  Use% Mounted on
/dev/hda2     2.5G    1.5G    1G         60%  /
/dev/hda1     100M    30M     70M        30%  /boot
```

Now, verify that the file tree in the boot partition is correct, look for */boot/boot*:

```
$ ls /boot
System.map-2.4.21  boot  grub  config  splash.xpm.gz  vmlinuz  vmlinuz-2.4.21
```

If there is not a */boot/boot* directory, create one, and copy over the files from the parent directory:

```
# cp -av /boot/ /boot/boot/
```

Some distributions, such as Debian, create a */boot* soft link to the parent directory:

```
$ cd /boot
$ ls -al boot
lrwxrwxrwx  1 root  root  1 Apr  16  08:50  /boot/boot -> .
```

It is okay to leave this alone and not create a new */boot* directory, even though this link creates an endless loop in the file tree. It's another way to ensure having a */boot* directory in the boot partition.

Discussion

Confused over all these *boot*s? Just keep in mind that a partition name is not a directory name, because a partition is not a directory, and a mountpoint can be given any

---

name. GRUB knows nothing about mountpoints—it reads filesystems before they are mounted. So if there is not a */boot* directory in the boot partition, GRUB does not see */boot/grub*, but */grub*. While it's not strictly necessary to have a */boot* directory, following this convention will make your life a lot easier.

See Also

- The GRUB Manual (*http://www.gnu.org/software/grub/manual/grub.html*)
- *info grub*

12.9   Creating the GRUB Boot Menu

Problem

As fun as it is to discover root devices and kernels from the GRUB command line, you would like to preserve your boot parameters in a configuration file and have a nice boot menu to use at startup. In this menu you will configure your chosen defaults, and have a menu of all of your installed operating systems to choose from.

Solution

Add boot entries to GRUB's configuration file, */boot/grub/menu.lst*. (Red Hat uses *grub.conf* and creates a soft link named *menu.lst*.)

GRUB calls the different boot entries *stanzas*. Here is a basic configuration:

```
title          Fedora 1 core
root           (hd0,0)
kernel         /boot/vmlinuz-2.4.22-1 root=/dev/hda1 ro
initrd         /boot/initrd-2.4.22-1.img
```

The title can be anything at all, and you must have one—it tells GRUB where each stanza starts, and it appears in the boot menu. The other two lines are the same values we used on the GRUB command line. It is not necessary to use the *boot* command in *menu.lst*.

You can list as many operating systems as you want; each one requires a stanza like this one. Make sure the kernel line points to the right partition and kernel executable. It's common to have several bootable kernels in the same root partition. And it is common (even good) for all the boot configurations to use the same boot partition.

Not all Linux distributions require a *ramdisk*, which is loaded by the *initrd* image. If */boot/initrd-** exists, you must use it.

Discussion

Remember that the root device, indicated by:

```
root           (hd0,0)
```

is the location of the */boot* directory, and *hd0,0* is GRUB's own numbering system. On the kernel line:

```
kernel      /boot/vmlinuz-2.4.22-1 root=/dev/hda2 ro
```

root is the root filesystem, using the kernel *dev* name.

See Also

- The GRUB Manual (*http://www.gnu.org/software/grub/manual/grub.html*)
- *info grub*

12.10 Customizing menu.lst

Problem

You want to change the look of the GRUB menu, and customize options such as timeouts and default boot entries.

Solution

Make your customizations in */boot/grub/menu.lst*. (Some systems use *grub.conf*.)

There are two sections: the global settings and the boot stanzas. Colors, timeouts, and default boot entries are defined in the global section.

This is a complete sample *menu.lst*, including global configuration options:

```
##GRUB configuration for windbag, created 10-22-2003
## global settings

## default num
default    0

## timeout sec
timeout    5

# Pretty colors
color cyan/blue white/blue

# Display a splash screen
splashimage (hd0,0)/boot/splash.xpm.gz
foreground    bbbbbb
background    000000

### Boot menu
## default
title    Libranet GNU/Linux, kernel 2.4.21
root     (hd0,0)
kernel   /boot/vmlinuz-2.4.21 root=/dev/hda1 ro hdb=scsi hdc=scsi
```

```
### new 2.6 test kernel
title     Libranet GNU/Linux, kernel 2.6.3-test1
root      (hd0,0)
kernel    /boot/bzImage-2.6.3-test1 root=/dev/hda1 ro

## Stock Red Hat 9
title       Red Hat 9
root        (hd0,4)
kernel      /boot/vmlinuz-2.4.22-1 root=/dev/hda5 ro
initrd      /boot/initrd-2.4.22-1.img
```

Discussion

These are definitions for the global configuration options:

default 0

> Sets your default boot entry. Stanzas are read in order, starting from zero, so *default 0* selects the first one.

timeout 5

> Specifies how long to wait before the default entry boots.

color cyan/blue white/blue

> Configures the colors for the GRUB boot menu. *cyan/blue* defines the foreground and background colors. *white/blue* defines the highlight colors for lines of text selected by the cursor. The available colors are listed in the GRUB manual and *info grub*.

splashimage (hd0,0)/boot/splash.xpm.gz
foreground bbbbbb
background 000000

> Yes, you can replace the splash screen that came with your distribution with an image of your choosing. (See Recipe 12.16 for how to create the image.) Use the *splashimage* option to set the filepath to the image. You'll also need to configure the foreground and background colors for the fonts, using standard HTML hex color codes.

Another *default* choice is *default saved*. When you use *default saved*, you must also add *savedefault* to the boot stanzas, like this:

```
title     Libranet GNU/Linux, kernel 2.4.21
root      (hd0,0)
kernel    /boot/vmlinuz-2.4.21 ro root=/dev/hda1
savedefault
```

This makes the last item booted the default for the next boot. Many distributions configure the boot stanzas to include *savedefault*, but they don't add *default saved*, so it doesn't work.

See Also

- The GRUB Manual (*http://www.gnu.org/software/grub/manual/grub.html*)
- *info grub*
- Recipe 12.16, "Creating a GRUB Splash Image"

12.11 Adding Windows 95/98/ME to a Linux System

Problem

You have a single computer, and you would like to dual-boot Windows 95/98/ME and Linux, because you use applications on both platforms. Or you have a small test network, and you want to install as many operating systems are you can in multi-boot configurations, so that you can test different combinations of operating systems without using a lot of computers. Or you already tried to add Windows 95/98/ME to your nice new Linux multiboot system, but it didn't even install—it complained about not being able to format the C: drive, which is a good thing, because it would have overwritten your Linux installations. You don't want to use an emulator like VMWare, which lets you run both at the same time without rebooting, because it's too expensive, or your hardware is too feeble.

Solution

There are a number of tricky bits to adding Windows 95/98/ME to a Linux system. You'll need to hide partitions, and restore GRUB to the MBR after the Windows installation, because Windows overwrites the bootloader. Windows 95/98/ME must have a primary partition prepared in advance. Unfortunately, GRUB does not boot CD-ROMs, so you'll need a Windows Startup diskette. (This is a very useful disk for all versions of Windows.) If you don't have one, it is easy to make one from 98 or ME:

1. Load a new, blank diskette.
2. Go to Control Panel → Add/Remove Programs.
3. Click on the Startup Disk tab.
4. Click on the Create Disk button.

Write-protect the disk, and it's ready to go.

To install Windows 95/98/ME on */dev/hda4*:

1. Boot to the GRUB command shell.
2. Insert the Windows 98 Startup diskette.
3. At the GRUB command line, hide all of your existing partitions:

```
grub> hide (hd0,0)
grub> hide (hd0,1)
grub> hide (hd0,2)
```

4. Now boot the Windows diskette:

```
grub> chainloader (fd0) +1
grub> boot
```

Be sure to enable CD-ROM support as the diskette boots.

5. Use MS-DOS *fdisk* on the Windows rescue diskette to create a primary DOS partition for Windows. When you're finished partitioning and back at the *A:\>* prompt, insert the Windows installation CD, change to the *D:* drive, and start the Windows Setup program:

```
A:\> D:
D:\> setup
```

6. Windows will overwrite the MBR, which is convenient for getting through the many reboots. When it's done, restore GRUB to the MBR. Boot to your GRUB floppy, and run the following comands:

```
grub> root (hd0,0)
grub> setup (hd0)
```

7. Remove the GRUB diskette and reboot, and your GRUB menu will reappear. Boot to Linux so you can edit *menu.lst*:

```
title   Windows 98 on /dev/hda4
hide (hd0,0)
hide (hd0,1)
hide (hd0,2)
unhide (hd0,3)
rootnoverify(hd0,3)
makeactive
chainloader +1
```

Discussion

Let's look at the last three options more closely:

rootnoverify

Don't try to read or mount the partition.

makeactive

Set the bootable flag on the partition. Windows needs this.

chainloader +1

Points to the bootloader of operating systems that GRUB does not directly support, like Windows.

If you're thinking "Wow, this sounds like a lot of work," you are right. There is an easier way to dual-boot Windows 95/98/ME with Linux: install Windows 95/98/ME first, then add Linux. If you install Linux last, the installer will load GRUB in the MBR for you and will automatically create an entry for Windows in the GRUB menu.

You cannot run more than one 95/98/ME, unless you use GRUB's partition-hiding on every one and have enough primary partitions to give each one its own.

See Also

- Microsoft Knowledge Base Article 217210: "How to Multiple Boot Windows XP, Windows 2000, Windows NT, Windows 95, Windows 98, Windows Me, and MS-DOS"
- Recipe 9.16, "Creating Linux Disk Partitions with fdisk"
- The GRUB Manual (*http://www.gnu.org/software/grub/manual/grub.html*)
- *info grub*

12.12 Adding Windows NT/2000/XP to a Multiboot System

Problem

You have a single computer and you would like to dual-boot Windows NT/2000/XP and Linux, because you use applications on both platforms. Or you have a small test network and you want to install as many operating systems as you can in multiboot configurations, so that you can test different combinations of operating systems without using a lot of computers. You don't want to use an emulator like VMWare, which lets you run both at the same time without rebooting, because it's too expensive or your hardware is too feeble. And you hope it's not as much hassle as Windows 95/98/ME.

Solution

Fear not, Windows NT/2000/XP is a lot easier. The installer is more intelligent—it will let you choose which partition to use, or create a new one. You can even add it to a system with Linux already installed, as long as you have enough free space and an unused primary partition.

Make a hard copy of your partition table, and note what you have installed on each partition. Windows won't recognize any of your Linux partitions, it will only print the sizes of them, so having it written down will help you keep track.

You won't need a boot floppy; just install it from CD like you normally would. When the installation is completed, you'll need to restore GRUB to the MBR. Load your GRUB boot floppy, then do:

```
grub> root (hd0,0)
grub> setup (hd0)
grub> reboot
```

Remove the boot floppy, reboot, and your GRUB menu will reappear. Boot to Linux, and create a *menu.lst* entry for Windows:

```
title          WindowsXP on /dev/hda4
rootnoverify   (hd0,3)
makeactive
chainloader +1
```

It is not necessary to hide partitions from Windows NT/2000/XP.

Discussion

When you want to multiboot more than one version of Windows, start with the oldest, and install them in sequence from oldest to newest. You can install only one of Windows 95/98/ME, because it does not support multibooting. Windows NT/2000/XP all support multibooting.

You can use a single primary partition for all of your Windows versions, by dividing it into several logical partitions. Use the Windows NT/2000/XP installer to do the partitioning and formatting; don't use Linux *fdisk*.

See Also

- Microsoft Knowledge Base Article 217210: "How to Multiple Boot Windows XP, Windows 2000, Windows NT, Windows 95, Windows 98, Windows Me, and MS-DOS"
- The GRUB Manual (*http://www.gnu.org/software/grub/manual/grub.html*)
- *info grub*
- Recipe 12.13, "Restoring GRUB to the MBR with a Knoppix CD"

12.13 Restoring GRUB to the MBR with a Knoppix CD

Problem

When you installed Windows on your Linux/Windows dual-boot system, Windows overwrote the MBR (master boot record), so your GRUB menu was replaced with the Windows boot menu, and now you can't boot to Linux. The GRUB documentation tells how to restore GRUB to the MBR, but it seems to assume that you have a floppy drive. And you don't. How can you restore GRUB to the MBR when your system does not have a floppy drive?

Solution

Use a Knoppix CD. Boot it up, and open a command shell. *su* to root—there is no password—and run GRUB:

```
# grub
Probing devices to guess BIOS drives. This may take a long time.
```

```
GNU GRUB  version 0.94  (640K lower / 3072K upper memory)
[ Minimal BASH-like line editing is supported.  For the first word, TAB lists
possible command completions. Anywhere else TAB lists the possible completions of a
device/filename. ]

grub>
```

Then run these three commands:

```
grub> root (hd0,0)
grub> setup (hd0)
grub> quit
```

When you reboot, your GRUB menu will reappear.

Discussion

Floppy drives are disappearing from all kinds of systems, especially laptops. Even the "desktop replacement" notebooks are omitting the floppy drive, in favor of combination CD-ROM/DVD-ROM/CD-R/RW drives.

See Also

- Knoppix home page (*http://www.knopper.net/*)
- The GRUB Manual (*http://www.gnu.org/software/grub/manual/grub.html*)
- *info grub*

12.14 Protecting System Files with a GRUB Password

Problem

You don't want your users to have access to the GRUB command shell, because they would be able to access all system files, regardless of permissions or access privileges.

Solution

Set a password in *menu.lst* to lock users out of the GRUB command shell.

First, from a Bash shell, use *grub-md5-crypt* to generate a hashed password:

```
# grub-md5-crypt
Password:
Retype password:
$1$RiAfJO$QTuAlS/BGqlkYHQADZejs1
```

Now paste the encrypted password into *menu.lst,* in the global configuration part, before the boot stanzas:

```
password --md5 $1$RiAfJO$QTuAlS/BGqlkYHQADZejs1
```

You can also use a plain text password, like this:

```
password bigsecretword
```

Obviously, this is less secure. If you use plain text, restrict file permissions to root only:

```
# chmod 600 menu.lst
```

When the system boots and the GRUB menu appears, hit *p* to enter the password and unlock the command shell. Users without the password will only be able to make selections from the boot menu; they will not have access to the GRUB command shell.

Discussion

File access permissions are attributes of the filesystem. GRUB operates outside of filesystems, so anyone with access to the GRUB command shell can read any file on the system.

If you lose your GRUB password, it's not the end of the world, because you can boot with a rescue disk and edit *menu.lst*—which illustrates the ancient Unix security dictum, "anyone with physical access to the box owns it."

See Also

- The GRUB Manual (*http://www.gnu.org/software/grub/manual/grub.html*)
- *info grub*

12.15 Locking Out Users from Individual GRUB Menu Entries

Problem

Your GRUB menu contains several entries. You don't want any user to be able to boot any entry; you would like to lock out users from some of the entries.

Solution

First set up a GRUB password (Recipe 12.14), then use the *lock* command in *menu.lst*:

```
title   Libranet GNU/Linux, kernel 2.4.21, single user mode
lock
root    (hd0,0)
kernel  /boot/vmlinuz-2.4.21 root=/dev/hda1 ro single
```

GRUB reads *menu.lst* in order, so everything after *lock* is blocked from users who do not have the password. Don't lock out the title, or no one will be able to boot to this entry. Users without the password will only be able to boot to unlocked entries. If they try locked entries, they will get an error message:

```
Error 32: Must be authenticated
```

It's a good idea to use titles that tell users which ones are restricted:

```
Libranet GNU/Linux, kernel 2.4.21, single user mode, AUTHENTICATION REQUIRED
```

Discussion

Using a GRUB password and *lock* is useful on shared workstations—for example, in classrooms, training labs, and the workplace. However, anyone with physical access to the box can use a bootable rescue disk to gain unrestricted access. This can be foiled by disabling the rescue disks in the system BIOS, but don't forget how many different boot devices there are now: floppy disks, CDs, USB devices, SuperDisks, Jaz/Zip disks, Ethernet Wake-on-LAN, and probably some more I haven't thought of. Then set a BIOS password when you're done.

Still, a determined user can open the case and reset the BIOS password with a jumper on the motherboard. You could put a physical lock on the case, but even then a really determined person could haul the whole works out the door.

How far you need to go on boot security is obviously something you need to evaluate for your particular situation.

See Also

- The GRUB Manual (*http://www.gnu.org/software/grub/manual/grub.html*)
- *info grub*

12.16 Creating a GRUB Splash Image

Problem

You're totally bored with the default GRUB splash screen that came with your distribution, and you'd like to use an image that you created.

Solution

You can create a GRUB splash image from any kind of image file. You must convert the image to a specific format and size, then make an entry in *menu.lst* that points to the image.

GRUB splash images must meet these specs:

- *xpm.gz* file type
- 640 × 480
- 14 colors only

Start with an image of your own creation, at least 640 × 480, in any graphical file format. Use ImageMagick and *gzip* to do the rest. In this example, we'll convert a *.jpg*:

```
$ convert -depth 14 -resize 640x480 image.jpg newimage.xpm && gzip newimage.xpm
```

Move the new file, *newimage.xpm.gz*, to the */boot* directory. Edit *menu.lst*, and add (or edit) an entry for the splash image:

```
# Display a splash screen
splashimage (hd0,5)/boot/newimage.xpm.gz
```

When you reboot, the GRUB menu will be adorned with your nice, new custom splash screen.

Discussion

ImageMagick does not create a backup of your original image, so you'll probably want to work from a copy.

ImageMagick is a suite of command-line utilities:

> *animate*
> *composite*
> *conjure*
> *convert*
> *display*
> *identify*
> *import*
> *mogrify*
> *montage*

There is no "imagemagick" command. See *imagemagick(1)* for full details.

Try a Google search on "grub splashimage" to find all sorts of interesting online splash image galleries, as well as tips and tricks for creating them.

See Also

- *imagemagick(1), gzip(1), info grub*
- The GRUB Manual (*http://www.gnu.org/software/grub/manual/grub.html*)

12.17 Booting Linux with LILO

Problem

You want to use LILO and need to know how to configure it to boot a Linux system.

Solution

Use *liloconfig* to generate a basic *lilo.conf*, then edit *lilo.conf* to add comments, titles, and any additional options you want.

Make sure you have the latest version of LILO, and as always, have a current backup of your data and bootable rescue disks at hand:

```
# /sbin/lilo -V
LILO version 22.4.1
```

After installing/upgrading, run *liloconfig*:

```
# liloconfig
```

It asks many questions, and gives many instructions. In this example, the root filesystem is on */dev/hda3*. Say yes to these four questions:

```
Install a partition boot record to boot Linux from /dev/hda3?
Use LBA32 for addressing big disks using new BIOS features?
Install a master boot record on /dev/hda?
Make /dev/hda3 the active partition?
```

Run *lilo* to write the changes to the MBR:

```
# /sbin/lilo -v
```

Reboot to test it. When the system comes back up, you'll probably want to edit */etc/lilo.conf*, because *liloconfig* does a rather barebones job on the boot stanzas. Here is a sample *lilo.conf*, first generated by *liloconfig*, then edited:

```
# Specifies the boot device
boot=/dev/hda3
# Location of the map file. This is a binary
# file generated by lilo, don't touch it
map=/boot/map
# Video resolution for the boot screen
vga=normal
# the LILO boot screen
message = /boot/boot_message.txt
# Show the LILO prompt for ten seconds
# before booting the default
prompt
timeout=100
# Access large disks beyond cylinder 1024
lba32

# Boot menu #
# default boot entry
default="Libranet-hd3"

# Stable 2.4 kernel
image=/boot/vmlinuz-2.4.21
label="Libranet-hd3"
root=/dev/hda3
read-only
```

```
# Test 2.6 kernel
image=/boot/bzImage-2.6.3
label="2.6-test-hd3"
root=/dev/hda3
read-only
```

There is a limit of 16 different images that can be configured in *lilo.conf*.

Discussion

This is what the original *liloconfig*-generated boot stanzas looked like:

```
# These images were automagically added. You may need to edit something.

image=/boot/vmlinuz
label="DEB 0"
read-only

image=/boot/vmlinuz-2.4.21
label="DEB 1"
read-only

image=/boot/bzImage-2.6.3
label="DEB 2"
read-only
```

liloconfig is good for setting up your first *lilo.conf*; after that, it is easier and better to edit it manually. Let's take a look at the four *liloconfig* questions you answered yes to:

Install a partition boot record to boot Linux from /dev/hda3?
 This refers to where the */boot* directory is located, and it must be a primary partition.

Use LBA32 for addressing big disks using new BIOS features?
 Definitely say yes to this, unless you are using a system BIOS that does not support large-block addressing. Mainboards built in 1998 and after should support LBA32. This is the option that lets LILO boot partitions that are beyond the 1024-cylinder limit. The 1024-cylinder limit is a limitation of the x86 architecture; see "The Large Disk Howto" on *tldp.org* for details.

Install a master boot record on /dev/hda?
 LILO stores the first-stage bootloader in the MBR; this bootloader then points to your other partition boot records.

Make /dev/hda3 the active partition?
 This marks the partition as bootable, which Linux does not care about, but Windows does.

Any time you make changes to */etc/lilo.conf*, you must re-run LILO to write the changes to the MBR:

```
# /sbin/lilo -v
```

The *-v* flag turns on verbosity, with levels ranging from 1 to 5:

```
# /sbin/lilo -v5
```

Another useful flag is *-t*, for test. Use this with *-v* to see what will happen before actually writing the changes to disk:

```
# /sbin/lilo -t -v2
```

See Also

- *lilo(8)*, *lilo.conf(5)*
- */usr/doc/lilo*, or */usr/share/doc/lilo*
- "The Large Disk Howto" on *tldp.org*

12.18 Multibooting Linuxes with LILO

Problem

You would like to run several different Linuxes on a single PC, and you want LILO for the bootloader.

Solution

The first Linux installed is the "host" system. You need to preserve it to keep LILO working. Make sure that the root filesystem containing the */boot* directory is on a primary partition, or LILO won't work.

Write down the location of the partition where the root filesystem of your next Linux is going to be installed. If you also know the exact name of the kernel, and the *initrd* image (if there is one), you're ahead of the game. While you're still in the host Linux, you can create a *lilo.conf* entry for Linux #2:

```
# Red Hat 9
image=/boot/vmlinuz-2.4.22-1
initrd=/boot/initrd-2.4.22-1.img
label="Red Hat 9"
root=/dev/hda6
read-only
```

Then write the changes to the MBR:

```
# /sbin/lilo -v
```

Now you can go ahead and install Linux #2, and because you already have a LILO boot menu entry for it, you can glide through however many reboots it takes to complete the installation.

When the installer gets to the bootloader installation, be sure to select "install to the first sector of the root partition," or however your installer words it. Do not overwrite the MBR.

If you don't know the exact kernel name and *initrd* image, you'll have to discover them from the host Linux. Go ahead and start the installation of Linux #2. When it comes to the first reboot, you'll end up back in the host Linux. Mount the new Linux #2 filesystem and read the */boot* directory:

```
# mount /dev/hda6 /mnt/tmp
# cd /mnt/tmp
# ls boot
System.map  initrd-2.4.22-1.img  System.map-2.4.22-1  vmlinuz  vmlinuz-2.4.22-1
```

There's your kernel and *initrd*. Make your *lilo.conf* entry, re-run */sbin/lilo*, and reboot. Now you can select your new Linux from the bootloader menu and finish the installation.

Discussion

Sometimes a *ramdisk* is required for the system to boot properly. If this is the case, there will be an *initrd* image. Note that not all distributions require an *initrd* image. If it's in */boot*, it's needed, and it requires an entry in *lilo.conf*.

See Also

- *lilo(8)*, *lilo.conf(5)*
- */usr/doc/lilo*, or */usr/share/doc/lilo*

12.19 Multibooting Windows and Linux with LILO

Problem

You want to dual-boot Linux and Windows, or multiboot several versions of each.

Solution

The easy way is to first install all versions of Windows that you want to run on the system. Always install them in order, starting with the oldest. Save the fourth primary partition for Linux.

You may install only one of Windows 95/98/ME, because they do not support multibooting. Windows NT/2000/XP all support multibooting and will create entries for each installed Windows in the Windows bootloader.

Install Linux last. Make the fourth primary partition into an extended partition, then create a logical partition for Linux. During the Linux installation, install LILO to the MBR, and LILO will automatically create an entry for Windows. Here is an example of what *lilo.conf* will look like:

```
# Stable 2.4 kernel
image=/boot/vmlinuz-2.4.21
label="Libranet-hd3"
```

```
root=/dev/hda5
read-only

# Windows
other = /dev/hda1
  label = "Windowses"
  table = /dev/hda
```

There is only one entry for Windows, because LILO only needs to point to the Windows boot menu.

Discussion

When you have more than one Windows installed, the Windows bootloader will always stay with the first one. So if Windows 95 is installed on */dev/hda1*, and Windows 2000 is installed on */dev/hda2*, LILO still needs to point to */dev/hda1*.

See Also

- *lilo(8), lilo.conf(5)*
- */usr/doc/lilo*, or */usr/share/doc/lilo*
- Microsoft Knowledge Base Article 217210: "How to Multiple Boot Windows XP, Windows 2000, Windows NT, Windows 95, Windows 98, Windows Me, and MS-DOS"

12.20 Creating a LILO Boot Diskette

Problem

You would like to create a LILO boot diskette, for easy recovery in case of trouble.

Solution

Use LILO's built-in boot diskette creator:

```
# cd /usr/lib/lilo
# make -f Makefile.floppy
```

Be sure to write-protect the diskette.

Discussion

The Linux world contains an amazing number and variety of bootable rescue disks. As long as you can boot the system, you can fix anything. Be sure to check the installation disks for your distribution, because they often come with rescue utilities customized for the distribution, including utilities for reinstalling the bootloader.

- *lilo(8), lilo.conf(5)*
- */usr/doc/lilo*, or */usr/share/doc/lilo*

12.21 Password-Protecting LILO

Problem

You don't want your users messing around with your carefully crafted bootloader configuration. You also want to prevent them from exploiting LILO's ability to allow root access without a password, which can easily be done by entering:

```
linux single
```

or:

```
linux init=/bin/sh
```

at the LILO prompt.

Solution

First, restrict *lilo.conf* to root only:

```
# chmod 600 lilo.conf
```

Then password-protect LILO. In the global section of *lilo.conf*, make these entries:

```
password=""
restricted
```

Re-run LILO to write the changes:

```
# /sbin/lilo
```

It will ask you to enter a password. Give it your root password. It will then create a */etc/lilo.conf.shs* file, containing a password hash accessible only to root.

Now when the system reboots, anyone trying to enter *linux single* or *linux init=/bin/sh* at the LILO prompt will be asked for the password.

Discussion

For additional boot-time security, disable all external boot devices in the system BIOS, and use a BIOS password. This is not perfect—after all, as we showed in Recipes 12.14 and 12.15, "Anyone with physical access to a box owns it." But it's good enough to keep ordinary users from mucking up the works.

See Also

- *lilo(8), lilo.conf(5)*
- */usr/doc/lilo*, or */usr/share/doc/lilo*

12.22 Backing Up the MBR

Problem

You would like to have a backup copy of your master boot record. And what good is that backup if you don't know how to restore it?

Solution

You can back up the MBR to a floppy disk. Mount the disk first, using the mount-point appropriate for your system, then use the *dd* command:

```
# dd if=/dev/hda of=/floppy/mbr bs=512 count=1
```

Restore it this way:

```
# dd if=/floppy/mbr of=/dev/hda bs=512 count=1
```

The filename of your backup can be anything you like: for example, */mbr-server01* labels it so you know which computer it belongs to. You can store many MBRs on a single floppy disk:

```
# ls /floppy
lost+found  mbr-server01  mbr-workstation04  mbr-host15
```

If you need to format a floppy disk first, do this:

```
$ mke2fs /dev/fd0
```

This creates a nice Linux-formatted disk, using the Ext2 filesystem.

Discussion

The *dd* command does a literal, byte-by-byte copy. It doesn't need to understand filesystems, so it can be used to copy block devices, like */dev/hda*.

If your system does not have a floppy drive, you can restore a borked MBR with a Knoppix disk, by reinstalling GRUB (Recipe 12.13).

See Also

- *dd(1), mke2fs(8)*
- Recipe 12.13, "Restoring GRUB to the MBR with a Knoppix CD"

System Rescue and Recovery with Knoppix

13.1 Introduction

Facing a nonbooting system is one of life's less pleasant sensations. Knoppix, a complete Debian-based Linux distribution on a live, bootable CD, is a first-rate recovery disk. You get over 2 GB of Linux utilities and drivers, compressed onto a 700-MB CD. It has great hardware detection, supports all the major filesystems, automatically finds your existing partitions, creates mountpoints, and automatically finds your DHCP server. If you need to configure networking manually, it has a nice utility called *netcardconfig*. Knoppix can't be beat for ease of use. Just pop it in, boot it up, and everything works.

Knoppix can be downloaded as a 700-MB *.iso*, or you can purchase commercially produced CDs, which is nice for folks with slow or expensive Internet service.

A entire creative community has grown up around Knoppix; on Knoppix.net you'll find a large number of specialty projects inspired by Knoppix, and howtos for creating your own custom bootable live CD.

13.2 Booting Knoppix

Problem

You want to customize Knoppix's boot process. First, you need to find out what boot-time options Knoppix has.

Solution

To see all boot options, hit F2 at the prompt.

You can just pop Knoppix into the drive and let it boot itself, but there are a large number of boot-time options at your disposal. The default keyboard layout is German, so you might want to change it to your own locale:

```
knoppix lang=uk
```

The default desktop is KDE. You can choose a different one:

```
knoppix desktop=icewm
```

Or boot to a console, and not run X:

```
knoppix 2
```

You can speed up the boot process a bit by disabling hardware detection for things you don't have:

```
knoppix nopcmcia noscsi
```

To boot with minimal hardware detection, use:

```
failsafe
```

You can combine as many options as you need:

```
knoppix lang=uk desktop=icewm nopcmcia noscsi
```

Discussion

You'll need about 20 MB of RAM to boot console Knoppix, and a minimum of 96 MB to run an X session satisfactorily. To run KDE, you'd better have 256 MB of RAM. Knoppix will find and use the swap partition on the hard drive, if there is one.

The fun thing about Knoppix is that if you don't like how it booted, or you want to try something different, you don't have to bother with a graceful shutdown—just pull the plug and start over.

Knoppix glitches

Running programs from a CD can cause some odd troubles, especially on notebooks. It is common for power management to mess up a Knoppix session: when you wake up the machine, Knoppix doesn't respond to commands any more. Try disabling power management, or simply hit the power switch and start over.

Sometimes Knoppix gets stuck during boot-up and hangs partway into KDE (or any X session) startup. Switch to the first virtual console (Ctrl-Alt-F1) to see the live system messages; this should tell you where the problem is. For example, Knoppix might hang on SCSI detection. In this case, reboot and disable SCSI detection:

```
knoppix noscsi
```

See Also

- Documentation on the Knoppix CD
- Knoppix.net (*http://www.knoppix.net/*)—the best Knoppix resource, with all kinds of tips and howtos
- Knopper.net (*http://www.knopper.net/*)—the official home page of Klaus Knopper, the creator of Knoppix

13.3 Creating a Knoppix Boot Diskette

Problem

Your system will not boot from a CD, but you would still like to use Knoppix. How do you get a Knoppix boot diskette?

Solution

Knoppix comes with a boot image all ready to copy to a diskette. Load and mount your Knoppix CD on any Linux system, load a new, blank diskette, and run:

```
# dd if=/cdrom/KNOPPIX/boot.img  of=/dev/fd0 bs=1440k
```

You can also create the boot diskette in Windows. Open a DOS window, then open the *KNOPPIX* directory on the CD:

```
c:> d:
d:> cd \KNOPPIX
```

Then create the diskette:

```
d:> mkfloppy.bat
```

Boot the system with the diskette, stick in the Knoppix CD when it tells you to, and you're in business.

Discussion

Including a DOS batch file to make a Knoppix boot diskette is a nice touch—another handy tool for your rescue kit.

See Also

- Documentation on the Knoppix CD
- Knoppix.net (*http://www.knoppix.net/*)
- Klaus Knopper's official homepage (*http://www.knopper.net/*)

13.4 Saving Your Knoppix Configuration on a USB Memory Stick

Problem

You would like to save your Knoppix configuration, such as network settings and desktop configuration, so you don't have to start over every time.

Solution

This is a perfect job for one of those little USB memory sticks. Boot Knoppix with the memory stick inserted. On the Knoppix menu, look for Configuration → Save KNOPPIX Configuration. Select *dev/sda1* as the device to save it to.

Now when you boot Knoppix, make sure your USB stick is inserted, and use the following boot command:

```
knoppix myconfig=/dev/sda1
```

You may also make Knoppix autodetect it:

```
knoppix myconfig=scan
```

Discussion

256- and 512-MB USB pen drives are getting dirt cheap. Carry one of these and a Knoppix disk, and you can make yourself at home almost anywhere.

See Also

- Documentation on the Knoppix CD
- Knoppix.net (*http://www.knoppix.net/*)
- Klaus Knopper's official homepage (*http://www.knopper.net/*)

13.5 Creating a Persistent, Encrypted Knoppix Home Directory

Problem

You really like running Knoppix from the CD, because it cannot be infested by viruses, Trojans, or rootkits, and you would like to use it in place of a hard drive installation. But there's a problem: where do you store personal data, email, and other things that you'd like to keep with you? You want a secure home directory in which to store email and other data files.

Solution

Run Knoppix → Configure → Create to make a persistent Knoppix home directory. You'll have the option of creating *home* on the hard drive, or on removeable media such as USB memory sticks, compact flash cards, or Zip disks. This creates a file called *knoppix.img*.

Say yes when it asks you if you want to create an AES-encrypted directory. The directory will be encrypted with a 256-bit key. You have to come up with a passphrase of at least 20 characters. Make it a sentence that you can remember, like "thisismylong-password," because you'll need it every time you boot.

To boot using your nice, new encrypted */home*, insert your removable media and type:

```
boot: knoppix home=/dev/sda1
```

If you also saved your Knoppix configuration, you can specify both:

```
boot: knoppix home=/dev/sda1  myconfig=/dev/sda1
```

Your new */home* directory will appear in Knoppix as */home/knoppix* and will be automatically mounted at boot. If you store your encrypted */home* in an existing Linux partition on the hard drive, the whole partition will be mounted.

Discussion

The default size of */home/knoppix* is 30 MB. Make it as large as you need.

See Also

- Documentation on the Knoppix CD
- Knoppix.net (*http://www.knoppix.net/*)
- Klaus Knopper's official homepage (*http://www.knopper.net/*)

13.6   Copying Files to Another Linux PC

Problem

You want to copy files from a troubled PC to another machine on your network. This is a good way to do an emergency backup of critical files when a PC appears to be dying or behaving strangely.

Solution

Boot up Knoppix. The troubled PC must then connect to the LAN. If you have a DHCP server, Knoppix will connect automatically.

If you need to configure a static IP address, run *netcardconfig* from the console, or use Knoppix → Network/Internet.

You'll need an SSH server set up on the receiving machine. (See the "Discussion" section of this recipe if you need to set this up.)

First, mount the filesystem containing the files you want to copy. Knoppix creates */etc/fstab*, puts all the mountpoints under */mnt*, and creates desktop icons for all filesystems. The easy way to mount the filesystem is to click on the desktop icon. Or you can peek into *etc/fstab* and use the command line. First change to root. There is no password:

```
knoppix@tty0[knoppix]$ su
root@ttyp0[knoppix]# mount /mnt/hda5
```

Then run the *scp* (secure copy) command:

```
# scp -rp /mnt/hda5/home/kmartin 192.168.1.5:/home/kmartin/tmp
```

It will complain:

```
Could not create directory '/home/kmartin/.ssh'.
The authenticity of host '192.168.1.5 (192.168.1.5)' can't be established.
RSA key fingerprint is a2:c6:77:2e:63:b2:ed:90:b2:9b:bc:e7:d4:22:ba
Are you sure you want to continue connecting?" (yes/no)?
```

Say yes. Then it will ask you for root's password on the SSH server. Enter the password, and the files will be copied.

You can also do this as an ordinary user, for the user's own account. At the Knoppix root prompt, create a new user:

```
root@ttyp0[knoppix]# useradd kmartin
```

Don't bother with a password—you only need the user's password on the SSH server. Now *kmartin* can move files into her own account on the SSH server. Only root can copy files into other users' accounts.

Discussion

The *-r* option for *scp* copies directories recursively. *-p* preserves permissions.

This is how to set up a quick-and-dirty SSH server. Install OpenSSH on the Linux machine to which you want to copy files. If it's already installed, upgrade to the latest version to get all the security fixes. Then start it up:

```
# /etc/init.d/ssh start
```

and it is ready to receive files. If you intend to use SSH routinely for remote administration, don't stop here—you'll need to take a few more steps to ensure a safe connection. See Chapter 17 for more recipes on running SSH.

Because you are running Knoppix in memory, there is no way to save SSH keys or hosts, so it will emit the same complaints every time. If you plan to make a habit of copying files via *scp*, see Recipe 13.5.

See Also

- *scp(1), ssh(1)*
- Recipe 13.5, "Creating a Persistent, Encrypted Knoppix Home Directory"

13.7   Copying Files to a Samba Share

Problem

You would like to copy files from a Linux PC to a Windows PC on your LAN using Knoppix.

Solution

You need to have Samba (Chapter 23) already configured and working on your LAN. Open a root shell:

```
knoppix@ttyp0[knoppix]$ su
root@ttyp0[knoppix]#
```

Create a local directory on which to mount the remote share, then mount the remote share:

```
root@ttyp0[knoppix]# mkdir /mnt/samba
root@ttyp0[knoppix]# mount -t smbfs -o \
uid=knoppix,workgroup=local,username=helix,password=tehsecuar \
//windbag/lan_share/mnt/samba
```

Substitute your own workgroup, username, password, hostname, and shared folder name. On Windows 95/98/ME, if you did not configure file sharing to require a password, use "guest" as the username and leave the password field blank.

Now you can open a couple of Konqueror windows for copying files or you can use the *cp* command:

```
root@ttyp0[knoppix]# cp -av /home/helix  /mnt/samba
```

Discussion

If you prefer a graphical interface, there are a couple of options. If you know the hostname and share name, enter them in Konqueror's Location bar:

```
smb://HOST/SHARE
```

Knoppix also includes LinNeighborhood for network browsing, under Internet → LinNeighborhood.

See Also

- Chapter 9 of *Using Samba*, by Jay Ts, Robert Eckstein, and David Collier-Brown (O'Reilly)
- The Official Samba-3 Howto and Reference Guide for Samba 3.x (*http://samba.org/*)
- Chapter 23, *File and Printer Sharing, and Domain Authentication with Samba*

13.8   Copying Files to a CD-R/RW

Problem

You have a CD writer on your PC, and you would like to burn files to a CD-R/RW.

Solution

The absolute easiest way is to use K3b. Start up Knoppix, and open System → K3b Setup. K3b will automatically find your CD drives; verify this in step 3 of the setup wizard. In step 6, add any non-root users you want to use K3b. (Remember, you need to create the users first.)

When you're finished with the setup wizard, close it, and open System → K3b. Click File → New Project. Simply drag and drop the files you want to copy, hit the Burn button, and you're done.

Discussion

K3b is a great CD/DVD-writing interface, one of the best on any platform. It is logically organized, and it hides all the grotty details of CD/DVD writing, so you don't have to navigate bales of windows and menus to burn a disc, or bother with odd terminology like "Joliet," "Rock Ridge," or "El Torito." While it is good to know the inner workings of a program, it is also nice when the computer does the work.

See Also

- Chapter 11, *CD and DVD Recording*
- The K3b home page (*http://www.k3b.org/*)

13.9   Editing Configuration Files from Knoppix

Problem

Someone with more confidence than knowledge (maybe even you) "fixed" something in a configuration file and now the system won't boot. You need to fix it. But how do you edit a file on a machine that won't boot?

Solution

This is a perfect job for Knoppix. You can open and edit any file on a PC from Knoppix.

Boot up your Knoppix disk to KDE. Right-click the icon on the desktop for the filesystem you want to use, left-click "Mount," then left-click "Change read/write mode."

Open a root shell, then navigate to the file you want to edit and open it with the editor of your choice:

```
knoppix@ttyp0[knoppix]$ su
root@ttyp0[knoppix]# cd /mnt/hda3/etc
root@ttyp0[etc]# kate inittab &
```

Now you can edit the file, just as you normally would.

It's easy to become confused over whether you are in Knoppix or your PC's filesystem. Check with *pwd*:

```
root@ttyp0[etc]# pwd
/mnt/hda3/etc
```

Remember that the filesystems on your PC's hard drives are all mounted under */mnt* in Knoppix.

Discussion

Knoppix comes with a variety of window managers: larswm, IceWM, XFce, Windowmaker, Fluxbox, and TWM. But only KDE comes with the Knoppix menu and desktop icons for all of your partitions.

Just like with any Linux, you can also do everything from the console. To mount a filesystem as readable/writable, use:

```
root@ttyp0[knoppix]# mount -o rw /mnt/hda3
```

To open a file for editing, use:

```
root@ttyp0[knoppix]# vim /mnt/hda3/etc/inittab
```

Knoppix autodetects your filesystems and partitions and creates an */etc/fstab* file, so you can look in there to find mountpoints.

See Also

- *mount(8)*
- Recipe 9.11, "Mounting and Unmounting Filesystems on Hard Drives"

13.10 Installing Software from Knoppix

Problem

You need to run *apt-get*, *apt-rpm*, *up2date*, or some other updater utility that needs to be run from inside its own root filesystem.

Solution

In Knoppix, you can *chroot* to the root filesystem on the hard drive. Open a Knoppix root shell, then do:

```
root@ttyp0[knoppix]# mount -o rw /mnt/hda6
root@ttyp0[knoppix]# chroot /mnt/hda6
root@Knoppix:/
```

This gives you a root shell in the filesystem on the hard drive, as though you were booted directly into it. You are no longer in the /mnt directory in Knoppix. Now you can run any command, as though the system had booted normally. That includes commands for updating software like *apt-get*.

Discussion

From an ordinary Knoppix session it's easy to keep track of your whereabouts, as all the filesystems on the hard drive are mounted under /mnt. But in *chroot*, you won't see Knoppix files. If you get confused, try poking around and reading filenames—you should recognize files that belong on the hard drive, and not to Knoppix.

See Also

- *chroot(8)*

13.11 Repairing a Lost Root Password

Problem

Oops, you lost your root password.

Solution

No problem whatsoever. Fire up Knoppix and open a root shell. Mount the filesystem containing /etc/shadow, and make it writable (see Recipe 9.10). Open /etc/shadow in your favorite editor, and find root's entry:

```
root:$1$7nMNZYci$E.U6ftxnAZUOrk29qvYpk0:12460:0:99999:7:::
```

Delete the password hash, which is between the first set of colons:

```
root::12460:0:99999:7:::
```

Now when you start up the system and log in as root, you will not be asked for a password.

Discussion

Don't forget to set a new root password.

This is yet another demonstration that "anyone with physical access to the box owns it." See Chapter 12 for tips on securing the boot process.

See Also

- *shadow(5)*
- Recipes 12.14 ("Protecting System Files with a GRUB Password"), 12.15 ("Locking Out Users from Individual GRUB Menu Entries"), and 12.21 ("Password-Protecting LILO") for how to set passwords on LILO and GRUB

13.12 Installing Knoppix to a Hard Disk

Problem

You really like using Knoppix, and you want to install it to a hard drive, just like a "real" Linux.

Solution

Fire up Knoppix and open a root shell. Type *knoppix-installer*. Follow the menus and prompts, and when you're done you'll have a thoroughly modern Debian system.

Discussion

This operates pretty much like any Linux installation. Check the release notes for your version of Knoppix, because up to Version 3.2 the installer script was *knx-hdinstall*. In 3.3 it changed to *knoppix-installer*. It could change again—the Linux world waits for no one.

See Also

- The Knoppix Wiki on *http://www.knoppix.net/docs/*—all the latest and greatest tips and howtos are here

13.13 Virus-Scanning Windows PCs with Knoppix

Problem

You want a quick, inexpensive method for running virus scans on Windows, independent of the operating system. You know that the installation disks for commercial antivirus products, like Symantec and McAfee, can be used to run a preinstallation virus scan, but the virus definitions are going to be months out of date.

Solution

Get yourself a copy of Knoppix 3.4 or newer. You'll need Internet connectivity to download fresh virus definitions. You can either run a scan-only or a scan-and-disinfect on Windows partitions with FAT16/32. On NTFS filesystems, you can only run a scan because write support for NTFS is still unreliable in Linux.

Boot up Knoppix. Go to KNOPPIX → Utilities → Install software. This brings up a menu of available packages to install; check *f-prot*.

After *f-prot* is installed, select KNOPPIX → Extra Software → *f-prot*. This brings up the *f-prot* menu; the first thing you want to do is 4, "Online Update."

After the new virus defintions are downloaded, select partitions or directories to scan. Knoppix automatically mounts all partitions on your system, so you can easily select the ones you want. To run a scan-only, hit the "scan" button—and go find something to do, because it will take awhile. When it's finished, you'll see a report showing the results of the scan.

To scan and disinfect, run *f-prot* from the command line instead of the graphical menu. First, make sure the partition is mounted read/write; simply right-click on the icon for the drive, which is on your Knoppix desktop, and left-click Actions → Change read/write mode.

Next, open a command shell and run this command, naming the partition you want scanned:

```
$ f-prot -disinf -list /mnt/hda1
```

The *-list* option shows the scan's progress and the *-disinf* option will disinfect the system. That's all there is to it.

Discussion

This approach has a number of advantages:

- You are working from a guaranteed clean operating system—and since it's on a nonwritable disk, it's impossible to compromise.
- Because you must power down the PC to boot Knoppix, any memory-resident nasties are evicted.
- It's free—so you can burn masses of disks and go on a virus-scanning spree.

f-prot has a Windows edition for $29, and liberal licensing terms for home users; it covers all your home computers. There is also a free Linux workstation edition; sure, we can mock and abuse Microsoft all we want, but all it would take is one evil genius writing a lethal Linux exploit and hordes of happy script kiddies distributing it all over the planet in a heartbeat, and we wouldn't be laughing anymore.

See Also

- Knoppix net, for bales of howtos (*http://www.knoppix.net*)
- *f-prot* home page (*http://www.f-prot.com*)

## CHAPTER 14

Printing with CUPS

14.1 Introduction

The Common Unix Printing System (CUPS) is a modern printing subsystem for Linux and Unix that replaces the hoary old Unix line-printer protocols. It runs on Unix, Linux, Mac OS, and Mac OS X, and it serves clients on nearly any platform, including Windows.

CUPS is thoroughly modern, supporting laser and inkjet printers as well as dot matrix and other legacy printers.

There are two versions of CUPS: the free GPL version, which is the default on most of the major Linux distributions, and a commercial edition. The commercial version comes with support, a larger selection of drivers, and nicer management interfaces.

Printer drivers in CUPS consist of one or more filters specific to a printer, which are packaged in PPD (PostScript Printer Description) files. All printers in CUPS—even non-PostScript printers—need a PPD. The PPDs contain descriptions about the printers, specific printer commands, and filters.

Filters are the heart and soul of CUPS. Filters translate print jobs to formats the printer can understand, such as PDF, HP-PCL, raster, and image files, and they pass in commands for things such as page selection and ordering. PPDs are text files—take a look in *Iusr/share/cups/model/* to see what they look like. Installed printers have PPDs in */etc/cups/ppd*.

Finding Drivers

Included in CUPS are generic PPDs for 9-pin and 24-pin Epson dot matrix printers, Epson Stylus and Color Stylus Photo printers, LaserJet and HP DeskJet printers, and even Dymo label printers. These will work for hundreds of printers, but they do not support all printer functions, such as duplexing, inkjet head-cleaning and alignment, or tray selection.

There are four good sources for printer drivers, if your printer manufacturer does not supply Linux drivers:

- Foomatic, at *http://linuxprinting.org*
- Gimp-Print, at *http://gimp-print.sourceforge.net*
- The commercial edition of CUPS, at *http://www.easysw.com/cups/*
- Windows PostScript drivers

Foomatic is a free printer-driver project that integrates with all the common Linux printing systems (CUPS, LPRng, LPD, GNUlpr, PPR, PDQ, CPS).

Gimp-Print originally started out as a Gimp plug-in, but it has expanded to support all Linux printing. Gimp-Print drivers are very high quality; if there is one for your color printer, it is probably the best choice.

Be sure to check the hardware compatibility list for your Linux distribution, or the printer database on linuxprinting.org, before purchasing a printer.

Gimp-Print and Foomatic are available as packages that you can install on your system, if they are not already included in your distribution. This ensures that you get a complete selection of drivers, plus all the required subsystems that make everything work together correctly. The RPMs are complete; Debian splits them into several smaller packages. Visit the Debian package search page to find them (*http:// packages.debian.org*).

You can use the Windows drivers for PostScript printers on Linux. Look for PPD files in your Windows system directory. Note that only PPDs for real PostScript printers will work. Many printers are only PostScript-compatible; your printer documentation will tell you.

You can test PPDs at *http://www.cups.org/testppd.php*. This site looks for syntax errors in PPD files. The errors it finds are usually things you can fix, such as a typo or incorrect command.

Networking Printers

There are four ways to share printers on a network:

- Share printers that are attached to users' PCs.
- Build a dedicated Linux printer server.
- Buy network-direct printers, such as the HP JetDirect series.
- Buy hardware printer servers, such as the Linksys EPSX3, that can connect any printer directly to your LAN.

This chapter covers the first two options. The last two are too diverse, and there are too many choices to try to cover here. Here are some things to keep in mind when you're deciding which one to use:

- Using a Linux box as a printer server gives you maximum flexibility and customization options.
- Network-direct printers, with built-in networking hardware, tend to be expensive and require proprietary network hardware.
- Network-direct printers are usually built for heavy-duty use.
- A hardware printer server lets you network any printers you want.

Using network-direct printers and hardware printer servers means less power consumption and smaller space requirements than using a PC as a dedicated printer server. You must shop carefully for Linux support, though, because some of them come with Windows-only management software. Anything that is managed via a web interface should work fine.

14.2 Installing a Printer on a Standalone Linux PC

Problem

You need to connect a printer to your Linux PC.

Solution

If you have a USB printer, it must be connected and powered up at boot time.

First, make sure that the CUPS daemon is running:

```
$ lpstat -t
scheduler is running
...
```

If it is not running, it says:

```
$ lpstat -t
lpstat: Unable to connect to server: Connection refused
```

If that is the case, start it with its *init* script:

```
# /etc/init.d/cupsys start
```

On Red Hat and Fedora, use:

```
# /sbin/service cups restart
```

The easiest way to install a new printer is with the CUPS web interface. Type the CUPS URL in any browser:

```
http://localhost:631
```

You'll need the root password. Click the Printers tab, then click "Add printer," which opens the Admin menu. There are three values to enter here:

```
Name: hp6L
Location: room-202
Description: bw-laser
```

Choose the name carefully—CUPS needs this name, and changing it will cause problems. Your printer name will be used on the next few configuration pages. I've entered "hp61" for my Hewlett-Packard LaserJet6L printer. The Location and Description are optional.

On the next page, define the "Device for <printername>." This means the physical connection: parallel port, USB, SCSI, serial port, or network. Select your deviceURI from the drop-down menu. In this example, that is "Parallel port #1 Hewlett-Packard HP LaserJet6L."

On the "Model/Driver for <printername>" menu, scroll to the model number of your printer, and select a driver from the list.

Now it should say "Printer <printername> has been added successfully." Click on the printer name to go the printer's control page, and print a test page. Your CUPS page should look like Figure 14-1.

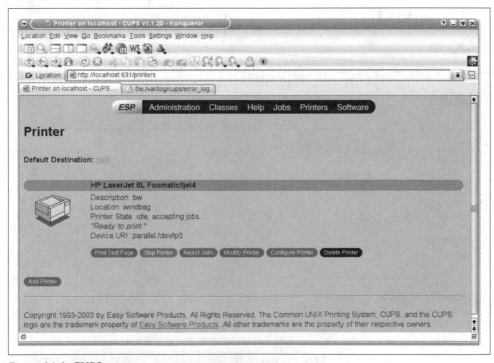

Figure 14-1. CUPS page

Discussion

If you prefer the command line, this long command does the same thing as the above example:

```
# lpadmin -p hp6L -L room-202 -D bw-laser -E -v parallel:/dev/lp0 \
-m HP-LaserJet_6-hpijs.ppd
```

Here are some definitions:

lpadmin -p
> Set the printer name.

-L
> Set the printer location.

-D
> Describe the printer.

-E
> Enable the printer and make it ready to receive jobs.

-v
> Set the device URI.

-m
> Specify which driver (PPD file) to use. Note that the filepath is hardcoded into CUPS; if you try to use a filepath like */usr/share/cups/model/laserjet.ppd*, it will fail, saying "lpadmin: add-printer (set model) failed: server-error-internal-error." Just use the PPD name, and make sure the PPD file you want is in */usr/share/cups/model/*.

If you have Gimp-Print and Foomatic installed (if you don't you probably should) you'll find additional PPDs in */usr/share/cups/model/gimp-print* and */usr/share/cups/model/foomatic*. They are compressed:

```
HP-LaserJet_6-hpijs.ppd.gz
```

You'll need to uncompress the file and move it to the */usr/share/cups/model* directory:

```
# gunzip HP-LaserJet_6-hpijs.ppd.gz && mv HP-LaserJet_6-hpijs.ppd \
/usr/share/cups/model/
```

It is not necessary to uncompress and move PPD files when you install printers using the CUPS web interface.

Generic drivers

These are the generic drivers that come with the free version of CUPS:

```
$ ls /usr/share/cups/model
epson24.ppd    laserjet.ppd  pxlcolor.ppd  stphoto.ppd   deskjet.ppd   epson9.ppd
okidat24.ppd  pxlmono.ppd    stphoto2.ppd  deskjet2.ppd  okidata9.ppd  stcolor.ppd
dymo.ppd    pcl-6.ppd    stcolor2.ppd
```

If you can't find a driver specific to your printer, one of these should work. (You did check your distribution's hardware compatibility list, or the database on linuxprinting.org, before purchasing the printer, right?)

See Also

- This chapter's "Introduction," for more information on printer drivers
- *CUPS Software Administrators Manual* (*http://localhost:631/documentation.html*)

14.3   Serving Linux Clients

Problem

You want to share the printers attached to your Linux PCs with other Linux clients on your LAN.

Solution

First, make sure CUPS is installed on all the computers with attached printers. These PCs must have static IP addresses and you'll need name resolution in place and working (*/etc/hosts* or a local DNS server).

Next, on the PCs with printers attached, edit */etc/cupsd.conf*. This sample *cupsd.conf* shows how to make the printers accessible to the local subnet. You can use this as it's shown, using your own network values:

```
LogLevel info
Port 631
<Location />
Order Deny,Allow
Deny From All
Allow From 127.0.0.1
Allow From 192.168.1.*
</Location>
BrowseAddress 192.168.1.255
```

Add this entry to restrict administrative access to the server only and not allow it from client machines:

```
<Location /admin>
AuthType Basic
AuthClass System
Order Deny,Allow
Deny From All
Allow From 127.0.0.1
</Location>
```

Restart *cupsd* after editing *cupsd.conf*:

 # /etc/init.d/cupsys restart

On Red Hat and Fedora, use:

 # /sbin/service cups restart

Print a test page. If you get the infamous "client-error-not-found" message, stop and restart the printer from the CUPS web interface.

CUPS printers will now automatically broadcast themselves on the network. Make sure that TCP port 631 is not blocked on either the server or the client machines.

Open the CUPS web interface (*http://localhost:631*) on any of the Linux client PCs, and all CUPS printers should automatically appear on the Printers page. You can now print a test page and print from applications.

Discussion

If there is a sample *cupsd.conf* on your system, don't let its size scare you. Chances are you'll never need most of the directives; just hang on to it as a reference, and create your own *cupsd.conf* from scratch.

All of the directives in *cupsd.conf* are listed and defined in the *CUPS Software Administrators Manual*, at *http://localhost:631/documentation.html*.

LogLevel info
> There are 10 levels of logging. *info* is the default; it logs errors and printer activity in */var/log/cups/error_log*.

Port 631
> This is reserved for IPP (Internet Printing Protocol).

<Location />
</Location>
> The *Location* directive specifies access control and authentication options. Note the positioning of the slashes—make sure you get them right, or things won't work.

Order Deny,Allow
Deny From All
Allow From 127.0.0.1
Allow From 192.168.1.*
> Your standard "deny all, allow as needed" scheme, limiting inbound connections to the local machine and the local subnet.

See Also

- The "Printing System Management" section in the *CUPS Software Administrators Manual* (*http://localhost:631/documentation.html*)

14.4 Sharing a Printer Without Using Name Resolution

Problem

You haven't bothered to create */hosts* files, or set up a local DNS server on your LAN, because you have no need for name resolution. The PCs on your LAN sit comfortably behind a NAT firewall, for sharing an Internet connection, and that's all they need. So how do you share a printer?

Solution

Give your printer server a static IP address. Add a ServerName directive to */etc/cupsd.conf* on the server, using its own IP address:

```
ServerName 192.168.1.5
```

Restart *cupsd*. On Debian, use:

```
# /etc/init.d/cupsys restart
```

On Red Hat and Fedora, use:

```
# /sbin/service cups restart
```

There is nothing to do on the client PCs, except wait a few seconds for CUPS to broadcast the printer. If you get the infamous "client-error-not-found" message, stop and restart the printer.

Discussion

By default, CUPS uses the hostname as the ServerName. If you are not using any kind of name resolution, your client PCs will not see any CUPS printers. Specifying the IP address as the ServerName fixes that. A side effect is that you may not be able to print a test page from the server; instead, you'll get the screen shown in Figure 14-2.

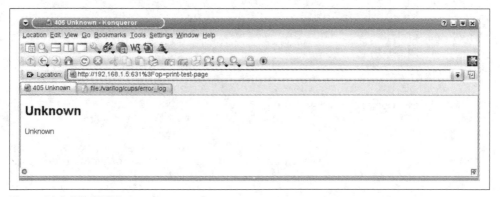

Figure 14-2. No CUPS page

However, you'll still be able to print from applications on the server. Client PCs won't notice anything odd.

If you don't need to set up a network filesystem such as NFS or Samba, or use DNS; it's perfectly okay, even if the other geeks laugh at you. A primary rule of security is "don't run what you don't need."

See Also

- *CUPS Software Administrators Manual* (*http://localhost:631/documentation.html*)

14.5 Serving Windows Clients Without Samba

Problem

You would like to connect your Windows clients to a Linux printer server, but you really don't want to set up Samba just to share printers.

Solution

CUPS can handle the job without Samba. You need your Windows installation CD or printer driver disk, and Windows clients need to have Internet Printing Services installed. This is the same as IPP (Internet Printing Protocol) on Linux.

Windows 95/98 users can get the download at *http://www.microsoft.com/windows98/downloads/*. Look for "Internet Print Services." The file you want is *wpnpins.exe*.

Windows ME supplies the Internet Printing Services software in the *Add-on* folder on the installation CD.

On Windows NT, go to Control Panel → Network → Services tab → Add Microsoft TCP/IP Printing.

On Windows2000/XP, install TCP/IP Print Services from Network and Dial-up Connections → Advanced Menu → Optional Networking Components → Other Network File and Print Services.

Next, fire up the Add Printer wizard. Select Network Printer, then add the printer URI. This consists of the IP address or server name, port number, and */printers/<printername>*. Be sure to use the exact name you gave the printer, like this:

```
http://192.168.1.5:631/printers/hp6L
```

There isn't a */printers* directory anywhere; that's just a convention used by CUPS.

When Windows first connects to the CUPS server, it will install its own local printer drivers and print its own test page, rather than the CUPS test page. So you may need a Windows CD or the driver installation disk.

Discussion

If you have name resolution working on your LAN, you can use the server name instead of the IP address:

```
http://windbag:631/printers/hp6L
```

See Also

- This chapter's "Introduction," for more information on printer drivers

14.6 Sharing Printers on a Mixed LAN with Samba

Problem

Your LAN has both Linux and Windows printers, and you want all of them to be accessible by both Linux and Windows clients.

Solution

You'll need both Samba and CUPS to make this work. See Recipe 23.22 and Recipe 23.23.

See Also

- *The Official Samba-3 Howto and Reference Guide (http://samba.org)*

14.7 Building a Dedicated CUPS Printer Server

Problem

Sharing printers connected to PCs works fine, but it places an extra load on the PCs, and the PCs must be running for printers to be accessible. And sometimes it means running all over to fix things. You want to set up a dedicated printer server, for easier centralized printer management.

Solution

A plain-vanilla Pentium-class PC with several attached printers makes a dandy CUPS printer server. There are two good ways to install multiple printers to a single PC:

- Use additional parallel-PCI cards, for connecting parallel-port printers.
- Add USB hubs for connecting more USB printers.

Set up a minimal Linux installation, with CUPS. Install all the Foomatic and Gimp-Print packages and drivers. (These are available both as RPMs and in Debian repositories.)

Then all you need to do is install the printers and configure CUPS. See the first four recipes in this chapter for how to install printers, and information on sharing with both Windows and Linux clients without needing to use Samba.

Discussion

A centralized printer server has a lot of advantages: all the printers are in one place, supplies can be stored close by, and users are not bothered by other people wanting to use their printers. And if you use Linux and CUPS for a print server, you don't need to set up Samba to share printers with Windows clients.

See Also

- *PC Hardware in a Nutshell*, by Robert Bruce Thompson and Barbara Fritchman Thompson (O'Reilly). This is a great hardware guide, even though it is Windows-centric, and their companion web site (*http://www.ttgnet.com*) includes a lot of useful updates to the book.
- The "Printing System Management" section in the *CUPS Software Administrator's Manual* at (*http://localhost:631/documentation.html*).

14.8   Distributed Printing with Classes

Problem

You have a user group that generates a lot of high-volume printing, and you need an easy way to give users a group of printers to use, without having to hassle with individual print queues.

Solution

Use *classes* to create, in effect, a single printer queue containing several printers. From the Admin page of the CUPS web interface, click "Add Class." Select printers for the class from your installed printers. Users can now send print jobs to the class, instead of to an individual printer, and the first available printers will take them. You can add or remove printers from this menu, and even create subclasses.

You can also do this from the command line. Create a class and populate it with printers this way:

```
# lpadmin -p printer1 -p printer2  -p printer3 -c art-dept
```

To add another printer to this class, use:

```
# lpadmin -p printer4 -c art-dept
```

Remove a printer with the *-r* option:

```
# lpadmin -p printer4 -r art-dept
```

To delete the entire class, use:

```
# lpadmin -x art-dept
```

Discussion

Obviously, you don't want to group geographically dispersed printers into the same class—they should be in the same room. It will get confusing enough, as users won't know which printers have their print jobs. The advantage is that if a printer gets jammed or otherwise becomes unavailable, jobs will still be printed without user intervention. It's also great for high-volume printing, as idle printers will automatically take over from busy ones.

See Also

- The "Printer Classes" section in the *CUPS Software Administrators Manual* (*http://localhost:631/documentation.html*)

14.9   Restricting Users from Printers and Classes

Problem

You have some printers you would like to restrict to selected users. You don't want people printing pictures of their kids on the design group's fancy graphics printer, for example.

Solution

Use the *lpadmin* command:

```
# lpadmin -p hp6L  -u allow:carla,jenn,dancer
```

This changes */etc/cups/printers.conf*:

```
# Printer configuration file for CUPS v1.1.20
# Written by cupsd on Fri Jan  7 00:36:36 2004
<DefaultPrinter hp6L>
Info
Location
DeviceURI parallel:/dev/lp0
State Idle
Accepting Yes
JobSheets none none
QuotaPeriod 0
PageLimit 0
KLimit 0
AllowUser carla
AllowUser jenn
AllowUser dancer
</Printer>
```

You can also restrict classes:

```
# lpadmin -p art-dept  -u allow:carla,jenn,dancer
```

This modifies */etc/cups/classes.conf*.

You can also deny users:

```
# lpadmin -p hp6L  -u deny:daryl,larry,otherlarry
```

Discussion

Don't try to edit *classes.conf* or *printers.conf* directly, because your changes will be lost. Use *lpadmin*.

See Also

- The "Managing Printers" section in the *CUPS Software Administrators Manual* (*http://localhost:631/documentation.html*)

14.10 Troubleshooting

Problem

Printing, especially network printing, is probably the most difficult and troublesome aspect of system administration. What tools are there for diagnosing and fixing problems?

Solution

Your first stop is */var/log/cups/error_log*. The default log level in *cupsd.conf* is *LogLevel info*. This logs errors and ordinary activity. If *LogLevel info* does not generate enough detail, the highest levels are *debug* and *debug2*.

Trying a different printer driver cures a large number of printing problems.

If test pages won't print, try printing other documents. A test page not printing indicates a problem somewhere, but if you can get your work done, you can probably live without the test page.

For network printing, make sure you have connectivity. Ping both IP addresses and hostnames. Try connecting manually to Samba shares. Try printing from the machine to which the printer is attached.

Run the *ppd* file for the printer through the PPD checker at *http://www.cups.org/testppd.php* to test for syntax errors.

If you can't decipher for yourself where the problem is, you can post log output and the steps you've tried in help forums. Here is a listing of the more useful ones:

http://printing.kde.org
> Specific to printing in KDE, but still a thorough resource for many aspects of printing with CUPS

http://gimp-print.sourceforge.net/p_Mailing_Lists.php3
> Help for Gimp-Print drivers

http://www.linuxprinting.org/forums.cgi
> Help forums for HP, Epson, Alps, and many more printers

http://www.cups.org/newsgroups.php
> CUPS newsgroups

As always, search the archives before posting your query. There is nothing new under the sun.

See Also

- *The Troubleshooting-CUPS-and-Asking-for-Help Howto*, by Kurt Pfeifle—a wonderful, comprehensive CUPS troubleshooting guide (*http://www.cups.org/cups-help.html*)

## CHAPTER 15

Configuring Video and Managing X Windows

15.1 Introduction

The X Window System is the foundation of Linux's graphical interface. All those nice window managers and desktop environments—XFce, Enlightenment, KDE, Gnome, and so forth—run on top of X.

The X Window System is an amazing piece of work. You can run in a graphical environment, have text consoles open at the same time, and easily switch back and forth between them. The X Window System does more than draw pretty pictures; it's a networking protocol as well. You can even log in to remote systems via X. (This is covered in Chapter 17.)

While the X Window System has been the Linux standard forever, there is a new windowing system finding acceptance: X.org. It is a fork of the XFree86™ project that found sudden popularity when the 4.4 release of XFree86 adopted a licensing change that was possibly incompatible with the GPL. Fedora and Mandrake were the first on board with X.org. By the time you read this, everyone may have kissed and made up, or it may all be a jumble, with yet another distribution difference to trap the unwary. You'll need to know which one is on your system. This command gives the version number for XFree86:

```
$ XFree86 -version
```

And this is for X.org:

```
$ X.org -version
```

X.org currently mirrors XFree86 very closely; the primary differences are in the configuration filenames and locations. However, the two will probably diverge more with time.

There is a lot of confusing terminology around the X Window System, as well as inconvenient capitalizations. Here are a few definitions:

XFree86 Project, Inc.
> The organization that produces XFree86, which is a freely redistributable open source implementation of the X Window System.

XFree86 4.x
> The current version of XFree86 on Linux.

X Window System
> The original network-aware windowing environment for Unix. It is also called "a network protocol that draws pictures."

X11
> The eleventh version of the X Window System.

X11R6
> The specifications for the X Window System.

X.Org Foundation
> A fork of the XFree86 project.

Make it easy on yourself, and just call it "X."

Hardware

All video adapters will work in Linux; even the most obscure card will work at a generic VGA level (640 × 480, 16 colors). All the major Linux distributions come with good video configuration tools that will detect your hardware and find drivers automatically. It is unlikely you'll ever need to edit *XF86Config*, except perhaps to enable hardware acceleration or to customize multihead displays.

The majority of video adapters have Linux drivers and will deliver good 2D performance, which means that for everyday tasks—email, web surfing, spreadsheets, word processing, and so forth—most any adapter will do. Getting 3D hardware acceleration support can take a little more effort, but if you play games like Tux Racer and Quake, or do 3D computer-aided design (CAD) or 3D modeling, hardware acceleration is essential.

Modern video cards are more powerful than PCs of yesteryear: a high-end model has 256 MB of RAM, a 256-bit bus, a 256-MHz GPU, and often even has its own cooling fan.

Video-card performance is limited by the type of motherboard slot it is plugged into. PCI cards are the slowest. AGP is much faster, and is found on all modern boards. There are several flavors of AGP:

AGP 1.0
> 1X = 266 MB/sec
>
> 2X = 533 MB/sec

AGP 2.0
  1X = 266 MB/sec

  2X = 533 MB/sec

  4X = 1.066 GB/sec

AGP 3.0
  1X = 266 MB/sec

  2X = 533 MB/sec

  4X = 1.066 GB/sec

  8X = 2 GB/sec

The AGP standards are backward- and forward-compatible; you can mix up new cards and old motherboards and old cards and new motherboards. However, putting a new, high-end card on an older board means you won't get all the performance you paid for.

Drivers

One way to get hardware video acceleration in Linux is by using Direct Rendering Infrastructure (DRI) and a Linux-supported video card. DRI is built in to XFree86. Currently, XFree86/DRI support is available for these chipsets: 3dfx, Gamma, Intel i8x0 motherboard chipsets, Matrox, ATI Rage, ATI Radeon, Mach64, and Sis300. Visit *http://xfree.org* and *http://dri.sourceforge.net* for up-to-date information on supported chipsets and howtos.

The other way to get hardware video acceleration is by using drivers supplied by the manufacturer. For example, nVidia supplies their own binary-only drivers and kernel modules, which are currently the only way to get hardware acceleration for nVidia adapters. You can use the the open source *nv* driver for nonaccelerated 2D operation.

ATI and Matrox both have some cards that are fully supported by open source drivers and some that require proprietary binary drivers to get full functionality. As always, do your homework before buying.

Terminology

Here's some terminology:

DAC
  Digital-to-analog converter. Usually a single chip that converts digital data to analog, for example in modems.

RAMDAC
  Random Access Memory digital-to-analog converter. The chip that converts digital signals to analog, for analog displays.

GPU

Graphics processing unit. The processor that does the intense computations required for 3D video.

SRAM

Static Random Access Memory. It's "static" because it does not need to be refreshed, unlike DRAM (Dynamic Random Access Memory). SRAM is considerably faster than DRAM, with access times as low as 10 nanoseconds, compared to 60 nanoseconds for DRAM.

AGP

Accelerated graphics port. AGP is based on the PCI bus. It is a dedicated channel to system memory, and it is considerably faster than PCI, which tops out at 133 MB/sec. Currently the fastest AGP slot is 8X, or 2 GB/sec.

15.2   Using Both X Windows and Consoles

Problem

You want both console sessions and X sessions.

Solution

Yes, Linux user, you can have it all. To switch from an X session to one of the consoles, simply hit Ctrl-Alt-F*n*, where F*n* is F1–F6. To switch between consoles, hit Alt-F*n*. To switch back to X, hit Alt-F7. The first X session is always *:0*. To open a second X session, do this from a console:

```
$ startx -- :1
```

Make sure there is a space on either side of the double hyphen. The X session you've just created belongs to the F8 key. Don't log into two X sessions as the same user, as strange and bad conflicts will occur. You can create as many X sessions as you have available consoles and system resources for.

When you start X from a console, all of the debugging messages and background mutterings can be seen on the console. KDE is especially talkative, like it's on a coffee jag. Most of it is not significant, but sometimes it's useful for troubleshooting.

Discussion

Most Linuxes install with seven *virtual consoles*. Take a look in */etc/inittab*:

```
# Note that on most Debian systems tty7 is used by the X Window System,
# so if you want to add more gettys go ahead, but skip tty7 if you run X.
#
1:2345:respawn:/sbin/getty 38400 tty1
2:23:respawn:/sbin/getty 38400 tty2
3:23:respawn:/sbin/getty 38400 tty3
4:23:respawn:/sbin/getty 38400 tty4
```

```
5:23:respawn:/sbin/getty 38400 tty5
6:23:respawn:/sbin/getty 38400 tty6
```

The majority of Linux systems bind the default X session to *tty7*. A notable exception is Knoppix, which uses only five virtual terminals.

What can you do with all of these? Express all of your personalities. Log in as several different users. Log in as yourself many times. Switch to another console to get out of trouble. Gloat about how flexible and versatile Linux is.

gettys and ttys

These words, like so much of Linux's terminology, are Unix history lessons. *getty* means *get tty*. *tty* is teletype. That's right, Linux sees your expensive new full-color, high-definition monitor, with built-in sound and FireWire ports, as a teletype—just some old thing to stream output to.

getty manages logins over serial connections. It opens a serial device, such as a text terminal, virtual terminal, or modem, and waits for a connection. It displays the login prompt; then, when you enter your username, hands off to the *login* program. There are many *gettys*: *mgetty*, *mingetty*, *ugetty*, *agetty*, *getty-ps*, *fbgetty*, and doubtless more. *mingetty* is a minimal *getty* designed only for virtual consoles. It won't talk to modems. *mgetty* is probably the best modem *getty*. How do you know which *getty* your system uses?

```
$ ps ax | grep getty
  456 tty2    S    0:00 /sbin/getty 38400 tty2
  457 tty3    S    0:00 /sbin/getty 38400 tty3
  458 tty4    S    0:00 /sbin/getty 38400 tty4
  459 tty5    S    0:00 /sbin/getty 38400 tty5
  460 tty6    S    0:00 /sbin/getty 38400 tty6
```

Why doesn't this show *tty1*? Because that's the terminal you're logged in on. *getty* only sticks around waiting for logins; it retires quietly once a login is completed.

This tells us we're running *getty* itself, and not a link to some other *getty*:

```
$ ls -go /sbin/getty
-rwxr-xr-x   1   14264 Sep 19 21:25 /sbin/getty
```

tty is a program. Go ahead, try it out in a console:

```
$ tty
/dev/tty3
```

Now try it in an X terminal:

```
$ tty
/dev/pts/2
```

tty tells you what virtual terminal you are in ("virtual" because in the olden days, they had real terminals that had no processing power of their own—they were merely interfaces to a great and mighty mainframe somewheres).

ttyS* is a serial port. The serial ports are numbered *ttyS0* through *ttyS04*. While we think of a serial port as the physical DB-9 connector, it's also a logical port with an IRQ and I/O address.

tty* names the virtual consoles: *tty1*, *tty2*, etc. While most Linux systems ship with 7, theoretically you could have up to 63 virtual consoles.

pts means pseudoterminal. These are X terminals, like *xterm, gnome-terminal, wterm, powershell*, and *Konsole*.

Because these are serial interfaces, horrid things like flow control, data flow paths, buffers, and other things that used to be of concern to users are involved. Thankfully, in these modern times, Linux handles all this for us (though these are still completely configurable, for those who wish to do so).

See Also

- *tty(1), tty(4), pts(4), console(4), getty(8), mingetty(8), mgetty(8)*
- *The Serial Howto (http://www.tldp.org/HOWTO/Serial-HOWTO.html)*

15.3 Installing a New Video Adapter

Problem

You are adding a second video adapter to a system, or replacing the old one with a different type of adapter. How do you configure it and get it working?

Solution

The best way is to use the graphical configuration tool that comes with your distribution. Let these excellent tools do the work. SuSE has SaX, Red Hat has *redhat-config-xfree*, Fedora uses *system-config-xfree*, and Mandrake's is XFdrake. Every distribution has its own utility; you'll get the best results by using it.

The second-best way is to edit *XF86Config* manually, changing only the parts that are pertinent to your new adapter. See the next recipe for how to edit *XF86Config*.

Discussion

You may find these X utilities to be helpful:

- XFree86 -configure
- */usr/X11R6/bin/xf86config*
- */usr/sbin/ddcprobe*

All of these must be run as root.

XFree86 -configure probes your hardware and automatically generates a new *XF86Config* file. It thoughtfully stores the file in a separate location, without overwriting your original *XF86Config* file, so that you can test it first.

xf86config requires that you know configuration data about your mouse, keyboard, video adapter, and monitor. It takes you through the setup line by line, asking questions until you're ready to explode. Most important are the name of your video card, the amount of video RAM, and the horizontal/vertical refresh rates for your monitor.

Run */usr/sbin/ddcprobe* to collect the information you need for your video card. It may also probe your monitor, but most likely it won't, so be sure to have your monitor's documentation at hand. If you don't have it, these values are common to modern multisync monitors and will get you up and running so you can Google for the correct figures:

- Horizontal Sync (kHz): 30–58
- Vertical Sync (Hz): 50–85

If your new configuration does not work, check */var/log/Xfree86.0.log* to see what went wrong. If you get stuck in a bad X session and can't log out, use Ctrl-Alt-Backspace to break free.

See Also

- XFree86 documentation (*http://www.xfree86.org/resources.html*)—look here to find the driver name for your adapter
- *X(7x)*

15.4   Editing XF86Config

Problem

You installed a new video adapter in a system, and you prefer to make the new settings manually. Your distribution utility doesn't do what you want, or you just want to edit a text file and be done with it.

Solution

X configuration is stored in the *XF86Config* file, which can be in a number of locations:

```
/etc/X11/XF86Config-4
/etc/XF86Config
/usr/X11R6/etc/X11/XF86Config-4
/usr/X11R6/etc/X11/XF86Config
```

Installing a new driver means changing a single section. This example shows changing from a Voodoo 3 adapter to an nVidia card. Simply change the Driver and the Identifier, by commenting out the old lines and adding your new values:

```
Section "Device"
#    Identifier    "3Dfx"
#    Driver        "tdfx"
    Identifier  "nVidia"
    Driver      "nv"
EndSection
```

The Identifier can be anything you like; the Driver must be the actual name of the driver. You'll find these at *http://www.xfree86.org/resources.html*.

Discussion

If you're using vendor-supplied drivers, you'll have to download the drivers and follow their installation instructions.

Commenting out old lines instead of deleting them makes it easy to undo your changes, if necessary.

See Also

- XFree86 documentation (*http://www.xfree86.org/resources.html*)—look here to find the driver name for your adapter

15.5 Enabling 3D Hardware Acceleration with XFree86/DRI

Problem

You want to play Tux Racer, TuxKart, or Quake 3, or do some 3D modeling, CAD, or other high-end video work. You have a supported card and you've installed the drivers, but you're still stuck in 2D.

Solution

Making 3D hardware video acceleration work correctly requires having a supported video adapter and editing *XF86Config* to load the appropriate kernel modules.

First, see if the DRI extension is working:

```
$ glxinfo | grep rendering
Xlib: extension "XFree86-DRI" missing on display ".0.0".
direct rendering: no
```

It is not, so the next step is to enter the following lines in *XF86Config*:

```
Section "Module"
...
```

```
      Load "dri"
      Load "glx"
  ...
  EndSection
  ...
  Section "dri"
    Mode 0666
  EndSection
```

Save your changes and restart X.

Test the new configuration by running *glxgears*, or by playing Tux Racer, TuxKart, or any game that requires hardware acceleration. Or you can run *glxinfo* again. Look for these lines:

```
$ glxinfo
direct rendering:..yes
...
OpenGL vendor string: VA Linux Systems, Inc.
OpenGL renderer string: Mesa DRI 20020221 Voodoo3 x86/MMX/3DNow!
OpenGL version string: 1.2 Mesa 4.0.4
...
```

This shows that hardware acceleration is working, because it names your hardware. If it were not, it would say this:

```
OpenGL vendor string: VA Linux Systems, Inc.
OpenGL renderer string: Mesa GLX Indirect
OpenGL version string: 1.2 Mesa 4.0.4
```

Most times, editing *XF86Config* this way cures the problem. If it doesn't, go to the next recipe for troubleshooting tips.

Discussion

Remember that your *XF86Config* file can be in a number of locations, depending on your distribution:

/etc/X11/XF86Config-4
/etc/XF86Config
/usr/X11R6/etc/X11/XF86Config-4
/usr/X11R6/etc/X11/XF86Config

XFree86, starting with Version 4.0, comes with DRI and the Mesa libraries built in, so you don't have to install any additional packages. Check your version:

```
$ XFree86 -version
XFree86 Version 4.3.0 (Debian 4.3.0-0ds2 20030304042836 dstone@aedificator)
Release Date: 27 February 2003
X Protocol Version 11, Revision 0, Release 6.6
Build Operating System: Linux 2.4.21-pre5 i686 [ELF]
Build Date: 04 March 2003
    Before reporting problems, check http://www.XFree86.Org/
to make sure that you have the latest version.
```

```
Module Loader present
OS Kernel: Linux version 2.4.21 (root@galaxy) (gcc version 3.2.3 20030316 (Debian
prerelease)) #1 Sun Aug 3 20:15:59 PDT 2003
```

If you're using XFree86 3.x, you really need to update. It's not worth trying to add DRI and the Mesa libraries to Version 3; it's better to upgrade the whole works.

See Also

- *XF86Config(7)*
- The DRI User Guide (*http://xfree.org/*)
- The Resources page at *http://xfree.org/*, for documentation for your version of XFree86 and for hardware-specific information, including drivers and configurations

15.6   Troubleshooting 3D Acceleration Problems

Problem

You went through the steps in Recipe 15.5, but you still don't have hardware acceleration.

Solution

Start from the beginning, and make sure all the pieces are in place.

Is your video card supported? See this chapter's "Introduction" for a list of supported models, and check *http://xfree.org* and *http://dri.sourceforge.net* for current information.

Did your driver modules load? Run *lsmod* to find out:

```
$ lsmod
Module           Size  Used by    Not tainted
tdfx             30432  17
agpgart          37312   0 (unused)
```

tdfx is a 3dfx Voodoo3 driver. *agpgart* is needed for the AGP subsystem to work. If your driver module or *agpgart* does not show up in *lsmod*, look in the */lib/modules* directory to see if the modules exist:

/lib/modules/2.4.21/kernel/drivers/char/agp/agpgart.0
/lib/modules/2.4.21/kernel/drivers/char/drm/tdfx.0

If either one is missing, you'll need to build and load it. (See Recipe 10.7.) Then restart X.

Is the *dri* subsytem working? If */proc/dri/0* exists, then it is:

```
$ ls /proc/dri/0
bufs  clients  mem  name  queues  vm  vma
```

If it doesn't, it may be that DRI was not enabled in the kernel. Check your kernel *.config* file. Look for:

```
# Hardware configuration
...
CONFIG_DRM=y
...
# DRM 4.1 drivers
...
CONFIG_DRM_TDFX=m
```

If *CONFIG_DRM=y* is not there, you'll need to rebuild the kernel. If the DRM module for your video card is not there, you can build and load it without rebuilding the kernel. Look in the kernel configurator for Character Devices, Direct Rendering Manager (XFree86 DRI support).

Unlike other kernel modules, all of these will be loaded by the X server. Make sure they are entered in the Modules section in *XF86Config*.

Always check */var/log/XFree86.0.log*. Look for error messages, and check that all the modules listed in the Modules section of *XF86Config* loaded. If you still can't figure it out, visit the Getting Help, Resources, and Community Lists pages on *http://xfree.org*.

Discussion

If you are using drivers supplied by the manufacturer of your video adapter, you'll need to look to them for support. Check your documentation, make sure you have the right driver, and look on the manufacturer's web site for user forums and support knowledge bases.

Enabling hardware acceleration for supported cards is a matter of having the correct kernel configuration and making sure the relevant kernel modules load. See Chapter 10 for how to build kernels and modules.

See Also

- The DRI User Guide (*http://xfree.org*)
- The Resources page at *http://xfree.org*, for documentation for your version of XFree86 and for hardware-specific information, including drivers and configurations

15.7 Configuring a Multihead Display

Problem

You would like to connect two monitors to a single system. You might want to have a single desktop span both monitors, or have two separate desktops, and maybe run different screen resolutions on each monitor.

Solution

XFree86 does it all. You'll need to have either two video cards or a single dual-head card installed and working. You'll also need two monitors, and XFree86 Version 4.x. Then edit *XF86Config* to create your desired multihead configuration.

To check your X version, use:

```
$ X -version
XFree86 Version 4.3.0...
```

You should configure your system to boot to a text console, so you can start X in whatever mode you want. You'll have four modes to choose from:

Traditional
    Two different desktops, which can have different resolutions and color depths

Xinerama
    A single desktop spanning across all screens, which must have the same resolutions and color depths

Clone
    Two displays, mirrored

Single
    Use only one monitor

First, back up your current *XF86Config*, then open it for editing. The PCI bus ID must be added to the Device entries:

```
Section "Device"
    Identifier  "3dfx"
    Driver      "tdfx"
    BusID       "PCI:1:0:0"
EndSection
...
Section "Device"
    Identifier  "nVidia"
    Driver      "nv"
    BusID       "PCI:0:12:0"
EndSection
```

This information comes from *lspci*:

```
$ /sbin/lspci
...
```

```
0000:00:12:0 VGA compatible controller: nVidia Corporation NV5M64 [RIVA TNT Model 64/
Model 64 Pro](rev 15)
0000:01:00.0 VGA compatible controller: 3Dfx Interactive, Inc. Voodoo 3 (rev 01)
```

Next, create a ServerLayout section. This example activates Xinerama at startup:

```
Section "ServerLayout"
   Identifier       "Xinerama"
   InputDevice      "Default Keyboard0"      "CoreKeyboard"
   InputDevice      "Default Mouse0"         "CorePointer"
   Option           "Clone"         "off"
   Option           "Xinerama"      "on"
 # Other screen position options are Below, Above, and LeftOf
   Screen           "Screen0" RightOf "Screen1"
   Screen           "Screen1"
 EndSection
```

To start X, boot to a text console and run:

$ startx

It will start up in full-color Xinerama.

Discussion

To start up in Traditional mode, set both Clone and Xinerama to "off," and change the Identifier to "Traditional."

To set Clone mode, turn off Xinerama, turn on Clone, and change the Identifier to "Clone."

Many video adapters are not capable of handling 3D acceleration in multihead mode. Check your documentation to find out if yours can.

PCI bus numbers that start with 0 are PCI cards. AGP cards start with 1.

Sometimes two video cards conflict and simply won't work together. If you think you have a problem, first run each card individually, to verify that they work. Then try moving the PCI card to a different slot. If that does not cure the conflict, you'll have to try different cards.

See Also

- *XF86Config(5x)*, for a complete description of all the available configuration options
- Recipe 7.4, "Starting and Stopping X," to learn how to configure your system to boot to either X or a text console

15.8 Choosing Different ServerLayouts at Startup

Problem

You don't want to be locked into the same old thing every time you start X. Maybe you want Xinerama. Maybe you want Traditional. Maybe you want to run a single monitor on occasion, and you want to be able to select which one.

Solution

Configure different ServerLayouts in *XF86Config*, then select the one you want with *startx* options:

```
$ startx -- -layout Single0
$ startx -- -layout Single1
$ startx -- -layout Clone
$ startx -- -layout Traditional
```

This layout starts a single monitor:

```
Section "ServerLayout"
  Identifier    "Single0"
  InputDevice   "Default Keyboard0"    "CoreKeyboard"
  InputDevice   "Default Mouse0"       "CorePointer"
  Screen        "Screen0"
EndSection
```

Start this layout like this:

```
$ startx -- -layout Single0
```

Now add a second Single layout, so that you can select either monitor at startup:

```
Section "ServerLayout"
  Identifier    "Single1"
  InputDevice   "Default Keyboard0"    "CoreKeyboard"
  InputDevice   "Default Mouse0"       "CorePointer"
  Screen        "Screen1"
EndSection
```

Start this layout like this:

```
$ startx -- -layout Single1
```

You can also create ServerLayouts for each of your multihead modes. This example starts Clone mode:

```
Section "ServerLayout"
  Identifier    "Clone"
  InputDevice   "Default Keyboard0" "CoreKeyboard"
  InputDevice   "Default Mouse0" "CorePointer"
  Option        "Clone" "on"
  Option        "Xinerama"off"
#Other screen position options are Below, Above, and LeftOf
```

```
    Screen        "Screen0" RightOf "Screen1"
    Screen        "Screen1"
EndSection
```

This example starts Traditional mode:

```
Section "ServerLayout"
    Identifier   "Traditional"
    InputDevice  "Default Keyboard0" "CoreKeyboard"
    InputDevice  "Default Mouse0" "CorePointer"
    Option       "Clone" "off"
    Option       "Xinerama"off"
#Other screen position options are Below, Above, and LeftOf
    Screen       "Screen0" RightOf "Screen "
    Screen       "Screen1"
EndSection
```

Recipe 15.7 shows the Xinerama ServerLayout.

Discussion

Here is a sample *XF86Config*, showing all the required elements and two ServerLayouts.

The core elements are the Input Device, Device, and Monitor sections. These are the sections where your devices are identified and linked to their drivers. The Screen section sets resolution and color depth. In the ServerLayout sections, you put together the pieces for your various modes by their Identifiers.

```
Section "Files"
    FontPath       "unix/:7100"
    FontPath       "/usr/lib/X11/fonts/misc"
    FontPath       "/usr/lib/X11/fonts/cyrillic"
    FontPath       "/usr/lib/X11/fonts/75dpi"
EndSection

Section "ServerFlags"
    Option   "DefaultServerLayout"  "Xinerama"
EndSection

Section "Module"
    Load    "ddc"
    Load    "GLcore"
    Load    "dbe"
    Load    "dri"
    Load    "extmod"
    Load    "glx"
    Load    "record"
    Load    "bitmap"
    Load    "speedo"
EndSection

Section "InputDevice"
    Identifier     "Default Keyboard0"
    Driver         "keyboard"
    Option         "CoreKeyboard"
```

```
    Option"        XkbRules"         "xfree86"
    Option        "XkbModel"         "pc104"
    Option        "XkbLayout"        "us"
    EndSection

Section "InputDevice"
    Identifier      "Default Mouse0"
    Driver          "mouse"
    Option          "CorePointer"
    Option          "Device"            "/dev/input/mice"
    Option          "Protocol""IMPS/2"
    Option"          Emulate3Buttons"     "true"
    Option          "ZAxisMapping"      "4 5"
EndSection

Section "Device"
    Identifier  "3dfx"
    Driver      "tdfx"
    BusID       "PCI:1:0:0"
EndSection

Section "Device"
    Identifier  "nVidia"
    Driver      "nv"
    BusID       "PCI:0:12:0"
EndSection

Section "Monitor"
    VendorName          "0195"
    ModelName           "SYL"
    Identifier          "Monitor0"
    HorizSync           30-70
    VertRefresh         0-160
    Option              "DPMS"
EndSection

Section "Monitor"
    VendorName          "0195"
    ModelName           "SYL"
    Identifier          "Monitor1"
    HorizSync           30-70
    VertRefresh         0-160
    Option              "DPMS"
EndSection

Section "Screen"
    Identifier      "Screen0"
    Device          "3dfx"
    Monitor         "Monitor0"
    DefaultDepth    24
    SubSection  "Display"
        Depth   24
        Modes   "1024x768"
```

```
            EndSubSection
        EndSection

        Section "Screen"
            Identifier      "Screen1"
            Device          "nVidia"
            Monitor         "Monitor1"
            DefaultDepth    24
            SubSection "Display"
                Depth    24
                Modes    "1024x768"
            EndSubSection
        EndSection

        Section "ServerLayout"
          Identifier    "Xinerama"
          InputDevice   "Default Keyboard0"      "CoreKeyboard"
          InputDevice   "Default Mouse0"         "CorePointer"
          Option        "Clone"         "off"
          Option        "Xinerama"      "on"
        #Other screen position options are Below, Above, and LeftOf
          Screen        "Screen0" RightOf "Screen1"
          Screen        "Screen1"
        EndSection

        Section "ServerLayout"
          Identifier    "Single0"
          InputDevice   "Default Keyboard0"    "CoreKeyboard"
          InputDevice   "Default Mouse0"       "CorePointer"
          Screen        "Screen0"
        EndSection
```

See Also

- *XF86Config(5x)*, for a complete description of all the available configuration options

15.9   Setting a Default ServerLayout

Problem

You like having all those X startup options, but you also want a default, so you don't have to be bothered with selecting one every time.

Solution

Create a ServerFlags section to set the default. This must come before the Server-Layout entries:

```
        Section "ServerFlags"
          Option     "DefaultServerLayout"  "Xinerama"
        EndSection
```

Then simply use:

```
$ startx
```

to start an X session.

15.10 Configuring startx

Problem

You like to boot to the console and then run *startx* when you want an X session. But you need to know how to configure *startx* to start the desktop or window manager of your choice.

Solution

Edit *.xinitrc* in your home directory. This will start Gnome:

```
exec gnome-session
```

You can list all of your installed window managers and desktop environments:

```
exec gnome-session
#exec startkde
#exec icewm
#exec icewm-experimental
#exec afterstep
#exec enlightenment
#exec blackbox
```

Entering all of your installed window managers makes it easy to change the default by uncommenting the one you want. Be sure that only one is uncommented at a time.

Discussion

Gnome, KDE, and XFce should be started from their startup scripts—*gnome-session, startkde,* and *startxfce*—rather than their executables.

If a user has no *~/.xinitrc* file, *startx* will look for the global *.xinitrc*, which will be tucked away somewhere in */etc*, like */etc/X11/xinit/.xinitrc*. X Windows file locations tend to be different on the various Linux distributions, so you might as well get used to hunting them down.

See Also

- *startx(1x)*

15.11 Changing Your Login Display Manager

Problem

You don't like your login display manager, and you want to try a different one. Perhaps your distribution installed *xdm*, which is rather bare-bones, and you'd like to try a login display manager with more features, like *gdm* or *kdm*. Or you've having problems, such as hanging at shutdown, and you think a different login manager might help.

Solution

The three main display managers are *xdm* (X display manager), *gdm* (Gnome display manger), and *kdm* (KDE display manager). To find out which one your system is using, use *ps*:

```
$ ps ax | grep dm
3796 ?    S    0.00  /usr/bin/kdm -nodaemon
```

Most distributions use */etc/X11/default-display-manager*. It should contain a single line:

```
/usr/bin/kdm
```

Change this to the display manager of your choice, using the full pathname:

```
/usr/bin/gdm
```

or:

```
/usr/bin/xdm
```

Red Hat and Fedora do it a little differently. Edit */etc/sysconfig/desktop,* and add this line:

```
DISPLAYMANAGER="GNOME"
```

or "KDE," or "XDM." Don't use the paths to the executables; that doesn't work.

Discussion

xdm, the X display manager, can be thought of as a graphical replacement for the login command. It requires only the X Windows System to run, unlike *gdm* and *kdm* (which require Gnome and KDE, respectively).

gdm and *kdm* do the same thing as *xdm*, plus allow users to shutdown or restart; select a different window manager or desktop; and customize the login screen with a picture or logo.

Red Hat and Fedora use the */etc/X11/prefdm* script to start the display manager, which is called from */etc/inittab*. */etc/X11/prefdm* looks to */etc/sysconfig/desktop* for the default display manager, as you can see by reading the script:

```
$ less /etc/X11/prefdm
...
```

```
preferred=
if [ -f /etc/sysconfig/desktop ]; then
    . /etc/sysconfig/desktop
      if [ "$DISPLAYMANAGER" = GNOME ]; then
        preferred=gdm
      elif [ "$DISPLAYMANAGER" = KDE ]; then
        preferred=kdm
      elif [ "$DISPLAYMANAGER" = XDM ]; then
        preferred=xdm
      fi
  fi
```

This is where we see that it wants *DISPLAYMANAGER = "GNOME"*, instead of */usr/ bin/gdm*.

If you peruse Red Hat's */rc*.d* directories, you'll notice there are no entries for any display manager. How can this be? Take a look at the bottom of */etc/inittab*:

```
# Run xdm in runlevel 5
x:5:respawn:/etc/X11/prefdm -nodaemon
```

The moral is, in Linux, there are always many ways to do things.

See Also

- Chapter 7, *Starting and Stopping Linux*, for recipes on how to change to different runlevels and how to configure runlevels to boot to a text console or to a display manager
- the *xdm* and XTerminal mini-howto (*http://www.tldp.org/HOWTO/XDM-xterm*)
- *gdm* homepage (*http://freshmeat.net/projects/gdm*)
- *kdm* handbook (*http://docs.kde.org/en/3.2/kdebase/kdm*)

15.12 Running Different Window Managers Simultaneously with Xnest

Problem

You have all these great window managers and desktop environments installed—KDE, Gnome, Enlightenment, Fluxbox, XFce, and such—and you would like to run some of them simultaneously. You know you can start up separate additional X sessions, or log out of X and start up in another window manager, but you wonder if there isn't a way to run them at the same time.

Solution

Xnest, the "nested X server," is just the tool for the job. Xnest allows you to run additional X sessions inside of already running X sessions.

Open a command shell in any X session—let's say you're running IceWM—and fire up Xnest:

```
$ Xnest -ac :1
```

You should see a blank screen with an X cursor in the middle. Now you can open a window manager. This example starts up WindowMaker:

```
$ wmaker -display :1
```

Now you can start up another one. From a command shell on IceWM, enter:

```
$ Xnest -ac :2
```

Some window managers or desktop environments, such as Gnome, need to start from an xterm in the Xnest window. First start up an xterm:

```
$ xterm  -display :2
```

Then start Gnome from the xterm:

```
$ gnome-session
```

You can start up yet another Xnest session from any available terminal in any of the windows:

```
$ Xnest -ac :3
```

You can continue to open more window managers until your system resources are exhausted and everything slows to a crawl. Figure 15-1 shows Gnome inside of IceWM, on KDE.

Discussion

X sessions are numbered from 0, so the default X session is always :0. The -ac option to Xnest specifies the session number for the new display. Keep track of your whereabouts by checking the *DISPLAY* value:

```
$ echo $DISPLAY
:0.0
```

The -ac option disables access controls. Otherwise, X will not let you open any applications. Xnest uses the same options as the X command—see *xserver(1x)*.

When you get several window managers going, you might see an error message like this, and the new one won't start:

```
$ gnome-session
gnome-session: you're already running a session manager
```

No problem. Just track it down and kill it:

```
$ echo $SESSION_MANAGER
local/windbag:/tmp/.ICE-unix/2774
$ rm /tmp/.ICE-unix/2774
```

and now Gnome will start.

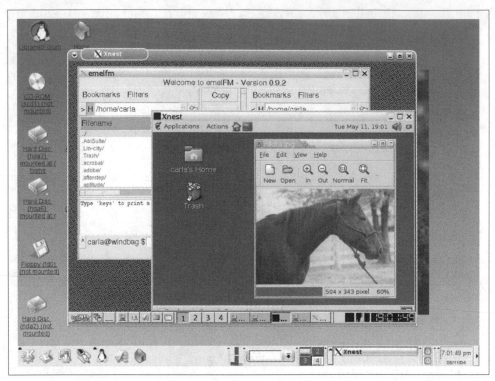

Figure 15-1. Gnome

See Also

- *xnest(1), xserver(1)*
- Window managers for X (*http://www.plig.org/xwinman*)

CHAPTER 16

Backup and Recovery

16.1 Introduction

Making good backups is a fundamental chore, and one that is too often messy and inconvenient. This chapter covers using *rsync* and Mondo Rescue for robust, easy backups and, just as important, easy restores.

rsync is extremely efficient. It only transfers changes in files, and it can perform on-the-fly compression. It excels at keeping file trees sychronized; unlike a lot of backup software, it even mirrors deletions. Because of these features, *rsync* is the tool of choice for updating and mirroring web sites, CVS trees, and other large, complex file trees.

There are two ways to use *rsync*: over *ssh*, for authenticated login and transport; or by running it as a daemon to create public archives, which do not use *ssh*. Using *ssh* requires users to have login accounts on every machine for which they need *rsync* access. When *rsync* is run in daemon mode, you can use its built-in authentication methods to control access, so that users do not need login accounts on the *rsync* server.

Mondo Rescue is a great utility for creating a bootable system restore disk. Use it to make a snapshot of your current system configuration, and a bare-metal rebuild is as easy as booting to a CD or DVD. You'll have all of your patches, configurations, and updates. Then pull your data from your *rsync* server, and you're back in business in record time. Mondo can also be used for a complete system backup, all by itself.

Tape backups have long been a mainstay, because they used to provide the most storage for the least money. But they are slow to write to, and even slower to restore from. If you're getting paid by the hour, it might not seem so bad to sit back and enjoy the endless whirring when you're looking for a little bitty text file at the end of the tape. But there are other disadvantages:

- Hard drives are much larger than tapes now, so you may have to use a tape auto-loader, which is expensive, or have a designated tape-changing minion, which can raise dependability issues.
- Users must depend on system administrators to restore files.

- Doing a bare-metal restore is complicated, because you must first install a file-system, then the tape drivers, and then do the restore.

- Even when a single tape is large enough to store a complete backup, you still have to change and store tapes, even if it's only on a weekly basis.

Tape has one advantage: longevity. CDs, DVDs, and hard drives cannot be counted on for long-term archiving. I wouldn't count on home-burned CDs/DVDs for longer than two years. Tapes should be good for 20 years, if stored carefully. Of course, there's no guarantee that there will be drives or software to read them in 20 years, but the tapes themselves should last just fine.

Longevity is the primary difficulty with all digital storage media, because even if the medium (tape, DVD, etc.) survives, there's no guarantee that the tools to read it will endure. Hardware is in a continual state of change, and file formats change too. Can you still read 5.25" floppy disks? WordStar files? VisiCalc? Even the most offbeat obsolete file can be read, if it's a plain ASCII file. But what are you going to do with proprietary binary datafile formats, like *.ppt* and *.pst*? If the vendor decides to stop supporting them, or goes out of business, you're out of luck.

Paper is still the long-term storage champion. (Yes, stone tablets, parchment scrolls, and clay tablets win hands-down for sheer durability, but let's stick to contemporary media.) However, movies and songs do not translate well to paper, and paper is hundreds of times bulkier than any digital storage medium.

So, as a practical matter, planning good short-term archiving and disaster recovery is usually the best we can do. *rsync* and Mondo Rescue are perfect for this. *rsync* is fast, compact, and completely automatic—no need to remember to swap discs or tapes. Restores are easy and fast. You can even set up user-accessible backup archives, so users don't have to pester you to restore files.

What about backing up your backup server? No problem. Setting up a remote *rsync* mirror for backing up the backups is a common strategy.

Also, there are more choices than ever for removable media, including removable drive trays for IDE drives, USB/FireWire portable drives, and flash storage devices. In sum, there are a lot of excellent options for designing your backup and recovery schemes.

16.2 Using rsync for Local File Transfers and Synchronization

Problem

You need to keep file trees synchronized on your workstation because your workstation is a staging ground for web directories, image galleries, source code trees, or other complex collections of files. So you use a working directory for editing files, and then copy the finished files to a separate upload directory. You would like something faster and more intelligent than *cp*, because *cp* takes a long time and you lose track of what needs to be copied.

Solution

Use *rsync* to keep file trees synchronized. *rsync* copies only changes, so it speeds up file copying, and it tracks changes inside files and in file trees.

Be sure you have the latest version, to get all the bugfixes and security patches. You definitely want 2.6 or later:

```
$ rsync --version
rsync  version 2.6.2  protocol version 26
...
```

This command copies a directory of web files to a staging directory that will later be uploaded to the web server:

```
$ rsync -av --stats  /home/pearlbear/webs  ~/web_upload
building file list ... done
...<all the files being copied fly by>...
Number of files: 254
Number of files transferred: 235
Total file size: 8923014 bytes
Total transferred file size: 8923014 bytes
Literal data: 8923014 bytes
Matched data: 0 bytes
File list size: 6490
Total bytes written: 8939848
Total bytes read: 3780
```

To verify the transfer, use:

```
$ ls ~/web_upload
webs
```

 There is a subtle gotcha here: */home/pearlbear/images* transfers the contents of */images* and the images directory itself. Adding a trailing slash (*/home/pearlbear/images/*) copies only the contents of the */images* directory, but not the directory itself. The trailing slash only matters on the source directory; it makes no difference on the destination directory.

If more files are added to */home/pearlbear/webs,* or any existing files are changed, simply re-run the same command. *rsync* will transfer only the changes.

You can specify more than one source directory to be copied:

```
$ rsync -av  /home/pearlbear/webs /home/pearlbear/web_images  ~/web_upload
```

You can also test your *rsync* command first with the *--dry-run* option:

```
$ rsync -av  --dry-run  /home/pearlbear/webs /home/pearlbear/web_images  ~/web_upload
```

Discussion

If any files are deleted from the source directory, *rsync* will not delete them from the destination directory unless you explicitly tell it to with the *--delete* flag:

```
$ rsync -av --delete /home/pearlbear/webs  ~/web_upload
```

The *-av* flags mean *archive*, which retains file permissions and ownership, and *verbose* output.

Be careful using the *--delete* flag; if you accidentally delete from the *rsync* archive a file that you wanted to keep, it's gone for good. Be especially careful with your file-paths, because *--delete* will happily erase an entire directory or file tree.

rsync is a great tool for keeping local archives synchronized. When you're authoring web pages, writing code, assembling files to burn to CD, or managing any kind of large collection of files, it's a real timesaver to have *rsync* track and synchronize all the changes.

Installation is simple—both RPMs and Debian packages are named *rsync*, and you only need the single package. The sources are statically linked, so there is no danger of dependency problems, however you elect to install it.

See Also

- *rsync(1)*

16.3 Making Secure Transfers with rsync and ssh

Problem

You want to use *rsync* to copy files to another PC over a LAN, or over the Internet, and you want encrypted transport and authentication.

Solution

Use *rsync* over *ssh*. *ssh* must be set up and working on all hosts.

Specify your source and destination, and specify *ssh* with the *-e* flag. This command transfers files over the local network, to *ljl*'s account on the remote PC "stinkpad":

```
ljl@compak:~$ rsync -av -e ssh  stationery  stinkpad:test
ljl@stinkpad's password:
building file list ... done
stationery/
stationery/ljl-return-address-small.sxw
stationery/ljl-holiday-label.sxw
stationery/ljl-return-address-MV-small.sxw
wrote 25984 bytes  read 68 bytes  7443.43 bytes/sec
total size is 25666  speedup is 0.99
```

Beware of filepath trickiness. *stinkpad:test* uploads the *stationery* directory and its contents to */home/ljl/test* on *stinkpad*. If */test* does not exist, *rsync* will create it:

```
ljl@stinkpad's password:
building file list ... done
created directory test
```

If you want to upload to a directory outside of your home directory, you'll need sufficient permissions for *rsync* to create a new directory, or you'll need it to be an existing directory that you can write to. Precede the upload directory with a forward slash, to make it relative to the root filesystem instead of to your home directory:

```
$ rsync -av -e ssh  stationery  stinkpad:/shared_uploads
```

To upload files over the Internet, use your login on the remote system and the full domain name:

```
$ rsync -av -e ssh  stationery  ljl@stinkpad.test.net:/shared_uploads
```

The syntax for copying files from a remote host is a little different. This copies the */scripts* directory and its contents from the remote host to your local */downloads* directory:

```
$ rsync -av -e ssh ljl@stinkpad.test.net:/shared_uploads/scripts  ~/downloads/
```

Discussion

Both authentication and transport are encrypted, so this is a nice, secure way to transfer sensitive files. The one downside is that users need shell accounts on all machines they are going to store files on or retrieve files from, so it's a bit of work to set up. A central server, with shared directories, is a good way to manage complex file sharing scenarios. You can control access with the usual Linux tools—file and directory permissions, and user groups, and you can use unique logins on the shared server, for extra security.

See Also

- *rsync(1)*

16.4   Building an rsync Backup Server

Problem

You want users to back up their own data. But you really don't want to give users shell accounts all over the place, just so that they can do backups. You'd also like to make it easier for them to share files, again without giving all your users shell accounts.

Solution

Use a dedicated PC for a central server, and run *rsync* in daemon mode. Users will not need login accounts on the server, and you can use *rsync*'s own access controls and user authorization for security.

rsync must be installed on all machines.

First, on the *rsync* server, edit or create */etc/rsyncd.conf* to create an *rsync* module defining the archive:

```
# global settings
log file = /var/log/rsyncd.log
# modules
[backup_dir1]
    path = /backups
    comment = server1 archive
    list = yes
    read only = no
```

Make sure that */backups* exists. Next, start *rsync* on the server in daemon mode:

```
# rsync --daemon
```

Now you can copy files from a remote machine to the server. In this example, the remote PC is "workstation," and the *rsync* server is "server1." First, verify that the *rsync* server is accessible:

```
sue@workstation:~$ rsync server1::
backup_dir1        server1 archive
```

This command copies Sue's */spreadsheets* directory to the module *backup_dir1*:

```
sue@workstation:~$ rsync -av  spreadsheets server1::backup_dir1
building file list.....done
spreadsheets/aug_03
spreadsheets/sept_03
spreadsheets/oct_03
wrote 126399 bytes  read 104 bytes  1522.0 bytes/sec
total size is 130228  speedup is 0.94
```

Now, view the nice, new uploaded files:

```
sue@workstation:~$ rsync server1::backup_dir1
drwx------        192  2003/02/12  spreadsheets
-rw-r--r--      21560  2003/09/17  aug_03
-rw-r--r--      21560  2003/10/14  sept_03
-rw-r--r--      21560  2003/11/10  oct_03
```

Sue can easily retrieve files from *server1* to her workstation:

```
sue@workstation:~$ rsync -av  server1::backup_dir1/sept_03  ~/downloads
receiving file list...done
sept_03
wrote 21560 bytes read 126 bytes 1148.0 bytes/sec
total size is 22031  speedup is 0
```

Discussion

This particular setup is perfectly functional, but not very secure. *backup_dir1* is wide open, so any *rsync* user can access it. Files are transmitted in the clear, so you shouldn't use this for sensitive files.

You can use *rsync*'s built-in simple authentication and access controls to limit access, so it's possible to set up reasonably private archives. See Recipe 16.5 to learn how to add some security.

This is what the *rsync* command options mean:

rsync server1::
> Double colons are used when connecting to an *rsync* server running in daemon mode. When you connect to an *rsync* server, you use the module names, rather than filepaths.

rsync -av
> *-a* means *archive mode*. This tells *rsync* to copy directories recursively, preserve permissions, copy symlinks, preserve group, preserve owner, and preserve time-stamps. *-a* is the same as *-rlptgoD*. *-v* is verbose.

--stats
> This option prints a verbose set of statistics on the file transfer, for those who wish to calculate the efficiency of the *rsync* algorithm.

/etc/rsyncd.conf should be familiar to Samba users, as it uses the same style as *smb.conf*. Global settings go at the top. Then you can define as many modules as you need. A *module* defines a single directory, with its options and access permissions:

[backup_dir1]
> The module name is enclosed in square brackets. Make this anything you like.

path = /backups
> The directory for this module. Always use absolute paths.

comment = server1 archive
> This is optional; say anything you want here.

list = yes
> This allows the module to be listed when users query the server. The default is no, which will hide the module.

read only = no
> The default is read-only. If you want to be able to upload files to this directory, turn off read-only.

See Also

- *rsync(1), rsyncd.conf(5)*
- The *rsync* home page (*http://rsync.samba.org*)

16.5   Securing rsync Modules

Problem

You followed Recipe 16.4, and you really like giving users the power to fetch their own files from the backup server, or delegating updates of web and FTP servers to someone else. But it's wide open to anyone using *rsync*—how do you secure the modules?

Solution

rsync comes with its own simple authentication and access controls. You'll create a new file containing username/password pairs, and add "auth users" and "secrets file" directives to */etc/rsyncd.conf*.

First create the password file on the *rsync* server. This example is for our fearless user, Sue. Make it *chmod 600*:

```
# rsync-users for server1
# created 2/7/2004
sue:sekkrit
```

Next, edit */etc/rsyncd.conf*. Give Sue her own module, and lock out everyone but her:

```
# global settings
log file = /var/log/rsyncd.log
#modules
[sue_backup]
    path = /backups/sue
    comment = Sue's private archive
    list = yes
    read only = no
    auth users = sue
    secrets file = /etc/rsync/rsync-users
```

To access the module, Sue must prefix the server name with her *rsync* username:

```
sue@workstation:~$ rsync sue@server1::sue_backup
Password:
drwx------        192   2003/02/12   spreadsheets
-rw-r--r--      21560   2003/09/17   aug_03
-rw-r--r--      21560   2003/10/14   sept_03
-rw-r--r--      21560   2003/11/10   oct_03
```

Now she can upload and download files just like before, as long as she remembers to use her *rsync* login. Don't forget the double colons, which are used when connecting to an *rsync* server.

Discussion

The username/password pairs are arbitrary and are not related to system user accounts, so it is quick and easy to create or edit modules and add or delete users.

For additional security, add these directives to *rsyncd.conf*:

strict modes = yes
> This enforces strict permissions on the password file. The file will not be checked by *rsync* if it is readable by any user other than the *rsync* daemon, and users will not be allowed access. The default is "yes," so it's not necessary to include this line, except as a reminder. If you don't want strict mode, you'll have to use *strict modes = false*.

hosts allow
> Use this to specify hosts that are allowed to access the *rsync* archives. For example, you can limit access to hosts on your domain:
> ```
> hosts allow = *.windbag.net
> hosts allow = 192.168.1.
> ```
> All hosts not allowed are denied, so you don't need a *hosts deny* directive.

hosts deny
> This usually isn't needed, if you use *hosts allow*. It is useful for denying access to specific hosts that cause annoyance, if you don't want to use *hosts allow*.

The password file is in cleartext, so it must be restricted to the superuser.

See Also

- *rsync(1)*, *rsyncd.conf(5)*
- The *rsync* home page (*http://rsync.samba.org*)

16.6   Building an Anonymous Public rsync Server

Problem

You want to distribute software or other files, using an *rsync*-enabled server to conserve bandwidth. So you'll need anonymous access for downloads, and restrictions on who can upload files to the server.

Solution

First, build an *rsync* server as described in Recipe 16.4. Then make all public modules read-only, and be sure that permissions on directories do not allow write access to anyone but user and group owners. To upload files to your server, use *rsync* over *ssh*.

Discussion

To make a module read-only, add this line to the section for the module in *rsyncd.conf*:

```
read only = yes
```

Remember, the syntax for uploading files via *ssh* is a little different than the syntax for uploading files when *rsync* is running in daemon mode. You'll want to specify the true directory name, not the module name, and use only a single colon:

```
$ rsync -av -e ssh  /webfiles  rsyncadmin@stinkpad.test.net:/www/public
Password:
```

Discussion

If you want to automate nightly uploads over *ssh*, see Recipe 16.9.

See Also

- *rsync(1), rsyncd.conf(5)*
- Chapter 17, *Remote Access*
- The *rsync* home page (*http://rsync.samba.org*)
- Recipe 16.4, "Building an rsync Backup Server"

16.7   Launching the rsync Daemon at Startup

Problem

You don't want to start the *rsync* daemon by hand all the time. But *rsync* does not come with an *init* script. How do you make it start at boot time?

Solution

Put this script in */etc/init.d,* then add it to your desired runlevels:

```
#!/bin/bash
# simple init script to run
# rsync in daemon mode

case "$1" in
    start)
        echo "Starting the rsync server..."
        exec /usr/bin/rsync --daemon
        ;;

    stop)
        echo "Stopping the rsync server...."
```

```
        killall /usr/bin/rsync
        ;;

    restart)
        $0 stop
        sleep 1
        $0 start
        ;;

    *)
        echo "Usage: $0 {start|stop|restart}"
        exit 1
        ;;
esac
```

Discussion

Remember to *chmod +x* to make this script executable.

See Also

- Chapter 7, *Starting and Stopping Linux*, to learn how to add *rsync* to your desired runlevels

16.8   Fine-Tuning File Selection

Problem

You would like to exclude some files (such as *.tmp* and *.bak* files) from being backed up, or you would like to create a list of included files.

Solution

Put your file lists in files, then call them with *rsync*'s *--exclude-from* or *--include-from* options.

The files can contain a list of files, regular expressions, or both:

```
*.tmp
*.temp
*.bak
/etc/skel
/etc/local
```

Then add the *--exclude-from* or *--include-from* option on the *rsync* command line:

```
$ rsync -ae ssh /home /etc --exclude-from=~/exclude-list backup.test.net:/home-etc
```

Discussion

It's best to use only one or the other; using both options is the fast track to confusion.

See Also

- *rsync(1)*

16.9 Automating rsync over ssh Backups

Problem

You would like to automate your *rsync* over *ssh* backups.

Solution

Write a script, create a *cron* job, and set up *keychain* to authenticate to your remote hosts. (See Recipe 17.7 to learn how to use *keychain*.)

Here is a simple script that backs up */home* and */etc,* using the "backupadmin" user created just for this job.The second line of the script tells *cron* to hook into *keychain* for remote authentication:

```
#!/bin/bash
source  /home/backupadmin/.keychain/$HOSTNAME-sh
rsync -av -e ssh  --delete --force /home /etc  stinkpad:home-etc-backup/
```

Once you have fine-tuned your file selection and tested your backup script, create a *cron* job to run the script. This runs it every night at 10 p.m.:

```
# crontab -e
0 22 * * *  /usr/local/bin/rsyncbackup.sh
```

Discussion

A lot of documentation tells you to create keys with null passphrases, so that you can schedule *ssh* transfers with *cron*. It's dangerous to do this, because anyone who gains access to your private key will be able to easily misuse it. *keychain* handles authentication for you, so you can properly protect your private keys with passphrases. The one downside to *keychain* is that it does not survive a reboot, so you have to enter your passphrase, or passphrases, at startup. But this is a security utility, after all— you don't want just anyone to be able to boot your machine and have unfettered access to your remote hosts.

Using the *--delete* flag means that all files deleted from the local archive will also be removed from the remote archive.

--force means that directories will be deleted even if they are not empty.

This is an easy way to perform secure, offsite backups. If all of your users' */home* and shared data directories are on a central server, it's even easier.

See Also

- *ssh(1)*, *rsync(1)*
- Recipe 16.8, "Fine-Tuning File Selection"
- Recipe 17.7, "Better Passwordless Logins with keychain"
- Hack #42, "Automated Snapshot-Style Incremental Backups with rsync," in *Linux Server Hacks*, by Rob Flickenger, for a really nice script that creates system snapshots at any interval you like (hourly, every four hours, daily, etc.)
- The Examples page at *http://samba.anu.edu.au/rsync*

16.10 Limiting rsync's Bandwidth Requirements

Problem

rsync can gobble up your bandwidth in nothing flat; imagine backing up a few gigabytes of ripped audio files on a busy network. What's an easy way to restrict it, without implementing full-blown traffic shaping?

Solution

Use the *--bwlimit* option:

```
$ rsync -a --bwlimit=256 rsync.test.net::testnetftp/ /ftp/mirror
```

Discussion

--bwlimit uses kilobytes per second, so be sure to take this into account when you're calculating what value to use. Remember that most network speeds are measured in kilobits, which are one-eighth the size of kilobytes.

See Also

- *rsync(1)*

16.11 Customizing Filepaths in rsync

Problem

You want to be able to specify filepaths, instead of dumping everything into a single directory.

Solution

Use the *-R* option:

```
$ rsync -aR -e ssh  /webfiles/site1  stinkpad.test.net:/www/public
```

This creates */www/public/webfiles/site1*, instead of */www/public/site1*.

Discussion

This is especially useful when you are transferring several directories and want to maintain separate filepaths for each one.

See Also

- *rsync(1)*

16.12 Installing rsync on Windows Clients

Problem

You're running a mixed LAN, and you would like to back up your Windows clients on your Linux *rsync* server.

Solution

On all the Windows clients, install Cygwin, *rsync*, OpenSSH, and a Linux text editor. Then make a few Windows-specific tweaks, and you can use *rsync* just like on Linux clients.

To get all of these, visit *http://www.cygwin.com* and download *setup.exe* to your Windows PC. Click "Install from Internet," then proceed through the installation steps until you get to the Select Packages menu. In the +Net menu, select *rsync* and OpenSSH. In the +Editors menu, select an editor.

Now you need to add Cygwin's path to Windows. On Windows 95/98/ME, add *C:\Cygwin\bin,* or whatever your path is, to the *SET PATH=* statement in *AUTOEXEC.BAT*. Then reboot.

On Windows NT, go to Control Panel → System → Environment tab. Add the path setting to the end, then click the Set button. Click OK. You won't need to reboot.

On Windows 2000/XP, go to Control Panel → System → Advanced tab, then click the Environment Variables button. Double-click on the *PATH* statement in the System Variable screen, append the path, then click OK. You won't need to reboot.

Remember to separate your *PATH* statements with semicolons. Now your Windows PC is ready to make *rsync* and *rsync* over *ssh* transfers.

To use Cygwin, open an MS-DOS command shell, and start up Cygwin like this:

```
C:\cygwin\cygwin.bat
administrator@powerpc ~$
```

This puts you in a nice, familiar Bash environment. Alternatively, you can run an application directly from the C: prompt:

```
C:\cygwin\bin\rsync -av -e ssh  stationery  stinkpad:test
```

Discussion

For running *rsync* on Windows, use all the same commands as on Linux. Just remember to be careful of filepaths—Windows uses backslashes instead of forward slashes, and drive letters:

```
C:\cygwin\bin\rsync -av -e ssh  stationery  stinkpad:test
```

Cygwin creates a nice native Linux environment on your Windows system, and it comes with a large assortment of Linux utilities. If Cygwin doesn't include a Linux program you want to use, you may be able to make it work by compiling it on Windows. See *http://www.cygwin.com* for details.

See Also

- *rsync(1)*
- Cygwin home (*http://www.cygwin.com*)

16.13 Creating a Message of the Day for rsync

Problem

You're running an *rsync* server, by running *rsync* in daemon mode, and you think it would be nice to greet users with a cheery daily message.

Solution

First create your MOTD, in a plain text file, then configure the path to the file in *rsyncd.conf*:

```
motd file = /etc/rsync/motd
```

When users connect to your server, they will see your message:

```
sue@workstation:~$ rsync server1::
Greetings from Asbury Park! I'm Bruce, and I'll be your rsync server today!

backup_dir1     server1 archive
sue_backup      sue's private stuff
```

Discussion

You don't have to settle for dull old text messages. ASCII art makes a nice MOTD; see Figure 16-1 for an example.

Figure 16-1. An ASCII message of the day

Create your own with the FIGlets ASCII generator, available at *http://www.figlet.org*.

See Also

- *rsync(1), rsyncd.conf(5)*

16.14 Creating a Bootable System Restore CD with Mondo Rescue

Problem

You need a simple method for creating a system image. You want a perfect clone to preserve your configurations, patches, and updates, so you can easily do a bare-metal restore, or migrate to a new hard drive, or roll out a number of identical installations. Your data are backed up separately, so you only want to preserve system and configuration files.

Solution

Use Mondo Rescue to create a custom bootable system CD.

Be sure there is enough free space on your hard drive to store the temporary CD image (at least 700 MB) per CD. Do not run any other programs (games, email, word processors, etc.) while running Mondo. Then, as root, run *mondoarchive* at the command line. Mondo will think about things for a minute or two, then open the window shown in Figure 16-2.

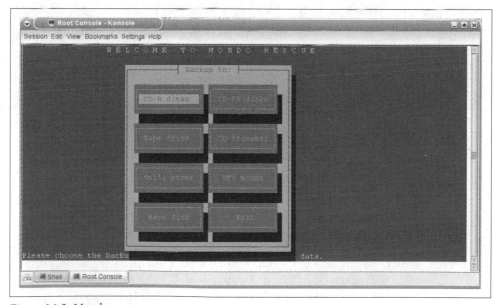

Figure 16-2. Mondo

Choose your backup medium. In this example, we'll use a CD-RW at SCSI address *0,1,0*. In the next window, it asks if your writer has "Burn-Proof" technology (*yes*). Next, choose the compression level (*Maximum*), then specify the speed of your CD (re)writer (*4*).

Tell it the SCSI address of your CD writer *0,1,0*. Next, you'll be asked which files you want to back up. Select /, or the entire root filesystem, because the next question is which files you want to exclude. */tmp* and */proc* are automatically excluded. You should also exclude */home* and any other data directories, such as shared data directories, mail spools, and logfiles.

Mondo will then ask whether you want to verify your backups after it has created them (*yes*) and whether you are confident that your kernel is a sane, sensible, standard Linux kernel (say *no* if you are using an older Debian kernel—see the "Discussion" section of this recipe for more information). Next it will ask if you are sure you want to proceed (*yes*).

When it asks you to enter your CD-ROM's */dev* device, give it the SCSI */dev* name—*/dev/scdn*—if your system has a 2.4 kernel. For 2.6 kernels, use */dev/hdn*. The backup can take up to a couple of hours. However, you can't wander away, because you'll need to push some buttons near the end.

Discussion

If you're running Mondo from the console and your screen blanks from inactivity, bring it back by hitting the Alt key.

cdrecord --scanbus shows the SCSI address of your drive. On systems with 2.4 kernels, look in */etc/fstab* to get the SCSI */dev* name, or dig through the output of *dmesg*.

To qualify as "sane," your kernel needs to include:

- *loopfs* support
- CD-ROM support
- ISO9660 filesystem support
- *initrd ramdisk* support (built-in)
- Virtual memory filesystem support (built-in)
- Floppy disk support (built-in)
- Ext2 filesystem support (built-in)
- Support for the backup media
- SCSI emulation in 2.4 kernels

Most stock kernels newer than 2.4.7 ought to be fine. Debian, in particular, didn't used to be well supported by Mondo, but Debian kernels from 2.4.18 should have all the required bits. If your kernel cannot be used to boot a Mondo Rescue CD, use the failsafe *mindi-kernel* (see Recipe 16.18). The *mindi-kernel* is used only to boot the Rescue CD; it does not replace your system kernel.

If you're not sure whether your drive supports "Burn-Proof" technology, run this command to show all of your drive's capabilities:

```
$ cdrecord --atip dev=0,1,0
Cdrecord 2.01a07 (i686-pc-linux-gnu) Copyright (C) 1995-2003 Jörg Schilling
scsidev: '0,1,0'
scsibus: 0 target: 1 lun: 0
...
Using generic SCSI-3/mmc CD-R driver (mmc_cdr).
Driver flags   : MMC-3 SWABAUDIO BURNFREE
Supported modes: TAO PACKET SAO SAO/R96P SAO/R96R RAW/R16 RAW/R96P RAW/R96R
...
```

Mondo has its own ideas about how GRUB should be set up, so GRUB users may need to create this soft link:

```
# ln -s /boot/grub/menu.lst /etc/grub.conf
```

Mondo insists on it and won't perform a backup without it, so it's best to humor it.

Mondo comes in source form, Debian packages, and RPMs. You'll need several packages:

> Mondo
> Mindi
> *afio*
> Newt
> *lzop*
> *syslinux*
> *cdrecord*
> *mkisofs*

Debian users will also see *apt-get* fetch:

> *buffer*
> *gawk*
> *mindi-busybox*
> *ms-sys*, *tint*
> *slang*

See Also

- *mondoarchive(1)*
- Your locally installed Mondo documentation (*/usr/share/doc/mondo/hml/ 1.6x-howto*)
- Mondo user forums (*http://forum.mondorescue.org*)

16.15 Verifying the Mondo Backup

Problem

You would like to verify that your new Mondo backup is good. It's always a good idea to verify that a backup is good; finding out that it's bad when you need to do a restore is *not* good for your health.

Solution

Use Mondo's *compare* command.

Boot up the Mondo disk on the same system that created it. At the command prompt, type:

```
# compare
```

This will take a while, depending on the size of the backup. When it's finished, review the changes by reading the */tmp/changed.txt* file. You can expect to see differences in logfiles, mail spools, */etc/mtab*, and other files that change frequently. There should not be changes in static system files, such as executables in */bin*, */sbin*, */usr/bin*, and */usr/sbin*, or in static configuration files in */etc*.

Discussion

Always test your backups! After running *compare*, restore a few files from the Mondo disk. If you have a spare PC that is the same hardware configuration, you can do a complete restore on it (the surest method).

See Also

- *mondoarchive(1)*
- Your locally installed Mondo documentation (*/usr/share/doc/mondo/hml/1.6x-howto*)
- Mondo user forums (*http://forum.mondorescue.org*)

16.16 Creating a Bootable System Restore DVD with Mondo Rescue

Problem

You would like to put your system backup on a single DVD, instead of several CDs.

Solution

Run Mondo Rescue from the command line, instead of using the graphical interface, and create an *.iso*. Then burn the *.iso* to DVD. In addition to the Mondo Rescue components listed in the "Discussion" section of Recipe 16.14, you'll need *dvd+rw-tools* and *cdrtools*.

The first command creates an *.iso*, and the second command copies it to the DVD:

```
# mondoarchive -OVmF -5 -S /tmp/scratch -T /tmp/mondo -E "/home /shared /var/www" \
-i -d /tmp/iso
# growisofs -dvd-compat -Z /dev/scd0=/tmp/iso
```

Discussion

This task can also be performed from the Mondo graphical interface. In the opening screen, select "Backup to Hard Disk." Using the command line gives you greater control; for example, you can turn off the prompt to create boot floppies and disable ejecting the drive tray.

This is what the various *mondoarchive* command flags mean:

-O Create a backup.

-V Verify the backup.

-m Don't eject the drive tray. Use this for unattended backups and for laptops, which usually do not have self-retracting disc trays.

-F Don't ask to create boot floppies.

-5 Compression level. The range is 0–9, with 0 being uncompressed and 9 the greatest level of compression. The default is 3.

-S Location of the scratch directory, where images are built before being archived.

-T The directory where other temporary files are stored.

-E List directories that are to be excluded from the backup. Removable mounts, */tmp*, and */proc* are automatically excluded.

-i Create *.iso* images.

-d The directory where the completed *.iso* is to be stored. The default is */root/images/mondo*.

See Also

- *mondoarchive(1), growisofs(1)*
- Your locally installed Mondo documentation (*/usr/share/doc/mondo/hml/1.6x-howto*)
- Mondo user forums (*http://forum.mondorescue.org*)

16.17 Using Mondo Rescue to Clone Linux Systems

Problem

You have a number of identical PCs, and you want to install identical custom Linux configurations on each one. It sounds easy, but in practice, installing the same custom configuration on two or more PCs is a pain and error-prone. Mondo Rescue makes it easy.

Solution

First, customize a single Linux installation to your specifications. Then create a Mondo CD or DVD from your customized system, and use it for your new installations. Boot to the Mondo disk, then select "Nuke" to perform the installation. It will overwrite anything that is already installed and create an exact copy of your customized Linux.

Discussion

This is a nice timesaver when you have a particular server configuration to replicate, or when you want to roll out a number of identical workstations. Don't forget to tweak network settings, such as hostnames and static IPs, and to set up user accounts as needed.

See Also

- *mondoarchive(1)*
- Your locally installed Mondo documentation (*/usr/share/doc/mondo/hml/ 1.6x-howto*)
- Mondo user forums (*http://forum.mondorescue.org*)

16.18 Using the mindi-kernel for a "Sane" Backup

Problem

Your Linux kernel is missing some of the elements Mondo needs to create a bootable rescue disk. You know this because when you tried to boot your Mondo rescue disk, it failed with a "VFS: Unable to mount root fs" error. What do you do next? How do you create a useable rescue disk?

Solution

Use the *mindi-kernel* to create your Mondo rescue disk.

The *mindi-kernel* is a failsafe 2.4.7 kernel provided by the Mondo authors. If you're using Mondo's graphical interface, it will ask you if you want to use the *mindi-kernel*. Say yes.

Use the *-k* flag to specify it at the command line:

```
-k FAILSAFE
```

Discussion

Debian users may need to install the *mindi-kernel* separately.

The *mindi-kernel* does not replace your system kernel; all it does is ensure a bootable rescue disk.

See Also

- *mondoarchive(1)*
- Your locally installed Mondo documentation (*/usr/share/doc/mondo/hml/1.6x-howto*)
- Mondo user forums (*http://forum.mondorescue.org*)

16.19 Restoring a System from a Mondo Rescue Disk

Problem

You need to do a complete system rebuild because your system has been compromised, or you just want to blow away your existing installation and restore it to a previous, known-good state.

Solution

To perform a complete system rebuild, boot to your Mondo rescue disk and type *nuke* at the command prompt. It will completely overwrite your system and restore it to the state saved on the Mondo disk.

Discussion

You can use Mondo to back up your entire system, including datafiles, or just the root filesystem. Using Mondo to preserve the root filesystem on a bootable CD, then backing up data separately on an *rsync* server, is an easy, fast way to do both back-ups and restores.

See Also

- *mondoarchive(1)*
- Your locally installed Mondo documentation (*/usr/share/doc/mondo/hml/1.6x-howto*)
- Mondo user forums (*http://forum.mondorescue.org*)

16.20 Restoring Selected Files from a Mondo Disk

Problem

You just need to replace a few selected files; you don't want to nuke your system and start over.

Solution

Boot your Mondo disk, and run it in *interactive* mode.

Type *interactive* at the prompt. Mondo will ask you which partitions to mount. Select the ones you want by editing the mountlist. Then follow the prompts:

```
Do you want to partition your devices? no
Do you want to format them? no
Do you want to restore everything? no
Do you want to restore something? yes
Which path do you want to restore? /etc/rsync
Select your restore path: /etc/rsync
```

Mondo will give you the option to try to boot your system directly from Mondo when you're finished restoring files, but it's usually simpler to remove the Mondo disk and reboot.

Discussion

You may wish to restore to the default path, which is */mnt/RESTORE*, and review the files before copying them to their final locations.

See Also

- *mondoarchive(1)*
- Your locally installed Mondo documentation (*/usr/share/doc/mondo/hml/1.6x-howto*)
- Mondo user forums (*http://forum.mondorescue.org*)

## CHAPTER 17

Remote Access

17.1 Introduction

Remote access is one of Linux's great features, and there are many ways to do it. For access over untrusted networks, don't use those old reliable standbys, telnet or X, because logins and data are sent in the clear. Your best bet is OpenSSH (Secure Shell), a suite containing a number of secure remote transfer programs: *scp* (secure copy), *ssh* (Secure Shell), and *sftp* (SSH file transfer protocol). *ssh* is the tool of choice for remote system administration; with *ssh*, you can log into remote systems and run them as though you were physically there. Logins and data are encrypted, and *ssh* will detect if any packets have been altered en route. Eavesdroppers can sniff and muck with all the packets they want—they won't get anywhere.

SSH isn't really a shell; it's a protocol. There are two incompatible versions of this protocol: *SSH-1* and *SSH-2*. OpenSSH supports both. This chapter covers SSH-2, because you should be using a current version of OpenSSH.

 SSH nomenclature can get a bit confusing. SSH, capitalized, is the protocol. *ssh*, *scp*, and so forth, in lowercase, are programs that use SSH. OpenSSH is the implementation of SSH used in this chapter.

Using SSH is not very complicated. If you're used to *rsh*, *rlogin*, or *rcp*, the command syntax is pretty much the same. You'll need *sshd*, the OpenSSH daemon, running on all machines to which you want to enable remote access, and you'll need shell accounts on the remote machines. You can log in as any user, as long you have the login and password.

OpenSSH uses public/private key pairs for authentication. Private keys are carefully guarded and never, ever shared. Always create a strong passphrase to encrypt and protect your private keys. A really strong passphrase is a nonsense sentence that combines words and numbers, like "t4is is mai 733t s3kkrit p4ssphr4se". As always, you must strike a balance between security and usability, because you may need to type your passphrase frequently.

Public keys are distributed to both remote SSH clients and remote SSH servers. For example, when you use *host-key authentication,* this means the public key of the server is stored on clients that are allowed to access it. All SSH sessions start with host-key authentication. Once the remote host's public key is copied to your local *~/.ssh* directory, you can log into any user account you have access to on the remote host, using the account logins.

If you want to use SSH keys for authentication, instead of user account logins, you generate your own public/private key pair, and copy your public key to all the remote hosts you wish to access. A couple of configuration steps, which are covered in this chapter, must be carried out to make this work. This is called *public-key authentication*.

If you're going to access a lot of remote machines, managing logins can be difficult. Recycling the same public key and passphrase all over the place presents a potential security problem, but tracking a lot of different passphrases can also be trouble. OpenSSH provides a way to avoid all this login drama, by using *public-key authentication, ssh-agent,* and *keychain*. These let you set up secure, passphraseless logins.

17.2   Setting Up OpenSSH the First Time

Problem

You need to establish a connection between your local workstation and a remote PC. The connection needs to be secure; you don't want your data exposed to prying eyes. (They're there, and you should be worried about them—even if you aren't para-noid.) So you want to set up OpenSSH.

Solution

Install OpenSSH on both machines. *sshd,* the *ssh* daemon, must be running on the remote host, so that it can receive connections. Copy the remote host's public key to the local machine's *~/.ssh/known_hosts* file, and you're in business.

Starting and stopping *sshd* on most *rpm*-based systems is done like this:

```
# /etc/init.d/sshd start
# /etc/init.d/sshd stop
```

On Debian, it's slightly different:

```
# /etc/init.d/ssh start
# /etc/init.d/ssh stop
```

Always check your *init* filenames, as they vary on different distributions.

Copying the remote host's public key to your local *~/.ssh/known_hosts* file is as simple as connecting to the remote host:

```
carla@windbag carla$ ssh stinkpad
The authenticity of host 'stinkpad (192.168.1.100)' can't be established.
RSA key fingerprint is a2:c6:70:3e:73:00:b3:ed:90:b1:9a:bc:e7:d5:32:ba.
Are you sure you want to continue connecting (yes/no)?
```

Type *yes*, and it will respond:

```
Warning: Permanently added 'stinkpad,192.168.1.100' (RSA) to the list of known hosts.
carla@stinkpad's password:
Linux stinkpad 2.4.21 #1 Sun Aug 3 20:15:59 PDT 2003 i686 GNU/Linux
Libranet GNU/Linux
Last login: Sat June  3 22:16:24 2004 from :0.0
carla@stinkpad:~$
```

Now you are logged into your account on the remote PC, and can work just as if you were sitting physically at the remote machine. (To learn how to run a remote X session, see Recipe 17.11.) To close the session, type *exit*.

Discussion

Using the simple ssh *<hostname>* login connects you to another host on your LAN, using the same login. You can connect as a different user with the *-l* flag:

```
carla@windbag ~$ ssh -l wilmaf stinkpad
```

To make an SSH connection over the Internet, you must use the full domain name:

```
carla@windbag ~$ ssh stinkpad.test.net
```

Making that initial connection, and copying the host's RSA key, is the riskiest part of setting up SSH. If an intruder managed to compromise your nameserver, she could possibly hijack your SSH session and capture your login. It's a pretty small risk, though, and you can verify the IP address before logging in the first time. To close off this hole, you can manually copy the host's public key to your local *~/.ssh/known_hosts* file first. You must edit it slightly; see the examples below.

Host keys are stored in */etc/ssh*. These are used to validate the identity of the remote host. This is all you need to allow users to access this machine. All they need is a copy of the public host key in their *~/.ssh/known_hosts* files and an account to log into. Some Linux distributions create two key pairs when you install OpenSSH—one RSA key pair and one DSA key pair:

```
$ ls /etc/ssh
ssh_host_dsa_key
ssh_host_dsa_key.pub
ssh_host_rsa_key
ssh_host_rsa_key.pub
```

If your system does not create these for you, or you wish to change them, see Recipe 17.3 to learn how to generate new host keys.

This is what the public *rsa* key looks like:

```
$ cat ssh_host_rsa_key.pub
ssh-rsa
AAAAB3NzaC1yc2EAAAABIwAAAIEA5pSqNmtqRzK2JaLr8qkIQ41nBDLI2JRJ6gRBmwg9gwK3S8xXnMUHIsu8w
h5S1oei8hs47x2I9cnNpxHfj1wQWwqP6lVyelDfD+y+uWIzoUGzUXN5IrqYZ70EdQ4Xn++Jl1kmFG6Ll6KySb
07OOXOnlCO9rNxisHL5GCOqi1+qM= root@windbag
```

The key itself must be one long, unbroken line—it must not have line breaks, as it does on this page. Copy it to a removeable disk, transfer it to your local *~/.ssh/ known_hosts* file, and modify it in this manner:

```
windbag.test.net,192.168.1.6 ssh-rsa
AAAAB3NzaC1yc2EAAAABIwAAAIEA5pSqNmtqRzK2JaLr8qkIQ41nBDLI2JRJ6gRBmwg9gwK3S8xXnMUHIsu8w
h5S1oei8hs47x2I9cnNpxHfj1wQWwqP6lVyelDfD+y+uWIzoUGzUXN5IrqYZ70EdQ4Xn++Jl1kmFG6Ll6KySb
07OOXOnlCO9rNxisHL5GCOqi1+qM=
```

As you can see, the hostname and IP address must be written at the beginning of the line, and the hostname must be deleted from the end of the line.

The *.pub*, or public, keys are world-readable, but private keys must be readable only by the key owner.

See Also

- *ssh(1)*
- *SSH, The Secure Shell: The Definitive Guide*, by Daniel J. Barrett and Richard Silverman (O'Reilly)

17.3   Generating New Host Keys

Problem

You looked in */etc/ssh* and didn't see any key files: your Linux distribution did not generate host keys when you installed OpenSSH. Or you just want to create new host keys yourself.

Solution

Use *ssh-keygen* to create a new key pair. This must be done as root, and you have to specify the name of the new key pair. You only need one key pair. Always specify a passphrase:

```
# ssh-keygen -t rsa -f /etc/ssh/ssh_host_rsa_key
Generating public/private rsa key pair.
Enter passphrase (empty for no passphrase):
Enter same passphrase again:
```

```
Your identification has been saved in /etc/ssh/ssh_host_rsa_key.
Your public key has been saved in /etc/ssh/ssh_host_rsa_key.pub.
The key fingerprint is:
6c:24:75:54:d3:21:17:c9:11:db:41:dd:95:3f:d0:ac root@windbag
```

This example uses the default key names, but you can call the keys anything you like. If you use different names, be sure to enter them in *etc/ssh/sshd_config*:

```
# HostKeys for protocol version 2
HostKey /etc/ssh/ssh_host_rsa_key
```

Comment out or delete any entries for keys that do not exist.

Discussion

See this chapter's "Introduction" for how to create a strong passphrase.

Once you have OpenSSH set up and working and you have distributed public keys, you don't want to change your private keys without a really good reason, because you'll have to distribute new public keys. If users try to connect with the old public key, they will get this message:

```
@@@@@@@@@@@@@@@@@@@@@@@@@@@@@@@@@@@@@@@@@@@@@@@@@@@@@@@@@@@
@    WARNING: HOST IDENTIFICATION HAS CHANGED!     @
@@@@@@@@@@@@@@@@@@@@@@@@@@@@@@@@@@@@@@@@@@@@@@@@@@@@@@@@@@@
IT IS POSSIBLE THAT SOMEONE IS DOING SOMETHING NASTY!
Someone could be eavesdropping on you right now (man-in-the-middle attack)!
It is also possible that the host key has just been changed.
Please contact your system administrator.
Add correct host key in <path>/known_hosts to get rid of this message.
Agent forwarding is disabled to avoid attacks by corrupted servers.
X11 forwarding is disabled to avoid attacks by corrupted servers.
Are you sure you want to continue connecting (yes/no)
```

It's a good idea to train your users to say *no* at the prompt, and to contact you to see what is going on.

See Also

- *ssh(1), ssh-keygen(1)*
- *SSH, The Secure Shell: The Definitive Guide*

17.4 Authenticating Via Public Keys

Problem

You would prefer to authenticate your SSH sessions with keys, rather than your system logins. This will let you use your SSH private-key passphrase instead of your system login, which means your system login is protected, and you can reuse the same public/private key pair for as many remote hosts as you need to connect to.

Solution

In this example, Valorie wishes to log in to *saturn* from *jupiter*. To do this, she must generate a new, personal private/public key pair with *ssh-keygen* on *jupiter*, then transfer a copy of her new public key to *saturn*.

This command generates a new RSA key pair, protected by a passphrase:

```
valorie@jupiter:~$ ssh-keygen -t rsa
Generating public/private rsa key pair.
Enter file in which to save the key (/home/valorie/.ssh/id_rsa):
Enter passphrase (empty for no passphrase):
Enter same passphrase again:
Your identification has been saved in /home/valorie/.ssh/id_rsa.
Your public key has been saved in /home/valorie/.ssh/id_rsa.pub.
The key fingerprint is:
79:1f:a5:5f:5f:17:e5:a8:bc:02:50:8c:3a:1e:e1:d1 valorie@jupiter
```

The new key pair is named */home/valorie/.ssh/id_rsa* and */home/valorie/.ssh/id_rsa.pub*. Now Valorie copies the new *id_rsa.pub* key to her account on *saturn*. Since this is her first entry in her *authorized_keys* file on *saturn*, she can use *scp*:

```
valorie@jupiter:~$ scp  ~/.ssh/id_rsa.pub  valorie@saturn:.ssh/authorized_keys
```

Now when Valorie logs into *saturn*, she will be asked for her private SSH key passphrase, instead of her system login:

```
valorie@jupiter:~$ ssh saturn
Enter passphrase for key '/home/valorie/.ssh/id_rsa':
Linux saturn 2.4.21 #1 Sun Aug 3 20:15:59 PDT 2003 i686 GNU/Linux
Libranet GNU/Linux

valorie@saturn:~$
```

To close the session, she can simply type *exit*.

Discussion

OpenSSH creates both RSA and DSA keys. Both support SSH2, which is the latest and greatest, so it doesn't matter which one you choose. RSA is the default.

A single key in *~/.ssh/authorized_keys* looks like this:

```
ssh-rsa AAAAB3NzaC1yc2EAAAABIwAAAIEAnYF8XfIqzuOIOXNwO71430hjOt4OuSN9NgWY8zlB7UkTQNu
AFXo2UWNU2WLDMPu3mJ6V1ixf49+wdfoENvWXNMuuAFiPHopHk2+PPHN75OLxlD8kvJc7BMTtYCU7GLj6lpH1
OyOglyUdMxO2GkjA45kPLYiXMpGNCclHRHVHU= valorie@jupiter
```

Remember, it must be one long, unbroken line. You can store as many keys here as you like.

Another way to copy a key to an *authorized_keys* file on a remote PC is to simply copy and paste. Open a normal SSH session:

```
$ ssh valorie@saturn
Password:
```

Then open a text editor on each side of the connection, and copy and paste.

You can do this for any account on the SSH server to which you have access. One public/private key pair should suffice; you can copy your public key to as many hosts as you need to, and use the same passphrase for all of them.

Keep track of where you are! It's easy to type a command thinking you're at the local machine when you're logged into a remote host.

Another point of confusion is which host is the client, and which host is the server. Any host that is running the *ssh* daemon, and is waiting to accept connections, can be thought of as the server.

Protect your keys! Public keys must be world-readable, but only owner-writable (mode 644). Private keys must absolutely not be anything but owner readable/writable (mode 600). Never, ever share your private keys.

Beware of text editors that automatically make backup copies. Either disable this feature, be very diligent about deleting the backup copies of keys and other sensitive SSH files, or make sure that permissions are set appropriately on the backups.

Public/private key pairs are a lovely stroke of genius that allow "hiding in plain sight." The public key encrypts, the private key decrypts. So you can (theoretically) strew your public keys all over the planet without harm.

See Also

- *ssh(1)*
- *SSH, The Secure Shell: The Definitive Guide*

17.5   Using Multiple Key Pairs

Problem

You would like to generate separate sets of keys for accessing different hosts, or different types of accounts. For example, you would like one SSH key for administering an FTP server, and a different one for accessing your private user accounts.

Solution

You can name your key pairs anything you like with *ssh-keygen*. *ssh-keygen* will automatically append *.pub* to the public key. Always create a passphrase!

```
akkana@windbag:$ ssh-keygen -t rsa -f /home/akkana/.ssh/ftp_key
Generating public/private rsa key pair.
Enter passphrase (empty for no passphrase):
Enter same passphrase again:
Your identification has been saved in /home/akkana/.ssh/ftp_key.
Your public key has been saved in /home/akkana/.ssh/ftp_key.pub.
```

```
The key fingerprint is:
95:d2:12:55:66:ba:ec:a8:5c:40:4b:1e:03:2b:6c:ea akkana@windbag
akkana@windbag:~$
```

When you create a key pair with non-default names, you need to enter the private key name in ~/.ssh/ssh_config. If this file does not exist, create it, and make an entry like this:

```
IdentityFile  ~/.ssh/ftp_key
```

Discussion

There should be a copy of the default *ssh_config* in */etc/ssh*. When you make changes, the simplest method is to append your options to the end of the file.

ssh_config is for both user-specific configurations and system-wide client options. Creating and storing a copy in a user's home directory configures user-specific options.

See Also

- *ssh(1), ssh_config(5)*
- *SSH, The Secure Shell: The Definitive Guide*

17.6 Passwordless Logins with ssh-agent

Problem

Typing passwords is a pain, and typing passphrases is even worse. You want to set up OpenSSH to open connections without having to enter a passphrase, and you want it to still be secure.

Solution

First, set up your private/public keys as in Recipe 17.3. Then use *ssh-agent*. *ssh-agent* handles authentication requests while you are gallivanting about the world, SSH-ing into various systems. You'll enter your passphrase once, at the beginning of your SSH session; when you log out of the session, you'll have to start over.

ssh-agent won't enable you to schedule SSH transfers from *cron*—see Recipe 17.8 to learn how to do this.

First, start up *ssh-agent*. You must name the shell you want to use:

```
$ shh-agent bash
```

You'll be returned to a normal-looking prompt. Now run *ssh-add*. This will load all of the keys in your ~/.ssh directory:

```
$ ssh-add
Enter passphrase for /home/jenn/.ssh/id_rsa:
```

```
Identity added: /home/jenn/.ssh/id_rsa (/home/jenn/.ssh/id_rsa)
Enter passphrase for /home/jenn/.ssh/apache_key:
Identity added: /home/jenn/.ssh/id_dsa (/home/jenn/.ssh/apache_key)
```

Now you can log into any of your SSH hosts without entering a passphrase:

```
jenn@windbag:$ ssh powerpc
Linux powerpc 2.4.21 #1 Sun Aug 3 20:15:59 PDT 2003 i686 GNU/Linux
Libranet GNU/Linux

Last login: Wed Feb  7 18:28:20 2004 from windbag.test.net
jenn@powerpc:~$
```

To shut down *ssh-agent*, just exit out of the *ssh-agent* shell:

```
$ exit
```

Discussion

Because the passphrases and keys are tied to a particular Bash shell process, they'll disappear when you log out of the *ssh-agent* shell. If you open a second shell to start another *ssh-agent*, you'll have to enter your passphrase again, even if the first one is still active.

You can see what keys are being used by *ssh-agent*:

```
$ ssh-add -l
1024 65:91:77:71:24:66:46:ea:cb:00:fe:83:ad:b8:4a:34 /home/jenn/.ssh/id_rsa (RSA)
1024 da:f7:27:6a:37:4e:a5:bb:1d:00:c7:a8:e9:fe:23:d8 /home/jenn/.ssh/apache_key (RSA)
```

You'll need to be back in the local *ssh-agent* shell for this to work, and not logged into a remote host. When you are logged in to a remote host, the remote host controls your terminal, and you'll get the "Could not open a connection to your authentication agent" error message.

You can specify a particular key to load:

```
$ ssh-add  /home/jenn/adminkeys/id_rsa_http
```

or you can delete a key from the active *ssh-agent* session (this does not delete the key from your system):

```
$ ssh-add -d /home/jenn/.ssh/id_dsa
Identity removed: /home/jenn/.ssh/id_dsa (/home/jenn/.ssh/id_dsa.pub)
```

To delete all keys, use:

```
$ ssh-add -D
All identities removed.
```

See Also

- *ssh(1), ssh-add(1), ssh-agent(1)*
- *SSH, The Secure Shell: The Definitive Guide*

17.7   Better Passwordless Logins with keychain

Problem

ssh-agent is nice, but you still have to enter a passphrase with every new shell you open, and when you log out you have to start over. Also, *ssh-agent* doesn't enable passphraseless SSH transfers to work with *cron*.

Solution

First, set up your system to use *ssh-agent*. Then use *keychain* to keep your SSH passphrases alive, system-wide, until you reboot. *keychain* also makes it possible to run SSH transfers from *cron*.

Download and install *keychain* from the usual sources; it comes in RPMs, *.debs*, and sources. Then edit your local *~/.bash_profile*, adding these lines:

```
keychain id_dsa
. ~/.keychain/$HOSTNAME-sh
```

Use the real name of your private key: *id_rsa*, *my_own_groovy_key,* whatever. Be sure to use the leading dot on the second line; this tells Bash to read the file named on the line.

That's all you have to do. Now when you log in to your local workstation, a *keychain* prompt will appear, asking for the passphrase of your key. *keychain* will handle authentications until the system reboots.

Discussion

You can name as many keys as you wish to use, like this:

```
keychain id_dsa  apache_key  ftp_key
```

You'll enter the passphrase for each one at system login. Then *keychain* will handle authentications as long as the system stays up, even if you log out and log back in a few times. When you restart the system, you start over.

A lot of documentation tells you to use null passphrases on keys generated for servers, to enable unattended reboots. The risk is that anyone who gets a copy of the private key will be able to easily misuse it. As always, you'll have to decide for yourself what balance of convenience and security is going to serve your needs.

See Also

- *ssh(1), ssh-add(1), ssh-agent(1), keychain(1)*
- *SSH, The Secure Shell: The Definitive Guide*

17.8 Passwordless Logins for cron Jobs

Problem

You want to schedule some backups or file transfers via SSH, using *cron*. How do you tell *cron* to look to *keychain* to handle authentication of remote hosts?

Solution

Use the same source line in your *cron* scripts that you used in your *.bash_profile*. This is a simple script that uses *rsync* to back up a user's home directory:

```
#!/bin/bash
source  /home/saz/.keychain/$HOSTNAME-sh
rsync -a -e ssh --delete --force rsync.test.net::home/saz/  /backups/saz
```

Slap it in a *cron* job, and you're fully automated until the next reboot.

Discussion

Again, using null-passphrase keys leaves your private keys wide open to being misused by anyone who gains access to them. Using *keychain* ensures that you can properly protect your SSH keys with passphrases and still automate SSH transfers.

See Also

- *ssh(1), keychain(1)*
- Chapter 16, *Backup and Recovery*
- *SSH, The Secure Shell: The Definitive Guide*

17.9 Shutting Down ssh-agent Automatically at Logout

Problem

As a security measure, you would like to ensure that any stray *ssh-agent* processes are killed automatically when you log out.

Solution

Make this entry in your ~/.bash_logout file:

```
kill $SSH_AGENT_PID
```

Discussion

Don't do this if you're using *keychain,* because the whole point of using *keychain* is to be able to log in and out without having to re-enter your passphrases.

If you don't have a *~/.bash_logout* file, create one. There should be a system-wide default logout file at */etc/skel/.bash_logout* to use as a model.

See Also

- *bash(1), ssh-agent(1)*
- *SSH, The Secure Shell: The Definitive Guide*

17.10 Customizing the Bash Prompt for ssh

Problem

Sure, you know that the prompt changes to display the remote hostname when you're logged in via SSH. But it's just a dumb little black-and-white prompt, and it's easy to make mistakes, so you want a customized, colorful prompt to indicate when you have an active SSH login.

Solution

Customize the Bash prompt on the remote PCs. This example turns the prompt red and adds "ssh" to it.

Add these lines to the *~./bashrc* for the remote account you want to log into:

```
if [ -n "$SSH_CLIENT" ]; then text=" ssh"
fi
export PS1='\[\e[0;31m\]\u@\h:\w${text}$\[\e[m\] '
```

When you log into this machine, the prompt will look like this, in red:

```
carla@server06:~ssh $
```

Only the prompt is red; all the other text will be your normal shell colors.

Discussion

Customizing the Bash prompt is practically a book topic in itself. The example in this recipe can easily be edited to suit your preferences. You don't have to use "ssh" or name the variable "text;" these can be anything you like. *\e[0;31m\]* determines the text color—just change the numbers.

\e[m\] turns off the colors, so that your commands and command output will return to the normal shell colors (Table 17-1).

Table 17-1. Bash prompt text colors

Black 0;30	Dark Gray 1;30
Blue 0;34	Light Blue 1;34

Table 17-1. Bash prompt text colors (continued)

Green 0;32	Light Green 1;32
Cyan 0;36	Light Cyan 1;36
Red 0;31	Light Red 1;31
Purple 0;35	Light Purple 1;35
Brown 0;33	Yellow 1;33
Light Gray 0;37	White 1;37

This customization works by checking for the presence of the *SSH_CLIENT* environment variable. Then Bash knows to use the custom SSH prompt instead of the default prompt. To see this for yourself, log into a remote host via SSH, then run:

```
user@remotehost$ echo $SSH_CLIENT
192.168.1.5 33232 22
```

This only works on the remote prompt. Running it at the local prompt will return a blank line:

```
user@localhost$ echo $SSH_CLIENT
```

because once you complete an SSH login, the remote machine controls your local terminal, and the SSH client is running on the remote PC. That is why you have to customize *~/.bachrc* on the remote hosts.

See Also

- *bash(1)*
- The Bash Prompt Howto (*http://www.tldp.org/HOWTO/Bash-Prompt-HOWTO/ index.html*)

17.11 Tunneling X over SSH

Problem

You like running remote X sessions, but you know that they are completely insecure, so you want to run X over SSH.

Solution

Follow the previous recipes to get SSH configured and running, then enable X forwarding on the SSH server, in */etc/ssh/sshd_config*. Then use the *-X* flag when you start your SSH session.

Put this line in */etc/ssh/sshd_config* on the SSH server:

```
X11Forwarding yes
```

Then connect to the server with the *-X* flag:

```
$ ssh -X saturn.test.net
```

Run this command to test that X forwarding is working:

```
$ echo $DISPLAY
localhost:10.0
```

If it weren't, it would return a blank line. Now you can run any X program installed on the server as though it were local. Try this for a simple test:

```
$ xeyes
```

Or run *glxgears*, or any X program that is installed on the server.

Discussion

Using SSH for remote X sessions is both simpler and more secure than running a plain-vanilla X session without SSH, which is not secure at all. However, it still carries some risks. Use this to connect only to trusted hosts, because a snoopy admin can easily capture your keystrokes or logins, or even connect to your local desktop and snoop even more. Make sure your local *~/.Xauthority* file is mode 600, to prevent unprivileged users on the remote host from also joining in the snooping.

Be sure that these entries are in your local */etc/ssh/ssh_config* file and any *~/ ssh/ ssh_config* files on your system:

```
Host *
ForwardX11 no
ForwardAgent no
```

It's important to ensure that X forwarding is turned off, except when you absolutely need it.

Depending on your physical distance from the remote server and the speed of your network connection, you may notice some lag in your keystrokes or mouse movements, as the X protocol is a bit of a network hog.

See Also

- *ssh(1)*
- *SSH, The Secure Shell: The Definitive Guide*

17.12 Connecting from a Windows PC

Problem

SSH on Linux is great. But you want to access your Linux PCs from Windows. How can you use OpenSSH on a Windows PC?

Solution

There are several ways to do this. The two we'll look at here are Cygwin and PuTTY.

Recipe 16.12 details how to install and run Cygwin. Cygwin creates a native Linux environment on Windows. You'll be able to run OpenSSH from Windows just like from a Linux box, both as a server and as a client. You can even run X over SSH.

PuTTY is a free SSH client for Windows. There is no server component. PuTTY is dead easy—just download, install, and double-click, then type in the name of the host to which you want to connect and click Open. Figure 17-1 shows the main PuTTY window.

Figure 17-1. PuTTY

Discussion

If all you need a is a simple SSH client, PuTTY is the quickest and easiest. *putty.exe* easily fits on a floppy disk, for portable SSH-ing.

- PuTTY home page (*http://www.chiark.greenend.org.uk/~sgtatham/putty/download.html*)
- Cygwin (*http://www.cygwin.com*)

17.13 Setting File Permissions on ssh Files

Problem

You want to be sure that your SSH files and keys have the correct, most secure permissions.

Solution

For user accounts in *~/.ssh*, use the following permissions:

~/.ssh	mode 700
~/.ssh/id_dsa and other private keys	mode 400
~/.ssh/id_dsa.pub and other public keys	mode 644
~/.ssh/ssh_config	mode 644
~/.ssh/known_hosts	mode 644
~/.ssh/authorized_keys	mode 644

Files in */etc/ssh* should have these permissions:

/etc/ssh	mode 755
/etc/ssh/sshd_config	mode 644
/etc/ssh/ssh_config	mode 644
/etc/ssh/ssh_host_dsa_key and other private keys	mode 400
/etc/ssh/ssh_host_dsa_key.pub and other public keys	mode 644
/etc/ssh/moduli	mode 644

Discussion

File permissions and ownership are fundamental security tools in Linux, so it's important to be careful and make sure to get them right. Again, beware of text editors that create automatic backup copies, and be careful when you delete files. If they sit in the Trash, they can easily be retrieved.

See Also

- *ssh(1), sshd(8)*
- *SSH, The Secure Shell: The Definitive Guide*

## CHAPTER 18

Version Control

18.1 Introduction

What is the point of using a version control system? A version control system is an efficient way to track changes in documents and to preserve a complete history of a project. It's like having a time machine; months later, you can easily roll back to an earlier system configuration, or code block, or manuscript version.

Version control systems are useful for all sorts of things: source code, binary files, configuration files, scripts, articles and books, songs, inventories, indexes—any kind of text document. You can keep your shopping lists in a version control repository, if you like. Because a version control repository keeps track of every change ever made, you can easily go back to any point in the lifetime of a particular project. And the version control system does the work—you don't have to depend on users to create and store copies of the different versions of documents. This is quite handy when you want to retrieve that brilliant code you wrote months ago, or that perfect configuration file, or that astonishingly fine arugula recipe.

Version control systems allow teams of users to work on a single project in a controlled manner. For example, you can break up a project into separate branches, which can later be merged. You can also merge different versions of files, though you need to be aware that the software doesn't know what the files mean and cannot intelligently resolve conflicts—it only knows how files differ, so merging files sometimes requires some human intervention to be managed correctly.

There are whole lot of free/open source version control programs out there. Here are the more popular ones:

- RCS (Revision Control System)
- CVS (Concurrent Versions System)
- Subversion
- GNU Arch
- Monotone

Commercial products include:

- BitKeeper
- Visual SourceSafe
- OpenCM
- CMSynergy
- Perforce
- ClearCase

RCS and CVS are the oldest and most widely used. They are fairly simple to set up and use, and they have been around long enough to be thoroughly torture-tested.

Subversion, GNU Arch, and Monotone all offer features not present in CVS: you can set up distributed repositories, as opposed to the central-server model of CVS, and they support atomic commits. With an atomic commit, changes happen all at once. When a user commits a change to the repository, the whole change is applied, and it is visible to other users only once completed. CVS applies changes a file at a time, so if a network outage interrupts the commit, the changes will be only partially applied.

While this feature is quite cool and useful, Subversion, GNU Arch, and Monotone are still somewhat immature. GNU Arch and Subversion are difficult to install and configure and not that easy to learn to use. Monotone has an interestingly different architecture—one major difference is it transfers files via an embedded network protocol, *netsync*, rather than using HTTP, NNTP, or SMTP. This eliminates a lot of gnarly setup steps and means that every installation of Monotone is ready to function either as a client or a server.

A forward-thinking person might set up some of these on some test machines, keep an eye on their development, and get the hang of using them, because these are the version control systems of the future.

BitKeeper is one of the more popular commercial products. Linux kernel development is done on BitKeeper. You can test-drive BitKeeper for free; its makers offer both a free 30-day evaluation and a somewhat dumbed-down free-of-cost version for personal use.

Although there are numerous alternatives, this chapter concentrates on RCS and CVS, the most mature and widely used version control systems. RCS is the backend to CVS, so it's easy to learn both of them. RCS is perfect for a single user with simple needs; CVS is good both for a single user, and to support teams of users working on complex projects.

Essential CVS (O'Reilly), by Jennifer Vesperman is an excellent CVS howto and command reference. If you have the budget for only one CVS book, this is the one you should buy.

18.2   Building a Simple Local RCS Repository

Problem

You're worried that someday you'll change some file, break something, and you'll forget how to undo the change. So you want a simple, local version control repository for tracking code changes, configuration files, scripts, and other documents for a single user. You don't need network access or support for multiple users—just something quick and easy to use for yourself.

Solution

Install RCS (Revision Control System) from RPMs, *.debs*, or sources. Then follow these steps to create your RCS repository.

First create a working directory, then create an RCS subdirectory:

```
$ mkdir projecthome
$ cd projecthome
$ mkdir RCS
```

Make sure you are in your working directory (*projecthome*) with some files to play with. This is how you check a file into the repository:

```
terri@workstation1:~/projecthome$ ci -u cupsd.conf
RCS/cupsd.conf,v <-- cupsd.conf
enter description, terminated with single '.' or end of file:
NOTE: This is NOT the log message!
>> LAN printer server, for windows and linux, no samba
>> .
initial revision: 1.1
done
```

When you want to edit the file, check it out of the repository, then open it in your favorite text editor:

```
terri@workstation1:~/projecthome$ co -l cupsd.conf
RCS/cupsd.conf,v --> cupsd.conf
revision 1.1 (locked)
done
terri@workstation1:~/projecthome$ kate cupsd.conf &
```

When you're finished, close and save the file, then check it in just like above. Add a comment for the log detailing your changes:

```
$ ci -u cupsd.conf
RCS/cupsd.conf,v <-- cupsd.conf
new revision: 1.2; previous revision: 1.1
enter log message, terminated with single '.' or end of file:
>> added administrative controls to prevent users from making changes to the server
>> .
done
```

Discussion

In a simple version control repository like this, you have only two directories to keep track of. Your working directory is where the working copies of documents are kept. The RCS directory is the actual repository. The files in the repository are given a *,v* suffix, like this:

```
$ ls RCS
cupsd.conf,v
```

The different revisions are tracked inside the file:

```
$ less cupsd.conf,v
head     1.3;
access;
symbols;
locks; strict;
comment @# @;
1.3
date     2004.06.15.03.33.46;    author terri;    state Exp;
branches;
next     1.2;
1.2
date     2004.06.13.30.47;    author terri;    state Exp;
branches;
next     1.1;
1.1
date     2004.06.12.03.27.01;    author terri;    state Exp;
branches;
next     ;
desc
@LAN printer server, for windows and linux, no samba
.....
```

Keep in mind that the files in your working directory are temporary versions. When a file has reached a state where you wish to preserve it, check it into the repository.

RCS's commands are mnemonic:

ci -u
    Check in and unlock

co -l
    Check out and lock

Using the *-u* flag on checkin preserves the copy in your working directory. The file in the working directory is set to read-only, which prevents accidents, and reminds you to check the file out of the repository for editing.

File locking means only one person at a time can check out and edit a file, so RCS is not suitable for a busy project with multiple users. However, it is perfect for small projects and single users, with the added advantage of being simple to learn.

See Also

- *rcsintro(1), ci(1), co(1)*
- Official RCS home page (*http://www.cs.purdue.edu/homes/trinkle/RCS*)

18.3   Retrieving Older File Revisions from RCS

Problem

It finally happened: you changed the recipe for the secret sauce, got it wrong, and can't put it right. But you've been using RCS, so you have several versions of the file in your repository, and you want to see a list of all the versions, the changelog entries, and the dates they were last edited. After figuring out which version you want, you need to check out that older working version.

Solution

When you have accumulated multiple revisions of a file, and you want to see a list of all of them, use *rlog*:

```
$ rlog cupsd.conf
RCS file: RCS/cupsd.conf,v
Working file: cupsd.conf
head: 1.2
branch:
locks: strict
access list:
symbolic names:
keyword substitution: kv
total revisions: 2;     selected revisions: 2
description:
LAN printer server, for windows and linux, no samba
----------------------------
revision 1.3
date: 2004/07/31 03:33:46;  author: terri;  state: Exp;  lines: +1 -1
corrected error in Allow directive
----------------------------
revision 1.2
date: 2004/07/27 05:29:27;  author: terri;  state: Exp;  lines: +2 -0
added administrative controls to prevent users from making changes to the server
----------------------------
revision 1.1
date: 2004/07/27 05:19:25;  author: terri;  state: Exp;
Initial revision
=============================================================
```

As you can see, this shows the importance of writing helpful comments. To check out a specific revision, specify the revision number:

```
$ co -l -r1.1 cupsd.conf
```

This overwrites your working copy of the file, which in this example is *projecthome/cupsd.conf*. If you don't want your working copy overwritten, preserve it by first checking it into the RCS repository.

To quickly display the file without having to check it out and open it in an editor, use the *-p* option:

```
$ co -p -r1.5 cupsd.conf
```

Discussion

When you have multiple versions of a file in your repository, the newest one will be checked out by default when you do not specify a revision number.

Once your repository is set up and working, you can see your files listed in the RCS directory and even open them in a text editor to see what RCS does to them. You'll see that even though you may have a dozen revisions of a file, there is only a single file in the repository. RCS changes only records inside the file; it does not make individual copies of each revision.

Using RCS is liberating; you don't have to waste mental energy remembering your changes because RCS will track them for you.

See Also

- *rcsintro(1), ci(1), co(1), rlog(1)*
- Official RCS home page (*http://www.cs.purdue.edu/homes/trinkle/RCS*)

18.4   Comparing File Versions in RCS

Problem

Your current version of a configuration file isn't working the way you want, or perhaps a text document doesn't have the content you thought you put in there, or your brilliant code has all of a sudden gone dull. You're pretty sure an older version has what you want, so you want to compare the new version with older revisions to find out where you went astray.

Solution

Use the *rcsdiff* command. This compares two revisions:

```
$ rcsdiff -r1.1 -r1.2 cupsd.conf
```

Make sure there are no spaces after the *-r* flags.

This compares the working file with a specific revision:

```
$ rcsdiff -r1.2 cupsd.conf
```

And this compares the current working file with the most recent revision:

```
$ rcsdiff cupsd.conf
```

Use this command to review your changes after you've edited the file, but before you check it in.

Discussion

If the *rcsdiff* output is long, you can always direct it to a file for leisurely perusal:

```
$ rcsdiff -r1.1 -r1.2 cupsd.conf > cupsdiff.txt
```

Here is an example of *rcsdiff*'s output:

```
$ rcsdiff -r1.1 -r1.3 cupsd.conf
==-========================================================
RCS file: RCS/cupsd.conf,v
retrieving revision 1.1
retrieving revision 1.3
diff -r1.1 -r1.3
9c9,17
< BrowseAddress 192.168.1.255
\ No newline at end of file
---
> BrowseAddress 192.168.1.255
>
> <Location /admin>
> AuthType Basic
> AuthClass System
> Allow From 127.0.0.1
> Order Deny,Allow
> Deny From All
> </Location>
```

It tells you right at the top what file versions you are looking at:

<   Means the line is unique to the first file.

>   Means the line is unique to the second file.

\   Prefixes comments from RCS.

See Also

- *rcsdiff(1)*
- Official RCS home page (*http://www.cs.purdue.edu/homes/trinkle/RCS*)

18.5 Managing System Configuration Files with RCS

Problem

You want to preserve all versions of your system configuration files so that you can easily roll back to an earlier configuration, or just to preserve all of your brilliant configuration ideas as they occur.

Solution

It is tempting to stuff all of /etc into an RCS repository, but that's unnecessary and wasteful. Back up /etc in your usual manner, then use RCS to store only files that you change. Start out by checking the files you are going to edit into RCS. Check them out to make your changes, then check them back in when you're finished. Copy the working file to its final home in /etc after checkin. Then you will have a complete revision history of every configuration file that you edit.

Discussion

This example walks through creating an RCS repository for two programs, Amavisd-new and Clam Anti-Virus. Each program will have its own subdirectory in the repository. All commands are run as root.

```
# mkdir /rcs_configs
# cd /rcs_configs
# mkdir -p amavis/RCS
# mkdir -p clamav/RCS
# cd /amavis
# cp /etc/amavis/amavisd.conf amavisd.conf
# ci -l amavisd.conf
RCS/amavisd.conf,v  <--  amavisd.conf
enter description, terminated with single '.' or end of file:
NOTE: This is NOT the log message!
>> original amavis config, used with clamav and postfix
>> .
initial revision: 1.1
done
# co -l amavisd.conf
# vim amavisd.conf
```

Make your edits, save and close the file, then check it back in:

```
# ci -u amavisd.conf
```

Copy your working file into /etc:

```
# cp amavisd.conf /etc/amavis/amavisd.conf
```

---

and you're ready to go. Your original copy and first revision are safely preserved, and you're all set up to easily save additional revisions.

You may keep everything in single directory, rather than creating subdirectories for each program. It's up to you how to organize your files. Just remember to always change to the correct working directory before you start, or you'll find your files getting scattered all over.

When using RCS, it's easy to get confused and lock files at checkin instead of checkout, or to check out files and forget to check them back in. If you make such an error, the next time you try to check out the file, you'll get a message:

```
# co -l amavisd.conf
RCS/amavisd.conf,v  -->  amavisd.conf
co: RCS/amavisd.conf,v: multiple revisions locked by carla; please specify one
```

So when you specify a revision, you still get warnings:

```
# co -l -r1.4 amavisd.conf
RCS/amavisd.conf,v  -->  amavisd.conf
revision 1.4 (locked)
writable amavisd.conf exists; remove it? [ny](n): y
co: RCS/amavisd.conf,v: warning: You now have 2 locks.
done
```

The easiest way to get to get out of this is to open the RCS file (in this example, *RCS/amavisd.conf,v*) and edit it directly. You'll need to make it writable first:

```
# chmod 644 amavisd.conf,v
```

Then edit the header. Look for this:

```
head    1.4;
acccss;
symbols;
locks
        carla:1.1
        carla:1.2; strict;
comment    @# @;
```

Delete the locks, so it looks like this:

```
head    1.4;
access;
symbols;
locks; strict;
comment    @# @;
```

Save and close the file, and be sure to reset it to read-only:

```
# chmod 444 amavisd.conf,v
```

That's the end of the locks.

See Also

- *rcsintro(1), ci(1), co(1)*
- Official RCS home page (*http://www.cs.purdue.edu/homes/trinkle/RCS*)

18.6   Using CVS for a Single-User Local Repository

Problem

You would rather use CVS for your local, personal repository because you plan to also use it for larger projects, and you want to stick to learning a single system. Or your personal repository is getting complex, so you need the additional abilities of CVS to manage it, such as more complex directory structures, and being able to checkout multiple files or entire directories at once.

Solution

CVS scales nicely from small personal projects to large projects without a problem. Installation is simple. Both RPMs and *.debs* are named "cvs"; if you prefer to install from sources, get them from *https://www.cvshome.org/*.

After installing CVS, create your personal repository with these commands:

```
$ mkdir ~/cvsroot
$ chmod -R 700 ~/cvsroot
$ cvs -d ~/cvsroot init
```

Now select a directory of files to store in your repository. Change to that directory, and import the directory into your CVS repository:

```
$ cd /scripts
$ cvs -d ~/cvsroot import scripts jenns_configs version_1
N scripts/useradd.txt
N scripts/postfix_ube.txt
N scripts/logparse.pl
No conflicts created by this import
```

During the import, your default editor will open, displaying this text:

```
CVS: -------------------------------------------------------
CVS: Enter Log.  Lines beginning with `CVS:' are removed automatically
CVS:
CVS: -------------------------------------------------------
```

Enter your project description here (e.g., "Jenn's system administration scripts for Slackware 9"). Make this detailed enough so that six months from now, it will still make sense.

To check out a file for editing, you must first create a working directory. This directory must be outside of the directory that holds your CVS repository. Then change to the working directory, and check out a file:

```
$ mkdir ~/sandbox
$ cd ~/sandbox
$ cvs -d ~/cvsroot  checkout  scripts/postfix_ube.txt
cvs checkout: Updating scripts
U scripts/postfix_ube.txt
```

Checking out files from the CVS repository creates a CVS sandbox in your working directory. The sandbox is the local working directory where all of your actual work takes place. When you check out files from CVS, a batch of CVS admininistrative files are installed in the sandbox. Always work from a sandbox; never enter a CVS repository to edit files. Your sandbox can have any name you choose.

The file you just checked out is in the *scripts* directory, so that is your sandbox, and you should change to that directory to edit the file:

```
$ cd scripts
$ vim postfix_ube.txt
```

When you're finished editing the file, save it in the normal fashion, and put it back in the CVS repository using the *commit* subcommand:

```
$ cvs commit
cvs commit: Examining .
/home/jenn/cvsroot/scripts/postfix_ube.txt,v  <--  postfix_ube.txt
new revision: 1.2; previous revision: 1.1
```

Again, your default editor will open, and you'll be asked to write a log entry detailing your changes.

As long as you are in the sandbox, which in this example is *~/sandbox/scripts*, you can omit specifying the name of the repository for checkouts and commits.

Discussion

This is the CVS command syntax:

```
cvs [ global_options ] command [ command_options ] [ command_args ]
```

CVS is all about record keeping. Take the time to make useful log entries—you will thank yourself many times during the life of your CVS project.

You can name your CVS root directory anything you like.

jenns_configs and *version_1* are the vendor tag and release number, respectively. While you may not care about these, CVS requires them. The vendor tag usually identifies whoever supplies the source files, and the version number is the starting version number for the project.

You can collect all the files you want for a new project in a temporary directory, then delete it after they are safely imported into the repository. Test the import by checking out a sandbox and verifying that the files in the sandbox are correct before you delete the originals. Once you have created your sandbox and imported the files into the repository, you don't need to keep the originals; they're just taking up space.

A single directory, and all of its files and subdirectories, is a *project*. Every project must be stored in a directory, even if it is just a single file.

You can check out single files, space-delimited lists of files, or entire directories:

```
$ cvs checkout scripts/postfix_ube.txt
$ cvs checkout scripts/postfix_ube.txt scripts/logparse.pl
$ cvs checkout scripts
```

Unlike RCS, checking out files in CVS does not lock them to prevent other users from checking them out at the same time. Thus, you can grab an entire directory without hindering other users.

See Also

- Local documentation—Overview (*/usr/share/doc/cvs/html-info/cvs_1.html*)
- Chapters 2 and 3 of *Essential CVS* (Chapter 2 is available for free from *http://www.oreilly.com/catalog/cvs/*)
- CVS home page (*https://www.cvshome.org*)

18.7   Adding New Files to a CVS Repository

Problem

You have created a new file, and you need to add it to your local CVS repository.

Solution

Run these commands from your working directory, or sandbox. In this example, the new file you have created is cleverly named "newfile," and it is in your sandbox:

```
$ cvs update
cvs update: Updating .
? newfile
$ cvs add newfile
cvs -d /home/jenn/cvsroot add newfile
cvs add: scheduling file `newfile' for addition
cvs add: use `cvs commit' to add this file permanently
$ cvs commit -m 'simple Ethereal filter for monitoring HTTPS traffic' newfile
/home/jenn/cvsroot/scripts/newfile,v  <--  newfile
initial revision: 1.1
```

Discussion

When you run the *update* command, the question mark shows which files have not yet been committed to the CVS repository.

The *update* command synchronizes changes from the repository to the sandbox (not the other way). Use the *status* command to see the differences first, without making any changes in your sandbox:

```
$ cvs status
```

The *commit -m* command demonstrates how to create a log entry for a single file on the command line, to avoid invoking a text editor. It's nice little timesaver.

Keep in mind that when you edit a file to a point where you want CVS to preserve it, the thing to do is check it into the repository. Don't leave it lying around in your sandbox. When you start work for the day, you should run *update* first thing to bring your local copies up-to-date.

Even when you're the only user of a repository, it's a good idea to keep your sandbox in sync with the repository. But in a shared repository, it's very important to stay synchronized—it's much easier to deal with small conflicts than larger ones, and if you're synched, conflicts are rarer.

See Also

- Chapter 3 of *Essential CVS*
- "A.18 update—Bring work tree in sync with repository" (*/usr/share/doc/cvs/html-info/cvs_16.html*)
- CVS home page (*https://www.cvshome.org*)

18.8   Deleting Files from a CVS Repository

Problem

You want to delete some files from your CVS repository.

Solution

Delete the file from your sandbox, then run the *cvs remove* command:

```
$ rm badfile
$ cvs remove badfile
cvs remove: scheduling 'badfile' for removal
cvs remove: use 'cvs'commit' to remove this file permanently
```

The next time you run a *commit*, the file will be moved to a special subdirectory called Attic. This preserves the file history and allows you to restore the file, should you change your mind.

Alternatively you can use a single command to delete the file from both your sandbox and repository:

```
$ cvs remove -f badfile
```

Discussion

You can't remove directories like you can remove files. Using the *-P* flag for *update* and *checkout* prevents empty directories from being downloaded to your sandbox. A common shortcut is to make this the default behavior in *~/cvsrc* (see Recipe 18.19).

CVS never really deletes anything. It's not supposed to. If you have a "spring cleaning" mindset you may find CVS a bit frustrating, because you're not supposed to clean its closets. The purpose of using a version control system is to maintain a complete history of a project.

See Also

- Chapter 2 of *Essential CVS*
- Recipe 18.19, "Customizing Your CVS Environment"
- CVS home page (*https://www.cvshome.org*)

18.9   Creating a Shared CVS Repository

Problem

CVS is nice for tracking your own files, but in the real world teams of people usually work together on projects. How do you set up a CVS repository that's shared by a group of users?

Solution

First create a CVS owner and group; these will own the repository. Then create the repository:

```
# groupadd cvsusers
# useradd -g cvsusers -u 105 cvs
# mkdir /cvsroot
# chown -R cvs /cvsroot
# chmod -R 770 /cvsroot
# cvs -d /cvsroot init
```

```
# chgrp cvsusers /cvsroot
# chmod g+s /cvsroot
```

Add users to the *cvsusers* group to give them access.

Now any user in the *cvsusers* group can import a project into the repository. This example adds the *techbook* project:

```
$ cd /techbook
$ cvs -d /cvsroot  import  techbook  cups_howto version_1
```

The new project will be owned by the person who imported it, and the *cvsusers* group:

```
$ stat /cvsroot/techbook
File: `techbook'
  Size: 136         Blocks: 1        IO Block: 4096   directory
Device: 306h/774d   Inode: 69624     Links: 2
Access: (2775/drwxrwsr-x) Uid: ( 1000/   carla)  Gid: ( 1005/cvsusers)
```

Discussion

The commands in this recipe must be run on the CVS server. See Recipe 18.11 to learn how to access a remote repository.

It's important to follow the above command sequence, to get the permissions correct. *cvs init* creates a large batch of administration files, with its own set of permissions, so you don't want to change them. (You can view them in the *CVSROOT* subdirectory.)

When you're creating a system or daemon user, remember to assign an appropriate UID (see Recipe 8.2, "Sorting Human Users from System Users").

You should set all users' *umask* values to 007 to eliminate any kind of world access to the CVS repository files. Just add this line to everyone's *~/.bashrc*:

```
umask 007
```

Setting the sticky bit restricts removing or renaming of files to the file owners, the group owners, or the superuser.

See Also

- Chapters 2 and 6 of *Essential CVS*
- Local documentation—"The Repository" (*/usr/share/doc/cvs/html-info/cvs_2.html*)
- CVS home page (*https://www.cvshome.org*)

18.10 Sharing a Single Repository Between Several Groups

Problem

You have several different project groups that each need their own CVS repository, and you want to put them inside a single master CVS repository to make it easier to do backups and administrative chores. You need to configure file permissions to keep users from wandering into the wrong repositories.

Solution

Follow Recipe 18.9, and create a new subdirectory for each individual repository. Adjust owner and group permissions on the individual repositories to control access:

```
# cd /3dgame
# cvs -d /cvsroot  import  3dgame  best_game_ever  version_1
# chown gamers:gamegroup /cvsroot/3dgame
```

Discussion

You can create a separate repository for each project, or put everything under a single CVS root. Backups are easier with a single CVS root, but having separate multiple repositories makes it a little easier to manage permissions and user access.

See Also

- Chapters 2 and 6 of *Essential CVS*
- Recipe 18.19, "Customizing Your CVS Environment"
- CVS home page (*https://www.cvshome.org*)

18.11 Accessing a Remote CVS Repository

Problem

You have your CVS server all set up and ready to go; now how do you give users secure, remote access?

Solution

Use OpenSSH. OpenSSH is the simplest, most secure method for accessing your CVS repository, both over your LAN and over the Internet. If you set up OpenSSH right from the start, you'll have only a single connection and authentication method to maintain for all remote connectivity. (See Chapter 17 to learn how to set up OpenSSH.)

Follow these steps to connect via SSH:

1. Install and configure OpenSSH on all hosts (the CVS server, and everyone who is going to connect to it).
2. Run OpenSSH on the CVS server in daemon mode.
3. Make sure that all users have login accounts on the CVS server.
4. Set up your keys, and test SSH logins to the server.
5. On the users' PCs, add this line to their ~./cvsrc files, or create ~./cvsrc files for them:

        CVS_RSH SSH

Suppose the remote CVS server is *cvs.project.net*. You would connect to the repository like this, from the parent directory of your local sandbox:

```
$ cvs -d :ext:jenn@cvs.project.net:/cvsroot checkout scripts
jenn@cvs.project.net's password:
```

If the CVS server is on your LAN, all you need is the hostname or IP address:

```
$ cvs -d :ext:jenn@cvs:/cvsroot checkout scripts
```

Discussion

If you have NFS implemented, you might be tempted to create NFS shares for your CVS repository. Don't do this. NFS is not secure, you'll encounter permissions hell, and there is a risk of data corruption. Also, it makes it too easy for users to accidentally delete CVS files.

OpenSSH gives you a number of methods for logging into remote hosts. You can use system logins, or (even easier) you can authenticate via public/private key pairs. Use the *keychain* program to handle key authentication for security and convenience, so you won't have to enter a password or passphrase at all (see Recipe 17.7).

OpenSSH encrypts the entire session—login and transport. It's easy to implement, and using the same mechanism for both LAN and Internet access simplifies the job of administering the CVS server.

See Also

- Chapter 17, *Remote Access*
- Recipe 17.7, "Better Passwordless Logins with keychain"
- CVS home page (*https://www.cvshome.org*)

18.12 Updating Your Working Files in CVS

Problem

Because you are working on a shared project, you want to be sure that your first checkout of the day brings all your sandbox files up to date, and incorporates changes made by other users.

Solution

At the start of the day, run the *update* command, with the *-n* flag (for "not really"), from your sandbox:

```
$ cvs -n  update -dP
cvs update: Updating .
cvs update: Updating CVSROOT
cvs update: Updating project
M project/oldfile
? project/newfile
```

This shows what files are different, and the status of each of these files. To synchronize your sandbox with the repository, re-run the command without the *-n* flag. This will merge, or attempt to merge, both sets of files.

To get even more information, run the following command:

```
$ cvs diff
```

This will display line-by-line changes.

Discussion

Running *update* routinely will keep your local working copies in sync with the repository copies. If you're concerned about other users making annoying changes (which is not a CVS problem, but a project-management problem), you can always review them first. Keep in mind that when you have edited a file to a point where you wish to preserve it, you should check it into the repository. Don't leave it lying around in your sandbox—the whole point of using CVS is to preserve many versions of the same file.

These are the possible states that files will be in:

U The file was updated successfully.

A The file was added but has not yet been committed.

R The file was removed but has not yet been committed.

M The file in the repository was different from your sandbox copy, and the changes were successfully merged.

C   A conflict exists between the repository copy and your copy, requiring human intervention.

?   The file is in your working directory but not the repository, and CVS doesn't know what to do with it. You'll see this when you have created a new file and not yet added it to CVS.

See Also

- Recipe 18.7, "Adding New Files to a CVS Repository"
- Chapter 3 of *Essential CVS*
- CVS home page (*https://www.cvshome.org*)
- Recipe 18.8, "Deleting Files from a CVS Repository"

18.13 Retrieving Specific Older Revisions from CVS

Problem

You want to check out a particular older revision of a file. It might be a configuration script that you want to roll back to, or an earlier version of some brilliant code, or the best version of a short story you've been working on. Whatever it is, you're not happy with the current version, so you want to review an earlier version or versions.

Solution

From your sandbox, use *cvs log* to see the available versions of the file:

```
$ cvs log newerfile

RCS file: /home/foober/cvsroot/project/newerfile,v
Working file: newerfile
head: 1.2
branch:
locks: strict
access list: .
symbolic names:
keyword substitution: kv
total revisions: 2;    selected revisions: 2
description:
----------------------------
revision 1.2
date: 2004-08-01 07:37:07 +0000;  author: foober;  state: Exp;  lines: +3 -0
added a new line for tracking specific hosts
----------------------------
revision 1.1
```

```
date: 2004-07-29 21:22:20 +0000;  author: foober;  state: Exp;
simple ethereal script to monitor HTTPS traffic
================================================================
```

Then fetch the version you want:

```
$ cvs update -r 1.1 newerfile
U newerfile
```

This downloads a static, unchangeable version of the file. You can see the "sticky tag" with the *cvs status* command; this is what marks a file as static, by locking it at a particular revision:

```
$ cvs status newerfile
================================================================
File: newerfile           Status: Up-to-date
    Working revision:    1.1        Sun Aug  1 07:47:17 2003
    Repository revision: 1.1        /home/foober/cvsroot/project/newerfile,v
    Sticky Tag:          1.1
    Sticky Date:         (none)
    Sticky Options:      -kkv
```

At this point, there are a lot of things you can do with this file: use it as a reference, copy things out of it, or make a copy of it. Don't try to edit it directly, because this will goof up the revision history.

If you make a copy, you'll need to remove the sticky tag from the copy. Simply open the copy in a text editor, and change "Sticky Tag: 1.1" to "Sticky Tag: (none)."

Then, when you're finished editing, commit the file in the usual manner:

```
$ cvs commit
```

Discussion

This recipe demonstrates the importance of making good, descriptive log entries. When the revisions start accumulating, the descriptions are the best tool you have to find what you want.

Use *cvs diff* to view the differences between revisions:

cvs diff newerfile
Show changes that have been made in this file.

cvs diff -r1.3 newerfile
Show changes in this file from Version 1.3 to the current version.

cvs diff -r1.3 -r1.5 newerfile
Show changes in this file between Versions 1.3 and 1.5.

See Also

- Chapters 3 and 5 of *Essential CVS*
- CVS home page (*https://www.cvshome.org*)

18.14 Building an Anonymous Read-Only CVS Repository with Pserver

Problem

In the spirit of "many eyes make all bugs shallow," you want to set up a public CVS repository, so that random users can download your nightly builds (or whatever you've stored there—your Great Collaborative Anime, World's Best Arugula Recipes, Finest Unheard Songs, etc.). Your anonymous users will be allowed to only check out files; they won't be able to do checkins.

Solution

Set up a CVS Pserver. You'll need *cvsd*, a functioning CVS server, and OpenSSH set up and running on the CVS server in daemon mode. *cvsd* is an add-on for running CVS in Pserver mode, tucked away in a nice *chroot* jail.

cvsd is available in Debian Testing and Unstable, and in a source tarball. When this was written, the only available RPMs were quite old (Version .6-2). This recipe was written for Version 1.0.2, so if you can't find a current RPM, you should install from sources. Sources (as well as *.debs*) are available from the *cvsd* home page (*http:// tiefighter.et.tude.nl/~arthur/cvsd*).

This is how to install from sources:

```
$ ./configure --prefix=/usr --sysconfdir=/etc
$ make
# make install
```

Create a *cvsd* user and group:

```
# groupadd cvsd
# useradd -d /cvs/home -s /bin/false -c "cvs pserver daemon" -g cvsd -u 110 cvsd
```

Then create your repository root directory and *chroot* jail. This must be a subdirectory of an empty directory, so that the *chroot* jail will work:

```
# mkdir /cvs
# cd /cvs
# cvsd-buildroot /cvs
```

Change ownership to the *cvsd* user and group, and set permissions:

```
# chown -R cvsd:cvsd /cvs
# chmod 775 /cvs
```

Next, initialize your new *cvsd* repository, and create the root directory for the repository. Put this in a subdirectory:

```
# cvs -d /cvs/home init
```

Now edit */etc/cvsd/cvsd.conf* as follows:

- The UID and GID should be *cvsd* and *cvsd*.
- *Umask* should be 027.
- *RootJail* must correspond to the root of your CVS repository (in this example, */cvs*).
- Edit one of the *Repos* entries to name the new root directory of your repository (in this example, */home*).

Next, add anonymous access to your repository. As root, create a sandbox directory somewhere, then check out the *CVSROOT* directory:

```
# mkdir /sandbox
# cd /sandbox
# cvs -d /cvs/home checkout CVSROOT
# cd CVSROOT
```

Create a *CVSROOT/readers* file, adding a *guest* user. There should be just one line of text in this file, the word "guest". Be sure to end the file with a couple of blank lines. Then use the *add* and *update* commands to add it to the repository:

```
# cvs -d /cvs/home update
# cvs -d /cvs/home add readers
# cd /sandbox
# cvs -d /cvs/home commit -m 'pserver guest access' CVSROOT/readers
```

Finally, give *guest* a null password:

```
# cvsd-passwd /cvs/home guest
```

Don't create a password; just hit Enter until it goes away. Now fire up *cvsd*, and connect as an ordinary user:

```
# /etc/init.d/cvsd start
$ cvs -d:pserver:guest:@localhost:/home login
Logging in to :pserver:guest@localhost:2401/home
```

If you type a colon after "guest", it won't prompt you for the empty password. Mind your filepaths: use */home*, not */cvs/home*.

Discussion

It is important to follow all the steps in order, to get the file permissions correct. You want the *chroot* filesystem in */cvs* to be owned by *cvsd*, but not the *CVSROOT* directory.

Populate your new public repository in the usual manner. Add authorized users to the *cvsd* group. They can then import project files locally, or over SSH.

Do not use the CVS Pserver for anything but anonymous public access, and never allow checkins via Pserver. Its authentication methods are wide-open cleartext, as you saw when you created the *readers* and *passwd* files. For extra insurance, to prevent write access via Pserver, create an empty *CVSROOT/writers* file.

Users connecting over the Internet must use the full domain name:

```
$ cvs -d:pserver:guest:@cvsserver.test.net:/home login
```

You'll have to post explicit instructions to tell them how to connect to your repository. Users can also go directly to checkout:

```
$ cvs -d :pserver:guest:@cvsserver.test.net:/home checkout .
```

OpenSSH is for your authorized users who will be maintaining the files in the repository. (They will use the access methods described in Recipe 18.11.) It is best to keep your public repository separate from your private, working repository, and to update it nightly via *rsync-over-ssh*. If someone manages to compromise your Pserver, you don't want to provide an easy path to your working CVS server.

See Also

- The Readme and the FAQ in the source tarball, which contain bales of essential information—you should get this even if you install *cvsd* from packages
- *cvsd* home page (*http://tiefighter.et.tudelft.nl/~arthur/cvsd*)
- CVS home page (*https://www.cvshome.org*)

18.15 Mirroring a CVS Repository

Problem

You don't want your public, anonymous Pserver repository to be your main working repository; you would rather mirror it nightly, so that you can keep your working repository safely sheltered somewhere else, and keep access strictly controlled.

Solution

Put your Pserver and working CVS server on two separate boxes. Use *rsync* over SSH, with *keychain* managing authentication, automated by *cron,* to do a nightly upload to the Pserver. You need:

- Two separate CVS repositories set up and working—the anonymous public server and the private working server
- OpenSSH set up and working for both repositories
- *rsync* installed on the working repository
- A mirroring script placed in a nightly *cron* job

This is the simplest *rsync* invocation, copying files from the working repository to the public repository. The user *cvsadmin* was created especially for this job:

```
#!/bin/bash
source  /home/cvsadmin/.keychain/$HOSTNAME-sh
```

```
rsync -av -e ssh  --cvs-exclude --delete --force /cvsroot  publiccvs.test.net:
cvsroot/
```

Save the script as *cvsmirror.sh* or whatever you like, make it executable, and stick it in a *cron* job. This runs the script every morning at 2 a.m.:

```
# crontab -e
0 02 * * * /usr/local/bin/cvsmirror.sh
```

Discussion

The *--cvs-exclude* option is a nice *rsync* feature that ignores the same files that CVS ignores.

This is a simple and perfectly serviceable script. One possible problem is running the mirror script while users are editing repository files. Any writes committed during the backup could be lost. CVS includes a locking mechanism, to lock files as read-only during a backup. This is rather complex to implement, but Chapter 6 of *Essential CVS* discusses the implementation in detail and provides locking and unlocking scripts.

You could probably get away with having the two repositories on the same box, but the risk is that anyone who compromises your Pserver could gain access to the whole system and get into your private, working CVS repository.

See Also

- Chapter 16, *Backup and Recovery*
- Chapter 6 of *Essential CVS*
- CVS home page (*https://www.cvshome.org*)

18.16 Storing Binary Files in CVS

Problem

CVS is great with plain ASCII text files, but you are running into problems with binary files, like binary executables, MS Word files, image files, and such. How can you store binary files in the CVS repository without CVS doing strange things to them and making them not work?

Solution

Use the *-kb* flags with the *add* command, like this:

```
$ cvs update  binaryfile
$ cvs add -kb binaryfile
$ cvs commit -m 'C proggie for timing tea' binaryfile
```

You should also check out binary files with the *-kb* flags. If you are working with binary files a lot, you can make this the default in your *~/.cvsrc*.

Discussion

Making *-kb* the default means you will have to use *cvs add -kkv* when adding non-binary files. If you forget to use the *-kkv* flags when adding a non-binary file, run the following command:

```
$ cvs admin -kkv textfile
```

to modify the file for future commits and updates.

CVS makes a number of changes to text files that do no good to binary files:

- It changes linefeeds to carriage return/linefeeds, for cross-platform compatibility.
- It performs keyword expansion, so that any string in a binary file that looks like a CVS keyword will be changed. Embedded strings in the form *$keyword$* and *$keyword:...$* are replaced with their actual values whenever you fetch a new revision of the file. This is definitely not something you want to happen to a binary file.

See Also

- Chapter 3 of *Essential CVS*
- Local documentation—"Keyword Substitution" (*/usr/share/doc/cvs/html-info/cvs_12.html*)
- Recipe 18.19, "Customizing Your CVS Environment"

18.17 Creating Release Snapshots with Tags

Problem

You need a way to mark a specific set of files as a set. They may be in different directories, or simply a subset of files in a directory. You can't just grab them by revision number, because the files belonging to a particular project can have all kinds of different revision numbers. And you want to be able to retrieve the selected files with a single command, instead of having to hunt them down individually.

Solution

CVS uses *tags* to collectively label a particular set of files. With a tag, you can easily retrieve all the revisions of all the files that correspond to a specific milestone, such as an official 1.0 release of a project.

All the files are linked by the tags, like pearls on a string, and can be retrieved with a single command. They do not have to be in the same directories; simply list the files you want tagged on the command line, as follows:

```
$ cvs tag rel_1.0_3dgame file1 file2 file2 file4
```

The easy way is to have all the files you want tagged sitting in your sandbox; then tag them this way:

```
$ cvs tag rel_1.0_3dgame
```

This will recurse directories and tag all of your checked-out files. To retrieve tagged files, yank the whole batch by tag name:

```
$ cvs checkout -r rel_1.0_3dgame
```

Discussion

Here's a bit of ASCII art to show how tags work. In this example, the files that belong to your upcoming 1.0 release are stored in several different places. They are marked with asterisks:

```
file1   file2   file3   file4

1.1     1.1     1.1     1.1
1.2     1.2     1.2     1.2
1.3     1.3*    1.3     1.3
1.4     1.4     1.4*    1.4
1.5*    1.5             1.5*
1.6                     1.6
```

This means you don't have to worry about creating perfect file trees to keep the files belonging to the release organized, which is pretty much impossible in any case.

See Also

- Chapter 4 of *Essential CVS*
- Local documentation—"4 Revisions" (*/usr/share/doc/cvs/html-info/cvs_4.html*)
- CVS home page (*https://www.cvshome.org*)

18.18 Creating Stable and Development Branches for a Project

Problem

You want to divide a programming project into two branches: one that is stable, in maintenance mode, and one that is under active development. This way you'll have a reliable, stable branch that is ready for production use, and a wild and crazy development branch where improvements and new features will be developed and tested. When features from the development branch are ready for prime-time, you can merge them back into the stable branch.

Solution

To create the wild and crazy development branch from the nice, stable *project* module, first make all your commits and have your sandbox up-to-date. Then run this command:

```
$ cvs rtag -b projectbranch project
```

Name the new branch first, and the module for which it is created second. This command operates directly on the repository, not on the sandbox.

You can also create a branch from tagged files, which were discussed in Recipe 18.17:

```
$ cvs tag -r rel_1.0_3dgame -b rel_1.0_3dgame_branch
```

To check out the branch files you'll need to create a separate sandbox. Create a new directory for the new sandbox, then check out the branch files:

```
$ cvd -r projectbranch project
```

Committing files back to the branch requires no special options:

```
$ cvd commit
```

Someday, you will want to merge your branches. This is how (the *-j* means "join"):

```
$ cvs checkout project
$ cvs update -j projectbranch
```

How do you know if you're working in a branch, or on the main trunk? Read the sticky tag:

```
$ cvs status
===================================================================
File: somefile   Status: Up-to-date

    Working revision:    1.2      Wed Jul 28 06:08:54 2003
    Repository revision: 1.2      /home/foober/cvsroot/project/somefile,v
    Sticky Tag:          project (branch: 1.2.6)
    Sticky Date:         (none)
    Sticky Options:      -kkv
```

Discussion

Creating a CVS branch is no small thing. You must keep track and pay attention to what you are doing. It's rather pointless if the files get all mixed up and you lose track of the branches you've created.

After branches are merged, the individual branches will still remain in the CVS repository. Remember, CVS is designed to never forget anything.

CVS is pretty good at merging branches, and the majority of the merges succeed without incident. However, it's not magical; the various people working on the project will still need to have manners, communicate progress with each other, and have something in the way of project goals to aim for.

See Also

- Chapter 4 of *Essential CVS*, which goes into detail on branching, merging, and keeping track of everything
- Local documentation—"Branching and Merging" (*/usr/share/doc/cvs/html-info/ cvs_5.html*)

18.19 Customizing Your CVS Environment

Problem

You want to customize your CVS environment: the default editor, filepaths, default repository, and perhaps some command options. You want less typing and more working, or maybe less typing and less working, but at least you'd like to set up your working environment to please yourself.

Solution

Create a *.cvsrc* file and store it in your home directory. Every user can do this to customize their CVS working environment. This example sets some basic defaults:

```
cvs -T /tmp
cvs -d /cvsroot
cvs -e nano
update -dP
checkout -P
cvs -z3
diff -c
```

These changes do not affect the CVS server at all; this is how you make your life easier on the client side.

Discussion

A lot of CVS documentation will instruct you to set your CVS environment variables in your system profile (e.g., in *~/.bashrc*). Using *~/.cvsrc* is usually preferable, because it's portable and simple to configure. *~/.cvsrc*, when present, overrides any CVS environment variables in *~/.bashrc*.

The above *~./cvsrc* does these things:

cvs -T /tmp

Sets the temporary directory where you want it.

cvs -d /cvsroot

Sets the path to the default repository, so you don't have to type *cvs -d <cvsserver>*. This saves you a bit of typing when you're importing new projects; after you initialize a new sandbox, you don't need to specify the repository anyway.

cvs -e nano

Sets the default editor.

update -dP

Checks out new directories but not empty directories.

checkout -P

Does not check out empty directories.

cvs z3

Sets the compression level. The range is 1–9. Note that higher compression levels place a greater load on the CVS server, and may cause nastiness to flow from the server admin.

diff -c

Formats diff output as context diffs, which are the easiest to read.

As you use your CVS repository, make note of the command options you use the most, so you can set yourself some sensible defaults and save some typing.

See Also

- *cvs(1)*
- Chapter 3 of *Essential CVS*
- The CVS Quick Reference on the last page of *Essential CVS*
- Local documentation—"Guide to CVS commands" (*/usr/share/doc/cvs/html-info/cvs_16.html*)
- Local documentation—"All environment variables which affect CVS" (*/usr/share/doc/cvs/html-info/cvs_19.html*)

18.20 Calculating Storage Size for a CVS Repository

Problem

You need to know how to calculate how much storage space to allocate for your CVS repository, and if you should put it on its own partition.

Solution

A simple rule of thumb is to allocate 10 times as much space as the expected final size of the project files. When you have a lot of users busy on a project, it's easy to generate a lot of activity and eat up a lot of disk space. The definitive answer is "the more the better."

The best place to put your repository is in a filesystem that is already segregated on its own partition, such as */var* or */home*. This makes it easy to back up and keeps it separate from the root filesystem, which is always good for data files. You can also create a top-level directory on its own partition, such as */cvsroot*, to make it easier to find.

See Also

- Chapter 2 of *Essential CVS*

CHAPTER 19
Keeping Time with NTP

19.1 Introduction

Keeping accurate time on a single PC, or on a LAN, is important for a number of reasons: maintaining accurate timestamps in logs, keeping databases happy, and ensuring that batch jobs and other automated processes run at the right times. Even more important than keeping precisely correct time is keeping all of your servers and workstations synchronized with each other.

Linux includes a motley collection of time and date utilities: *ntpdate*, *hwclock.sh*, *date*, *822-date*, *tzselect*, *tzsetup*, *vcstime*, *uptime*, *zdump*, *ddate*, *rdate*, *ctime*, and doubtless several more. In olden times, we ran *hwclock.sh*, *rdate*, or *ntpdate* at boottime, or put them in *cron* jobs for periodic updating. *ntp*—the Network Time Protocol—replaces all of that. It is best to disable any of the other utilities that are set to run automatically, whether from *rc*.d* files or *cron*, and let *ntp* be your sole timekeeper. With one exception: *ntpdate* is still useful for making large corrections. If your system time is off by more than 20 or 30 minutes, *ntp* will take several hours, or even days, to correct it, whereas *ntpdate* takes care of large corrections instantly.

The command *ntpd -g* is supposed to replace *ntpdate*, but it doesn't work well for corrections of more than an hour. If your system time is off by several hours, the *ntp* documentation tells you to correct it manually. If that works for you, fine; in this chapter, we'll cover how to make the computer do the work.

ntp is implemented on Linux by *ntpd*, the Network Time Protocol daemon. It is nearly "set it and forget it;" once you have it configured and running, you shouldn't have to do more than make an occasional check to verify it's keeping time correctly.

It is good time server etiquette to configure a single host on your LAN to synchronize with a group of external time servers, and to then use this host to serve your LAN. This prevents you from placing an undue burden on the public time servers, and it keeps your LAN hosts in sync with each other.

In the olden days, admins had to select a list of public time servers to use, from *http://www.eecis.udel.edu/~mills/ntp/servers.html*. However, due to abuse and users not respecting access policies, *http://pool.ntp.org* was created. *www.pool.ntp.org* creates DNS round-robins to automatically spread the load. A nice side benefit is that it's easier to configure.

19.2   Building a Local Time Server

Problem

You want to set up a local time server. It will synchronize with a public time server, and your LAN clients will connect to the local machine. The PC acting as the local time server has a full-time Internet connection.

Solution

First, install or upgrade *ntp* on the PC that is going to act as a time server for your LAN. You'll also want *ntpdate*.

Next, make sure the *ntp* daemon is not running:

```
# /etc/init.d/ntpd stop
```

On Debian, use:

```
# /etc/init.d/ntp-server stop
```

Make these entries in */etc/ntp.conf*, and create the driftfile and logfile if they do not already exist. root should own them (*chmod 644*).

```
#/etc/ntp.conf
driftfile  /etc/ntp.drift
logfile  /var/log/ntp.log

server pool.ntp.org
server pool.ntp.org
server pool.ntp.org
```

Make the initial time correction with *ntpdate*:

```
# ntpdate pool.ntp.org
```

Then start up *ntpd*:

```
# /etc/init.d/ntpd start
```

On Debian, use:

```
# /etc/init.d/ntp-server start
```

Use *ntpq* to see which servers you're connected to:

```
# ntpq -p
   remote refid st t when poll reach delay offset jitter
```

```
=========================================================
+clock.fmt.he.ne .GPS. 1 u 37 64 377 105.562 26.771 2.539
+dewey.lib.ci.ph reaper.twc.weat 2 u 25 64 377 398.666 -30.285 51.555
*clock.sjc.he.ne .CDMA. 1 u 21 64 377 98.269 15.298 4.000
```

Be patient, because it takes a few minutes for a server list to appear and up to 30 minutes for the first correction to take place. The * and + prefixes indicate that the connections were successful and synchronization is occurring.

 If you are running any databases, be sure to consult with your database admins before making any significant time changes. Large, sudden changes are generally unhealthy for databases, so it may be better to run only *ntpd* and allow it to make changes in its normal slow, incremental manner.

Discussion

Be sure to get the *ntp rpm*, not *xntp*. *ntp* is newer and replaces *xntp*. Debian users need *ntp-simple*, *ntp-doc*, and *ntp-server*.

ntpd makes small, incremental changes over a period of time. By itself, it will take hours, or even days, to adjust the system time, depending how far off it is. If the system time is off by more than 60 minutes, *ntpdate* is the quickest way to make the initial correction. *ntpdate* will not run if *ntpd* is running.

The maintainers at ntp.org are trying to deprecate *ntpdate*, claiming that *ntpd -g*, which is *ntpd's* "burst" command, does the same thing. Unfortunately, it doesn't handle corrections larger than 60 minutes any faster than *ntpd*, so *ntpdate* is still useful.

Using the same entry in *ntp.conf* three times—*server pool.ntp.org*—puts three different hits on the DNS pool at your disposal, so you'll never have to worry about servers being unavailable.

pool.ntp.org is a worldwide DNS round-robin of participating time servers. See Recipe 19.5 for more pool options, and how to get the best performance.

See Also

- Your local documentation, at */usr/share/doc/ntp-doc/html*, or online at *http://www.ntp.org/documentation.html*
- The home page for the *pool.ntp.org* project (*http://www.pool.ntp.org*)
- The ntp.org web site (*http://www.ntp.org/*), for more information than you'll ever want about how *ntp* works
- See the archives of *comp.protocols.time.ntp*, and also get help with new questions

19.3   Connecting to a Local Time Server

Problem

You were tired of seeing a different incorrect time on every machine in your shop. So you set up a local time server—now how do you connect the clients?

Solution

Install or update *ntp* on the client PCs, and make sure the *ntp* daemon is not running:

```
# /etc/init.d/ntpd stop
```

On Debian, use:

```
# /etc/init.d/ntp-server stop
```

Edit */etc/ntp.conf* to point to the local time server:

```
# /etc/ntp.conf
driftfile  /etc/ntp.drift
logfile  /var/log/ntp.logdriftfile

#use either hostnames or IPs
server 192.168.1.101
```

You can also include a fallback, in case the time server becomes unavailable:

```
# local fudge if network servers not available
# stratum 10 means low priority
server  127.127.1.0
fudge   127.127.1.0 stratum 10
```

ntp will continue to keep the time, based on past performance, until the server becomes available.

Now run *ntpdate*, pointing to the local server:

```
# ntpdate 192.168.1.101
```

Start up *ntpd*:

```
# /etc/init.d/ntpd start
```

On Debian, use:

```
# /etc/init.d/ntp-server start
```

Again, it may take a few minutes for a query to show any results:

```
# ntpq -p
 remote refid st t when poll reach delay offset jitter
==============================================================
 *clock.sjc.he.ne .CDMA. 1 u 21 64 377 98.269 15.298 4.000
```

Discussion

It is a good practice to also add some access controls; see the next recipe for */etc/ntp.conf* access rules and some sample *iptables* rules.

Windows clients should use the free Automachron *sntp* (Simple Network Time Protocol) client. It works on all versions of Windows, is easy to configure, and is free of cost (although if you use it, it would be a nice gesture to click the PayPal link on the author's web site and send him a few dollars). Download it from *http://www.oneguycoding.com/automachron*.

Automachron has a nice feature for dialup connections—the "Wait for dialup connection" setting. It won't attempt to synchronize until a connection is established. It is also easy to set the synchronization intervals.

See Also

- Recipe 19.4, "Adding Access Controls"
- Your local documentation at */usr/share/doc/ntp-doc/html*, or online at *http://www.ntp.org/documentation.html*
- The ntp.org web site (*http://www.ntp.org*)
- The Usenet group comp.protocols.time.ntp

19.4 Adding Access Controls

Problem

You want to be sure your local clients look like clients, and not *ntp* servers. You want them to receive time service only, and from only the specified servers.

Solution

Add some access rules in */etc/ntp.conf*, or you may add a couple of *iptables* rules to the client's firewall to allow time service only, and to disallow everything else.

To use *ntp*'s access controls, add these lines to */etc/ntp.conf*:

```
# default access policy
# this denies all ntp traffic that is not
# explicitly allowed
restrict default ignore

# allow time service from this server
# do not allow peering
# do not allow runtime configuration changes
# do not allow remote logging
restrict 192.168.1.101 nopeer nomodify notrap
```

```
# we trust localhost
restrict 127.0.0.0 mask 255.0.0.0
```

Remember to restart *ntpd* after making changes to *ntp.conf*.

An alternative to adding access rules to *ntp.conf* is to use these *iptables* rules. If the client machines are running *iptables*, add these rules to create a client that accepts only time service and rejects everything else:

```
iptables -A INPUT -p udp --dport 123 -m state --state ESTABLISHED -j ACCEPT
iptables -A INPUT -p udp --dport 123 -j REJECT
```

The first rule accepts all responses to sent *ntp* packets, and the second denies all others. Any host attempting to initiate a connection will be blocked, but responses to the client's own requests will be allowed.

Discussion

Here are some of the *ntp.conf* configuration options explained:

peer [hostname or IP]
> The specified host is polled in symmetric active mode, which means peers synchronize each other. Never peer with a public time server.

server [hostname or IP]
> The specified server is polled in client mode, so that only the client machine receives time synchronization.

restrict
> Define restrictions on specific hosts, and override defaults. When a default is specified, *restrict [host]* with no options is the same as *allow all [host]*.

ignore
> Ignore all *ntp* packets.

nomodify
> Do not allow runtime configuration changes. Queries that return information are permitted.

nopeer
> Do not allow peering. This means the only servers allowed to supply time service are the ones specified by the *server* directive, and other hosts cannot use use this machine as a time server.

notrap
> Do not trap mode 6 control messages. In effect, this disables remote logging.

noquery
> Ignore all NTP mode 6 and 7 packets. In other words, do not allow queries, remote logging, or runtime configuration requests. Time service is not affected.

The main reasons for using access controls are to prevent your clients from becoming the timekeepers to the world, and to keep order and sanity in your network.

See Also

- Your local documentation at */usr/share/doc/ntp-doc/html*, or online at *http://www.ntp.org/documentation.html*
- The home page for the *pool.ntp.org* project (*http://www.pool.ntp.org*)
- The ntp.org web site (*http://www.ntp.org*)
- The Usenet group comp.protocols.time.ntp

19.5   Deciding Which NTP Pools to Use

Problem

So you'd like to know about other choices for *ntp* pools. It seems that connecting to a global pool runs the risk of using servers that are too far away for good performance.

Solution

There are three classes of *ntp* pools available:

Global
> pool.ntp.org

Regional
> europe.pool.ntp.org
>
> north-america.pool.ntp.org
>
> oceania.pool.ntp.org
>
> asia.pool.ntp.org

Country
> us.pool.ntp.org
>
> de.pool.ntp.org
>
> fr.pool.ntp.org
>
> br.pool.ntp.org
>
> ...

There is not yet a definitive list of country pools. You can check to see if one exists for your country with *ping*:

```
$ ping nl.pool.ntp.org
PING nl.pool.ntp.org (194.109.206.206): 56 data bytes
64 bytes from 194.109.206.206: icmp_seq=0 ttl=49 time=240.8 ms
```

See *http://www.iana.org/cctld/cctld-whois.htm* for a list of country codes.

As a general rule, use a pool when it has at least three servers. You can find this out with *dig*:

```
$ dig de.pool.ntp.org
; <<>> DiG 9.2.4rc2 <<>> de.pool.ntp.org
;; global options:  printcmd
;; Got answer:
;; ->>HEADER<<- opcode: QUERY, status: NOERROR, id: 13116
;; flags: qr rd ra; QUERY: 1, ANSWER: 8, AUTHORITY: 6, ADDITIONAL: 6
;; QUESTION SECTION:
;de.pool.ntp.org.      IN      A

;; ANSWER SECTION:
de.pool.ntp.org.     5400    IN     A      81.169.174.99
de.pool.ntp.org.     5400    IN     A      134.99.176.3
de.pool.ntp.org.     5400    IN     A      195.185.228.210
de.pool.ntp.org.     5400    IN     A      213.133.108.8
de.pool.ntp.org.     5400    IN     A      217.160.141.61
de.pool.ntp.org.     5400    IN     A      80.190.100.192
de.pool.ntp.org.     5400    IN     A      80.237.234.15
de.pool.ntp.org.     5400    IN     A      81.169.158.205
...
```

To investigate further, run *ping* a few times to get an idea of roundtrip times:

```
$ ping de.pool.ntp.org
PING de.pool.ntp.org (217.204.76.170): 56 data bytes
64 bytes from 217.204.76.170: icmp_seq=0 ttl=238 time=221.7 ms
64 bytes from 217.204.76.170: icmp_seq=1 ttl=238 time=224.3 ms
64 bytes from 217.204.76.170: icmp_seq=2 ttl=238 time=223.8 ms
```

Then run *traceroute* a few times. Track the number of hops, and look for timeouts:

```
$ traceroute de.pool.ntp.org
traceroute: Warning: de.pool.ntp.org has multiple addresses; using 199.184.165.135
1  80.239.142.1 (80.239.142.1)  0.236 ms  0.129 ms  0.115 ms
2  ge-0-2-0.pr1.k88.fra.de.eurotransit.net (82.96.89.245)  0.317 ms  0.259 ms  0.248 ms
3  ffm-k88-i2-geth3-2.telia.net (213.248.79.65)  0.417 ms  0.243 ms  0.241 ms
...
11  195.185.228.210 (195.185.228.210)  9.191 ms  8.925 ms  9.094 ms
```

11 hops and no timeouts is pretty good. Each test should be run several times to get a reasonably accurate picture.

Discussion

The nice thing about using the *ntp* pools is that they do the work for you. Once your system is configured, you shouldn't have to fuss with it. And time server abuse is mitigated, so everyone is happy. If you have a good full-time Internet connection and want to be part of a pool, see *http://www.pool.ntp.org* for the details. The more time servers there are, the less load there is on each one.

See Also

- Your local documentation at */usr/share/doc/ntp-doc/html*, or online at *http://www.ntp.org/documentation.html*
- The home page for the *pool.ntp.org* project (*http://www.pool.ntp.org*)
- The ntp.org web site (*http://www.ntp.org*)
- The Usenet group comp.protocols.time.ntp

19.6 Connecting to a Time Server from an Intermittent Connection

Problem

You do not have a full-time Internet connection; you're still on a dialup account, you have a limited DSL account, or you travel. How can you synchronize to an *ntp* server?

Solution

ntp will still work for you. Install *ntp* and *ntpdate*. Make sure the *ntp* daemon is not running. Configure */etc/ntp.conf*, and create the driftfile and logfile if they do not already exist:

```
#  /etc/ntp.conf
driftfile  /etc/ntp.drift
logfile  /var/log/ntp.log

server pool.ntp.org
server pool.ntp.org
server pool.ntp.org
```

root should own the driftfile and logfile (*chmod 644*).

Debian users (or users of any system that puts PPP scripts in the */etc/ppp/ip-up.d/* directory) can copy this script:

```
#!/bin/bash
# ntp-dialup script for Debian
# put this in /etc/ppp/ip-up.d/
# set the correct time immediately
# and run /etc/init.d/ntp-server every time PPP starts

/usr/sbin/ntpdate pool.ntp.org
  if [ -x /etc/init.d/ntp-server ]; then
   /etc/init.d/ntp-server restart
  fi
```

root should own this script (*chmod 744*). The script will run every time you start PPP.

On Red Hat and Fedora, you'll need to edit or create the */etc/ppp/ip-up.local* script, adding these lines:

```
#!/bin/bash
# add these lines to /etc/ppp/ip-up.local
# on Red Hat and Fedora
# set the correct time immediately
# and run /etc/init.d/ntpd every time PPP starts

/usr/sbin/ntpdate pool.ntp.org
  if [ -x /etc/init.d/ntpd]; then
   /etc/init.d/ntpd restart
  fi
```

When you connect, *ntpdate* will run and correct the time within the first minute or two. Then the *ntp* daemon will continue running in the background:

```
11 Feb 11:38:18 ntpdate[6796]: adjust time server 163.1.87.28 offset -0.018303 sec
ntpdate is updating the time
Starting NTP server: ntpd.
```

If this is a dialup server serving an Ethernet LAN, you can now configure the client machines as per Recipe 19.3.

Discussion

These scripts contain a bit of a kludge, by using *restart* instead of *start*. *ntpd* binds itself to whatever IP address is assigned when *ntpd* starts up. When a PC has a dynamically assigned IP address, *ntpd* does not track when the lease expires and the address changes. So, if you leave your PC running all the time and need to dial up periodically, *ntpd* will lose the connection. *restart* ensures that *ntpd* will shut down completely and then restart, and thus will pick up the current IP address with each new dialup connection.

These scripts can easily be adapted for a PC that is dialing into a private network that has a local time server. In your PPP scripts, simply point *ntpdate* to the local server, and edit */etc/ntp.conf* to point to the local server.

See Also

- Recipe 19.4, "Adding Access Controls"
- The manuals for your distribution, for how to run scripts that start up with PPP
- Your local *ntp* documentation, at */usr/share/doc/ntp-doc/html*, or online at *http://www.ntp.org/documentation.html*; on Debian, you may need to install *ntp-doc*
- The home page for the *pool.ntp.org* project (*http://www.pool.ntp.org*)

- The ntp.org web site (*http://www.ntp.org*)
- The Usenet group comp.protocols.time.ntp

19.7 Setting Up Multiple Local Time Servers

Problem

Your local time server is getting overwhelmed, so you need to add more servers. And you would like the additional servers to peer, so that your network hosts are always synchronized with each other.

Solution

In this example, two internal servers—*server1* and *server2*—synchronize with *us.pool.ntp.org* and with each other:

```
# /etc/ntp.conf for server1

driftfile  /etc/ntp.drift
logfile  /var/log/ntp.log

# default access policy
# this denies all ntp traffic that is not
# explicitly allowed
restrict default ignore

# ntp server list
server pool.ntp.org
server pool.ntp.org
server pool.ntp.org
peer server2

# allow time service from peer
# but not run-time configuration changes
# disable remote logging
restrict server2 nomodify notrap

# allow localhost unrestricted
restrict 127.0.0.0 mask 255.0.0.0
```

/etc/ntp.conf for *server2* is identical, except the *server2* entries must be replaced with *server1*. Configure LAN clients as described in Recipe 23.2, using the peers as the server entries:

```
# /etc/ntp.conf for clients
driftfile  /etc/ntp.drift
logfile  /var/log/ntp.log

server  server1
server  server2
```

Discussion

You can set up as many additional peers as you like; workstations can even peer with each other. For your own sanity, keep it as simple as possible. Don't try to peer with the public time servers! They have no reason to trust your servers, and you do not want to annoy time server admins. The idea behind peering is to hit the public servers as little as possible, while adequately serving the local network.

See Also

- The manuals for your distribution, for how to run scripts that start up with PPP
- Your local *ntp* documentation at */usr/share/doc/ntp-doc/html*, or online at at *http://www.ntp.org/documentation.html*
- The ntp.org web site (*http://www.ntp.org*)
- The Usenet group comp.protocols.time.ntp

19.8   Using NTP Keys for Authentication

Problem

You're not comfortable running your local servers without some sort of authentication scheme. While *ntp* exploits are rare, you would feel better having some method of ensuring that your clients and servers can verify that they are who they claim to be.

Solution

Use *ntp*'s built-in key authentication scheme, *ntpkeys*.

First, configure the server (in this example *server1*):

```
# /etc/ntp.conf
...
crypto pw seekritword
keysdir /etc/ntp/keys
...
```

Because the password is stored in cleartext, *ntp.conf* should be *chmod 600*.

Create the key on *server1*:

```
# ntp-keygen -T -I -p seekritword
```

This may take a few minutes. Now, copy the newly generated file *ntpkey_IFFpar_server1.4558615255* to */etc/ntp* on all clients of *server1*. (Your timestamp will be different.) Because this is a secret key, you'll want to transfer it in a secure manner.

Floppy disks work fine. (Don't forget to secure the floppy disk when you're finished.)

Now configure the client machines. First, create two symlinks to the new key:

```
# ln -s ntpkey_IFFpar_server1.4558615255 ntpkey_iff_server1
# ln -s ntpkey_IFFpar_server1.4558615255 ntpkey_iff_client1
```

Now edit the server line in the client's */etc/ntp.conf,* adding the *autokey* keyword:

```
server server1 autokey
```

Restart *ntpd* on all participating machines and find something else to do for awhile, as the server and clients will take a little time to get the new authentication scheme synchronized and working. Within an hour or two, everything will be operating normally.

Discussion

This is what the *ntp-keygen* flags mean:

-*T* Generate a trusted certificate. By default, the program generates a nontrusted certificate.

-*I* Use the IFF identification scheme, overwriting any key files that already exist.

-*p* Set the password.

If you want to use authentication with public time servers, you'll need to do two things:

1. Find public servers that support authentication.
2. Configure the servers individually in *ntp.conf,* instead of using *ntp* pools.

See *http://www.eecis.udel.edu/~mills/ntp/servers.html* for a current list of public time servers. Warning: pay attention to their access policies! Do not connect to Stratum 1 servers, unless you meet their criteria. Always use Stratum 2 for ordinary time service.

The *keys* file is the obvious headache and weak point of this whole scheme. As the *ntp* documentation says, "The big trouble with the authentication facility is the *keys* file. It is a maintenance headache and a security problem. This should be fixed some day. Presumably, this whole bag of worms goes away if/when a generic security regime for the Internet is established."

In the real world, the chances of *ntp* being exploited are low. Even if a public time server is spoofed and sends you wrong time signals, you have some built-in protections: *ntp* makes small changes, and you're getting service from a pool of servers, so any mistakes, whether deliberate or not, are quickly corrected.

See Also

- The "ntp-keygen—Generate Public and Private Keys" section of the NTP manual, either at */usr/share/doc/ntp-doc/html*, or online at *http://www.ntp.org/documentation.html*
- The ntp.org web site (*http://www.ntp.org*)
- The Usenet group comp.protocols.time.ntp

## CHAPTER 20

Building a Postfix Mail Server

20.1 Introduction

The Linux world has many excellent programs for handling email: Sendmail, Exim, qmail, and Postfix are the top four mail transfer agents (MTAs). This chapter covers Postfix. Like most of the post-Sendmail generation of MTAs, Postfix is designed from the ground up to be secureable and robust. It scales nicely from the single user who wants more control over her personal mail all the way up to the largest service provider.

Here's a bit of terminology:

MTA

Mail transfer agent. This moves email between servers. Sendmail, Exim, qmail, and Postfix are MTAs. An MTA must support SMTP.

SMTP

Simple Mail Transfer Protocol. This moves messages between mail servers.

MUA

Mail user agent, also called "mail client." Mutt, Pine, Kmail, Evolution, and Balsa are MUAs. This is the user's program for composing, sending, and receiving email. MUAs can fetch mail from a local folder, or from a remote server via POP and IMAP.

MDA

Mail delivery agent. This is an intermediary between an MTA and a MUA. Procmail and Fetchmail are two popular MDAs. An MDA is not required; it is used for extra functionality, such as filtering, sorting, and autoresponding.

POP

Post Office Protocol. Moves messages from the server to the user's inbox. A POP server is simple to operate and does not need a lot of horsepower.

IMAP

Interactive Message Access Protocol. The message store remains on the server. An IMAP server needs a lot of RAM and lots of storage space.

TLS

Transport Layer Security is an evolution of SSL (Secure Sockets Layer). It provides encrypted transport for SASL-authenticated logins.

SASL

Simple Authentication and Security Layer, for authenticating users. SASL does the authenticating, then TLS provides the encrypted transport of the authentication data.

These are the official ports for different mail protocols:

tcp/25

SMTP

tcp/110

POP3

tcp/995

POP3 over SSL

tcp/143

IMAP

tcp/993

IMAP over SSL

There are several ways to build a Linux mail server. Most admins take the modular approach and build it from a collection of specialized programs. That is what we will do in this chapter. Another option is to use the Courier package, because it is a complete package that contains an MTA, POP3, IMAP, and a mailing list manager. Or purchase a distribution that puts it all together for you, like SuSE OpenExchange.

20.2 Building a POP3 Mail Server

Problem

You want to set up a POP3 mail server—nothing fancy, just a basic server for Internet mail for a single domain, with TLS/SSL support for more secure logins.

Solution

Here are the requirements:

- Postfix
- Courier-IMAP, which supplies both POP3 and IMAP
- OpenSSL
- *famd*, the file alteration monitor daemon

See Recipe 20.3 for Debian instructions.

Install or upgrade OpenSSL and *famd* first.

Next, remove any installed MTAs and POP/IMAP servers. Look first for Sendmail, as it is still the default on a lot of installations. Go ahead and break dependencies, because Postfix will satisfy them.

Then stop any running processes belonging to the old MTA:

```
$ ps ax | grep sendmail
root 10204 0.0 0.7 5296 1980 ? S 19:27 0:00 sendmail:accepti
$ su
# kill 10204
```

Now install Postfix. If you build from sources, be sure to compile in SASL support. (See the *SASL_README* in the tarball.)

After installing Postfix, make a backup copy of */etc/postfix/main.cf*:

```
# cp /etc/postfix/main.cf  /etc/postfix/main.cf-old
```

Erase everything in the original, and copy in these lines. Be sure to enter filepaths and host/domain names appropriate for your system:

```
command_directory = /usr/sbin
mail_owner = postfix
default_privs = nobody
# enter your domain name here
mydomain = tuxcomputing.com
# enter your own fully-qualified domain name here
myhostname = windbag.tuxcomputing.com
myorigin = $mydomain
alias_maps = hash:/etc/aliases
alias_database = hash:/etc/aliases
inet_interfaces = all
mydestination = $myhostname, localhost.$mydomain $mydomain
mynetworks_style = subnet

# very important! Courier must have maildirs, not mbox
home_mailbox = Maildir/
mail_spool_directory = /var/mail
mtpd_banner = $myhostname ESMTP $mail_name
mailbox_size_limit = 0
recipient_delimiter = +
```

Create aliases for root and postmaster in */etc/aliases*:

```
# See man 5 aliases for format
root:foober@test.net
postmaster:root
```

Then create the alias database:

```
# newaliases
```

and run the built-in syntax checker:

```
# postfix check
```

Some distributions start Postfix automatically after installation. To start it manually, use the *postfix* command:

```
# postfix start
```

If Postfix is already running, restart it:

```
# postfix reload
postfix/postfix-script: refreshing the Postfix mail system
```

Then verify that Postfix is running:

```
$ ps ax | grep postfix
26342 ?        Ss     0:00 /usr/lib/postfix/master
```

Next, verify that the *smtp* daemon is working:

```
$ telnet localhost 25
Trying 127.0.0.1...
Connected to localhost.localdomain.
Escape character is '^]'.
220 windbag.test.net ESMTP Postfix (Libranet/GNU)
EHLO windbag.test.net
250-windbag.test.net
250-PIPELINING
250-SIZE 10240000
250-VRFY
250-ETRN
250-XVERP
250 8BITMIME
^]
telnet> quit
Connection closed.
```

Now install Courier-IMAP. To install from RPMs, you'll need *courier-imap-common* and *courier-imap-pop3*. If you build from sources, be sure to read *00README.NOW.OR.SUFFER*.

After installation, generate the POP3 TLS/SSL certificate. First, edit */etc/courier/pop3d.cnf,* entering your own site information:

```
[ req_dn ]
C=US
ST=NM
L=Albuquerque
O=mailserver
OU=Automatically-generated POP3 SSL key
CN=Windbag
emailAddress=postmaster@tuxcomputing.com
```

Now generate the key:

```
# mkpop3dcert
Generating a 1024 bit RSA private key
.............................................++++++..++++++
writing new private key to '/usr/lib/courier/pop3d.pem'-----
1024 semi-random bytes loaded
Generating DH parameters, 512 bit long safe prime, generator 2
This is going to take a long time
.....+.......+........+.............+...+.........................................+.....
.......        ...
subject= /C=US/ST=NM/L=Albuquerque/O=Courier Mail Server/OU=Automatically-generated
POP3 SSL key/CN=windbag/emailAddress=postmaster@tuxcomputing.com
notBefore=May 20 18:08:13 2004 GMT
notAfter=May 20 18:08:13 2005 GMT
MD5 Fingerprint=D4:A5:53:48:09:65:C4:F0:11:8F:31:9E:FB:9F:EB:8A
#
```

Some distributions start Courier automatically after installation. Use these commands to start Courier manually, if necessary:

```
# /etc/init.d/courier-pop3d start
# /etc/init.d/courier-pop3d-ssl start
```

Verify the filenames, as they vary on different distributions.

Now you have a fully functioning POP3 mail server.

Discussion

The various Linux distributions customize Postfix and Courier in their own weird little ways, so be sure to verify filepaths and filenames.

If you're used to having mail queued in */var/spool*, you're going to find that Courier is different. The mail queues are in each user's home directory:

```
# ls /home/foober
Desktop  Maildir
# ls /home/foober/Maildir
courierimapkeywords     courierimapuiddb      cur  tmp
courierimapsubscribed   courierpop3dsizelist  new
```

New mail sits in */Maildir/new* until the user retrieves it. This is configured in Postfix, in *main.cf*:

```
home_mailbox = Maildir/
```

A POP3 mail server can be any old Pentium, or even a 486. It's best to put a mail server on its own dedicated box. A mail server must be exposed to untrusted networks, so anything on the same machine is exposed to some risk. Also, because this configuration of Postfix uses system passwords, giving it its own box means that email accounts will have their own separate passwords. You don't want users to have the same passwords for email as for logging into their workstations or LANs, because that's a big security hole.

When you generate the Courier SSL certificate, it is self-signed, which means no "trusted" third party vouches for the authenticity of your certificate. This is perfectly okay for most uses. If you think you need a genuine, signed, commercially generated SSL certificate from a vendor such as VeriSign or Thawte, it will cost you several hundred dollars per year. An alternative is to check with your ISP or web host to see if they offer lower-cost shared certificates.

See Also

- Recipe 20.3, "Building a POP3 Mail Server on Debian," for Debian instructions
- Local Courier documentation (*/usr/share/doc/courier-doc*)
- Postfix Basic Configuration (*/usr/share/doc/postfix/html/basic.html*)
- Courier-IMAP home page (*http://www.inter7.com/courierimap.html*)
- Postfix home page (*http://www.postfix.org*)

20.3   Building a POP3 Mail Server on Debian

Problem

You want to run a Postfix/Courier POP3 server on Debian, and you need to know the Debian way of doing this.

Solution

Debian automates most of the process. Install or upgrade *famd*, OpenSSL, and Postfix:

```
# apt-get install famd openssl postfix postfix-doc postfix-tls
```

Debian will walk you through a basic Postfix configuration and start it up. Next, back up */etc/postfix/main.cf*:

```
# cp /etc/postfix/main.cf  /etc/postfix/main.cf-old
```

Erase everything in the original, and copy in these lines. Be sure to enter filepaths and host/domain names appropriate for your system:

```
command_directory = /usr/sbin
mail_owner = postfix
default_privs = nobody
# enter your domain name here
mydomain = tuxcomputing.com
# enter your own fully qualified domain name here
myhostname = windbag.tuxcomputing.com
myorigin = $mydomain

alias_maps = hash:/etc/aliases
alias_database = hash:/etc/aliases
```

```
inet_interfaces = all
mydestination = $myhostname, localhost.$mydomain $mydomain
mynetworks_style = subnet

# very important! Courier must have maildirs, not mbox
home_mailbox = Maildir/
mail_spool_directory = /var/mail
mtpd_banner = $myhostname ESMTP $mail_name
mailbox_size_limit = 0
recipient_delimiter = +
```

Create a mail alias for root in */etc/aliases*:

```
# See man 5 aliases for format
root:foober@test.net
postmaster:root
```

Then create the alias database:

```
# newaliases
```

Run the built-in syntax checker:

```
# postfix check
```

Next, restart Postfix:

```
# postfix reload
postfix/postfix-script: refreshing the Postfix mail system
```

Now install Courier:

```
# apt-get install courier-authdaemon courier-base courier-doc courier-pop courier-
pop-ssl courier-ssl
```

Debian will automatically generate the keys and start the Courier daemons. However, you should edit */etc/courier/pop3d.cnf*, and manually generate a new certificate with the updated data. Recipe 20.2 tells how to do this.

Discussion

postfix reload is the fastest, least intrusive way to activate changes to *main.cf*. Use it when the system is under load and you don't want to disrupt service.

Always check the Debian packages search page, at *http://packages.debian.org*. Debian has its own package naming conventions and tends to split up packages into many small components.

See Also

- Recipe 20.2, "Building a POP3 Mail Server," for manually generating a Courier certificate
- The Debian packages search page (*http://packages.debian.org*)
- Postfix Basic Configuration (*/usr/share/doc/postfix/html/basic.html*)

- Local Courier documentation (*/usr/share/doc/courier-doc*)
- Recipe 20.4, "Testing the SMTP/POP3 Mail Server"

20.4 Testing the SMTP/POP3 Mail Server

Problem

You want to verify that the various server components are working.

Solution

Our old friend *telnet* and our new friend *openssl s_client* will do the job. Test the SMTP server with *telnet*:

```
$ telnet localhost 25
Trying 127.0.0.1...
Connected to localhost.localdomain.
Escape character is '^]'.
220 windbag.test.net ESMTP Postfix (Libranet/GNU)
ehlo windbag
250-windbag.test.net
250-PIPELINING
250-SIZE 10240000
250-VRFY
250-ETRN
250-XVERP
250 8BITMIME
mail from: foober@test.net
250 Ok
rcpt to: carla@test.net
250 Ok
data
354 End data with <CR><LF>.<CR><LF>
Date: Jan 15, 2004
From: foober
Reply-to: foober@test.net
Message-ID: six
Subject: telnet test
Hi Carla,
Did you get this?
.
250 Ok: queued as 6069F2290C
quit
221 Bye
Connection closed by foreign host.
```

Also test plain, unencrypted POP3 with *telnet*:

```
$ telnet localhost 110
Trying 127.0.0.1...
Connected to localhost.localdomain.
```

```
Escape character is '^]'.
+OK Hello there.
user carla
+OK Password required.
pass sekritword
+OK logged in.
stat
+OK 2 1275
list
+OK POP3 clients that break here, they violate STD53.
1 638
2 637
.
retr 1
+OK 638 octets follow.
Return-Path: <stinkpad@test.net>
X-Original-To: carla@test.net
Delivered-To: carla@test.net
Received: from 192.168.1.100 (unknown [192.168.1.100])
 by windbag.test.net (Postfix) with ESMTP id 409E722884
 for <carla@test.net>; Thu, 15 Jan 2004 15:29:54 -0700 (PDT)
From: stinkpad <stinkpad@test.net>
To: carla@test.net
Subject: telnet test
Date: Thu, 15 Jan 2004 15:29:50 -0700
User-Agent: KMail/1.5.4
MIME-Version: 1.0
Content-Type: text/plain;
  charset="us-ascii"
Content-Transfer-Encoding: 7bit
Content-Disposition: inline
Message-Id: <200401151529.50714.stinkpad@test.net>

Hi Carla,
Did you get this?


.

quit
+OK Bye-bye.
Connection closed by foreign host.
```

Test TLS/SSL support with *openssl s_client*. Use the POP3 mail commands:

```
$ openssl s_client -connect localhost:995
CONNECTED(00000003)
depth=0 /C=US/ST=NM/L=Albuquerque/O=Courier Mail Server/OU=Automatically-generated
POP3 SSL key/CN=windbag/emailAddress=postmaster@test.net
verify error:num=18:self signed certificate
...
<many lines of certificate data and protocols>
---
+OK Hello there.
user carla
+OK Password required.
```

```
pass sekritword
+OK logged in.
```

Continue just as you would with any POP3 session.

You can test client connectivity by hostname or IP:

```
$ telnet windbag 25
$ telnet 192.168.1.5 110
$ openssl s_client -connect windbag:995
```

Discussion

Here are some of the more common POP3 commands:

list
> Show a list of messages, by number, with the number of bytes in each message.

top msg lines
> Display the message header of message *msg* and display *lines* many lines. For example, *top 3 5* displays the headers of message 3 and the first 5 lines of the body of the message.

retr msg
> Display the message, selected by number (e.g., *retr 2*).

dele n
> Delete message number *n*.

rset
> Undelete any messages that are marked for deletion.

quit
> Delete messages marked for deletion, and log out.

See Also

- RFC 1939 for a complete description of POP commands
- This chapter's "Introduction," for a list of ports for the different mail protocols
- *telnet(1)*

20.5 Sending Internet Mail

Problem

How do you configure Postfix to send Internet mail? You've set up the server, but mail isn't flowing yet.

Solution

This is more complicated than it used to be, thanks to spammers. If your ISP does not require SMTP authentication, you can relay outbound mail via their SMTP server. Add a *relayhost* directive to */etc/postfix/main.cf*:

```
relayhost = isp.smtpserver.com
```

Use the SMTP server specified in your ISP account information.

If your ISP requires SMTP authentication, see Recipe 20.7.

Discussion

Beware of restrictive Terms of Service (TOS). They may forbid running servers of any kind. If your service provider does not allow you to run servers, you'll either need to move to a provider that does allow it or use a third-party service for "smart hosting" (a commercial SMTP relaying service).

Another option is to configure each individual mail client to use your ISP account for outgoing mail, because most mail clients can be configured to remember the SMTP login. However, there are a couple of drawbacks to doing this:

- You won't have any control over or logging of outbound mail.
- Internal mail won't be delivered directly, but rather bounced all over the Internet.

See Also

- Recipe 20.7, "Installing Cyrus-SASL for SMTP Authorization"
- The Postfix book (*/usr/share/doc/postfix/html/index.html*)

20.6   Receiving Internet Mail

Problem

Your nice new mail server is ready to go to work—how do you make it receive Internet mail?

Solution

You need three things: a static IP, a registered domain name, and DNS records pointing the world to your mail server. In your DNS configuration you need an A record for the server IP, and an MX record for the mail server. This is what BIND entries look like:

```
$ORIGIN tuxcomputing.com.
windbag     A    10.11.12.23
mx          10   windbag
```

djbdns entries look like this:

```
+www.tuxcomputing.com:10.11.12.23
@windbag.tuxcomputing.com:10.11.12.23:a
```

See Chapter 24 for more on DNS.

Discussion

There are many ways to manage DNS. Your ISP can do it, or you can use third-party DNS services such as Dyndns.org or your domain name registrar. You can also run your own public DNS server, and arrange with trusted friends to exchange secondaries.

See Also

- Chapter 24, *Managing Name Resolution*
- The Postfix book (*/usr/share/doc/postfix/html/index.html*)

20.7 Installing Cyrus-SASL for SMTP Authorization

Problem

You want to add Cyrus-SASL to your mail server, so you can set up *smtp-auth*. You want your users to authenticate themselves, and you want Postfix to authenticate to an external relay.

Solution

RPM users need these packages:

- *cyrus-sasl-2.x*
- *cyrus-sasl-plain-2.x*

Debian users, see Recipe 20.8.

Before installing Cyrus-SASL, verify that your version of Postfix supports SASL and TLS. Run *ldd* on the *smtpd* executable to find out. Look for *libsasl2*, *libssl*, and *libcrypto*:

```
$ ldd /usr/lib/postfix/smtpd
...
  libssl.so.0.9.7 => /usr/lib/i686/cmov/libssl.so.0.9.7 (0x4006f000)
  libcrypto.so.0.9.7 => /usr/lib/i686/cmov/libcrypto.so.0.9.7 (0x4009e000)
  libsasl2.so.2 => /usr/lib/libsasl2.so.2 (0x4018f000)
...
```

If Postfix links to these libraries, go ahead and install Cyrus-SASL. If it doesn't, you have two options:

- Rebuild Postfix from sources. Read the *README* and *SASL_README* files. Be sure to install Cyrus-SASL first, before compiling Postfix.
- Replace your Postfix with an up-to-date RPM package that has everything built in.

After installing Postfix and Cyrus-SASL, start up *saslauthd*:

```
# /etc/init.d/saslauthd start
```

Now add these lines to *main.cf*:

```
smtpd_sasl_auth_enable = yes
smtpd_sasl2_auth_enable = yes
smtpd_sasl_security_options =noanonymous
broken_sasl_auth_clients = yes
smtpd_sasl_local_domain =$myhostname

smtpd_recipient_restrictions =
        permit_sasl_authenticated
        permit_mynetworks
        reject_unauth_destination
```

and activate the changes:

```
# postfix reload
```

Then verify that Postfix sees the new SASL libraries:

```
$ telnet localhost 25
Trying 127.0.0.1...
Connected to localhost.localdomain.
Escape character is '^]'.
220 windbag.test.net ESMTP Postfix (Libranet/GNU)
EHLO windbag.test.net
250-windbag.test.net
250-PIPELINING
250-SIZE 10240000
250-VRFY
250-ETRN
250-STARTTLS
250-AUTH LOGIN PLAIN
250-AUTH=LOGIN PLAIN
```

```
250-XVERP
250 8BITMIME
```

The *STARTTLS* and *AUTH* lines are just what you want to see. Now you can move on to Recipe 20.9 for the next step.

Discussion

You can use *AUTH LOGIN* and *PLAIN*, because logins will be encrypted by TLS (see Recipe 20.9).

main.cf has over a hundred possible configuration options. Don't go nuts; it's not necessary to use all of them. Use the minimum needed to get the job done. You can check out many sample configurations in */usr/share/doc/postfix/examples/sample-smtpd.cf.gz*.

smtpd_recipient_restrictions can have multiple options separated by commas, either all on one line or broken up into multiple lines. Each line must start with whitespace.

See Also

- */usr/share/doc/postfix/examples/*, for descriptions of all the *main.cf* options
- */usr/share/doc/postfix/examples/sample-auth.cf.gz*, for explanations of the authentication options
- The Postfix book (*/usr/share/doc/postfix/html/index.html*)

20.8   Installing Cyrus-SASL on Debian

Problem

You need to know The Debian Way of adding Cyrus-SASL to your mail server.

Solution

First, install the SASL packages:

```
# apt-get install  libsasl2  sasl2-bin  libsasl2-modules
```

Then, edit */etc/default/saslauthd* to look like this:

```
# This needs to be uncommented before saslauthd will be run automatically
  START=yes

# You must specify the authentication mechanisms
# you wish to use.
# This defaults to "pam" for PAM support, but may
# also include
```

```
# "shadow" or "sasldb", like this:
# MECHANISMS="pam shadow"

MECHANISMS="pam"
```

Next, add these lines to *main.cf*:

```
smtpd_sasl_auth_enable = yes
smtpd_sasl2_auth_enable = yes
smtpd_sasl_security_options = noanonymous
broken_sasl_auth_clients = yes
smtpd_sasl_local_domain =$mydomain

smtpd_recipient_restrictions =
        permit_sasl_authenticated
        permit_mynetworks
        reject_unauth_destination
```

and activate the changes:

```
# postfix reload
```

Then verify that Postfix is seeing the new libraries:

```
$ telnet localhost 25
Trying 127.0.0.1...
Connected to localhost.localdomain.
Escape character is '^]'.
220 windbag.test.net ESMTP Postfix (Libranet/GNU)
EHLO windbag.test.net
250-windbag.test.net
250-PIPELINING
250-SIZE 10240000
250-VRFY
250-ETRN
250-STARTTLS
250-AUTH LOGIN PLAIN
250-AUTH=LOGIN PLAIN
250-XVERP
250 8BITMIME
```

The *STARTTLS* and *AUTH* lines are just what you want to see. Now you can move on to Recipe 20.9 for the next step.

Discussion

You can use *AUTH LOGIN* and *PLAIN*, because logins will be encrypted by TLS (see Recipe 20.9).

See Also

- */usr/share/doc/postfix/examples/*, for descriptions of *main.cf* options

- */usr/share/doc/postfix/examples/sample-auth.cf.gz*, for explanations of the authentication options
- The Postfix book (*/usr/share/doc/postfix/html/index.html*)

20.9 Setting Up smtp-auth to Authenticate Users

Problem

You want your users, especially remote users, to have to authenticate themselves to your Postfix server to prevent unauthorized relaying.

Solution

You'll need four things:

- Cyrus-SASL2
- OpenSSL
- Postfix compiled to support Cyrus-SASL
- A server certificate and keys

See Recipe 20.7 if you have not installed Cyrus-SASL. When SASL is installed and working, the next step is to generate an SSL server certificate. Find and enter the */ssl/ misc* directory:

```
# cd /usr/lib/ssl/misc
# ls
CA.pl  c_info  c_name  der_chop  CA.sh  c_hash  c_issuer  demoCA
```

The script that generates the keys is *CA.pl* (or, you might see *CA.sh,* which is a wrapper for *CA.pl* that adds a little extra functionality). Choose one and make a backup copy:

```
# cp  CA.sh  CA.sh-old
```

Edit the script, adding the *-nodes* flag everywhere there is a *$REQ* line:

```
-newcert)
    # create a certificate
    $REQ -new -nodes -x509 -keyout newreq.pem -out newreq.pem $DAYS
...
-newreq)
    # create a certificate request
    $REQ -new -nodes -keyout newreq.pem -out newreq.pem $DAYS
    RET=$?
...
else
    echo "Making CA certificate ..."
```

```
$REQ -new -nodes -x509 -keyout ${CATOP}/private/$CAKEY \
    -out ${CATOP}/$CACERT $DAYS
```

This eliminates the creation of a passphrase. You may not want to have to enter a passphrase every time the server restarts, or have an unattended reboot stall because it's waiting for a passphrase. You may skip this step and use a passphrase; obviously, using a passphrase increases security.

Now generate your new certificate:

```
# ./CA.sh -newca
# ./CA.sh -newreq
# ./CA.sh -sign
```

The result, after much output, is *newreq.pem*, *newcert.pem*, and *demoCA/cacert.pem*. Copy these to */etc/postfix*:

```
# cp newcert.pem /etc/postfix/
# cp newreq.pem /etc/postfix/
# cp demoCA/cacert.pem /etc/postfix/
```

Next, add these lines to */etc/postfix/main.cf*:

```
smtpd_use_tls = yes
smtpd_tls_auth_only = yes
smtpd_tls_key_file = /etc/postfix/newreq.pem
smtpd_tls_cert_file = /etc/postfix/newcert.pem
smtpd_tls_CAfile = /etc/postfix/cacert.pem
smtpd_tls_loglevel = 3
smtpd_tls_received_header = yes
smtpd_tls_session_cache_timeout = 3600s
tls_random_source = dev:/dev/urandom
```

Activate the changes:

```
# postfix reload
```

and test the server:

```
$ telnet localhost 25
Trying 127.0.0.1...
Connected to localhost.localdomain.
Escape character is '^]'.
220 windbag.test.net ESMTP Postfix (Libranet/GNU)
EHLO windbag.test.net
250-windbag.test.net
250-PIPELINING
250-SIZE 10240000
250-VRFY
250-ETRN
250-STARTTLS
250-XVERP
250 8BITMIME
STARTTLS
S: 220 Ready to start TLS
```

Now configure your user's mail clients, and you're done. Most mail clients can be configured to store the login and password, so all your users need to do is click the send button.

Discussion

Postfix installations are pretty consistent across the various package formats and Linux distributions, but it's still a good idea to verify all the filepaths in */etc/postfix/main.cf*.

See Also

- */usr/share/doc/postfix/examples/*, for descriptions of the *main.cf* options
- */usr/share/doc/postfix/examples/sample-auth.cf.gz*, for the explanations of the authentication options

20.10 Using smtp-auth to Authenticate Postfix to Another Server

Problem

You want to relay off your service provider's SMTP server, but it requires a login and password. You already have *smtp-auth* set up and working for your users.

Solution

Create or edit */etc/postfix/sasl_passwd*, and store your login information in it:

```
mail.tuxcomputing.com   carla:sekritword
```

Set restrictive file permissions:

```
# chown root:root /etc/postfix/sasl_passwd && chmod 600 /etc/postfix/sasl_passwd
```

Now convert it to a hashed DB:

```
# postmap hash:/etc/postfix/sasl_passwd
```

This creates */etc/postfix/sasl_passwd.db*.

Add one more line to */etc/postfix/main.cf*:

```
smtp_sasl_password_maps = hash:/etc/postfix/sasl_passwd
```

and activate the changes:

```
# postfix reload
```

Now Postfix will authenticate itself to your relay server.

Discussion

/etc/postfix/sasl_passwd may have multiple entries for different hosts, as long as each one has a different hostname:

```
mail.tuxcomputing.com    carla:sekritword
smtp.goodeats.com        carla:sekkritword
mail.saddles.net         horselady:secritword
```

See Also

- */usr/share/doc/postfix/examples/*, for descriptions of the *main.cf* options
- */usr/share/doc/postfix/examples/sample-auth.cf.gz*, for explanations of the authentication options
- Recipe 20.7, "Installing Cyrus-SASL for SMTP Authorization"
- Recipe 20.9, "Setting Up smtp-auth to Authenticate Users"

20.11 Configuring a Fully Qualified Domain Name

Problem

You're not sure how to configure a fully qualified domain name on your system. You know there are several files to edit, but you aren't quite sure what they are or what to put in them.

Solution

On most Linux systems, you must edit */etc/hostname* and */etc/hosts*. */etc/hostname* sets only the system's hostname:

```
windbag
```

/etc/hosts sets the domain name:

```
127.0.0.1      localhost.localdomain localhost
192.168.1.5    windbag.test.net  windbag
```

On Red Hat and Fedora, you must edit */etc/sysconfig/network* instead of */etc/hostname*:

```
HOSTNAME=windbag
```

Check your configurations as follows:

```
$ hostname
windbag
$ hostname --fqdn
windbag.test.net
```

```
$ dnsdomainname
test.net
```

You must reboot for hostname changes to take effect.

Discussion

/etc/sysconfig/network and */etc/hostname* are read at boottime to set the hostname.

You can change the domain name anytime and have it take effect by restarting networking. On Debian, use:

```
# /etc/init.d/networking restart
```

On Red Hat and Fedora, use:

```
# /etc/init.d/network restart
```

However, this is not foolproof, because some applications will not be updated with a networking restart. A reboot is usually best.

See Also

- *hosts(5), hostname(1)*

20.12 Building an IMAP Mail Server

Problem

Your users are a footloose lot, and they want to be able to log into their mail server from wherever they happen to be, see all their mail and folders, and not have to worry about having their mail scattered all over different PCs.

Solution

An IMAP server is one way to meet this need. (Webmail is another; see Recipe 20.18.) If you have an RPM-based sytem, like Fedora, and followed Recipe 20.2, you have an IMAP server installed. Debian users (Recipe 20.3) need to install two additional packages:

```
# apt-get install courier-imap courier-imap-ssl
```

Next, generate your TSL/SSL key, then start up the server:

```
# mkimapdcert
# /etc/init.d/courier-imap start
# /etc/init.d/courier-imap-ssl start
```

Check your *init* scripts for the exact filenames, as these vary on different Linux distributions.

Test it with *telnet*:

```
$ telnet localhost 143
Trying 127.0.0.1...
Connected to localhost.localdomain.
Escape character is '^]'.
* OK [CAPABILITY IMAP4rev1 UIDPLUS CHILDREN NAMESPACE THREAD=ORDEREDSUBJECT
THREAD=REFERENCES SORT QUOTA IDLE ACL ACL2=UNION STARTTLS] Courier-IMAP ready.
Copyright 1998-2004 Double Precision, Inc.  See COPYING for distribution information.
a001 login carla sekritword
a001 OK LOGIN Ok.
a002 examine inbox
* FLAGS (\Draft \Answered \Flagged \Deleted \Seen \Recent)
* OK [PERMANENTFLAGS ()] No permanent flags permitted
* 0 EXISTS
* 0 RECENT
* OK [UIDVALIDITY 1085106842] Ok
* OK [MYRIGHTS "acdilrsw"] ACL
a002 OK [READ-ONLY] Ok
a003 logout
* BYE Courier-IMAP server shutting down
a003 OK LOGOUT completed
Connection closed by foreign host.
```

To test your IMAP-over-TLS/SSL support, use:

```
$ openssl s_client -connect localhost:993
```

See RFC 3501 for a complete description of IMAP commands.

You now have a working IMAP server. See Recipe 20.13 for how to connect your users.

 You must have the file alteration monitor daemon (*famd*) running, so that *Maildir* folders will continually update themselves. *famd* is standard on most Linux systems; run *ps ax | grep famd* to make sure it's running.

Discussion

You'll need something better than the antique Pentium you used in Recipe 20.2 because an IMAP server requires more horsepower and lots more storage space than a POP3 server. And you definitely do not want to share the box—let the IMAP server have it all to itself. Because hardware requirements vary according to user demand, precise calculations are difficult. As a general rule, a 1.5-GHz CPU, 256 MB RAM, and a 30-GB drive can serve 100 users. Keep an eye on disk space, as that is usually the first to go.

See Also

- Local Courier documentation (*/usr/share/doc/courier-doc/htmldoc/imapd.html*)
- RFC 3501, for a complete description of IMAP commands.
- Recipe 20.13, "Connecting Your Users"

20.13 Connecting Your Users

Problem

You have your mail server up and running—now how do users connect to it?

Solution

All you have to do is point their email clients to your server. Every mail client has a different setup menu, but they all need the same information:

- Login name
- Password
- Server name or IP address
- Encryption or no encryption
- Server port number

Figure 20-1 shows the Balsa Mail setup menu.

Most Linux mail clients autodetect encryption and automatically set the correct port.

Discussion

Linux is chock-full of nice mail clients: Mutt, Pine, Kmail, Balsa, Mozilla Mail, Evolution, and Sylpheed, to name a few. Mozilla Mail is a good choice for standardizing on mixed networks, as it runs on Linux, Windows, and Mac OS X.

See Also

- Mozilla (*http://mozilla.org*)
- Thunderbird (*http://www.mozilla.org/projects/thunderbird*)
- Kmail (*http://kmail.kde.org*)
- Mutt (*http://www.mutt.org*)
- Evolution (*http://www.novell.com/products/evolution*)
- Balsa (*http://www.newton.cx/balsa*)

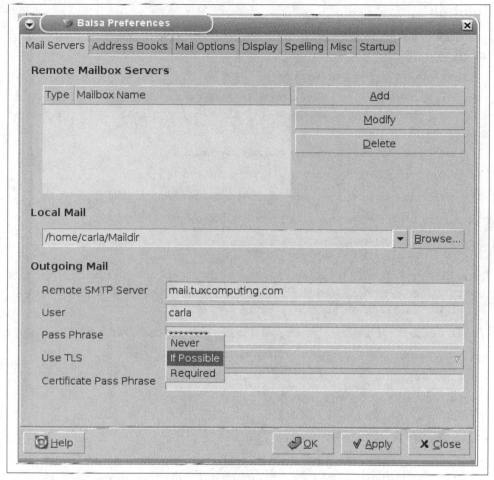

Figure 20-1. Balsa Mail configuration

- Pine (*http://www.washington.edu/pine*)
- Sylpheed (*http://sylpheed-claws.sourceforge.net*)

20.14 Sharing IMAP Folders

Problem

You want to set up shared folders on your IMAP server, and let your users create their own shared folders.

Solution

Use Courier's *maildirmake* command. First, as root, create a shareable *Maildir* with the big *-S* flag:

```
# maildirmake -S /var/mail/sysadmins
```

Then create a shareable folder (yes, these are plain old Linux directories, but Courier calls them folders) in the *Maildir* with the little *-s* flag. *write* gives read/write permissions to everyone:

```
# maildirmake -s write -f reports /var/mail/sysadmins
```

You can add another folder, with read permissions only, using:

```
# maildirmake -s read -f policies /var/mail/sysadmins
```

Note that *maildirmake* creates *dot,* or hidden, directories:

```
# ls -a /var/mail/sysadmins
. .. .reports .policies  cur  new  tmp
```

Permissions can be fine-tuned on the individual folders, just like with any Linux directory. (See Recipe 9.7 to learn how to adjust permissions on shared directories.) To remove shared folders, just delete them.

Users can also share folders. Their shared folders remain in their own home directories:

```
$ maildirmake --add images=/var/mail/sysadmins $HOME/Maildir
```

Users may "unshare", or break the link to the shared directory, with *--del*:

```
$ maildirmake --del images  $HOME/Maildir
```

Discussion

If you want a full-blown groupware/email server, it is possible to assemble all the pieces by hand from free/open source components. There are also a number of pre-fab Linux groupware packages available, some free of cost, some commercial. This is a small sampling—there are many more in various stages of development:

PHP GroupWare
  http://www.phpgroupware.org

OpenGroupware
  http://www.opengroupware.org

The Kolab Project
  http://kolab.org

SuSE OpenExchange
  http://www.suse.com

SKYRiX Groupware
   http://www.skyrix.com

Novell Linux
   http://www.novell.com/linux

See Also

- *maildirmake(1)*

20.15 Using Postfix's Virtual Mailbox Domains

Problem

You would like to host more than one domain on your Postfix server, or you want to get away from using Linux system accounts for your mail user accounts. That is, you'd like to be able to give users email accounts without having to create actual Linux accounts on your mail server. Giving out as few accounts as possible makes your systems more secure.

Solution

Use Postfix's *virtual mailbox domains*. This lets you create virtual mailboxes without having to create system user accounts. Then set up your users' logins in *userdb* in Courier, for either POP or IMAP.

First, add these lines to */etc/postfix/main.cf*, substituting your own domain name or names, and directories:

```
virtual_mailbox_domains = tuxcomputing.com  test.net  foober.com
virtual_mailbox_base = /var/mail/vhosts
virtual_mailbox_maps = hash:/etc/postfix/vmailbox
virtual_minimum_uid = 1000
virtual_uid_maps = static:5000
virtual_gid_maps = static:5000
virtual_alias_maps = hash:/etc/postfix/virtual
```

Now edit or create */etc/postfix/vmailbox*. In this file, you pair up your usernames with their local mail storage directories, which in this example are under */var/mail/vhosts*:

```
akkana@tuxcomputing.com        tuxcomputing.com/akkana/
dancer@tuxcomputing.com        tuxcomputing.com/dancer/
telsa@test.net                 test.net/telsa/
telsa.gwynne@test.net          test.net/telsa/
val.henson@foober.com          foober.com/valh/

# catch-all address for the domain- you'll be sorry,
# you'll get nothing but spam and virii
@foober.com                    foober.com/catchall
```

The trailing slashes indicate *Maildir*s. (Remove them to create *mbox* format, like in the catchall example.) Then convert the file to a Postfix lookup table:

```
# postmap /etc/postfix/vmailbox
```

Now you need to create your users' logins. This is done not in Postfix, but in Courier. Create or edit */etc/courier/userdb*. Add your new users to */etc/courier/userdb*, using the following format. Be sure to insert a tab stop after the login name, and give each one a unique UID/GID:

```
telsa    uid=1100gid=1100|home=/var/mail/vhosts/telsa|shell=/bin/bash|imappw=|pop3pw=
```

There must be no spaces anywhere on the line.

Now comes the tedious part. You need to generate a new password for each new user, using *userdbpw*. This example creates *md5*-hashed passwords:

```
$ userdbpw -md5
Password:
Reenter password:
$1$G41nVriv$GzWaLKidkoVIE2DxMxHBx1
```

Now copy this into */etc/courier/userdb*:

```
telsa    uid=1100gid=1100|home=/var/mail/vhosts/telsa|shell=/bin/
bash|imappw=$1$G41nVriv$GzWaLKidkoVIE2DxMxHBx1|pop3pw=$1$G41nVriv$GzWaLKidkoVIE2DxMxH
Bx1
```

Don't forget to write down your username/password pairs! When you're finished, stop *authdaemond,* and convert */etc/courier/userdb* file to a hashed database:

```
# /etc/init.d/courier-authdaemon stop
# makeuserdb
```

Now configure Courier to use */etc/courier/userdb* for authentication, in addition to system passwords. Do this in */etc/courier/authdaemonrc*:

```
##NAME: authmodulelist:0
#
# The authentication modules that are linked into
# authdaemond.  The
# default list is installed.  You may selectively
# disable modules simply
# by removing them from the following list.  The
# available modules you
# can use are: authcustom authcram authuserdb authldap
# authpgsql authmysql authpam

authmodulelist="authuserdb" "authpam"
```

Finally, restart *authdaemonrc*:

```
# /etc/init.d/courier-authdaemon start
```

Now your users can configure their mail clients, and you're done.

Discussion

Always double-check filepaths, as there are some differences on the different distributions.

There are four possible services that you can give users access to in */etc/courier/userdb*: *systempw, pop3pw, esmtppw,* and *imappw.* Only users with system accounts can use *systempw.* If you like, you may limit system users to mail service only by replacing *systempw* with any of the other three options.

If you have many domains, you can list them in a text file, one domain per line, and point *virtual_mailbox_domains* to the file:

```
virtual_mailbox_domains = /etc/postfix/virtual_domains
```

Having Courier authenticate with both */etc/courier/userdb* and */etc/passwd* can really slow things down. You can migrate your existing users into */etc/courier/userdb* to speed up authentications. First, migrate your existing users:

```
# /usr/sbin/pw2userdb > oldusers.text
```

This dumps the contents of */etc/shadow* into a text file, in the correct format for Courier, like this:

```
carla    uid=1000|gid=1000|home=/home/carla|shell=/bin/
bash|systempw=$1$.Mi$1huUDUGHKJjs78475fhyXg2xtoFdmO|gecos=carla schroder,,,
1000=    carla
www-data          uid=33|gid=33|home=/var/www|shell=/bin/sh|systempw=*|gecos=www-data
33=      www-data
postfix uid=102|gid=102|home=/var/spool/postfix|shell=/bin/false|systempw=!
102=     postfix
```

Take this and create or edit the file */etc/courier/userdb.* Simply copy and paste the entries you want to use.

20.16 Creating a Mail List with couriermlm

Problem

You want to set up some mail lists on your Postfix/Courier mail server.

Solution

You'll need *couriermlm* (Courier mailing list manager), *dot-courier,* and *cron.*

Users can create a list in any directory where they have write permissions. You might want to set up list directories for your users outside of their home directories, for example in */var.*

Run this command to create a directory for a new mailing list:

```
$ couriermlm create /var/lists/php_list  ADDRESS=php@test.net
```

This creates a directory chock-full of templates and subdirectories:

```
$ ls -xa php_list
.                       ..
adminrequest.tmpl       archive
bounces                 commands
confsubj.tmpl           digestsubj.tmpl
fetch.tmpl              fetchsubj.tmpl
headeradd               help.tmpl
idxheader2html.tmpl     idxheaderhtml.tmpl
idxheadertxt.tmpl       idxsubject.tmpl
modqueue                modrejbody.tmpl
modreject.tmpl          modrejheader.tmpl
modsubject.tmpl         modtext.tmpl
modtext2.tmpl           options
sub.tmpl                sub2.tmpl
sub3.tmpl               sub4.tmpl
sub5.tmpl               sublist
subreportfooter.tmpl    subreporthdr.tmpl
subreporthdr1.tmpl      subreporthdr2.tmpl
subreporthdr3.tmpl      tmp
unsub.tmpl              unsub2.tmpl
unsub3.tmpl             unsublist
warn1headers.tmpl       warn1text.tmpl
warn1text2.tmpl         warn2msg.tmpl
```

Read the following template files, and edit them as necessary to suit your needs:

help.tmpl
> The message that Courier sends in response to help requests.

sub.tmpl
> Subscription is a two-step process, requiring confirmation to minimize bogus and forged subscriptions. *sub.tmpl* is the first reponse to a subscription request.

sub.tmpl
> The final confirmation message, containing additional list instructions.

headeradd
> Put any additional mail headers you want on list messages here.

headerdel
> Put any mail headers you want deleted here.

If you're running a public list and don't want to expose subscribers' personal addresses to spammers, use *headerdel* and *headeradd* together:

```
# headerdel
Reply-To:
From:
```

```
# headeradd
Reply-To:php@test.net
From:php@test.net
```

Next, set up */etc/crontab* to run *couriermlm's hourly* and *daily* commands:

```
# m h dom mon dow   user    command
@midnight           alice   couriermlm daily /var/lists/php_list
@hourly             alice   couriermlm hourly /var/lists/php_list
```

Finally, create some *dot-courier* files to direct administrative list mails to the appropriate user. These files go in the list manager's home directory. In this example, the *php@test.net* list is administered by user *valorie*. First, *valorie* creates */home/valorie/.courier-php*. That tells the location of the *php* list:

```
/usr/bin/couriermlm msg /var/lists/php_list
```

Next is */home/valorie/.courier-php-owner*:

```
valorie@test.net
```

And finally, */home/valorie/.courier-php-default*:

```
/usr/bin/couriermlm ctlmsg /var/lists/php_list
```

This directs all the administrative list mail, such as subscribe/unsubscribe and help requests, to the correct mail list.

Discussion

The *hourly* and *daily* commands clean up any stale entries in the */var/lists/php_list/ commands* directory.

List users will use the following commands, in the *list-command@domain* format:

```
php-help@test.net
php-subscribe@test.net
php-unsubscribe@test.net
```

This is where those *dot-courier* files come into play, by directing these requests to the right places.

See Also

- *courier(8)*, *dot-courier(5)*

20.17 Administering a couriermlm List

Problem

You need to know the basic list-maintenance commands, such as those for manually unsubscribing a user, viewing subscriber information, and setting list options.

Solution

This command reference covers basic list chores.

To manually unsubscribe a user, use:

```
$ couriermlm unsub /var/lists/php_list lori@test.net
```

To generate a subscriber list, use:

```
$ couriermlm export /var/lists/php_list > php_subscribers.txt
```

Use the following command to restore the subscriber list from a file, if it is ever damaged or lost:

```
$ couriermlm import php_subscribers.txt
```

To post a message to the whole list, use:

```
$ couriermlm msg /var/lists/php_list
```

To display a single subscriber's record, use:

```
$ couriermlm info /var/lists/php_list  dancer@test.net
```

This command sets the list as moderated, so that all posts must be reviewed by the list admin before they are posted. Posts waiting for approval sit in the */var/lists/php_list/ modqueue* folder:

```
$ couriermlm set /var/lists/php_list  POST=mod
```

The default is to allow only subscribers to post. You can open the list to the world:

```
$ couriermlm set /var/lists/php_list  POST=all
```

By default, all messages are archived, and anyone can view them. This command purges archives after seven days and limits access to subscribers:

```
$ couriermlm set /var/lists/php_list  PURGEARCHIVE=7 POSTARCHIVE=subscribers
```

This also shows how list options can be grouped into a single command.

Discussion

Once a list is set up and running, there's not much to do except keep an eye on your users. Watch for flamewars and spammers. It is good to have a list policy, with clear rules about behavior. Put this in *sub2.tmpl*, so that all new subscribers see it.

See Also

- *courier(8)* and *dot-courier(5)*, for additional commands and list options

20.18 Squirreling Around with Webmail

Problem

Your remote users want even more freedom, and don't want to be tied down to a mail client. So you'd like to set up web access to email.

Solution

Give them Squirrelmail; then they can log in from any web browser, anywhere.

Prerequisites:

- A working IMAP server
- PHP4
- A working Apache web server

To install Squirrelmail simply copy the Squirrelmail files to your system. The usual location is wherever you store your other web files (e.g., */var/www/squirrelmail*), though it really doesn't matter where they go. Then run Squirrelmail's configuration script:

```
# /usr/sbin/squirrelmail-configure
```

This is for setting your own preferences, such as company name, color themes, and filepaths.

Squirrelmail is simply a batch of PHP4 files, which means Apache does the real work and must be configured to support PHP4. In this example, the existing web site is *www.tuxcomputing.com*, as this entry in *httpd.conf* shows:

```
### Section 2: 'Main' server configuration
ServerName www.tuxcomputing.com
DocumentRoot /var/www
```

Open *httpd.conf*, and uncomment or create these entries:

```
LoadModule php4_module /usr/lib/apache/1.3/libphp4.so

# make sure index.php is included
<IfModule mod_dir.c>
  DirectoryIndex index.html index.htm index.shtml index.cgi index.php
</IfModule>

  AddType application/x-httpd-php .php
  AddType application/x-httpd-php-source .phps
```

Save your changes and restart Apache.

Next, create a soft link named */var/www/webmail* to */usr/share/squirrelmail*, or wherever your Squirrelmail directory is:

```
# ln -s /usr/share/squirrelmail  /var/www/webmail
```

Now users can log in to their webmail at *http://www.tuxcomputing.com/webmail*.

Discussion

Squirrelmail is a PHP4 interface to Apache, not a standalone application. You'll need Apache knowledge.

As of this writing, there were still issues with PHP4 on Apache 2.x, so until those are resolved, Apache 1.3 is recommended.

If you want to enable *http://webmail.tuxcomputing.com*, instead of *http://www.tuxcomputing.com/webmail*, you'll need a DNS entry pointing to it, and you'll have to create a *VirtualHost* entry in *httpd.conf*. This example uses a name-based virtual host:

```
"NameVirtualHost *:80
<VirtualHost *:80>
  ServerName webmail.tuxcomputing.net
  DocumentRoot /var/www/webmail
</VirtualHost>
```

See Also

- Local Squirrelmail documentation (*/usr/share/doc/squirrelmail*)
- Squirrelmail home page (*http://www.squirrelmail.org*)
- Chapter 22, *Running an Apache Web Server*

20.19 Table of SMTP Response Codes and SMTP Commands

Table 20-1 is a quick reference for the different SMTP response codes. Complete information about these is in RFC 2821. I recommend studying RFC 2821, as it describes every step of the SMTP transaction in detail. You can also see these codes in action during a *telnet* session, as in Recipe 20.4.

Table 20-1. Code categories

Code category	Description
2xx	Positive completion reply. The requested action has been successfully completed.
3xx	Positive intermediate reply. Send more information.

Table 20-1. Code categories (continued)

Code category	Description
4xx	Transient negative completion reply. The command was not accepted; please try again.
5xx	Permanent negative completion reply. The command was not accepted. Go away and don't try again.

Table 20-2 lists the specific codes.

Table 20-2. Specific codes

Code	Description
211	System status or system help reply.
214	A help message for a human reader follows.
220	*<domain>* Service ready.
221	*<domain>* Service closing transmission channel.
250	Requested mail action okay, completed.
251	User not local; will forward to *<forward-path>*.
252	Cannot VRFY user, but will accept message and attempt delivery.
354	Start mail input; end with *<CRLF>.<CRLF>*.
421	*<domain>* Service not available, closing transmission channel.
450	Requested mail action not taken: mailbox busy or unavailable.
451	Requested action aborted: local error in processing.
452	Requested action not taken: mailbox full.
501	Syntax error, no parameters allowed.
502	Command not implemented.
503	Bad sequence of commands.
504	Command parameter not implemented.
521	*<host>* does not accept mail.
530	Must issue a *STARTTLS* command first. Encryption required for requested authentication mechanism.
534	Authentication mechanism is too weak.
538	Encryption required for requested authentication mechanism.
550	Requested action not taken: mailbox unavailable.
551	User not local; please try *<forward-path>*.
552	Requested mail action aborted: exceeded storage allocation.
553	Requested action not taken: mailbox name not allowed.
554	Transaction failed.

Table 20-3 lists the SMTP commands.

Table 20-3. SMTP commands

Command	Description
HELLO (HELO)	Identifies the sender-SMTP to the receiver-SMTP by hostname.
MAIL (MAIL)	Identifies the sender, and begins the mail transaction.
RECIPIENT (RCPT)	The name of the person to whom the message is addressed.
DATA (DATA)	The message itself, containing the usual elements that you see in a mail client: From, To, Date, CC, Reply-to.
RESET (RSET)	Aborts the current mail transaction. Any stored sender, recipients, and mail data are discarded, and all buffers and state tables are cleared. The receiver must send an OK reply.
VERIFY (VRFY)	Asks the receiver to confirm that the recipient has a mailbox on the system. Spammers like to exploit this, so Postfix provides a way to disable it (Recipe 21.4).
NOOP (NOOP)	Asks the receiver to send an OK response.
QUIT (QUIT)	Requests that the receiver send an OK reply and then ends the transmission.

## CHAPTER 21

Managing Spam and Malware

21.1 Introduction

Spam and malware really take the fun out of the Internet. It seems that no human invention, no matter how cool, is immune from being spoiled by idiots.

Malware is a general term that covers viruses, Trojan horses, worms, malicious executables on web pages, and any other kind of nasty that can infect a system from a mail client or web browser. Currently, this means primarily Outlook, Outlook Express, and Internet Explorer. Eliminating these from a Windows system goes a long way toward making it less insecure.

This chapter covers adding a number of spam and virus-fighting tools to your Postfix server: Clam Anti-Virus, SpamAssassin, DNS blackhole lists, and whitelists. You can mix and match to your heart's content. Make sure you are running the latest versions of everything—especially Postfix, which should be Version 2.0 or newer.

There are three ways to apply restrictions on incoming mail:

1. SMTPD restrictions
2. Header/body checks
3. Content filters

The farther down the chain you go, the more work is placed on the server. There are limits to what can be effectively done at each level. Expect to invest a bit of time and do some tweaking until you get it right.

Your basic strategy is:

- Protect your bandwidth.
- Protect your mail server from being overloaded.
- Protect your proxies and mail servers from being used to relay spam.
- Keep yourself from being a source of contagion.

The last is the most important. No one else cares how messed up your system is, as long as you don't become a source of contagion to the entire Internet.

It's a ridiculous amount of effort to exert just to keep your inboxes reasonably free of pestilence, but if you have any Windows hosts on your network, you have to do it.

Do you need to do all this if you are not running any Windows systems? You can probably omit Clam Anti-Virus, though it doesn't hurt to have it running. Linux isn't immune from attack, though attacks via email viruses are highly unlikely. As of this writing, there are no significant Linux email viruses. Attacks on Linux systems usually come through the back door. An attacker has to find a way to gain access to the system, then gain enough privileges to commit mischief. Opening in document mode is the Linux standard, so even if you've configured your mail client to associate file types with applications, you still can't activate an executable directly from an email. And if an ordinary user should activate a malicious email attachment, by saving it to a directory, doing *chmod +x*, and then running it, it would still need root privileges to do anything significant. (Remember how Postfix insists that root's mail goes to an alias?)

Furthermore, even if a Linux email virus managed to install and propagate itself and infect other hosts, it would fizzle out pretty quickly. It simply would not find a warm welcome, not the way Windows viruses do. Still, it never hurts to be careful. All it takes is one evil genius to write a lethal exploit; armies of willing script kiddies will quickly take care of unleashing it on the world.

Again, taking care of the basics is fundamental:

- Use the minimum necessary privileges for the job—do not take the name of root in vain.
- Remember that strong passwords are effective.
- Keep a tight leash on *sudo* users.
- Be careful with file ownerships and permissions.

See Also

- Virus Library, for a comprehensive, easily searchable collection of viruses, Trojan horses, worms, and so forth (*http://www.viruslibrary.com*)
- Security Focus, home of the BugTraq list and many more excellent resources (*http://www.securityfocus.com*)
- The SANS (SysAdmin, Audit, Network, Security) Institute (*http://www.sans.org*)

21.2   Basic Checklist: Preparing to Build Spam Malware Defenses

Problem

You administer a mixed LAN, with clients running Windows, Linux, and maybe a few other platforms as well. You're most concerned about your Windows machines, because as much as you would like to lock them down in quarantine and deny them all network access to protect the rest of the LAN, it can't be done. So how can you harden your LAN against email and web infection?

Solution

Start with your Windows hosts. Remove:

- Outlook
- Outlook Express
- Internet Explorer

Replace these with any of the following fine free email clients and web browsers:

- Eudora
- Pegasus
- Mozilla Mail
- Netscape Mail
- Opera Mail
- Opera web browser
- Mozilla web browser
- Netscape web browser
- Firefox web browser

You have now closed off the major malware ports of entry, and you can move on to the next steps.

Discussion

Locking down Outlook/Outlook Express/Internet Explorer is theoretically possible, but in my estimation it's too risky. If all you need are a mail client and a web browser, there are many first-rate alternatives. IE has fallen far behind other web browsers in functionality, so you're not even getting a benefit for the increased risk.

If you need the groupware features of Outlook because you are running an MS Exchange server, you might give Novell Evolution a test drive. It runs on Linux, so it's not an option for your Windows hosts, but if you're considering migrating some desktops, or want to integrate your Linux users, it's a great choice. It connects to an Exchange server via the Evolution Connector, which is currently free from Novell. You'll get all the features of Outlook and none of the vulnerabilities. See *http://www.novell.com* for more information.

SuSE OpenExchange is a fine candidate for a cross-platform, out-of-the box mail and groupware server. Instead of using standalone mail clients, users can connect via a well-organized web interface, so you don't have to worry about mail clients or client compatibility at all. It also supports all POP/IMAP clients, for those who cannot live without them. Because OpenExchange is assembled from standard free/open components, you can replicate it yourself if you have the know-how. (Chapter 20 tells how do to some of this.)

If you want to standardize on a single web browser or mail client, look no further than Mozilla. It is standards-compliant, fully featured, and runs on Windows, OS X, Linux, OS/2, Solaris, HPUX, AIX, and many more platforms.

Also, keep an eye on Novell. They appear to be serious about supporting Linux and about developing good, enterprise-quality network integration and management products.

See Also

- Chapter 20, *Building a Postfix Mail Server*
- Securing Outlook, Part One: Initial Configuration (*http://www.securityfocus.com/infocus/1648*)
- Securing Outlook, Part Two: Many Choices to Make (*http://www.securityfocus.com/infocus/1652*)
- SuSE (*http://www.suse.com/us*)
- Novell Linux (*http://www.novell.com/linux*)

21.3   Safely Testing New UBE Controls in Postfix

Problem

You want to try some new unsolicited bulk email (UBE) controls in Postfix, because you want to reject as much noxious traffic as possible at the SMTP level, to minimize the load on your server. But you're concerned about bouncing the wrong messages and losing mail you want to receive.

Solution

Postfix has two ways of turning off bounces during testing: globally, and per configuration item. To disable rejects globally, add this line to */etc/postfix/main.cf*:

```
soft_bounce = yes
```

This converts 5xx error codes to 4xx. Then you must monitor your logs to see exactly what happens. (See Recipe 20.19 for a description of SMTP response codes.)

To configure individual configuration items, use the *warn_if_reject* qualifier:

```
smtpd_recipient_restrictions =
    reject_invalid_hostname,
    reject_non_fqdn_hostname,
    warn_if_reject  reject_non_fqdn_sender,
```

Again, read your logs—Postfix will log a warning, but still deliver the message.

Always run *postfix reload* after making changes to *main.cf*.

Discussion

Postfix's log files are must-reads for the mail admin at all times, and especially during testing.

Fending off unwanted traffic at the SMTP level is efficient, but it's also error-prone, because there are so many misbehaving and misconfigured mail servers. The chances are good that you'll reject mail that you want to keep, so keep an eagle eye on the logs so you know what's going on. This is a quick, easily modifiable regexp to help search for specific messages:

```
# egrep '(reject|warning|error|fatal|panic):' /var/log/maillog
```

See Also

- RFC 2821—Simple Mail Transfer Protocol
- Postfix's *SMTPD_ACCESS_README* and *access(5)*
- *Postfix: The Definitive Guide*, by Kyle D. Dent (O'Reilly)

21.4   Basic UBE Configurations for Postfix

Problem

You want to block as much spam at the SMTP level as possible to minimize the load on your server, so you need to know some basic checks to add to */etc/postfix/main.cf*.

Solution

Add these checks, or some of these checks, to */etc/postfix/main.cf*:

```
smtpd_helo_required = yes
disable_vrfy_command = yes

smtpd_recipient_restrictions =
    reject_invalid_hostname,
    reject_non_fqdn_hostname,
    reject_non_fqdn_sender,
    reject_non_fqdn_recipient,
    reject_unknown_sender_domain,
    reject_unknown_recipient_domain,
    reject_unauth_pipelining,
    permit_mynetworks,
    reject_unauth_destination
```

Always run *postfix reload* after making changes to *main.cf*.

With the exception of the last three lines, which are safe and should always be used, you don't have to use all of these directives. See the "Discussion" section of this recipe to find out what the directives do—they are not specific to spammers, but will also reject mail from misconfigured mail servers, which are all too common.

Discussion

These directives are for Postfix version 2.0 and newer; the syntax for 1.x is different. It is important to keep Postfix upgraded to the latest stable version, to get security and performance updates.

Be sure to follow Recipe 21.3 for the correct, nondestructive testing procedures.

Here's a rundown of what the */etc/postfix/main.cf* settings mean. To learn more about the SMTP commands and transaction sequence, read RFC 2821 and Recipe 20.19.

smtpd_helo_required = yes
> Require the client to send the HELO or EHLO command before sending the MAIL FROM or ETRN command. Many spammers play dumb tricks with HELO, so this will get rid of them.

disable_vrfy_command = yes
> Do not allow remote servers to verify local addresses. Only spammers care about this.

smtpd_recipient_restrictions =
> This operates on the RCPT TO command. By default, Postfix delays all reject actions until after RCPT TO, so for the sake of simplicity and clarity, you can put most of your UBE controls here. Postfix makes these checks, in order:

- *smtpd_client_restrictions*
- *smtpd_helo_restrictions*
- *smtpd_sender_restrictions*
- *smtpd_recipient_restrictions*
- *smtpd_data_restrictions*

Not surprisingly, these checks follow the order of SMTP transactions.

reject_invalid_hostname

> Reject when the client HELO/EHLO uses improper hostname syntax. Spammers often play tricks with HELO/EHLO.

reject_non_fqdn_hostname

> Reject when the fully-qualified domain name is not used. Spammers often use "localhost" or a fake IP address in place of the FQDN.

reject_non_fqdn_sender

> Reject when the sender's domain in MAIL FROM is not in FQDN form.

reject_non_fqdn_recipient

> Reject when the address in the client RCPT TO command is not in FQDN form.

reject_unknown_sender_domain

> Reject when the sender's mail address has no DNS A or MX record; it's probably a fake.

reject_unknown_recipient_domain

> Reject when the recipient mail address has no DNS A or MX record; it's probably a fake.

reject_unauth_pipelining

> Foil spammers who would use pipelining to speed delivery of their garbage (especially dictionary attacks).

permit_mynetworks

> Permit when the client address matches any network listed in *$mynetworks*.

reject_unauth_destination

> Reject unless the recipient is in your domain. This is determined by checking that one of the following is true:
>
> - RCPT TO matches *$relay_domains* or a subdomain
> - RCPT TO matches *$mydestination*, *$inet_interfaces*, *$proxy_interfaces*, *$virtual_alias_domains*, or *$virtual_mailbox_domains*. This prevents some spoofing and all unauthorized relaying.

Running a mail server is a complex, tricky affair, and not all mail admins are as well trained as they should be. Because it is common for mail servers to be misconfigured, and because Postfix can't tell the difference between misconfigured servers and spammers, you may find that trying to implement UBE controls at this level is more trouble than it's worth.

See Also

- RFC 2821, for a complete description of SMTP commands and codes
- Recipe 20.19, "Table of SMTP Response Codes and SMTP Commands"
- Recipe 21.3, "Safely Testing New UBE Controls in Postfix"
- "Postfix Configuration—UCE Controls" (*http://www.postfix.org/uce.html*)
- Postfix's *SMTPD_ACCESS_README* and *access(5)*
- Chapter 11 of *Postfix: The Definitive Guide*

21.5 Creating Whitelists

Problem

Because you are setting up all kinds of mail filtering and virus-scanning measures, you are worried about losing wanted mail. How can you make sure wanted messages get through?

Solution

Postfix handles this with *map* files and the *smtpd_sender_restriction* directive in */etc/postfix/main.cf*.

Put your wanted addresses in a plain text file, one per line, like this:

```
myfriend@mypal.com              OK
myotherfriend@thatplace.com     OK
mychum@techies.net              OK
wanteddomain.com                OK
.wanteddomain.com               OK
mychum@                         OK
```

In this example, the text file is named */etc/postfix/whitelist*. Now convert it to a nice fast indexed binary database file:

```
# postmap /etc/postfix/whitelist
```

Then add this line to */etc/postfix/main.cf*:

```
smtpd_sender_restriction =
    check_sender_access  hash:/etc/postfix/whitelist
```

Postfix supports three different database formats. To find out which one your system is using, do the following

```
$ postconf | grep database_type
default_database_type = hash
```

Discussion

Postfix's database files can be in one of three formats: *hash, btree,* or *dbm. hash* and *btree* have *.db* extensions. *dbm* is split into two files, *.pag* and *.dir. hash* is usually the Linux default.

Setting up whitelists of important addresses is the first thing you should do when you're setting up any kind of mail filtering. This is an efficient method for ensuring that mail from people or domains that you want to receive mail from will get through.

The format of your whitelist is based on the */etc/postfix/access* file. The *check_sender_access* directive compares the whitelist to the MAIL FROM command during the SMTP transaction (this command, of course, can be spoofed, but it's still a useful check). The example in this recipe demonstrates three types of address selection:

Everything from one user at one address
    myfriend@mypal.com

Everything from a single domain
    wanteddomain.com

Everything from a domain, including subdomains (note the leading dot)
    .wanteddomain.com

Everything from a single user, from any domain
    mychum@

OK means accept the message.

See Also

- RFC 2821, for a complete description of SMTP commands and codes
- Recipe 20.19, "Table of SMTP Response Codes and SMTP Commands"
- Postfix's *SMTPD_ACCESS_README* and *access(5)*
- Chapter 11 of *Postfix: The Definitive Guide*

21.6 Using DNS Blackhole Lists

Problem

You're going nuts, because it seems like all the mail you receive from a certain service provider, or even an entire country, is nothing but spam. You have good whitelists in place, and you want to discard this garbage while wasting as few system resources as possible.

Solution

Postfix makes it easy. Simply list your selected DNSRBLs (DNS blackhole lists) in *main.cf*, under the *smtpd_recipient_restrictions* directive:

```
smtpd_recipient_restrictions =
.....
        reject_rbl_client   relays.ordb.org,
        reject_rbl_client   list.dsbl.org,
        reject_rbl_client   sbl.spamhaus.org
```

Make them the very last entries in *smtpd_recipient_restrictions*, if there are other entries. *smtpd_recipient_restrictions* entries are processed in order, so you want your whitelists and other checks to operate first, to make sure wanted mail gets through.

Discussion

Selecting a DNSRBL is a process on which you should spend a bit of time. Read their policies, and check out their user forums. Everyone has different criteria for listing and de-listing offenders. The Open Relay Database (*http://www.ordb.org*) is reliable, though spammers do not exploit open relays now as much as they used to. Spamhaus and Spamcop are fairly conservative; SPEWS (Spam Prevention Early Warning System) is the most hard-core and unforgiving. There are many others; start your research with these three, and do a bit of Googling to find more. You won't block all spam with blocklists, they're just one tool in your kit.

The good part about DNSRBLs is that discarding traffic at the SMTP level places the least load on your server. Spam floods have crashed many a server, or acted as denial-of-service attacks. Heading 'em off at the pass conserves your bandwidth and system resources. The bad part is that it's Draconian—you will lose legitimate mail.

Here's a quick lesson in how DNSRBLs work. Depending on the criteria established by the DNSRBL maintainer, individual IP addresses or entire netblocks are added to the blocklist. The idea is not to simply block traffic from spammers, because it is impossible to block only spammers at the IP level. (It's impossible to block only spammers at any level.) Spammers buy entire blocks of IP addresses, then shift their operations from one netblock to another, leading you in a frustrating game of "whack a mole." There are two goals: to block unwanted traffic, and to put pressure on the service providers to get rid of the spammers. Blocklists are effective in both respects. If it were not for blocklists, spam would be even worse than it is now, if that's conceivable.

Unfortunately, the effectiveness of DNSRBLs has been diluted by the proliferation of compromised Windows PCs. This has created a huge, distributed pool of spam-spewing proxies, so it's harder to block spammers at any level.

If you expect to receive mail from strangers—for example, you have contact information on your web site for potential customers—don't use blocklists. You're better off relying on SpamAssassin (see Recipes 21.9 and 21.10).

Spammers and service providers who are affected by DNSRBLs scream bloody murder, calling it an infringement of their free speech rights and all sorts of other nonsense. However, it's your server and your rules, and they have no right to trespass.

See Also

- Postfix's *SMTPD_ACCESS_README* and *access(5)*
- The Spamhaus Project (*http://www.spamhaus.org*)
- SPEWS (*http://spews.org*)
- spamcop (*http://www.spamcop.net*)
- Open Relay Database (*http://www.ordb.org*)

21.7 Rejecting Messages with Attachments

Problem

You want to block messages with certain attachments at the SMTP level.

Solution

Use Postfix's *mime_header_checks*, using the following regexp:

```
# this must be one unbroken line
/filename=\"?(.*)\.(bat|cmd|com|dot|exe|hta|scr|pif|vbe|vbs)\"?$/
REJECT keep your malware off my network
# this must be one unbroken line
/^\s*Content-(Disposition|Type).*name\s*=\s*"?(.+\
.(asd|hlp|ocx|reg|bat|c[ho]m|cmd|exe|vxd|pif|scr|hta|jse?|sh[mbs]|vb[esx]|ws[fh]|))"?
\s*$/
    REJECT Attachments that contain or end in "$3" are prohibited on this server.
"$2" is the name of the rejected file
```

Put this in a file and call it */etc/postfix/mime_header_checks*.

Then add it to *main.cf*:

```
mime_header_checks = regexp:/etc/postfix/mime_header_checks
```

Remember to run *postfix reload* after changing *main.cf*.

Edit the list of file types to suit your own needs. The list in the example does not include any MS Office document file formats, such as *.xls, .xlk, .doc, .wdb, .wri, .wrs, .ppt*, and so forth; you may wish to add some of these.

Discussion

You can, with one simple regexp, reject all messages with attachments:

```
/filename=\"/  REJECT all messages with attachments are rejected
```

Just keep in mind that this will also reject messages with Vcards, messages with GPG signatures that are attached rather than inline, HTML messages that attach images as separate files, and Outlook/Outlook Express messages that use MS-TNEF (MS-TNEF is useless to anyone not running Outlook/Outlook Express, because it's a proprietary rich-text format that no one else can read). Keep in mind that even if you don't care about rejecting all these things, the senders will not know that their messages were rejected, unless they read their mail logs.

Why list only Microsoft file types? That's up to you—you can list anything you want. Certainly, Windows is the hands-down winner at extending a warm, friendly welcome to malware via email.

See Also

- Postfix's *SMTPD_ACCESS_README*, and *access (5)*
- Chapter 11 of *Postfix: The Definitive Guide*
- Microsoft Knowledge Base Article, 291369, for Microsoft's own "Unsafe File List"
- Appendix C, *Microsoft File Types*

21.8 Setting Up Clam Anti-Virus on a Postfix Server

Problem

You want a good anti-virus scanner on your Postfix mail server, to automatically scan all incoming mail and to reject infected mail.

Solution

Use Clam Anti-Virus and Amavisd-new on your Postfix server. Amavisd-new is a Perl wrapper that acts as an SMTP proxy, to manage the message flow between Clam AV and Postfix. Clam AV cannot directly scan incoming emails by itself.

Note that this is a radical departure from the previous recipes that describe how to set up UBE controls and whitelists in Postfix. All of that will now be handled by Amavsid-new, not Postfix.

RPM users need *clamav* and *amavisd-new*. Debian users need *amavisd-new, clamav, clamav-base, clamav-daemon*, and *clamav-freshclam*.

Back up your configuration files before making any changes. Then set up Amavisd-new. Create */var/log/amavis.log*, and assign ownership to the "amavis" user and group, which should have been created by the package manager.

Next, edit */etc/amavis/amavisd.conf*. In Section 1, set *$mydomain* and *$myhostname* to your own values, and uncomment the following lines:

```
$forward_method = 'smtp:127.0.0.1:10025'; # where to forward checked mail
$notify_method = $forward_method; # where to submit notifications
```

Disable virus quarantines in Section IV, because virus-infested messages will be rejected at the SMTP level. There's no point in saving them, as the vast majority are autogenerated with forged return addresses:

```
$QUARANTINEDIR = undef;
$virus_quarantine_to = undef;
```

Also in Section IV, disable all auto-notifications to senders. Most return addresses are forged; it's pointless to send out "Hey, you sent me a virus!" notices. This rejects virus-infested messages without notification of any kind:

```
$final_virus_destiny = D_DISCARD; # (defaults to D_BOUNCE)
```

Next, find Section VII and uncomment the Clam AV section. Comment out all virus scanners you are not using:

```
### http://www.clamav.net/
['Clam Antivirus-clamd',
  \&ask_daemon, ["CONTSCAN {}\n", "/var/run/clamav/clamd.ctl"],
  qr/\bOK$/, qr/\bFOUND$/,
  qr/^.*?: (?!Infected Archive)(.*) FOUND$/ ],
```

Now make sure Amavisd-new is stopped, and check the configuration with the built-in debugger:

```
# /etc/init.d/amavis stop
# amavis debug
```

This spits out a configuration summary; all you need to worry about are error messages. Next, start it back up and connect with *telnet* to confirm that Amavisd-new is running:

```
# /etc/init.d/amavis start
$ telnet 127.0.0.1 10024
Trying 127.0.0.1...
Connected to 127.0.0.1.
Escape character is '^]'.
220 [127.0.0.1] ESMTP amavisd-new service ready
```

Amvisd-new is running, so quit *telnet*:

```
^]
telnet> quit
Connection closed.
```

Next, configure Postfix to use Amavisd-new, which will now function as an SMTP proxy server. Add this to the end of */etc/postfix/master.cf*:

```
smtp-amavis unix -    -    n    -    2 smtp
    -o smtp_data_done_timeout=1200
    -o disable_dns_lookups=yes
127.0.0.1:10025 inet n - n - - smtpd
    -o content_filter=
    -o receive_override_options=no_unknown_recipient_checks,no_header_body_checks
    -o local_recipient_maps=
    -o relay_recipient_maps=
    -o smtpd_restriction_classes=
    -o smtpd_client_restrictions=
    -o smtpd_helo_restrictions=
    -o smtpd_sender_restrictions=
    -o smtpd_recipient_restrictions=permit_mynetworks,reject
    -o mynetworks=127.0.0.0/8
    -o smtpd_authorized_xforward_hosts=127.0.0.0/8
    -o strict_rfc821_envelopes=yes
```

Then add this line to */etc/postfix/main.cf*:

```
content_filter = smtp-amavis:[127.0.0.1]:10024
```

And do a complete stop/start cycle for Postfix:

```
# /etc/init.d/postfix stop
# /etc/init.d/postfix start
```

The final step is to make the "amavis" user the owner of Clam AV. It won't work otherwise. First, open */etc/clamav/clamav.conf* and */etc/amavis/amavisd.conf,* and make sure that *amavisd.conf* references the "LocalSocket" file:

```
## /etc/clamav/clamav.conf
LocalSocket /var/run/clamav/clamd.ctl


## /etc/amavis/amavisd.conf
### http://www.clamav.net/
['Clam Antivirus-clamd',
  \&ask_daemon, ["CONTSCAN {}\n", "/var/run/clamav/clamd.ctl"],
  qr/\bOK$/, qr/\bFOUND$/,
  qr/^.*?: (?!Infected Archive)(.*) FOUND$/ ],
```

Now you must make the "amavis" user the owner of all directories that Clam AV uses. In this example, that is:

- *LogFile /var/log/clamav/clamav.log*
- *PidFile /var/run/clamav/clamd.pid*
- *DatabaseDirectory /var/lib/clamav/*

For example:

```
# chown -R amavis:amavis /var/log/clamav/
```

Be careful! Only change directories that belong *only* to Clam AV; any files in shared directories must be changed individually. Now open */etc/clamav/freshclam.conf*, and do the same with any directories listed there. Finally, hunt down any files belonging to Clam AV in */etc/logrotate.d/*. For example:

- */etc/logrotate.d/clamav-daemon*
- */etc/logrotate.d/clamav-freshclam*

The filenames may vary. Inside each file, find this line:

```
create 640 clamav adm
```

Change it to:

```
create 640 clamav amavis
```

Save your changes, and restart both *clamd* and *freshclam*. On Debian, use:

```
# /etc/init.d/clamav-daemon reload
# /etc/init.d/clamav-freshclam reload
```

On Red Hat and Fedora, use:

```
# /etc/init.d/clamd reload
# /etc/init.d/freshclam reload
```

And you're done. Now you can start sending test messages and watching your logs.

Discussion

You'll save yourself a lot of work if you install from packages, rather than sources. If you must install from sources, read all the documentation. You'll have to manually create all kinds of users, directories, and *init* scripts.

The *-o content_filter=* and *-o smtpd_xxx_restrictions=* directives in *master.cf* override the directives in */etc/postfix/main.cf*. You do not want duplications, because they will either waste system resources or create loops—and Clam AV, together with Spam-Assassin, will do a better, less error-prone job of filtering mail than the Postfix UBE checks described in the previous recipes.

The two Clam AV components of greatest interest are *clamd*, the scanning daemon, and *freshclam*, which automatically fetches virus definition updates. These are configured in */etc/clamav/clamav.conf* and */etc/clamav/freshclam.conf*, respectively. The defaults should be fine, there really isn't much to tweak, except that you should find a different update mirror for *freshclam.conf*, at *http://www.clamav.net/mirrors.html*. Be kind—don't use the default mirror.

See Also

- The Postfix *FILTER_README*, which describes how mail is moved between Postfix and Amavisd-new in detail
- Local Amavisd-new documentation (*/usr/share/doc/amavisd-new*, *amavisd-new(8)*, and */usr/share/doc/amavisd-new/README.postfix*)
- Local Clam AV documentation (*/usr/share/doc/clamav*)
- Clam Anti-Virus (*http://www.clamav.net*)
- Amavisd-new (*http://www.ijs.si/software/amavisd*)

21.9   Setting Up SpamAssassin on Postfix with Amavisd-new

Problem

You know that UBE checks at the SMTP level, while useful and efficient, are limited, and you want something smart enough to shoot down spam without requiring a lot of monitoring and tweaking. It needs to integrate into your existing Postfix/Amavisd-new/Clam AV setup.

Solution

SpamAssassin is just what you want. Because this is going onto a system running Amavisd-new, which acts as an SMTP proxy, you install SpamAssassin, then configure it in */etc/amavis/amavisd.conf*. You won't use */etc/SpamAssassin/local.cf*.

To get started, install SpamAssassin, then edit */etc/amavis/amavisd.conf*. In Section 1, comment out:

```
@bypass_spam_checks_acl  = qw( . );
```

Section IV tells Amavisd-new what to do with messages marked as spam. This setting delivers them to the recipients:

```
$final_spam_destiny = D_PASS; # (defaults to D_REJECT)
```

This setting drops them at the server, with no notice to the sender:

```
$final_spam_destiny = D_DISCARD; # (defaults to D_REJECT)
```

Section VII configures SpamAssassin:

```
$sa_tag_level_deflt  = -999; # add spam info headers if at, or above that level
$sa_tag2_level_deflt = 5.0; # add 'spam detected' headers at that level
$sa_kill_level_deflt = -999; # triggers spam evasive actions
```

```
# string to prepend to Subject header field when message exceeds tag2 level
$sa_spam_subject_tag = '***SPAM*** ';
```

And finally, the "amavis" user must own SpamAssassin files:

```
# chown -R amavis:amavis /usr/share/spamassassin
```

Discussion

The question of whether to drop spam at the server or pass it on to users is up to you. If you allow delivery, users can easily set up filters in their mail clients to route the spam to wherever they want to put it, filtering on the "***SPAM***" subject line.

A third option is to reject the spam, and also send a 5xx nondelivery message:

```
$final_spam_destiny = D_REJECT
```

This is the correct behavior for an MTA, but I don't see any point in wasting bandwidth on SMTP messages to fake addresses just to adhere to protocol.

The fourth, and absolute worst, option is to bounce the spam. Since the vast majority of spammers use fake return addresses, and any tiny fraction who use honest return addresses won't care, all this does is waste bandwidth and clog the Internet uselessly.

Postfix accepts mail on port 25, then forwards it to 127.0.0.1:10024 where Amavisd-new is listening. Amavisd-new puts SpamAssassin and Clam AV through their paces, then hands the mail back to the Postfix instance running on 127.0.0.1:10025. The second Postfix instance reinjects mail into the queue without any further interference.

If you miss your Postfix whitelists, which were overridden when Amavisd-new was installed (see Recipe 21.8), you can reimplement them in */etc/amavis/amavisd.conf* (Section V: Per-recipient and per-sender handling, whitelisting). However, I suggest giving SpamAssassin and Clam AV a good test drive before adding more controls. Most likely they will do the best job, with the lowest error rate.

See Also

- The SpamAssassin Wiki (*http://wiki.apache.org/spamassassin/FrontPage*), for howtos and help
- Local Amavisd-new documentation (*/usr/share/doc/amavisd-new*, *amavisd-new(8)*, and */usr/share/doc/amavisd-new/README.postfix*)

21.10 Setting Up SpamAssassin Without Amavisd-new

Problem

You're not using Amavisd-new, so how can you use SpamAssassin with Postfix?

Solution

Use Courier-Maildrop to pass traffic between Postfix and SpamAssassin. After installing Courier-Maildrop, edit or create */etc/maildroprc*, adding these lines:

```
if ( $SIZE < 26144 )
{
    exception {
        xfilter "/usr/bin/SpamAssassin"
    }
}

if (/^X-Spam-Flag: *YES/)
{
    exception {
        to "$HOME/Maildir/.junkmail/"
    }
}
else
{
    exception {
        to "$HOME/Maildir/"
    }
}
```

The *.junkmail* folder, or whatever you want to call it, must already exist. *$SIZE < 26144* specifies a minimum message size to send to SpamAssassin; you can tweak this to suit your needs.

Then add this line to */etc/postfix/main.cf*, to tell Postfix to use Maildrop for delivery to Linux system accounts:

```
mailbox_command = /usr/bin/maildrop -d ${USER}
```

Run *postfix reload*, and you're finished.

The default SpamAssassin configuration is a good starting point; run it for a while without changing anything. See the "Discussion" section of this recipe for a sample configuration and explanations of the options.

Discussion

If you're hosting virtual domains on your Postfix server, don't use the *mailbox_command* directive. Instead, add these lines to *main.cf*:

```
maildrop_destination_recipient_limit = 1
virtual_transport = maildrop
```

Then add the following lines to */etc/master.cf*:

```
maildrop  unix -    n    n    -    -    pipe
  flags=DRhu user=vhosts argv=/usr/bin/maildrop -d ${recipient}
```

There's a tricky bit here, in *user=vhosts*. Maildrop must run as the same user that owns the virtual mailboxes, which should be a unique user created just for the job. It must not be the "nobody," "postfix," or root user. (See Recipe 20.15.)

Restart Postfix, and you're done.

Configuring SpamAssassin is pretty simple. The global configuration file is */etc/spamassassin/local.cf*. Here is a sample configuration:

```
required_hits 8.0
rewrite_subject 1
use_terse_report 1
report_safe 0
skip_rbl_checks 0
use_bayes 1
auto_learn 1
```

Here's a rundown of what the above options mean:

required_hits 8.0
> The higher the number, the fewer messages SpamAssassin will mark as spam. You can adjust this up or down as you get SpamAssassin trained.

rewrite_subject 1
> Adds "*****SPAM*****" to the subject line.

use_terse_report 1
> Use a shorter report format.

report_safe 0
> Adds SpamAssassin reports to the message headers, without altering the rest of the message. Set this to 2 if you have any Windows clients. Level 2 converts the messages to an attachment or type text/plain, which adds a level of protection.

skip_rbl_checks 0
> By default, SpamAssassin checks DNSRBLs; this setting turns them on. Set this to 1 to turn them off if you are doing DNSRBL checks somewhere else.

use_bayes 1
> Use the built-in Bayes classifier. You definitely want this enabled; it is what makes SpamAssassin so smart.

auto_learn 1
> Feed high-scoring mails to the Bayes classifier.

Complete options are spelled out in *perldoc Mail::SpamAssassin::Conf*. That's a command, if you're not familiar with Perldocs:

```
$ perldoc Mail::SpamAssassin::Conf
```

Perldocs are also available online and in man page format.

See Also

- Postfix's *MAILDROP_README*
- *Mail::SpamAssassin::Conf(3)*
- *maildrop(1)*

## CHAPTER 22

Running an Apache Web Server

22.1 Introduction

This chapter covers Apache 2.0. Apache 1.3 is the most widely used HTTP server in the world; it's dependable, robust, and extremely well documented. In fact, it's so well documented you don't need me to rehash the same old stuff. Apache 2.0 is a significant upgrade from 1.3; architecturally, there are many changes and improvements, and it's a bit easier to configure than 1.3. This chapter covers compiling Apache from sources; hosting multiple domains; serving up pages in different languages with Content Negotiation; using dynamic shared objects (DSOs), which are analogous to loadable kernel modules; and various other Apache tasks.

This chapter does not cover scripting or writing web applications. Those are large topics that are well taught by fine books such as these (all published by O'Reilly):

> *Apache Cookbook*, by Ken Coar and Rich Bowen
> *Apache: The Definitive Guide*, Third Edition, by Ben Laurie and Peter Laurie
> *Java Servlet and JSP Cookbook*, by Bruce W. Perry
> *JavaServer Faces*, by Hans Bergsten
> *Perl Cookbook*, Second Edition, by Tom Christiansen and Nathan Torkington
> *PHP Cookbook*, by David Sklar and Adam Trachtenberg
> *Tomcat: The Definitive Guide*, by Jason Brittain and Ian F. Darwin
> *Upgrading to PHP 5*, by Adam Trachtenberg
> *Web Database Applications with PHP and MySQL, Second Edition*, by Hugh E. Williams and David Lane

When you're planning to build a web site, the first decision is what operating system to run it on. Apache runs on Windows, Unix, OS/2, and even BeOS. Since this is a Linux book, let's assume you'll run Apache on Linux. Your remaining decisions are a little harder:

- Use Apache 1.3, or Apache 2.x?
- Install from sources or packages?
- Self-host, or use a service provider?

Use Apache 1.3, or Apache 2.x?

This is one of those "too many good choices" scenarios. Apache 1.3 is rock solid, well supported, and over-abundantly documented—a rare luxury in computing. It's also endlessly extensible and customizable via add-on modules. "If it ain't broke, don't fix it" is still a good maxim, especially in computing.

On the other hand, Apache 2 is a significant departure from the architecture of Apache 1.3. It's faster, it's more efficient, and it scales up a lot better than 1.3. The downside is that 1.3 modules don't work with 2.0 without being recompiled or, in some cases, rewritten. The good news is that it's been around long enough to have a sizable number of useful modules available and ready to go to work. And it's only going to get better, as more developer energy is directed toward 2.0 and less toward 1.3.

Currently, the major remaining problem module is PHP. The maintainers of PHP warn you to not use PHP and Apache 2.0 on a production system, but by the time you read this, PHP 5 should be production-ready. Why should you care about PHP? If you plan to serve only static pages, you don't need it. However, if you want to generate dynamic content and build web applications, it's a good alternative to Perl, as it is a scripting language invented especially for web development. Learn all about it at *http://us3.php.net* or in *Apache: The Definitive Guide*.

Apache 2.0 differences

The most interesting changes to Apache 2.0 are its new multithreading architecture, which is configured using multiprocessing modules (MPMs), and a simplified configuration file. Most of the confusing and redundant directives have been removed from *httpd.conf*, so it's a lot easier to understand.

The default MPM is "Prefork." If you wish to try one of the others, you need to select it at compile time. These are the three MPM modes for Linux:

Prefork: The 1.3 model
> A single parent process spawns child processes to handle requests. Spare children are kept sitting around just in case. Excess children are killed off after a prescribed length of time. (This is what the docs say. Really.) This is the 1.3 way of doing things. It permits using thread-unsafe libraries, so you can still use old modules that don't support multithreading.

Worker: Hybrid multiprocess and multithreads
> This is a hybrid multiprocess multithreaded server. It uses threads to serve requests, and because threads use fewer system resources than processes, it can handle a larger workload. Yet it retains much of the stability of a process-based server by keeping available multiple processes, each with many threads. Because threads share memory space, programs must be written to be "thread-safe."

PerChild

A fixed number of processes spawn varying numbers of threads. This is the most scalable option. Most radically, it allows daemon processes serving requests to be assigned a variety of different user IDs, which presents some interesting possibilities for secure, high-performance virtual hosting. It is also the trickiest option. If you are an ace programmer, Apache invites you to participate in testing and developing this module.

Prefork is the default, but users running high-demand servers might be interested in testing the Worker MPM. See *http://httpd.apache.org/docs-2.0/mod/worker.html* to learn how to implement the Worker MPM.

There are also platform-specific MPMs. If you are running Apache on one of these, be sure to select the appropriate MPM for the operating system:

BeOS
beos

Netware
mpm_netware

OS/2
mpmt_os2

Windows
mpm_winnt

Install from Sources or Packages?

Installing from packages is quickest, if you don't mind being stuck with whatever the package maintainer decides you should have. But it is not the easiest option—all the different distributions use different filenames and package names, so the Apache documentation doesn't make sense until you figure out the differences.

Installing from sources is a bit more work: you need to manually create a startup script, create an Apache owner and group, and set all of your compile-time options, including file locations. However, you have precise control over what goes in and, equally important, what is left out. And with Apache 2.0, it's no longer necessary to recompile the binary when you wish to add or remove a module. A new feature is Dynamic Shared Objects (DSO), which are analogous to loadable kernel modules. Simply add or remove the modules as you need, without touching the *httpd* binary.

Self-Host or Use a Service Provider?

There are quite a number of hosting options to choose from. First, you can host your web server on a physically local machine, such as a machine in your home or office. This option offers convenience and control—if anything goes wrong, you're right there to deal with it. On the other hand, maintenance, security, and service are all up to you. And if your Internet connection goes down, there is no one but you to call up your upstream provider and nag them to fix it. The biggest downside is that bandwidth is expensive.

Another option is to use a commercial web-hosting service, where you pay a monthly fee for a certain amount of storage, bandwidth, and features on a shared server. This can be a nice option, if you find a quality web host. Typically, you get rafts of features: webmail, FTP, MySQL, PHP, CGI, Perl, POP/IMAP, SpamAssassin, streaming media, forum software, and more. If you plan to host more than one web site, look at CPanel reseller plans. CPanel is a web-based administration tool that is especially good for managing multiple sites. Shop carefully—the world is full of folks who get into the business without any idea of what they are getting into. Check out the Web Hosting Talk forums at *http://www.webhostingtalk.com* to learn about who's good and who's scammy. Don't go for the cheapest hosts—you can get good deals, but you generally get what you pay for. There is no such thing as "unlimited bandwidth," or any such nonsense.

The next option is to lease hardware and connectivity in a commercial data center and to install and maintain all the software yourself. You should see some cost savings for bandwidth, since you'll be on a shared line. A good facility will have backup power, redundant Internet connectivity, and good physical security. They will also monitor customers' bandwidth and server usage, and keep a tight rein on hogs and service abusers.

A shared server costs the least, but the disadvantages are obvious: you might not get a shell account, which means administration via a clunky web interface; and all it takes is one dunce customer to goof up the entire box by running system-hogging scripts or getting compromised. However, in a well-run data center, this can be a cost-effective solution. Look for a service provider offering User-Mode Linux (UML) hosting; this quite effectively isolates the different users from each other, and everyone gets shell accounts.

A leased, dedicated server is usually expensive, but if the lease cost includes on-site administration, it can be a good deal. Hardware maintenance is the responsibility of the data center, which may be a real hassle-saver for you.

If you want a dedicated server and don't want to share with other customers, usually the most cost-effective plan is to buy your own machine and rent rack space. Many data centers offer on-site administration and hardware support on an as-needed basis.

Beware of weirdo bandwidth billing methods. Be very clear up front how you will be charged for your bandwidth usage. One common dodge is to play games with aggregate usage: you think you're getting 1 gigabyte of data transfer per month, but the provider might have sneaky daily or even hourly "burst" limits, and penalties for exceeding them. Another dodge is vague service-level agreements. These should specify a guaranteed uptime and how quickly they will respond to an error ticket.

Make sure you have a written agreement that explicitly spells out every little thing, and if there is anything you don't understand, don't sign until they clarify it to your satisfaction.

Keep in mind that the more you want, the more it will cost—there are no free rides, and definitely be suspicious of too-good-to-be-true deals.

22.2   Installing Apache 2.0 from Sources

Problem

You want to install Apache 2.0 from sources, so that you can customize it exactly the way you want. That means you need to know the *configure* options, and what modules are available. You also want to take advantage of DSOs (Dynamic Shared Objects), so you can add or remove modules later without having to recompile the *httpd* binary.

Solution

Apache 2.0 installs via the usual *configure-make-make install* routine. However, it has a large of number of compile-time options, so you'll spend some time selecting the ones you want. You'll also need to know the defaults. The configuration below shows a typical installation.

First, download and unpack the Apache tarball. (The current stable version is *httpd-2.0.50*.)

Next, make a list of all the files on your system:

```
# find / | grep -v -e ^/proc/ -e ^/tmp/ -e ^/dev/ > apache2-preinstall.list
```

You'll also make a post-install list, so you can *diff* the two lists and see exactly what files Apache installed.

Change to the directory where you unpacked the tarball, and display all the configuration options:

```
# ./configure --help | less
```

The default is to put everything in */usr/local/apache2*. This configuration puts things in more standard locations, and modifies the default modules slightly:

```
#./configure --prefix=/etc/httpd \
--exec-prefix=/usr \
--bindir=/usr/bin \
--sbindir=/usr/sbin \
--mandir=/usr/share/man \
--sysconfdir=/etc/httpd/conf \
--includedir=/usr/include/httpd \
--libexecdir=/usr/lib/httpd/modules \
```

```
--datadir=/var/www/ \
--with-mpm=prefork \
--enable-mods-shared="rewrite" \
--disable-cgi
```

Now run *make* and *make install*:

```
# make
# make install
```

Then make another list after installation:

```
# find / | grep -v -e ^/proc/ -e ^/tmp/ -e ^/dev/ > apache2-postinstall.list
```

Now start up Apache:

```
# apachectl start
```

And open the default web page by entering *http://localhost* in your browser. It should look like Figure 22-1.

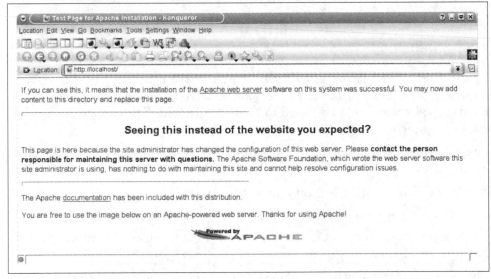

Figure 22-1. Default Apache web page

You now have a working web server.

Discussion

If you don't want to add any DSOs during configuration, but you want to enable DSO capability for adding modules later, use this line in *./configure*:

```
--enable-so
```

There is no downside, except using more disk space, to building all available modules at installation. Adding or removing them is then as simple as editing *httpd.conf*, then restarting Apache (see the next recipe). To build all modules at compile time, do this:

```
--enable-mods-shared=all
```

There are many RPMs and *.debs* for Apache, so you may install from packages if you prefer. A rather large problem you will encounter is that the various package maintainers use all kinds of different filenames and have their own ideas as to where Apache's files should go. This isn't too awful if your Linux distribution provides good documentation, like Red Hat and SuSE do. But if you don't have good localized documentation, you're going to spend a fair amount of time just trying to find things.

If you run *./configure* again with new settings, be sure to run *make clean* first, or your old configs will still be hanging around, getting in the way.

The above configuration does these things:

--prefix=/etc/httpd
--exec-prefix=/usr
> These set the default installation directories. Documentation and configuration files go into the Apache default directories in */etc/httpd*, and executables go in */usr*, if you do not specify a different path. This recipe specifies paths for all installation directories; it sets the defaults as a safety net to catch anything that might get missed.

--bindir=/usr/bin
--sbindir=/usr/sbin
--mandir=/usr/share/man
--sysconfdir=/etc/httpd/conf
--includedir=/usr/include/httpd
--libexecdir=/usr/lib/httpd/modules
--datadir=/var/www/
> Because Apache defaults to */usr/local/apache2* for everything, man pages and executables won't be in your existing Path. This example puts everything in the usual Linux places. However, stuffing everything under */usr/local/apache2* makes it simple to delete the whole works and start over, which might be useful for testing.

--with-mpm=prefork
> This chapter's "Introduction" describes the three Apache threading/process models: Prefork, Worker, and PerChild. Prefork is similar to the traditional Apache 1.3 model. This is the default, and it is the safe, conservative choice. You'll still get the benefit of the many improvements in Apache 2.0. The Worker and PerChild MPMs are for high-demand servers, and are still somewhat experimental.

--enable-mods-shared="rewrite"
> When you use *enable-mods-shared*, DSO capability is automatically included. This builds the module *rewrite* as a DSO instead of building it statically into the

httpd binary. *rewrite* lets you set up URL redirects; for example, when you overhaul a web site and want to set up automatic redirections from old URLs to new ones. DSOs need a *LoadModule* directive in *httpd.conf*; *rewrite* looks like this:

```
LoadModule rewrite_module /usr/lib/httpd/modules/mod_rewrite.so
```

--disable-cgi

This server won't be running scripts, so it doesn't need CGI.

See Also

- Chapter 4, *Installing Programs from Source Code*
- Complete configuration options (*http://httpd.apache.org/docs-2.0/programs/ configure.html*)

22.3   Adding New Modules After Installation

Problem

You configured your Apache server to support DSOs (Dynamic Shared Objects), and now you want to add some additional modules. They might be Apache modules or third-party modules.

Solution

For this example, let's say you've changed your mind and want to add *mod_cgi*, so you can run scripts. No problem, because you remembered to enable DSO capability at installation (see the previous recipe). This is a built-in Apache module, so you must run this command from the top level of your Apache build tree, installing the module to the *libexecdir* you configured at installation:

```
# ./configure --prefix=/usr/lib/httpd/modules/ --enable-cgi=shared
# make install
```

Then you must add the following directive to *httpd.conf*:

```
LoadModule rewrite_module /usr/lib/httpd/modules/mod_cgi.so
```

Restart Apache, and you're done.

Adding a third-party module can be done in two ways. If you preserved your Apache build tree, use this syntax:

```
# ./configure --add-module=module_type:/mod_foo.c --enable-foo=shared
# make install
```

Or use the *apxs* utility to build a third-party module outside of your build tree:

```
# apxs -c mod_foo.c
# apxs -i -a -n foo mod_foo.la
```

The real world, unfortunately, is not always this clear-cut. Many third-party Apache modules have specialized configuration and installation options, so be sure to follow the module instructions.

Removing a module is as simple as commenting out its entry in *httpd.conf*, then restarting Apache.

Discussion

There is a utility called ApacheToolbox that eases module management. It has nice menus for checking off what you want to install, then it does the download and installation for you. Find it at *http://www.apachetoolbox.com*.

See Also

- Recipe 22.5, "Accessing the Apache User's Manual Locally"
- *http://localhost/manual/dso.html*
- *http://localhost/manual/mod/*
- The Apache 2.0 documentation (*http://httpd.apache.org/docs-2.0*)

22.4 Setting Apache File Permissions and Ownership

Problem

You want to be sure that file permissions on your Apache installation are sane and secure.

Solution

Follow this checklist:

First, make sure that the *httpd* binary is owned only by root, is not writable, and is not readable by non-root users:

```
# chown root:root /usr/sbin/httpd
# chmod 511 /usr/sbin/httpd
```

Next, create an unprivileged user just for *httpd*:

```
# useradd -c "httpd owner" -d /dev/null -s /bin/false -u httpd
```

Open */etc/httpd/conf/httpd.conf*, and configure *httpd* to run under this user. Look for "Section 2: 'Main' server configuration":

```
User httpd
```

Next, create a unique user and group to own your web page directories; in this example *"web"*:

```
# groupadd -g 60 web
# useradd -c "Web Server" -d /var/www/ -g web -s /bin/false -u web
# chown -R web:web /var/www/http
# chmod -R 755 /var/www/http
```

Remember to add users who are authorized to edit your web pages to the *web* group. Finally, restart Apache:

```
# apachectl restart
```

That takes care of the basics.

Discussion

The *httpd* binary is owned by root, but it only runs with root permissions for long enough to launch child processes, which run under a user with minimal privileges. *httpd* does not touch the network at all; all the work is handled by its children. The default is the *nobody* user—don't use *nobody*, as it's used far too often, and is a favored cracker target. Also, you never want to share a system user; always create unique users for your various daemons and servers.

You can use the usual Linux filesystem permissions to control which users have access to your web page files and subdirectories.

Apache is a very secure application. The more typical places to find vulnerabilities are in the underlying operating system, or when you start adding server-side scripting, adding web forms, and generating dynamic content with PHP, Perl, Python, and so on.

See Also

- *http://httpd.apache.org/docs-2.0/misc/security_tips.html*
- Section 2.3 of *Apache: The Definitive Guide*

22.5   Accessing the Apache User's Manual Locally

Problem

You appreciate the fine job the Apache maintainers have done with the documentation, and how it is nicely indexed on *http://httpd.apache.org/docs-2.0/*. But it sure would be handy to have a local copy, so you can depend on it being available.

Solution

When you install from sources, the Apache manual is installed into your *--datadir*. If you configured your installation according to Recipe 22.2, this is */var/www/http/manual*. You can read the manual pages by entering this directory, but the hyperlinks won't work. A nicer way to use it is to start up Apache, then read it in a web browser—simply open your browser and go to *http://localhost/manual*.

Discussion

If you install Apache from packages, you'll need a separate documentation package. On Debian, it's *apache2-doc*. RPM users need to look for *apache2-manual* or *httpd-manual*.

Examples of current versions are *apache2-manual-2.0.50-3mdk.i586.rpm* and *httpd-manual-2.0.50-2.1.i386.html*.

See Also

- *http://httpd.apache.org/docs-2.0/*

22.6   Setting Up a Simple Public Web Server

Problem

You want to build a simple public web server for a single domain, serving up static HTML pages.

Solution

After installing Apache 2.0, confirm that the location of your web site directory in *httpd.conf* is set correctly and that the directory exists:

```
DocumentRoot    /var/www/bratgrrl
```

Copy your web pages to your DocumentRoot directory (in this case */var/www/bratgrrl*). Then start up Apache:

```
# apachectl start
```

Configure DNS to point to your web server, and you're done.

Discussion

To run a public web server, you need a registered domain name and a static IP address for your web server. It can be a public, routable IP, or a private IP behind a

NAT gateway. Yes, you can play fun DNS tricks on a dial-up account with a dynamically assigned IP using services such as *dyndns.org*, if your terms of service allow you to run servers and if you just want to run a pretend web site as a learning exercise. Don't do this for a serious web site.

Hosts on your LAN can access your web site by either IP address or hostname:

```
http://windbag
http://192.168.1.5
```

This is good way to test connectivity and to preview your web pages.

If you installed Apache from packages, look in */etc/init.d* for the startup script. It probably has one of the following names.

```
# /etc/init.d/apache2
# /etc/init.d/httpd
# /etc/init.d/httpd2
```

Typically these are simple start/stop/restart/reload/force-reload scripts that verify file locations and call *apachectl*. (Be aware that many distributions rename *apachectl* as *apache2ctl*.)

Be sure that your *init* script calls *apachectl*, and not the *httpd* binary. The Apache maintainers recommend starting and stopping Apache with *apachectl* only:

> As of Apache 2 it is recommended to use only the *apachectl* script for (re-)starting or stopping the server.

See Also

- Chapter 24, *Managing Name Resolution*
- *http://httpd.apache.org/docs-2.0/mod/core.html#documentroot*
- *http://localhost/manual/mod/core.html.en#documentroot*

22.7   Redirecting URLs to a New Directory

Problem

You've just given your web site a massive overhaul. It was a cluttered, disorganized mess, so you rebuilt it from the ground up. But now all the links are different, so all those bookmarks visitors have made to your pages, and all those links in online articles and search engines are useless. What can you do about it?

Solution

Add *Rewrite* directives to *httpd.conf*. This example redirects the old URLs to the new ones:

```
RewriteEngine on
RewriteRule ^/olddir/(.*)$ /newdir/$1
```

In plain English, this means that *http://www.bratgrrl.com/olddir/*, and every file and directory that follow *olddir/*, will be redirected to *http://www.bratgrrl.com/newdir/*.

Discussion

This is a good basic *Rewrite* rule that takes care of one of the most common redirection needs. As you can see, if you're moving entire directories at a time, it's fairly simple. If you have bales of individual files going to different locations, you have a lot of rules to write.

See Also

- The URL Rewriting Guide (*http://localhost/manual/misc/rewriteguide.html*)

22.8   Giving Users Individual Web Directories

Problem

You want your users to have their own individual web directories that site visitors can access via *www.domain.com/~user,* because this is the quickest and simplest way to give users public web pages. You don't need to mess with DNS or virtual hosts; just set up the user's directory, and you're done.

Solution

Set up your user directories in */var/www/users*, or wherever you store your site files. Give each user his own subdirectory (e.g., */var/www/users/peters*). Stick a copy of any *index.html* file in */peters*, for testing. Then make this entry in *httpd.conf*:

```
UserDir /var/www/users
```

Restart Apache, and try this in a web browser:

```
http://localhost/~peters/
```

You should see your test index page.

Discussion

Remember to set the permissions on each user's directory so that legitimate users can get in, and unauthorized users are kept out. Set ownership to the user and the user's personal group, mode 755, because web pages must be world-readable.

See Also

- *http://localhost/manual/howto/public_html.html*

22.9 Starting Apache at Boot

Problem

Okay, it's no big deal to type *apachectl start*. Still, you would like Apache to start automatically at boot. You installed Apache from sources—where is the *init* script?

Solution

apachectl is your *init* script. Just drop a copy of it into */etc/init.d*, or make a soft link, then add it to the runlevels in which you want it to start. (See Chapter 7 to learn how to configure runlevels.)

Discussion

Debian users can modify */etc/init.d/skeleton* to create a startup script for any service or daemon.

See Also

- *http://localhost/manual/invoking.html*

22.10 Hosting Multiple Domains with Apache

Problem

You want to host several different domains on a single Apache server, sharing a single IP address. You've already registered all your domain names and have DNS in place for each one.

Solution

Use Apache's *VirtualHost* directives to set up name-based virtual host support. Here is a sample *httpd.conf* entry for serving two different domains:

```
NameVirtualHost *:80

<VirtualHost *:80>
ServerName  www.tuxcomputing.com
ServerAlias  tuxcomputing.com  *.tuxcomputing.com
DocumentRoot /var/www/tuxcomputing
ServerAdmin  admin@tuxcomputing.com
</VirtualHost>

<VirtualHost *:80>
ServerName  www.bratgrrl.com
ServerAlias  bratgrrl.com  *.bratgrrl.com
DocumentRoot  /var/www/bratgrrl
ServerAdmin  admin@bratgrrl.com
</VirtualHost>
```

Each domain has its own separate root directory where the site files are stored. This allows you to easily set up subdomains, such as *webmail.bratgrrl.com* and *wacko.games.tuxcomputing.com*. However, this does not work by magic—you need to create DNS A records for each domain and subdomain.

 Once you start using virtual hosts, each of your domains must have a *VirtualHost* directive. If you start out with a single domain, you'll have to create a *VirtuaHost* entry for it. *VirtualHost* directives override the global directives in *httpd.conf*. Almost any *httpd.conf* directive can be used in your *VirtualHost* stanzas, so you can customize each virtual host as you need.

Discussion

Name-based virtual hosting is the easiest way to serve up multiple domains from a single Apache server. Configuring A records for a lot of subdomains can get a bit wearisome, but it's better than using a domain wildcard. A domain wildcard allows all traffic that includes your domain name to hit your servers. For example:

randomstuff.bratgrrl.com
really.weird.randomstuff.bratgrrl.com

Spammers will abuse a domain wildcard beyond belief, so you want to be careful to configure only your exact domain names in your DNS records. It is acceptable to use domain wildcards in your *VirtualHost* directives, because only domain names explicitly defined in DNS will ever see any traffic.

Here is what each directive does:

NameVirtualHost *:80
> This tells Apache to listen for requests for these virtual hosts on all network interfaces, on port 80. It is best to specify an IP address or, as in this case, a wildcard. Don't use domain names, because the server will then have to do DNS lookups, which will slow it down. Never leave it blank. Any IP/port setting here must also match the *Listen* directive. For example:
>
> ```
> Listen 80
> Listen 192.168.1.5:8080
> ```
>
> *NameVirtualHost* can use either of these. Remember that when you use a non-standard port, such as 8080, users must specify the port in their URLs:
>
> > *http://www.games.tuxcomputing.com:8080*

<VirtualHost *:80>
> This must match the *NameVirtualHost* values.

ServerName www.tuxcomputing.com
> This should match a DNS A record.

ServerAlias tuxcomputing.com *.tuxcomputing.com
> Here you can define other server names; users can now connect to *www.tuxcomputing.com*, or *tuxcomputing.com*, or *<any subdomain>.tuxcomputing.com*. Note that every subdomain must have a specific DNS A record pointing to it—don't use DNS wildcards! This is asking for trouble with spammers and other loathsome subhumans who infest the Internet, looking for things like this to exploit.

DocumentRoot /var/www/tuxcomputing
> This specifies the local directory where the site files are stored.

ServerAdmin admin@tuxcomputing.com
> This provides a contact address to which users can report problems.

See Also

- *http://localhost/manual/vhosts/name-based.html*
- Chapter 4 of *Apache: The Definitive Guide*

22.11 Using Individual Log Files for Virtual Hosts

Problem

Your virtual hosts are pretty busy, and sorting out a single log file is getting difficult. How can you give each virtual host its own log file?

Solution

Alter the *httpd.conf* entries for each virtual host so that they have their own log files:

```
<VirtualHost *:80>
ServerName  www.tuxcomputing.com
ServerAlias  tuxcomputing.com  *.tuxcomputing.com
DocumentRoot /var/www/tuxcomputing
ErrorLog  /var/www/tuxcomputing/logs error_log
AccessLog  /var/www/tuxcomputing/logs access_log combined
ServerAdmin  admin@tuxcomputing.com
</VirtualHost>
```

Discussion

Note that the AccessLog specifies a particular log format with the nickname "combined." There are four ready-made *LogFormat* directives in *httpd.conf*:

```
LogFormat "%h %l %u %t \"%r\" %>s %b \"%{Referer}i\" \"%{User-Agent}i\"" combined
LogFormat "%h %l %u %t \"%r\" %>s %b" common
LogFormat "%{Referer}i -> %U" referer
LogFormat "%{User-agent}i" agent
```

If these do not please you, you can easily create your own. See *http://localhost/ manual/mod/mod_log_config.html* for a complete description of the available variables. This is what the variables in the "combined" *LogFormat* mean:

%h
: Remote host

%l
: Remote logname, from *identd*

%u
: Remote user

%t
: Time

\"%r
: First line of request

\" %>s
: Status—on redirections, this is the status of the original request

%b
: Bytes sent, excluding HTTP headers

\"%{Referer}i\"
: Contents of the Referer line in the HTTP header

\"%{User-Agent}i\"
: Contents of the *User-agent* line in the HTTP header

See Also

- *http://localhost/manual/mod/mod_log_config.html*
- Recipe 4.9 in *Apache Cookbook*

22.12 Keeping LAN Web Sites Off the Internet

Problem

You have a personal web site on your LAN where you keep your calendars, documents, and amusingly edited *.jpg*s of your coworkers. Or perhaps your company has departmental web sites that are not meant to be exposed to the outside world. Even though your LAN is chock-full of firewalls and bristling with security, you want to be sure that these web sites are not accessible outside the LAN.

Solution

There are two different ways to do this, depending on the type of web site. For an Apache virtual host or a standalone Apache web site, follow this recipe. For a *UserDir*-type site (described in Recipe 22.8), see Recipe 22.13.

Restricting access to your LAN, subnet, or certain domain names is done with simple deny/allow access rules, filtering on IP address, like this:

```
<VirtualHost *:80>
ServerName  www.bratgrrl.com
ServerAlias  bratgrrl.com  *.bratgrrl.com
DocumentRoot  /var/www/bratgrrl
ServerAdmin  admin@bratgrrl.com
order deny, allow
allow from 192.168.1.
deny all
</VirtualHost>
```

or using a domain name:

```
allow from oreilly.net
```

Discussion

Many businesses rely on all manner of internal web sites that are not for public consumption. Even with elaborate firewalls in place, it only takes a minute to add some extra insurance with access rules.

UserDir pages, which use URLs like *oreilly.net/~carla*, are protected at the directory level, rather than by the domain name (see the next recipe).

See Also

- Chapter 5 of *Apache: The Definitive Guide*
- Recipe 22.13, "Password-Protecting Individual Directories"

22.13 Password-Protecting Individual Directories

Problem

You don't want to restrict access to an entire domain, just some pages in a particular directory. For example, you may have a *UserDir*-type web page (see Recipe 22.8) that you wish to protect, because it contains certain work documents that don't need to be available to any old nosy coworker. You want to restrict access to you only, or perhaps to select other persons—how do you do this?

Solution

Apache comes with some simple user authentication methods that operate on directories: Basic and Digest. These are strictly lightweight security; don't use them for pages containing very sensitive information, or for any kind of web site where money or customer data are involved. Basic and Digest are fine for use on a LAN, where all you want to do is keep coworkers out of stuff that doesn't concern them.

Basic sends passwords in cleartext, which are trivially easy to snoop, so this recipe uses Digest, which employs an MD5 hash.

Setting up user authentication on directories has two parts: creating a *<Directory>* section in *httpd.conf*, and creating a password file with *htpasswd*.

Let's say you keep your calendars, contact lists, and important documents on *http://oreilly.net/~michael*. The real directory path is */var/www/users/michael*. First, create your *<Directory>* entry in *httpd.conf*:

```
<Directory /var/www/users/michael>
 AuthType Digest
 AuthName "Michael's Protected Files"
 AuthUserFile /etc/httpd/htpasswd/passwords
 Require user michael
 </Directory>
```

Now create your password file, which is already named above:

```
$ htpasswd -c /etc/httpd/htpasswd/passwords michael
New password:
Re-type new password:
Adding password for user michael
```

The -c flag creates a new file. Now only Michael, or anyone with Michael's password, can access *http://oreilly.net/~michael*.

To allow other users in, create logins with *htpasswd*, omitting the -c flag:

```
$ htpasswd /etc/httpd/htpasswd/passwords maria
```

and change the "Require user" directive to:

```
Require valid-user
```

This will authorize any user in your password file.

Discussion

Pay special attention to the *AuthName* directive. All directories with the same *AuthName* won't need to reauthenticate you after you log in the first time. This is a time-saver but it's also a security hole, so be sure to pay attention to your *AuthNames*.

What if you do not have access to *httpd.conf*, and you don't want to continually pester your hardworking Apache admin for changes and updates? Have your kindly, benevolent Apache admin set you up to use *.htaccess*, and then you can control access yourself. *.htaccess* is for setting configurations on directories, rather than domains.

The benevolent admin needs to make this entry in *httpd.conf*. This example enables all users in */var/www/users* to use *.htaccess* files:

```
<Directory /var/www/users>
    AllowOverride AuthConfig
</Directory>
```

Make sure there is no *AllowOverride None* directive, which disables *.htaccess*. Remember to restart Apache after making changes to *httpd.conf*.

This particular configuration has the benefit of speeding up server performance by restricting *.htaccess* to the */var/www/users* directory. If *.htaccess* is enabled globally in *httpd.conf*, like this:

```
AllowOverride AuthConfig
```

Apache will search all of its directories for *.htaccess* files, which can incur a significant performance hit.

Once the admin has made the above changes, Michael can create an *.htaccess* file containing the exact same directives as in the recipe above. He will put this file in his top-level directory; in this example, */var/www/users/michael*.

Using Digest authentication comes with an additional benefit: it gives you another reason to get rid of Internet Explorer, which does not support it for URLs that use *querystring*. These are URLs with question marks, like this:

http://catsearch.atomz.com/search/catsearch/?sp-a=sp1000a5a9&sp-f=ISO-8859-1&sp-t=cat_search&sp-q=apache&search=Go

That's the URL you get when you go to *http://linux.oreilly.com* and do a search for "apache." A plain ole static URL (such as *http://linux.oreilly.com*) usually works in IE, so it's not an issue for simple, static web pages. Even so, IE is a huge security hazard, and a notorious non-supporter of web standards—if you needed another reason to ditch it, here you go.

If you wish to standardize on a single web browser, the Mozilla browser supports Digest authentication just fine, and it runs on many different platforms. It adheres to W3C standards and comes with all sorts of nice user features that IE does not, such as tabbed browsing and meaningful cookie, pop-up, and password management.

Other excellent web browsers that are standards-compliant, are much more secure than IE, and have rafts of superior user features are Firefox, Amaya, Galeon, Konqueror, Opera, and Netscape. Amaya is designed to be an easy-to-use editor as well as a browser. Firefox, Amaya, Opera, and Netscape are cross-platform, available for Linux/Unix, Mac OS X, and Windows.

If you wish to use Basic authentication, which sends passwords in cleartext and works in all browsers, see the "Authentication, Authorization and Access Control" page in the Apache manual.

For serious heavy-duty security, you need SSL. This is rather complex to learn and set up. To learn how to set up an Apache server using SSL for secure transactions, start at the Apache SSL/TLS Encryption section of the Apache manual at *http://localhost/manual/ssl/*. Then see *Web Security, Privacy & Commerce,* by Simson Garfinkel (O'Reilly).

See Also

- Authentication, Authorization and Access Control (*http://localhost/manual/howto/auth.html*)
- Apache SSL/TLS Encryption (*http://localhost/manual/ssl*)
- W3C home page (*http://www.w3.org*)
- *Web Security, Privacy & Commerce*

22.14 Using robots.txt to Control Web Crawlers

Problem

You like that search engines find your web sites, and index them, and make it easy for visitors to find you. But some of them are driving you nuts by visiting too often, so you want to exclude them. Also, there are some directories or pages on your site that you don't want indexed.

Solution

Write a *robots.txt* file containing your restrictions, and place it in your root web site directory. A *robots.txt* file looks like this:

```
# all spiders/bots/crawlers etc.
# are not allowed to index these pages
User-agent: *
Disallow: /error/
Disallow: /users/
Disallow: /cgi-bin/
Disallow: /*.doc$
Disallow: /tmp/
# exclude these ill-mannered bots that
# suck up bandwidth
User-agent: BadBot/
Disallow: /
User-agent: VeryBadBot/
Disallow: /
```

Discussion

The two conventions used in a *robots.txt* file are *User-agent* and *Disallow*. Cruise your web logs to find specific user agents. Some examples are:

```
"GET /robots.txt HTTP/1.1" "http://www.whois.sc/" "SurveyBot/2.3 (Whois Source)"
"GET /foo.htm HTTP/1.0" "Googlebot/2.1 (+http://www.googlebot.com/bot.html)"
"GET /foo HTTP/1.0"  "-" "msnbot/0.11 (+http://search.msn.com/msnbot.htm)"
```

The user agents are SurveyBot/, Googlebot/, and msnbot/. If you wished to name them specifically, your entries would look like this:

```
User-agent: SurveyBot/
Disallow: /cgi-bin/
User-agent: msnbot/
Disallow: /
```

Search engines may not behave in accordance with your *robots.txt* file. The major ones are pretty good, but there are many scammy ones that follow no rules. If there are files you don't want indexed, *robots.txt* is useful, but don't make the mistake of thinking you can protect sensitive pages this way. Sensitive information should not be on a public web site.

Keep an eye on your logs. If someone is really giving you fits, see the next recipe to learn how to exclude them completely using Apache's built-in access rules.

See Also

- *http://www.robotstxt.org*, the authoritative source for information on bots and *robots.txt*, including a database of web robots at *http://www.robotstxt.org/wc/ active/html/index.html*

22.15 Blocking Obnoxious Visitors

Problem

You're getting pummeled by annoying site-scoopers, or search-engine bots, or other troublemakers who are blowing your bandwidth allowance right out of the water. How can you block them from accessing your site?

Solution

Use Apache's access controls in *httpd.conf*. Use this method to deny specific IP addresses or hosts:

```
Order allow,deny
Allow from all
Deny from 12.34.56.78
# this one keeps linking to our graphic images
Deny from *.booger.baddomain.net
# darned foo.com searchbot has been hammering us
Deny from search.foo.com
```

Discussion

When reviewing your logs, it's often an unpleasant surprise to see how much traffic is search-engine bots, or people grabbing your entire site with *wget* or other web site suckers. A lot of search-engine bots ignore *robots.txt* and crawl web sites as often and as thoroughly as they like. Automated tools are wonderful, but too many people turn them loose on the Internet with little thought for the consequences.

To learn how to use Webalizer, a tool that will make your log analysis easier so that you can spot these troublemakers quickly, see Recipe 22.21.

- *http://localhost/manual/howto/auth.html*

22.16 Making Custom Error Pages

Problem

When a visitor to your web site hits a bad link, you want her to see a nice, customized error page with the same look as the rest of your site, instead of the default stern, cold Apache 404 page:

    Not Found
    The requested URL /foo was not found on this server.
    Apache/2.0.50 (Unix) Server at http.bratgrrl.com Port 80

In fact, you would like your error pages to mirror the look of your web site and be friendly and informative.

Solution

Create your custom page (in this example *404-custom.html*), then set the *ErrorDocument* directive in *httpd.conf* to point to this page:

    ErrorDocument 404 /error/404-custom.html

The */error* directory is the default location for error pages.

Discussion

Don't change the default error pages that come with Apache. (Look in your *DocumentRoot* directory to see the default error pages. In the examples in this chapter, that is */var/www/error*.) You can customize these pages a bit, as discussed in the next recipe, but for a major overhaul it is better to create new ones, because the default pages are internationalized. Even if you don't want to use them now, you might as well save them just in case. Apache can use these internationalized pages to automagically deliver error messages in the language of your site visitors via Content Negotiation (see Recipe 22.19).

To use the internationalized default error pages, open *httpd.conf* and find the following lines:

    # The internationalized error documents require mod_alias, mod_include
    # and mod_negotiation. To activate them, uncomment the following 30 lines.

Then do what they say.

Instead of serving up an error page, you may specify a simple message in *httpd.conf*:

```
ErrorDocument 403 "Nobody here, you go away now"
```

See Also

- *http://localhost/manual/mod/core.html.en#errordocument*

22.17 Customizing Apache's Default Error Pages

Problem

You would like to use Apache's default error pages, and you want to enable Content Negotiation (discussed in Recipe 22.19) so that error messages will be delivered in the language of your site visitors. But they are sure are stern and ugly—isn't there some way to dress them up, without breaking the page code?

Solution

The Apache maintainers think of everything. In the examples used in this chapter, the default error pages are in */var/www/error*. If you go to this directory, you'll see the */include* directory. This contains three files: *bottom.html*, *spacer.html*, and *top.html*. You may freely customize *bottom.html* and *spacer.html* with text, images, links, or whatever you desire.

Discussion

It's a nice service to your visitors to customize your error pages; it gives them useful information, and lets them know where in cyberspace they are. If you're thinking of completely redesigning the pages, however, it's best to create your own from scratch (see the previous recipe).

See Also

- *http://localhost/manual/content-negotiation.html*

22.18 Making Full-Length Directory Indexes

Problem

You have some pages that contain indexes of downloadable files. Apache displays your directories like this, chopping off the filenames:

```
Parent Directory        27-Jul-2004 09:39       -
libpam-smbpass_3.0.5..> 27-Jul-2004 09:17    298k
```

```
libsmbclient-dev_3.0..> 27-Jul-2004 09:17   581k
libsmbclient_3.0.5-1..> 27-Jul-2004 09:17   467k
```

How can you make it show the entire filename?

Solution

In *httpd.conf*, find:

```
# IndexOptions: Controls the appearance of server-generated directory
# listings.
IndexOptions FancyIndexing VersionSort
```

and add the *NameWidth* directive:

```
IndexOptions FancyIndexing VersionSort NameWidth=*
```

Using the asterisk tells it to expand to the width of the longest filename. You might want to set a limit of something like 40 characters, to keep it readable in case a very long filename slips in:

```
IndexOptions FancyIndexing VersionSort NameWidth=40
```

Discussion

You can also configure this for individual virtual hosts; *VirtualHost* directives override the global directives.

See Also

- *http://localhost/manual/mod/mod_autoindex.html*

22.19 Using Content Negotiation to Deliver Pages in Different Languages

Problem

Your web site visitors speak a number of different languages, and you would like Apache to recognize the correct language for each visitor and serve up pages in that language.

Solution

Apache has all the tools to make this work on the server side. You need to supply pages translated into whatever languages you wish to serve. Then configure a *type map* file to point to the different pages. This file must have a *.var* extension.

On the client side, your visitors need to configure their web browsers to have a language preference.

The default Apache index page is a good model to see how this works (see Figure 22-1 in Recipe 22.2). Find your *htdocs* directory. This contains all the variations of the default *index.html*:

```
/var/www/index.html.ca
/var/www/index.html.cz.iso8859-2
/var/www/index.html.de
/var/www/index.html.dk
/var/www/index.html.ee
/var/www/index.html.el
/var/www/index.html.en
/var/www/index.html.es
/var/www/index.html.et
/var/www/index.html.fr
```

Now open the */var/www/index.html.var* file:

```
URI: index.html.ca
Content-language: ca
Content-type: text/html

URI: index.html.cz.iso8859-2
Content-language: cs
Content-type: text/html;charset=ISO-8859-2

URI: index.html.de
Content-language: de
Content-type: text/html

URI: index.html.dk
Content-language: da
Content-type: text/html
```

As you can see, all you need are the filepaths, a *Content-language* directive specifying the language, and the *Content-type: text/html* directive for each file.

The last entry in the file should function as a default, in case the Content Negotiation does not work. This should point to a page that has links to your index pages in the various languages:

```
URI: fallback.html
Content-type: text/html
```

Finally, this line needs to be uncommented in *httpd.conf* (which it should be by default):

```
AddHandler type-map .var
```

Discussion

Many multilanguage sites also have links to their various language pages on their front pages (for example, see *http://httpd.apache.org/docs-2.0*).

While Content Negotiation is an official part of the HTTP/1.1 standard, it is not universally supported. Not all web browsers support it, and not all users bother to configure their browsers appropriately. Using Content Negotiation also slows down performance. It's a really nice feature, but if it bogs down your server too much, you may as well stick to plain old links to your different language editions.

Figure 22-2 shows how to configure language preferences in Mozilla.

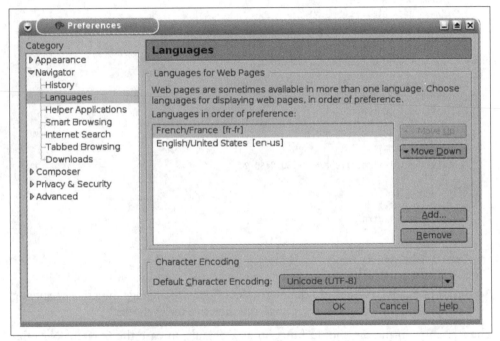

Figure 22-2. Configuring language preferences in Mozilla

When the user of this browser visits an Apache-served web site that offers multilanguage pages, she will automatically be served the French language pages. This is what Apache sees in the HTTP headers:

```
Accept-Language: fr; q=1.0, en; q=0.5
```

If there are no French-language pages, Apache will dish out the second choice, English. If the content negotiation fails, the visitor will get a 406 error:

```
Not Acceptable
An appropriate representation of the requested resource /foo/index.html could not be
found on this server.
Available variants:
```

```
index-en.html
index-fi.html
index-de.html
index-sv.html
```

Of course, you can create a custom 406 page to suit your needs (see Recipe 22.16).

See Also

- RFC 2616, "Hypertext Transfer Protocol—HTTP/1.1"
- *http://localhost/manual/content-negotiation.html*

22.20 Using Favicons

Problem

All of your favorite web sites use favicons—for example, *http://www.freebsd.org* has a cute little devil that shows up in the URL bar of visitors' browsers and in their bookmarks. You want to make favicons for your web sites, too.

Solution

This requires creating a *favicon.ico* image in the precisely correct format—it must be a real *.ico* file, not a renamed bitmap or *.jpg*—and adding some entries to *httpd.conf* and to the headers of your web pages.

Your favicon must be 16 × 16 pixels in size, in 16 colors (4-bit), and be named *favicon.ico*. You need an image editor that is able to create *.ico* files, such as the Gimp, Babygimp, or Kiconedit. Kiconedit is especially nice and easy to use, though you'll also need the base KDE installation to use it.

Once you have created your beautiful *favicon.ico*, store it in your root *datadir*, which in the examples in this chapter is */var/www/*. (See Recipe 22.2 to see a list of the configuration options used in this chapter.)

Next, add this entry to *httpd.conf*:

```
AddType image/x-icon .ico
```

Then add these lines to the headers of your web pages:

```
<link rel =icon href="/favicon.ico" type="image/x-icon">
<link rel="shortcut icon" href="/favicon.ico" type="image/x-icon">
```

The first line will display your favicon next to the URL of your web site in your visitors' web browsers, and the second line makes your favicon appear in visitors' bookmarks.

Discussion

If you aren't into creating your own favicons, a Google search for "favicon clip art" or "favicon gallery" will find you lots of ready-made icons to choose from.

If you are running virtual hosts, each one can have its own favicon. Just remember to add the *AddType image/x-icon .ico* line to each *VirtualHost* directive.

See Also

- Kiconedit (*http://w1.1358.telia.com/~u135800018/prog.html#KICONEDIT*)
- The Gimp (*http://www.gimp.org*)
- Babygimp (*http://babygimp.sourceforge.net*)

22.21 Viewing Apache Access Logs with Webalizer

Problem

Crawling through *access_log* is somewhat less than fun. It's huge, it's plain text, and your eyes glaze over. Isn't there some kind of nice graphical log viewer and analyzer, with colors and graphs?

Solution

Use Webalizer. Webalizer automatically creates HTML pages of hyperlinked color graphs, generated from your Apache *access_log*.

Download and install Webalizer in the usual manner; it comes in sources and packages. After installation, test it with this command:

```
# webalizer /etc/httpd/logs/access_log
Webalizer V2.01-10 (Linux 2.4.21) locale: C
Using logfile /etc/httpd/logs/access_log (clf)
Creating output in /var/www/webalizer
Hostname for reports is 'windbag'
Reading history file... /var/www/webalizer/ webalizer.hist
Reading previous run data... webalizer.current
Saving current run data... [08/08/2004 15:31:06]
Generating report for August 2004
Generating summary report
Saving history information...
107 records (97 ignored) in 0.15 seconds
```

Now enter */var/www/webalizer/index.html* in a web browser, and you will see a page like Figure 22-3.

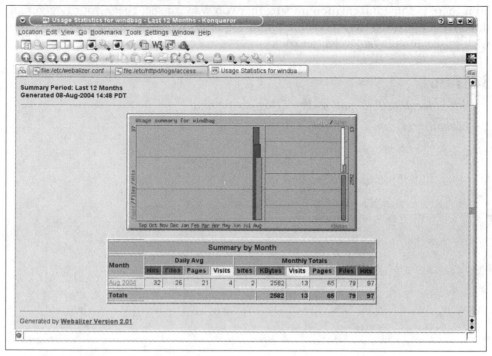

Figure 22-3. Viewing access_log with Webalizer

This shows only a few days' worth of activity, since this is from a web site created just for illustrating this chapter. As more history accumulates, you'll be able to view graphs of nearly any statistic captured in your log, by months, days, and hours.

Now you should configure */etc/webalizer.conf*. Make sure the filepaths are correct for your system:

```
LogFile          /etc/httpd/logs/access_log
OutputDir        /var/www/webalizer
HistoryName      /var/www/webalizer/webalizer.hist
```

You may specify only a single log file. Now you can generate an updated Webalizer page simply by typing:

```
# webalizer
```

Discussion

The *LogFormat* directives in *httpd.conf* control what data is passed to Webalizer:

```
LogFormat "%h %l %u %t \"%r\" %>s %b \"%{Referer}i\" \"%{User-Agent}i\"" combined
CustomLog logs/access_log combined
```

So if there is some information missing that you want to see, check your *LogFormat* directives. Webalizer also has some simple log filters for customizing what stats you wish to see; look in */etc/webalizer.conf*.

See Also

- *http://localhost/manual/mod/mod_log_config.html*
- *webalizer(1)*

## CHAPTER 23

File and Printer Sharing, and Domain Authentication with Samba

23.1 Introduction

Samba is used for providing file and print sharing and authentication services for Windows LANs, and for networking Windows with Linux/Unix. Samba functions much like a Windows NT domain controller, if you prefer a domain-style LAN, or an ordinary Windows peer network, where all the hosts can directly share files and printers with each other. It also functions nicely as a standalone file or print server, as part of a domain or workgroup.

You can mix Linux hosts into any of these scenarios: peer network, domain, or central file server. Files are easily shared between Linux and Windows. Sharing printers is a little trickier, but the combination of CUPS and Samba makes it much less painful.

As Windows NT4 Server nears the end of its support cycle (December 31, 2004), wise admins are migrating to Samba. It's a perfect drop-in replacement for an NT4 domain controller.

Samba server runs on every Unix variant, including Mac OS X. Any platform that supports the Common Internet System/Server Message Block (CIFS/SMB) protocol, such as VMS, AmigaOS, and NetWare, can be a Samba client.

Samba is now on version 3.x. If you're still using 2.x, you really need to upgrade. Outwardly, 3.x looks the same—the configuration options are the same, and it installs the same way. But under the hood, it's a beefier, much-improved engine.

Samba has another useful application that hardly anyone talks about: file sharing between Linux hosts. The Network File System (NFS) is the old standby for file sharing on Unix. It still does the job, but you ought to give Samba a try. It's more secure, and easier to set up and use. It's also quite a bit more flexible—users can update shares and log on and off without giving Samba fits.

Samba's configuration options are legion. The secret to Samba happiness is keep it simple. Start small and slowly, and add configuration options only as you really need them. Yes, the world is full of Samba geeks who love to show off their elaborate configurations. You're welcome to do the same, if that's what you enjoy. But for simply running nice, stable, reliable servers, complex configurations aren't necessary.

Samba 3 is a big improvement over Samba 2. Some of the improvements in Samba 3 are:

- Faster performance, especially on a 2.6 Linux kernel
- Native integration with Active Directory
- Support for Unicode character sets

Samba 3 cannot replace Active Directory; it does not have all the user, network, monitoring, and resource management tools that AD has. However, it can fit nicely into an Active Directory domain as a file server and be managed just like any other Active Directory member. It's a bit tricky to make it work, so I recommend practicing on a test network first. AD relies on Kerberos for authentication, so you'll need a good understanding of Kerberos (refer to Chapter 6 in the excellent and thorough *The Official Samba-3 HOWTO and Reference Guide*—available for free on *http://www.samba.org*, or you can purchase a printed book).

Unicode support is a big deal, because it means users can store documents in languages that don't use the ASCII character set and retain filenames in their own languages (Hebrew, Arabic, Russian, and so forth).

System Requirements

Samba doesn't need the latest, greatest CPU. It does like a lot of RAM and fast disk I/O. How much you should invest in the hardware depends on how many users will be hitting it, how much space you need for file storage, and how critical it is to keep it running. Since you wisely will not be running X on your Samba server, for a small LAN—say, 50 users or less—an old Pentium 300 running a three-disk IDE RAID 5 array, with 256 MB of RAM, makes a good, robust central file/print server. With RAID 5, you get striping for speed and a parity check for data integrity. Of course, you can always use a nice SCSI array, if you want to spend the money. Linux supports SCSI well, and you'll get better performance and longer life.

The quick-and-dirty way to check your Samba server's performance is with *ping*. If you get *ping* times over 100 milliseconds, your server is getting too busy.

A Brief History of Protocols

It all started way back in the olden days at IBM and Sytec, with NetBIOS (Network Basic Input Output System). This provided the interface between applications and network hardware. Then Microsoft tweaked it to allow file sharing over a LAN, producing the direct ancestor of CIFS/SMB. The original name was CIFS, then it became SMB.

Then IBM made more improvements, and came out with NetBEUI (NetBIOS Enhanced User Interface), which allowed packets to be passed over Ethernet and Token Ring. Remember, in those days no one knew that Ethernet would become queen, so all these new network protocols were being invented and tested. NetBIOS and TCP/IP turned out to be a particularly effective team: NetBIOS shoveled LAN packets, and TCP/IP made packets routable, which meant they could travel over wide-area networks.

Somewhere along the way Microsoft added user authentication and service announcements, so that connected hosts would announce their presence to each other. "Yo! I'm here!" may not be the most elegant solution, but it's practical.

Computer lore tells us that in the early 1990s, Andrew Tridgell, the primary author of Samba, needed to network his own DOS and Unix boxes. Unsatisfied with the available tools, he invented Samba. And the rest is history.

23.2 Building a Simple Anonymous Samba File Server for Windows

Problem

You have a Windows LAN, and you want reliable file sharing without spending a mint on a Windows server license, or having to upgrade hardware. Name resolution, TCP/IP, and Client for Microsoft Networks are installed and working, and all hosts can ping each other by either hostname or IP address. You don't want to hassle with passwords and permissions and all those dreadful things. You just want a nice, wide-open, anonymous file server so your users can store and retrieve files easily.

Solution

Install Samba on a Linux machine designated to be the file server. Then create file shares on the Samba server. Windows clients must all be members of the same work-group—in this chapter, the imaginatively named "workgroup." The Windows clients must have TCP/IP networking and Client for Microsoft Networks installed and working.

If you install Samba from sources, there is a single source tarball, *samba-latest.tar.gz*, which you can get from *http://www.samba.org*.

RPM users need *samba*, *samba-client*, and *samba-doc* for the server.

Debian users need *samba*, *samba-common*, *smbclient*, and *samba-doc*.

After installation, create a directory on the Samba box to store your shared files, and populate it with some files for testing:

```
# mkdir -m 777 /sharedstuff
```

Then configure Samba for anonymous access. Back up your original */etc/samba/ smb.conf*, and replace it with this:

```
[global]
    workgroup = workgroup
    netbios name = windbag
    server string = anonymous lan file server
    security = share
    browseable = yes
    hosts allow = 192.168.1.

[share1]
    path = /sharedstuff
    comment = testfiles
    read only = No
    guest ok = Yes
```

Substitute your own workgroup name and subnet. The *netbios* name can be anything you want, up to 15 characters; this is what appears in Network Neighborhood/ My Network Places. The *share* name must be no more than 12 characters.

Save and close *smb.conf*, then check for syntax errors with the following command:

$ testparm

It should not report any errors. If it does, check for typos and incorrect command syntax.

Now restart Samba, using:

 # /etc/init.d/samba restart

On Red Hat or Fedora, use:

 # /etc/init.d/smb restart

Always check your *init.d* filenames.

Now test to see if it's working. On the Samba server, run this command to list the shares on the server. Hit Return when it asks you for a password, because there is no password:

```
$ smbclient -L windbag
Password:
Domain=[WORKGROUP] OS=[Unix] Server=[Samba 3.0.5-Debian]

        Sharename      Type      Comment
        ---------      ----      -------
        share1         Disk      testfiles
        IPC$           IPC       IPC Service (anonymous lan file server)
        ADMIN$         IPC       IPC Service (anonymous lan file server)
Domain=[WORKGROUP] OS=[Unix] Server=[Samba 3.0.5-Debian]

        Server                   Comment
        ---------                -------
        WINDBAG                  anonymous lan file server
```

```
Workgroup           Master
---------           -------
WORKGROUP           WINDBAG
```

The available shares are listed under "Sharename." *IPC$* and *ADMIN$* are administrative share protocols; they are not file shares.

If your Samba server is connected to the LAN, your other hosts will also be listed under "Server."

Open Network Neighborhood/My Network Places on a Windows PC, and your Windows users will see "workgroup," "windbag," and "share1" on *windbag*. They can now easily fetch files from the share and store files on the share.

Discussion

It may take a few minutes for Samba to broadcast itself to your network. If Network Neighborhood appears empty at first visit, give it a couple of minutes.

This is an insecure setup. Using the *hosts allow* directive limits access to your local subnet, so there is a smidgen of protection from evil outside influences. But the files on the share are wide open, and anyone can read, change, or delete them. This is the type of setup a lot of users like, so here it is.

You can create a read-only share, so that users can fetch but not upload documents, with the *writeable = no* directive or the *read only = yes* directive in *smb.conf*, whichever you prefer.

Share directives override global directives, and both override the defaults, which are listed in *smb.conf(5)*.

Your share names, which are enclosed in square brackets, can be no more than 12 characters, including spaces. Anything longer than that will cause errors in Windows 95/98/ME and Linux. *[global]*, *[homes]*, and *[printers]* are reserved share names with special meanings. Otherwise, share names can be anything you want.

Here are descriptions of some of the directives in *smb.conf*:

netbios name = windbag
> This is the computer name that will appear in Network Neighborhood. Using the hostname keeps it simple, but you may use any name you like, up to 15 characters.

server string = anonymous LAN file server
> Make this anything you want; it should be descriptive enough to tell users what the server is for.

security = share

> A single password applies to the entire share, so anyone who knows the password can get in. If there is no password, anyone can access the share. In this recipe, there is no password.

browseable = yes

> This allows shares to be listed in LAN browsers such as Network Neighborhood and LinNeighborhood.

See Also

- *smb.conf(5)*, an indispensible reference
- Chapters 2 and 12 of *The Official Samba-3 HOWTO and Reference Guide* (*http:// samba.org* or the *samba-doc* package)

23.3 Building a Windows/Linux Peer Network

Problem

You think an anonymous file server is nice, but even better is a peer-to-peer network, where users are able to share files directly with each other. You want your Windows and Linux users to be able to do this without passwords or other impediments—just click and go.

Solution

Linux hosts need only to install both the server and client components of Samba, then set up shares just like the Samba server in Recipe 23.2.

Your Windows hosts need to make sure that file sharing is enabled on their systems, and then set up their shared directories. Windows NT/2000 users need to enable their "guest" accounts to give outside users access to their shares. Windows XP users must enable sharing by running the Network Setup Wizard. Each PC must belong to the same workgroup; in this chapter, that is "workgroup."

Now your Windows hosts can simply browse Network Neighborhood/My Network Places to find all shared resources on the LAN. Linux users, refer to Recipes 23.17 and 23.18 to learn how to connect to a Samba peer network.

Discussion

Don't have NetBEUI or Novell Networking (IPX/SPX) installed, unless you are sure you need them. They get in the way and slow down performance.

When a PC first boots up, it can take a few minutes for its shares to be broadcast to everyone, so have a little patience.

See Also

- Recipe 23.2, "Building a Simple Anonymous Samba File Server for Windows"
- Recipe 23.4, "Enabling File Sharing on Windows PCs"
- Recipes 23.17 ("Connecting Linux Clients to a Samba File Server or Peer Network") and 23.18 ("Connecting Linux Clients to Samba Workgroups with Command-Line Tools") for more information on file sharing with Linux hosts
- Chapter 3 of *Using Samba*

23.4   Enabling File Sharing on Windows PCs

Problem

You need to know how to set up file sharing on Windows PCs, so that other users on your LAN can access your shared files.

Solution

Follow this summary to learn how to enable file sharing on the various incarnations of Windows.

To enable file-sharing on Windows 95/98/ME, go to Control Panel → Network. Make sure that network cards are configured, TCP/IP Networking is installed, Client for Microsoft Networks is installed, and File and Printer Sharing are installed. It should look like Figure 23-1.

Click the "File and Print Sharing" button, and check the "share files" box.

Next, confirm that the hostname and workgroup are correctly configured, as in Figure 23-2. Finally, set "Share Level" access, as in Figure 23-3.

To create a shared directory, open Windows Explorer and right-click on the directory to be shared, then left-click "Sharing." "Sharing" will appear in this menu only when file and printer sharing are enabled.

For Windows NT/2000, go to Settings → Network and Dial-up Connections to verify that TCP/IP Networking, Client for Microsoft Networks, and File and Printer Sharing For Microsoft Networks are all installed and configured. Right-click on "Local Area Connection," then left-click "Properties" to see this (Figure 23-4).

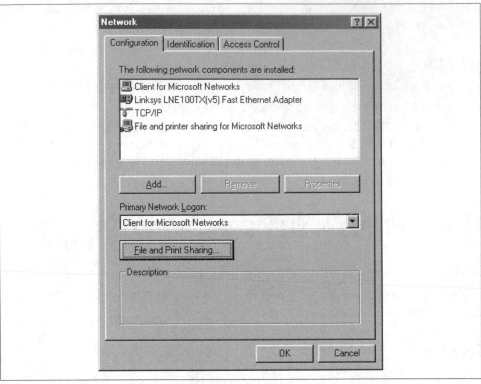

Figure 23-1. Check that network cards are configured and the appropriate items are installed (Windows 95/98/ME)

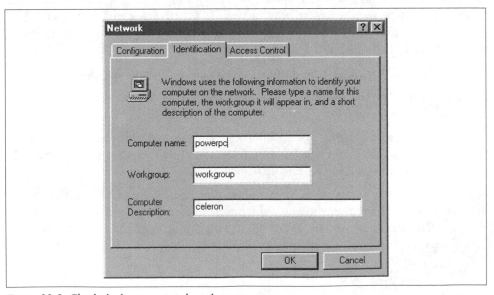

Figure 23-2. Check the hostname and workgroup

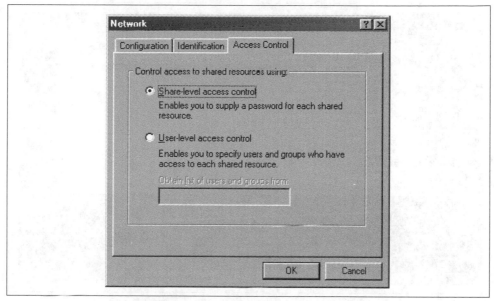

Figure 23-3. Set "Share Level" access

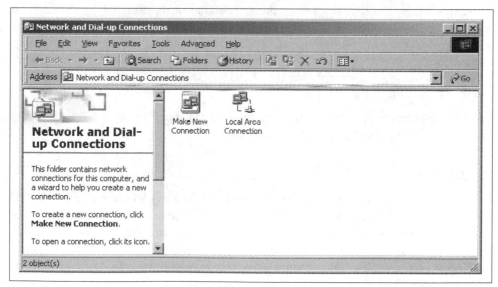

Figure 23-4. Check the Network and Dial-up Connections settings (Windows NT/2000)

Confirm the workgroup name in Advanced → Network Identification. Then go to Control Panel → Administrative Tools → Computer Management → Local User and Groups → Users. Double-click on "Guest," and make sure the account is enabled (Figure 23-5).

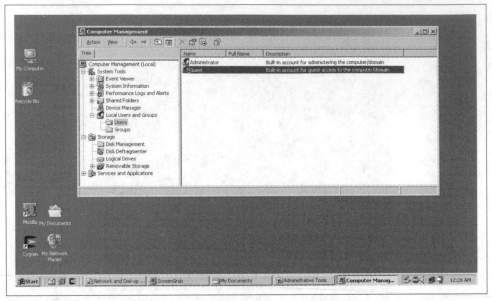

Figure 23-5. Check that the "Guest" account is enabled

Windows XP is different from the others. File sharing is disabled by default. To enable it, go to My Network Places → Set Up a Home or Small Office Network. This brings up the Network Setup Wizard. Follow the wizard to set up the workgroup name and file sharing. This enables Simple File Sharing, which is like Share-Level access in Windows 9x, except that the Windows system folders and program files cannot be shared.

To share files, the easiest way is to copy them to *Documents and Settings\All Users\ Documents*. This is the default shareable folder.

Discussion

Users who grew up in the casual, carefree days of Windows 95 often find NT/2000/ XP to be rather stifling and restrictive, and miss the ease of simply sharing an entire hard drive. This can still be done on NT/2000/XP; you just have to work at it a little harder. In Windows Explorer, right-click the drive you want to share. Select "Sharing," then click the New Share button. Give the drive you want to share a meaningful name, like "Fred C drive," and a descriptive comment. These comments appear in Network Neighborhood and in Linux LAN browsers, so make them helpful.

Of course, sharing your entire drive is completely insecure. But for folks who like to do it, there it is.

See Also

- Recipes 23.17, "Connecting Linux Clients to a Samba File Server or Peer Network," and 23.28, "Connecting Linux Clients to Samba Workgroups with Command-Line Tools," for information on LAN browsing with Linux hosts
- Chapter 3 of *Using Samba*
- Microsoft Knowledge Base Article 307874, for how to disable simplified sharing and set permissions on a shared folder in Windows XP; this also describes how to share a folder or a drive with other users
- Windows 95 Networking How-To Guide, a series of howtos that also apply to Windows 98 and ME (search for it on Google or Microsoft.com)
- Home and Small Office Networking with Windows XP, an excellent resource for users who need some Windows networking howtos (search for it on Google or Microsoft.com)

23.5   Adding Authentication to a Samba Server

Problem

You are not comfortable with the freewheeling, wide-open methods of file sharing described in the previous recipes. You want a nice central file server with all the shares tucked safely away on it, and you want to control who has access to the shares.

Solution

First of all, you must edit *smb.conf* to add user-level security and to require encrypted passwords. (Both of these are the 3.0 defaults, but it's always good to be explicit.) Then you must create Samba users with *smbpasswd*. Your Samba users must also have Linux system accounts on the server, so these must be created first. Both Windows and Linux users must have Samba accounts.

This example modifies the configuration from Recipe 23.2:

```
[global]
    workgroup = workgroup
    netbios name = windbag
    server string = lan file server
    security = user
    encrypt passwords = yes
    browseable = yes
    hosts allow = 192.168.1.

[share1]
    path = /sharedstuff
    comment = testfiles
    read only = No
```

Restart Samba after editing *smb.conf*.

Now you can create a Samba user and password:

```
# smbpasswd -a andrew
New SMB password:
Retype new SMB password:
Added user andrew.
```

 Any users that you add with *smbpasswd* must already have system accounts on the Samba server. If they are not in */etc/passwd*, you will get this error:

```
Failed to initialise SAM_ACCOUNT for user <foo>.
Failed to modify password entry for user <foo>
```

Continue adding users and defining your shares. Don't forget to write down the passwords to give to your users.

Discussion

This two-password-database clunkiness is due to the difference between Unix and Windows passwords, and the way each platform manages file permissions. They are very different critters, so the *smbpasswd* file is a bridge between the two. The next recipe shows how to use *mksmbpasswd* to convert */etc/passwd* to */etc/samba/ smbpasswd*.

Samba also supports XML, LDAP, and MySQL for password backends. See Chapter 10 in *The Official Samba-3 HOWTO and Reference Guide* on *samba.org* for details.

See Also

- *smb.conf(5)*, *smbpasswd(5)*, *smbpasswd(8)*
- Chapter 8, *Managing Users and Groups*

23.6   Batch-Converting System Users to Samba Users

Problem

You're not too thrilled at the idea of manually creating Samba accounts for all of your users, like the previous recipe describes. Isn't there a utility to make the conversion automatically?

Solution

Yes, sort of. Samba comes with the *mksmbpasswd* script, which converts all the entries in */etc/passwd* to the correct *smbpasswd* format and copies them to */etc/samba/smbpasswd*. It does not copy the passwords (it can't, because they are encrypted and stored in */etc/shadow*), so you still need to set these individually. The new accounts are disabled until you create passwords.

First, make a copy of */etc/passwd*:

```
# cp /etc/passwd /etc/passwd-old
```

Now go through */etc/passwd-old* and delete all the system user accounts, and any users you don't want to use the Samba server. They don't need to have Samba accounts; they're just potential security holes. Next, make the conversion to */etc/samba/smbpasswd*:

```
# cat /etc/passwd-old | /usr/sbin/mksmbpasswd > /etc/samba/smbpasswd
```

To activate the new Samba accounts, use *smbpasswd*:

```
# smbpasswd henna
New SMB password:
Retype new SMB password:
```

Don't forget to write the passwords down to give to your users.

Discussion

The usual advice is to run *mksmbpasswd* only once, to make the first conversion. If you edit your working copy of */etc/passwd-old* carefully, to avoid duplications, you can use *mksmbpasswd* to append additional users, with the double angle brackets:

```
# cat /etc/passwd-old | /usr/sbin/mksmbpasswd >> /etc/samba/smbpasswd
```

Remember to preserve and protect your original copy of */etc/passwd*.

See Also

- *mksmbpasswd(8), smbpasswd(5), smbpasswd(8)*
- Chapter 10 of *The Official Samba-3 HOWTO and Reference Guide*

23.7 Managing Samba Logins from Windows 95/98/ME

Problem

A charming Windows 95/98/ME gotcha is that it won't let you send a Samba user-name—it asks only for a password, so you cannot log in as a different user. How do you make it take both a Samba username and password?

Solution

Windows 95/98/ME sends Samba the Windows username. There is no way to send Samba a different username than the one used to log into Windows. The simplest workaround is to create a new account on Windows with the same name as your Samba user and log in as that Windows user.

You can even do this on the fly, if you're roaming around your workplace and logging in from random PCs. However, this creates a large security hole: Windows helpfully caches the Samba password, so you never need to trouble yourself with entering it again—nor does anyone else who uses the same machine.

Discussion

You can mitigate Windows 95/98/ME's security deficiencies a wee bit by using access control lists in *smb.conf*. See Recipe 23.9 to learn how to do this.

See Also

- Recipe 23.9, "Controlling Share Access with Access Control Lists"
- Windows 95 Networking How-To Guide, a series of howtos that also apply to Windows 98 and ME (search for it on Google or Microsoft.com)

23.8 Dealing with Windows Encrypted Password Confusion

Problem

You know that the default for Samba is to use encrypted passwords, and you also know that some Windows versions support only cleartext, not encrypted passwords. Samba must use either encrypted passwords or cleartext; it cannot use both. Which versions of Windows support what, and what is your best choice?

Solution

These versions of Windows support only cleartext, not encrypted passwords:

Windows 95 pre-OSR2
Windows NT 3.x
Windows NT4 pre-SP3

Fortunately, there is a patch available for Windows 95. See Microsoft Knowledge Base Article 165403; you want the *Vrdrupd.exe* patch.

Up-to-date NT4 users are on SP6, so that leaves only Windows NT 3.x users out in the cold. You can configure Samba to support cleartext passwords, if you really want to. To do this, you must install Registry hacks on all the non-NT3 Windows clients to enable them to use cleartext passwords. Editing the Windows Registry is always perilous, and this may break other applications that depend on encrypted passwords. The best advice is, don't do it. But if you really really want to—say, if all you have is a LAN populated by NT3 workstations—edit *smb.conf* to say *encrypt passwords = no*. Then see the */usr/share/doc/samba-doc/registry/* directory for a complete collection of prefab Windows Registry hacks for your non-NT3 hosts.

See Also

- Microsoft Knowledge Base Article 256986, a description of the Microsoft Windows Registry

23.9 Controlling Share Access with Access Control Lists

Problem

You would like to limit who can access a particular Samba share, either by username or group name.

Solution

Use the *valid users* directive in *smb.conf*, as follows:

```
[share1]
    path = /sharedstuff
    comment = testfiles
    read only = No
    valid users = andrew  foober  dana
```

Unix groups are indicated by a plus sign (+):

```
valid users = +sambausers
```

The groups must exist on the server, in *etc/group*. They are ordinary Linux groups; you don't need to create special Samba groups.

You may also exclude users or groups, using *invalid users*:

```
invalid users = root  +wheel  +bannedusers
```

Remember to restart Samba after changing *smb.conf*.

Discussion

If you have no network information services (NIS) groups, use the plus sign to tell Samba to look only for Unix groups.

Using @ (for example, *@bannedusers*) tells Samba to first search the NIS database, then Unix.

To use only NIS groups, use the ampersand: *&bannedusers*.

See Also

- *smb.conf(5)*

23.10 Creating Public Shares for Users

Problem

You have several project teams or departments that would like to share files, so you would like to create some Samba shares for them to use.

Solution

Simply create the shares, then use Samba's access controls to control access to the shares:

```
[qa-group]
    comment = qa group's shared files
    path = /var/share/qagroup
    valid users = helix  patti  devdas  @qausers
    browseable = yes
    writable = yes
```

Discussion

Users who are authorized to access the share can freely upload and download documents. You can set these shares to be non-browseable with *browseable = no*, so that only valid users can see the shares. Extremely sensitive documents should not be on a Samba share; it's better to use OpenSSH or *rsync-over-ssh* (see Chapters 16 and 17).

See Also

- *smb.conf(5)*

23.11 Accessing Users' Home Directories in Samba

Problem

You want your users to be able to access their home directories on the Samba server, so they always have access to their personal files, no matter where they log in from.

Solution

Add these lines to *smb.conf*:

```
[homes]
    comment = User's Home Directories
    valid users = %S
    browseable = No
    read only = No
```

Linux users can connect to their home directories with *smbclient*:

```
$ smbclient //windbag/homes -U <username> <password>
```

So, if user Andrew's password is *bigsecret*, he can access his home directory as follows:

```
$ smbclient //windbag/homes -U andrew bigsecret
```

Then use *smbmount* and *smbumount* to mount the share and make the files available (see Recipe 23.18).

smb4k and LinNeighborhood (discussed in Recipe 23.17) are excellent Linux graphical browsers for accessing *homes* shares.

Windows users merely need to find the server in Network Neighborhood, then log in in the usual manner.

Discussion

Because the *homes* shares are not browseable (*browseable = No*), they will not appear in any LAN browser until you log in. Then, only your home directory is displayed; you won't see the other users' directories. So users only need to know the name of the server, not the names of their shares.

valid users = %S means that all Samba users can get to their home directories. If you wish to restrict users, you may use the usual methods to grant or deny access to specific users and/or groups:

```
valid users = andrew  dana  helen  helix
valid users = +sambagroup
invalid users = daryl  larry  +badusers
```

See Also

- *smb.conf(5)*

23.12 Building a Primary Domain Controller with Samba

Problem

You want to set up a Samba primary domain controller for your LAN to provide domain authentication.

Solution

A domain controller provides a single central password database, so once users log in, they have access to domain resources without having to reauthenticate themselves as they access file or printer shares in the domain. The hardworking sysadmin can also easily lock out users, if necessary.

Because file and printer shares are configured centrally on the Samba server, access to shares is easy to manage. Unlike in a peer network, the sysadmin has complete control of network shares.

 Windows XP Home cannot join any domain—neither a Windows domain, nor a Samba domain. Windows NT 3.x does not support encrypted passwords, so you cannot join NT 3.x clients to a normal Samba domain. The best choices for domain clients are Windows 2000 and XP Pro.

There are five steps to the setup process:

1. Install Samba.
2. Configure *smb.conf*.
3. Create user and machine accounts.
4. Create directories.
5. Fire it up and connect clients for testing.

Installing Samba is the easy part. You can install from sources or packages, whatever you prefer.

Here is a complete, minimal *smb.conf* for your new domain controller. This configures authentication and users' *homes* shares. It does not define file or printer shares. The workgroup name becomes your new domain name:

```
[global]
    workgroup = holstein
    netbios name = windbag
    server string = Samba PDC
    domain master = yes
    os level = 64
    preferred master = yes
    local master = yes
    domain logons = yes
    logon script = netlogon.bat

    security = user
    encrypt passwords = yes
    log file = /var/log/samba/log
    log level = 2
    max log size = 50
    hosts allow = 192.168.1.

[netlogon]
    comment = Network Logon Service
    path = /var/samba/netlogon
    guest ok = Yes
    browseable = No

[homes]
    comment = User's Home Directories
    valid users = %S
    browseable = no
    writeable - yes
```

See the "Discussion" section of this recipe for a copy of the logon script, *netlogon.bat*.

Save and close *smb.conf*, then run *testparm* to check for syntax errors:

```
# testparm
```

Then restart Samba.

Next, create these administrative groups, using system group numbers:

```
# groupadd -g 112 sadmins
# groupadd -g 113 machines
```

Then create the *netlogon* directory:

```
# mkdir -m 0775 /var/samba/netlogon
# chown root.sadmins /var/samba/netlogon
```

Each PC in your new Samba domain must have a machine account. First, create Linux accounts on the Samba server for every PC. The dollar sign indicates that this is a "trust," or machine, account:

```
# useradd -g machines -d /dev/null -c "stinkpad" -s /bin/false stinkpad$
# passwd -l stinkpad$
```

Then add each account to the Samba password database. Leave the dollar sign off the machine name:

```
# smbpasswd -a -m stinkpad
Added user stinkpad$.
```

Finally, create a root account on Samba with *smbpasswd*. You need this every time you join a new Windows NT/2000/XP machine to the domain, because you must make your first domain login as the Samba root user. Don't forget to do this, or your Windows NT/2000/XP PCs will not be able to join the domain.

Log in to the domain as soon as possible, in order to synchronize with the server and to prevent someone else from possibly hijacking the account. *stinkpad* and Samba will exchange authentication tokens, so that Samba will always recognize *stinkpad*. That is where the "trust" happens.

The steps for joining clients running different versions of Windows to a Samba domain are all different; see the next three recipes to learn how.

Discussion

There are a couple of easy tests you can run to confirm that your Samba domain controller is working. First, always run *testparm*:

```
$ testparm
Load smb config files from /etc/samba/smb.conf
Processing section "[netlogon]"
Processing section "[homes]"
Loaded services file OK.
Server role: ROLE_DOMAIN_PDC
```

Server role: ROLE_DOMAIN_PDC is the line you want to see. Then run *smbtree* on the server:

```
$ smbtree -N
added interface ip=192.168.1.5 bcast=192.168.1.255 nmask=255.255.255.0
Got a positive name query response from 192.168.1.5 ( 192.168.1.5 )
Got a positive name query response from 192.168.1.5 ( 192.168.1.5 )
HOLSTEIN
Got a positive name query response from 192.168.1.5 ( 192.168.1.5 )
        \\WINDBAG                        Samba PDC
```

To test connectivity, run *smbtree* from another Linux host on the LAN.

This is a bare-bones configuration. You can easily add file and printer shares as you need, just like for any Samba server.

The *netlogon* share contains a script that is automatically downloaded to Windows clients. It mounts the users' *homes* shares on their local Z drives. This is the whole script:

```
REM NETLOGON.BAT
net use z: \\linux\samba /yes
```

Be sure to name it *netlogon.bat*, and store it in */var/samba/netlogon*.

These are the directives that tell Samba it is a primary domain controller (PDC):

```
domain master = yes
os level = 64
preferred master = yes
local master = yes
domain logons = yes
```

Remember, There Can Be Only One—don't put two PDCs on the same domain, or nothing will work right. You may have multiple Samba file servers, but only one PDC.

See Also

- *smb.conf(5)*
- Chapter 4 of *The Official Samba-3 HOWTO and Reference Guide*

23.13 Connecting Windows 95/98/ME to a Samba Domain

Problem

Your new Samba primary domain controller (PDC) is ready to roll—how do you connect a Windows 95/98/ME client?

Solution

This is the easiest one of all. First, be sure to log into Windows as the same user you're going to use to log into Samba. Next, confirm that networking is set up correctly (see Recipe 23.14). Then, go to Control Panel → Network → Client for Microsoft Networks → Properties. Check "Logon to NT Domain." Enter the domain name (*holstein*, in our example). Check "Logon and restore network connections." Click OK, and it will ask you for your Windows CD. Reboot to activate the changes. After rebooting, you can log into the domain.

Discussion

Remember that the workgroup name in *smb.conf* is your new domain name.

See Also

- Recipe 23.4, "Enabling File Sharing on Windows PCs," for more information on configuring Windows networking
- Chapter 3 of *Using Samba*

23.14 Connecting Windows NT/2000 Clients to a Samba Domain

Problem

Your new Samba primary domain controller (pdc) is ready to roll—how do you connect a Windows NT/2000 client?

Solution

Remember that root user you created a Samba account for in Recipe 23.12? Now you're going to use it. On Windows NT, go to Control Panel → Network → Identification → Change. Select the Domain button and enter the domain name, which is the workgroup name in *smb.conf*. Then select "Create a Computer Account in the Domain." Finally, log into the domain as the Samba root user. This is necessary to initialize the "trust" between the server and client machines.

On Windows 2000, right-click My Computer, click Properties, go to the Network Identification tab, and click the Network ID button. This will open the Network Identification Wizard, which will take you through all the necessary steps. Again, your first domain login must be as the Samba root user.

Discussion

Remember that the workgroup name in *smb.conf* is your new domain name.

After connecting successfully to a domain, you can initiate subsequent logins with Ctrl-Alt-Del. Note that you can either log into the domain, or log into the local machine without logging into a domain.

See Also

- Recipe 23.4, "Enabling File Sharing on Windows PCs," for more information on configuring Windows networking
- Chapter 3 of *Using Samba*

23.15 Connecting Windows XP Clients to a Samba Domain

Problem

Your new Samba primary domain controller (pdc) is ready to roll—how do you connect a Windows XP client?

Solution

First of all, you'd better have XP Pro, because XP Home cannot connect to any domain (neither Windows nor Samba).

For XP Professional, you need to take some extra configuration steps, and also install a Registry hack. Here's the procedure:

1. Open the Local Security Policy editor, at Administrative Tools → Local Security Policy.
2. Find "Domain member: Digitally encrypt or sign secure channel (always)." Disable it.
3. Find "Domain member: Disable machine account password changes." Disable it.
4. Find "Domain member: Require strong (Windows 2000 or later) session key." Disable it.
5. Look in */usr/share/doc/samba-doc/registry* for *WinXP_SignOrSeal.reg*. Copy it to Windows, and apply it by double-clicking. Alternatively, you can edit the Registry by hand. Look for this key, and make sure the *dword* value is *0*:
6. [HKEY_LOCAL_MACHINE\SYSTEM\CurrentControlSet\Services\Netlogon\ Parameters]
7. *"requiresignorseal"=dword:00000000*
8. Now right-click My Computer, select Properties, then click the Network ID button and run the Network Wizard.

For your first login to the domain, connect as the Samba root user (see Recipe 23.12).

Discussion

Remember that the workgroup name is your new domain name.

After connecting successfully to a domain, you can initiate subsequent logins with Ctrl-Alt-Del. Note that you can either log into the domain, or log into the local machine without logging into a domain.

See Also

- Recipe 23.4, "Enabling File Sharing on Windows PCs," for more information on configuring Windows networking
- Chapter 3 of *Using Samba, Second Edition*

23.16 Enabling Roaming Profiles

Problem

You move around a lot and log in from different machines, and you would like some way of having Samba present you with the same desktop environment. You'd like to have all of your menus, shortcuts, and pretty backgrounds in place, just as though you were chained to a single PC all day.

Solution

Configure roaming profiles in *smb.conf*. Add these lines to the *global* section:

```
logon home = \\%L\%U\.profiles
logon path = \\%L\profiles\%U
```

Next, create a *profiles* share:

```
[profiles]
    path = /var/profiles
    writeable = yes
    browseable = no
    create mask = 0600
    directory mask = 0700
```

Make sure that */var/profiles*, or whatever directory you want to use, exists and has these permissions:

```
# mkdir -m 1757 /var/profiles
```

Save your changes, and restart Samba. That's all it takes—now you will be greeted by your familiar desktop environment no matter where you log in.

Discussion

logon home is for Windows 95/98/ME. *logon path* applies to Windows NT/2000/XP. The variable-substitution macros automatically pick up your domain and username, so this is a nice generic configuration you can use anywhere.

The *create mask* and *directory mask* permissions ensure that only file owners will be able to read or write to their own profiles.

Profiles are enabled by default in Windows NT/2000/XP. To enable them in Windows 95/98/ME, go to Control Panel → Passwords → User Profiles tab. Check "Users can customize their preferences and desktop settings."

Enabling roaming profiles can cause problems. Profiles do not work consistently between the different versions of Windows, so anyone who logs in from different Windows systems will probably see some odd behavior. For example, changes made to the Start menu or desktop shortcuts might not appear the same from every machine used to log in. Also, if users accumulate a lot of files on their desktops, they'll clog the network and take up a lot of space on the Samba server.

Having roaming profiles is nice, but not essential; they're just cosmetic. If they are more trouble than they're worth, you may disable them in good conscience.

See Also

- *smb.conf(5)*

23.17 Connecting Linux Clients to a Samba File Server or Peer Network

Problem

The Linux users on your LAN need to be able to access your Samba file server, or gain access to the domains or workgroups. And they want nice, simple-to-use graphical LAN browsers for finding things.

Solution

Linux hosts need to have Samba installed (see Recipe 23.2). Then, there are several good graphical LAN browsers to choose from:

smb4k

> This gets my vote as the best Linux graphical LAN browser. It has a nice, clean appearance, and it's easy to use. The one possible downside is that it requires

KDE, so if you're not already a KDE user, you'll need to install *kdebase* and Konqueror.

LinNeighborhood
> This is a nice, easy, point-and-click GUI frontend for Samba and *smbmount*. Lin-Neighborhood is independent of any window manager or desktop environment, so it will run in any X environment.

Konqueror, the KDE file manager
> Enter *smb://* in the URL bar to show all available workgroups. Konqueror depends on LISA, the LAN information manager service, which is installed by default in most distributions. "lisa" packages are available in both *.deb*s and RPMs, if you need to add it.

Nautilus, the Gnome file manager
> Enter *smb://* in the URL bar to show all available workgroups.

Discussion

If Linux users wish to share files, set up the shares like any Samba file server, as in Recipe 23.2. The client portion of Samba can be installed separately, for users who only need share access and don't want to share files themselves.

If *smb4k* doesn't automatically find your workgroup, go to Settings → Configure *smb4k* → Network → Network Search and click "smbclient." The default is *nmblookup*, but *smbclient* often works better. See Figure 23-6 for a picture of *smb4k*.

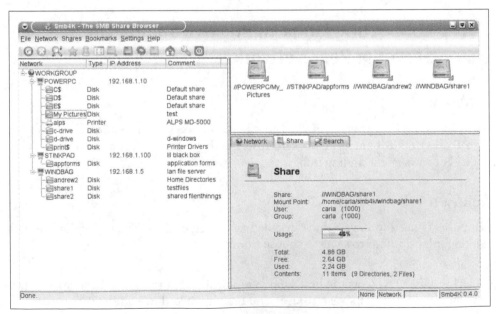

Figure 23-6. The smb4k browser

LinNeighborhood usually requires a bit of configuration. Go to Edit → Preferences. Under the Scan tab, enter the name of your master browser, which in this chapter is "windbag." On the Miscellaneous tab, you can enter a default username and select your default mount directory. This should be in your home directory, something like */home/carla/mnt*. On the Post Mount tab, configure your default file manager. Be sure to hit Save on every tab, and after you close the Preferences menu, click Edit → Save Preferences.

You can bring up a menu for logging in as different users on different shares simply by clicking on the share you want.

Figure 23-7 shows LinNeighborhood in action. Every PC in your workgroup is displayed. Double-click or right-click on the directory you want to use. This will open the Mount dialog, which lets you use the default mount directory or specify a new one.

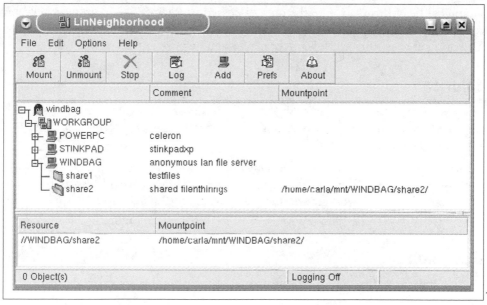

Figure 23-7. The LinNeighborhood network browser

The nice thing about Konqueror and Nautilus is that you don't need to explicitly mount the shares; you just manipulate the files as though they were stored locally. This can get tricky, though. For example, when you access a read-only share in Konqueror, it appears to let you edit or add files to the share. But it's an illusion—they do not really get changed or added. You can save any changes to your local drive, but not to the share.

See Also

- Smb4K—A SMB share browser for KDE (*http://smb4k.berlios.de*)
- LinNeighborhood (*http://www.bnro.de/~schmidjo*)
- Konqueror (*http://www.konqueror.org*)
- Nautilus (*http://www.gnome.org/projects/nautilus*)

23.18 Connecting Linux Clients to Samba Workgroups with Command-Line Tools

Problem

Graphical LAN browsers, like the ones discussed in Recipe 23.17, are nice, but you really want a command-line tool for browsing Samba shares and transferring files. You don't always run an X session, or maybe you just prefer the console.

Solution

Use *smbclient* to list available shares and to transfer the files you want. With *smbclient*, you don't need to mount shares to get or upload the files; it's just like using File Transfer Protocol (FTP).

Another option is to use *smbtree* and *smbmount/smbumount*. *smbtree* is an ASCII-text LAN browser, so you don't need to run X to use it. Use *smbtree* to display the hosts and shares in your workgroup, then use *smbmount/smbumount* to mount and unmount the shares you want to use.

Discussion

To use *smbclient*, first give it the hostname of your Samba server to show a list of shares:

```
$ smbclient -N -L windbag
...
        Sharename       Type        Comment
        ---------       ----        -------
        share1          Disk        testfiles
        share2          Disk        more testfiles
        share3          Disk        testfiles galore
...
```

Then connect to the share you want:

```
$ smbclient -N //windbag/share1
Domain=[WORKGROUP] OS=[Unix] Server=[Samba 3.0.5-Debian]
smb: \>
```

To list the files, use *ls*:

```
smb: \> ls
  .                               D        0  Sat Aug 14 16:47:24 2003
  ..                              D        0  Sat Aug 14 16:46:14 2003
  chatscripts                     D        0  Sat Aug 14 16:47:24 2003
  calendar                        D        0  Sat Aug 14 16:47:05 2003

                47838 blocks of size 65536. 17571 blocks available
```

Files are transferred by using the familiar old FTP commands:

```
smb: \> cd chatscripts
smb: \chatscripts\> ls
  .                               D        0  Sat Aug 14 16:47:24 2004
  ..                              D        0  Sat Aug 14 16:47:24 2004
  provider                        A      656  Tue Aug 19 15:14:46 2003

                47838 blocks of size 65536. 17571 blocks available
smb: \chatscripts\> get provider provider-copy
```

This command downloads the file *provider* to your local working directory and renames it *provider-copy*. To upload the *provider-copy* file when you're finished, without changing the name, use:

```
smb: \chatscripts\> put provider-copy
```

You can call up a list of commands with the question mark:

```
smb: \> ?
```

To terminate your session, use:

```
smb: \> quit
```

smbtree looks like this:

```
$ smbtree -N
WORKGROUP
    \\WINDBAG                     anonymous lan file server
          \\WINDBAG\ADMIN$          IPC Service (anonymous lan file server)
          \\WINDBAG\IPC$            IPC Service (anonymous lan file server)
          \\WINDBAG\share2          shared filenthinngs
          \\WINDBAG\share1          testfiles
    \\STINKPAD                    lil black box
          \\STINKPAD\ADMIN$         IPC Service (lil black box)
          \\STINKPAD\IPC$           IPC Service (lil black box)
    \\POWERPC                     celeron
          \\POWERPC\IPC$            Remote Inter Process Communication
          \\POWERPC\PRINTER$
```

When you see the share you want, mount the share on your system with *smbmount*, using a directory created for this purpose, and mind your slashes:

```
$ mkdir samba
$ smbmount //powerpc/c-win98 samba -o guest
```

To unmount the share when you're finished, use:

```
$ smbumount  samba
```

-o guest prevents Samba from asking for a password. Use this on anonymous shares that don't need authentication. If a login is required, enter your username:

```
$ smbmount //windbag/andrew  samba -o andrew
added interface ip=192.168.1.5 bcast=192.168.1.255 nmask=255.255.255.0
Password:
```

smbmount must be SUID for ordinary users to be able to use it. If your installation did not do this already, set the SUID bit this way:

```
# chmod +s smbmount
```

See Also

- *smbmount(8)*, *smbumount(8)*, *smbtree(1)*

23.19 Connecting Linux Clients to a Samba Domain with GUI LAN Browsers

Problem

You want to connect to a Samba domain with one of the nice graphical utilities in Recipe 23.17, but you don't know how to send Samba your login and password.

Solution

With Konqueror and Nautilus, all you need to do is browse the network. When you click on the domain icon, a login box will pop up.

In *smb4k*, right-click on the domain you wish to access, then left-click "Authentication." This opens a login box that lets you log in as any Samba user.

In LinNeighborhood, right-click on the domain you wish to enter, then left-click "scan group as user." This opens a login box that lets you log in as any Samba user.

See Also

- Smb4K—A SMB share browser for KDE (*http://smb4k.berlios.de*)
- LinNeighborhood (*http://www.bnro.de/~schmidjo*)
- Konqueror (*http://www.konqueror.org*)
- Nautilus (*http://www.gnome.org/projects/nautilus*)

23.20 Connecting Linux Clients to a Samba Domain with Command-Line Tools

Problem

You need to connect to a Samba domain—how do you send Samba your login and password with *smbtree*, *smbclient*, and *smbmount?*

Solution

You can send the username and password of any Samba user with these commands. So you can view your *homes* share with *smbtree*, for example, even though it is not browseable, and then connect with *smbclient*:

```
$ smbtree -U andrew
added interface ip=192.168.1.5 bcast=192.168.1.255 nmask=255.255.255.0
Password:
Got a positive name query response from 192.168.1.5 ( 192.168.1.5 )
Got a positive name query response from 192.168.1.5 ( 192.168.1.5 )
Got a positive name query response from 192.168.1.5 ( 192.168.1.5 )
HOLSTEIN
Got a positive name query response from 192.168.1.5 ( 192.168.1.5 )
        \\WINDBAG                    Samba PDC
                \\WINDBAG\andrew              User's Home Directories
                \\WINDBAG\ADMIN$             IPC Service (Samba PDC)
                \\WINDBAG\IPC$               IPC Service (Samba PDC)
$ smbclient //windbag/andrew  -U andrew
Password:
Domain=[HOLSTEIN] OS=[Unix] Server=[Samba 3.0.5-Debian]
smb: \>
```

Or, instead of using *smbclient*, you can mount the share with *smbmount*:

```
$ smbmount //windbag/andrew  samba -o andrew
added interface ip=192.168.1.5 bcast=192.168.1.255 nmask=255.255.255.0
Password:
```

To unmount it when you're finished, use:

```
$ smbumount  samba
```

Discussion

You may also put your password on the command line, after your username, but that exposes it to any snoopy eyeballs:

```
$ smbmount //windbag/andrew samba -o andrew bigsecret
```

See Also

- *smbmount(8)*, *smbumount(8)*, *smbtree(1)*

23.21 Keeping Samba and Linux Passwords in Sync

Problem

Your Samba users know they can use *smbpasswd* to change their own passwords, but when they do this, their Linux passwords on the Samba server do not change. You would like a method to keep them synchronized.

Solution

Add these lines to the *global* section of *smb.conf*:

```
unix password sync = yes
passwd program = /usr/bin/passwd %u
passwd chat = "*Enter OLD password*" %o\\n "*Enter NEW password*" %n\\n "*Reenter NEW
password*" %n\\n "*Password changed*"
```

This calls *passwd* to change the users' passwords in */etc/passwd* when they change their Samba passwords. *passwd chat* controls the change process and gives feedback. You can modify this to suit your own needs.

Discussion

This is a one-way trip; it does not update the Samba passwords when users change their Linux passwords.

The macro substitutions used in *passwd chat* are these:

%u Username.

%o Old password.

%n New password.

\n Newline, escaped. This breaks the *passwd chat* output into separate lines, instead of printing it all on one line.

For a complete list of Samba's substitution macros, see *smb.conf(5)*, in the "Variable Substitutions" section.

See Also

- *smb.conf(5)*

23.22 Sharing Linux Printers with Windows

Problem

You want your Windows users to have access to Linux-connected printers in your Samba workgroups or domains.

Solution

You need both CUPS and Samba to do this. Here's what you need to do:

1. Install printers on your Linux boxes in the normal manner via CUPS (see Chapter 14).
2. Install CUPS on the Samba server.
3. Configure CUPS for Samba.
4. Create a *printers* share in *smb.conf* on the Samba server.

To configure CUPS for Samba, run the following command:

```
# ln -s `which smbspool` /usr/lib/cups/backend/smb
```

This example *printers* share shares all printers on the network:

```
[printers]
    comment = All Printers
    printing = cups
    printcap name = cups
```

Restart Samba after editing *smb.conf*.

Now Windows users can run the Add Printer Wizard to install printers from the network. They will need to install Windows drivers locally, so they will need Windows CDs or driver installation disks.

Discussion

Make sure you create a *printers* share, not "printer"; *printers* is a special reserved Samba share, like *homes* and *global*.

When you install CUPS, be sure to include a complete complement of drivers by installing the Foomatic and Gimp-Print packages. Note that you can use a standalone CUPS printer server, without Samba, for both Windows and Linux clients (see Chapter 14). However, you need Samba to make Windows printers available to Linux (see Recipe 23.23).

With CUPS, sharing printers is much easier than it was under the old System V or Berkely printing systems. You don't have to mess about with raw queues or complex Samba shares. Just install them in the usual manner via CUPS, add the *printers* share to Samba, and they will magically appear in Network Neighborhood on the Windows PCs.

See Also

- Chapter 14, *Printing with CUPS*
- Recipe 23.23, "Sharing Windows Printers with Linux"

23.23 Sharing Windows Printers with Linux

Problem

You run a mixed Windows/Linux LAN, and you want your Linux users to be able to print to the Windows-connected printers.

Solution

You need both CUPS and Samba to do this. Here's what you need to do:

1. Install printers on your Windows boxes, and share them in the normal manner.
2. On Windows NT/2000/XP, make sure that the "guest" account is enabled, and make sure that "Everyone" has permission to print to the shared printers.
3. Install CUPS on the Samba server (see Chapter 14).
4. Configure CUPS for Samba.
5. Create a *printers* share in *smb.conf* on the Samba server.

To configure CUPS for Samba, run the following command:

```
# ln -s `which smbspool` /usr/lib/cups/backend/smb
```

These lines in *smb.conf* share all printers on the network:

```
[printers]
    comment = All Printers
    printing = cups
    printcap name = cups
```

Restart Samba after editing *smb.conf*.

Next, install the Windows printers on the Samba server with CUPS. Open the CUPS web interface (*http://localhost:631/admin*). Log in as root.

Click "Add Printer" and enter the printer name, which in this example is "Alps." Enter the location and description, then go to the next window, which is the Device window. Click on the drop-down menu, scroll to the bottom, and select "Windows Printer Via Samba."

In the next window, "Device URI for Alps," enter the device URI. "Alps" is connected to *powerpc* on Windows 2000, so you must enter the "guest" username and hostname:

```
smb://guest@powerpc/alps
```

In the next two windows, select the printer driver.

Print a test page from the server. Then move to a Linux client and open the CUPS web interface. If you configured CUPS correctly, the printer will appear. Print a test page from the Linux client. Now any Linux client on the LAN can use this printer.

Discussion

Printers connected to Windows 95/98/ME do not need a username, nor do they have guest accounts. All you need to do is share the printer. Recipe 23.4 goes into more detail on enabling sharing in the various Windows versions.

Note that you can use a standalone CUPS printer server, without Samba, for both Windows and Linux clients (see Chapter 14). However, you need Samba to make Windows printers available to Linux.

See Also

- Recipe 23.4, "Enabling File Sharing on Windows PCs"
- Chapter 14, *Printing with CUPS*

23.24 Running Windows Applications on Linux with CrossOver Office

Problem

You have Samba set up and running, and everything is working great. Users are sharing files, and networked printers are not being troublesome. But there's still a glitch in the file sharing: incompatible file formats. Sure, OpenOffice does a good job of converting even complex MS Office documents. But it can't convert Visual Basic scripts, or application interfaces written in Visual Basic. There's no way to use Adobe Photoshop files in Linux, or Quicktime, or Windows Media Player.

Maybe someday you want to migrate all users away from MS Office and run a 100% Linux shop. Or maybe you'll always have a mixed network, and you want your users to be able to freely share files, whatever platform they are created on. Whatever your future plans are, what can you do now to smooth over these file-format incompatibilities?

Solution

Install CrossOver Office to allow your Linux users to run Windows applications directly on Linux. Installation is easy; this recipe uses the free CrossOver Office Standard Edition demo to illustrate.

First, download your demo or purchased version. Then, to allow all users on your system to use CrossOver Office, run the installation script as the root user:

```
# sh install-crossover-standard-demo-3.0.1.sh
Verifying archive integrity...OK
Uncompressing CrossOver Office
Standard..................................................................................
...........................................................................................
.......................................................
install
```

This brings up the menu in Figure 23-8.

Figure 23-8. CrossOver Office setup menu

Click "Begin Install." When the installation is nearly over, you'll see the menu in Figure 23-9. Select "Exit now and allow individual users to install their own Windows applications." This allows all users on the system to use CrossOver Office.

Next, as an ordinary user, run the setup program to install your chosen Windows applications. On KDE and Gnome, look in the start menu for Crossover → Office Setup. This takes you through some basic system setup screens, then opens the menu shown in Figure 23-10.

So all you need are your installation disks for your chosen Windows applications, and to click on "Install." Follow the steps, and in short order your Windows programs will be installed.

When your Windows programs need a reboot, CrossOver Office even emulates this, with Crossover → Simulate Windows Reboot.

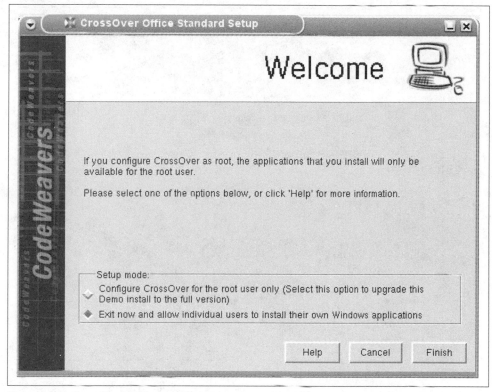

Figure 23-9. CrossOver Office installation

The installer creates start menu entries in both KDE and Gnome, including entries for your installed Windows applications. If you are using a different window manager, see the "Discussion" section of this recipe about creating them manually.

Discussion

CrossOver Office by default installs into */opt/cxoffice*, and users will have their own *~/.cxoffice* files, for customizing their CrossOver Office environments. Use these file-paths for manually creating menu entries in window managers other than KDE or Gnome:

Help
    /opt/cxoffice/doc/index.html

CrossOver Office Setup
    /opt/cxoffice/bin/cxsetup

Reset CrossOver Office
    /opt/cxoffice/bin/cxreset

Figure 23-10. CrossOver Office software installation

Simulate Windows Reboot
   /opt/cxoffice/bin/cxreboot

Uninstall CrossOver Office
   /opt/cxoffice/bin/cxuninstall

CrossOver Office is a great tool for the mixed LAN. You can run Windows applications on Linux, and gain the benefit of a more stable, more secure operating system. Users won't have to be retrained on native Linux applications. And you can save the cost of a Windows license.

Data migration is the biggest bottleneck when you're considering migrating from Windows to Linux. Microsoft Office users who have accumulated archives of custom Visual Basic scripts and macros are probably not going to look forward to learning new scripting languages, and doing everything over. If you are planning to migrate users away from Windows to Linux, CrossOver Office lets you take your time, and make the move with minimal disruption.

CrossOver Office is not free of cost. The Standard edition is $39.95, and includes six months of technical support. The Professional edition costs $74.95, and comes with one year of technical support. If you want multiple users on a single PC to use Cross-Over Office, the Professional edition is the better choice. It allows all applications to be shared. The Standard edition requires a separation installation for each user's chosen Windows applications.

Currently, over 1,000 applications will install and run on CrossOver Office. Visit the compatibility page at *http://www.codeweavers.com/site/compatibility/* to look up specific applications. Be warned that not all applications will run well, or have their entire feature set supported. Even the officially supported applications may have a hiccup or two.

CrossOver Office officially supports:

> Adobe Acrobat Reader 5.0
> Adobe Photoshop 6
> Adobe Photoshop 7
> Authorware Web Player
> Cortona VRML Client
> DCOM 95
> Dreamweaver MX
> Flash MX
> Flash Player
> Internet Explorer 6.0
> Lotus Notes 5
> Lotus Notes 6.5.1
> MDL Chime
> MODPLug
> Microsoft Excel Viewer 97/2000
> Microsoft Office 2000
> Microsoft Office 97
> Microsoft Office XP
> Microsoft PowerPoint Viewer 97/2000
> Quick View Plus
> QuickBooks 2000
> Quicktime 6.3
> Quicken
> RealPlayer 8 Basic
> Shockwave Player 8.5
> Superscape Viscape Universal
> Trillian
> VP3 For Quicktime 5
> Windows Media Player 6.4

eFax Messenger
ebrary Reader
iPIX Netscape Plugin Viewer

CrossOver Office is an adaptation of WINE (Wine Is Not a Emulator). WINE has a program loader, which loads and executes your Windows binaries, and a set of libraries that implements Windows API calls using their Unix or X11 equivalents. This enables running Windows programs on Linux without having to build a native Linux port. Because so many Windows applications are built with Windows tools, like Visual Studio, using the Microsoft Foundation Class Library, porting usually means an extensive, if not complete, rewrite. Which most vendors and program authors are understandably loathe to do. WINE enables running Windows binaries directly on Linux, with no rewriting or porting.

But, while development on WINE is rapid, it's still a long way from being finished, or user-friendly. Much tweaking is needed to get individual programs running correctly. CrossOver Office tunes WINE to run selected applications reliably, and provides an easy-to-use interface for installing and removing Windows programs.

See Also

- WINE home page (*http://www.winehq.com/*)
- CrossOver Office, by Codeweavers (*http://www.codeweavers.com/site/products/*)

## CHAPTER 24

Managing Name Resolution

24.1 Introduction

Name resolution includes the Domain Name System (DNS) and *hosts* files. The Dynamic Host Configuration Protocol (DHCP) goes hand-in-hand with name resolution. Name resolution resolves names to IP addresses, and DHCP takes over the tedious chore of assigning IP addresses to individual hosts. Servers need static IP addresses. Workstations do just fine with dynamically assigned addresses—just plug 'em in and let DHCP do the work.

DNS powers the Internet. All it does is *name resolution*, or translation of names to numbers. As simple as the concept is, a huge infrastructure has evolved to implement it. We could get along fine without DNS—after all, we've been using complex postal mail addresses and phone numbers all of our lives. But there are many advantages to using name resolution. Several names can be mapped to a single IP address. Names are easier to remember. And we can indulge in giving our servers fanciful hostnames, like the names of Tolkien characters, or astronomical terms, or mythological characters. (Okay, so that last one isn't vitally important—but it is fun.)

Implementing DNS

One difficulty with learning to run a DNS server is that the vast majority of the documentation is BIND-centric. Berkeley Internet Name Domain (BIND) is the oldest and most widely used DNS server. It seems as though BIND is considered to be the DNS protocol, rather than just an implementation of it.

This chapter contains recipes for two different DNS servers: BIND and *djbdns*. I believe that *djbdns* is the superior choice. It's modular, small, very fast, and very secure. It's also simple to configure and very dependable, because it runs from supervisory daemons that automatically restart it if it should die unexpectedly. Replicating a *djbdns* server securely and efficiently is easy—you use standard Linux utilities such as *rsync-over-ssh*, which means you can easily set up authenticated datafile transfers using SSH keys.

BIND has been around forever, and it is widely deployed. However, it's one big monolithic program, so you cannot customize the installation to suit your needs. About all you can do is configure it differently for different uses, which is not completely effective in shutting down the parts you don't need. This presents security risks, and BIND has a long history of security problems. Furthermore, it uses odd proprietary methods for replicating zone files to backup servers (secondaries), instead of nice, reliable, standard Unix utilities. Even back in the days before *rsync*, there was no shortage of dependable methods for transferring files, so the reason for the evolution of these BIND-specific file transfer protocols is a mystery.

Despite its drawbacks, BIND has the advantage in sheer volume of books and documentation, with Cricket Liu's books being the standards: the *DNS & BIND Cookbook* and *DNS and BIND*, which is now on its fourth edition (both published by O'Reilly), are must-haves for the BIND admin.

A DNS Glossary

DNS refers to three things: the DNS protocol; name resolution; and the entire system that implements it, which consists of domain name registrars, root servers, authoritative servers, IANA and the regional Internet registries, ICANN, and all the caching DNS servers that spread the load and keep things moving. Here are some terms to familiarize yourself with:

IANA
> Internet Assigned Numbers Authority. It all starts here—this is the group that coordinates the allocation of IP addresses worldwide. Both IPv4 and IPv6 addresses are part of the brew now. IANA dispenses blocks of IP adresses to the Regional Internet registries:
>
>> APNIC (Asia Pacific Network Information Centre): Asia/Pacific Region
>> ARIN (American Registry for Internet Numbers): North America and Sub-Saharan Africa
>> LACNIC (Latin American and Caribbean IP Address Registry):Latin America and some Caribbean Islands
>> RIPE NCC (Réseaux IP Européens): Europe, the Middle East, Central Asia, and African countries located north of the equator

ICANN
> Internet Corporation for Assigned Names and Numbers. Among many other duties, ICANN oversees domain name allocation and registration.

Root servers
> There are 13 root DNS servers. Run the *dig* command with no options to generate a list. All but three are hosted in the United States. However, the C, F, I, J,

and K servers are geographically dispersed clusters using *anycast*, so the actual number of root servers is much larger, and they are distributed all over the planet. *anycast* is a network addressing and routing scheme that routes data to the nearest or best destination.

Authoritative server, or content server
This is the DNS server controlled by you, the ace hostmaster for your domain, that contains all your name-to-IP address mappings. The root name servers do not store actual DNS records. All they do is point to authoritative name servers, or name servers that know the route to the authoritative name servers.

Caching server, or caching DNS resolver
Caching servers make this huge amount of traffic and complexity manageable. If every DNS request for a domain had to hit the authoritative server, the whole works would soon grind to a halt. This does not happen because the Internet is infested with DNS caching servers. Caching servers are very hardworking—they query external servers to satisfy DNS requests, and they also store the results of DNS lookups in memory, so that they can directly answer subsequent requests.

24.2 Enabling Local Name Resolution with hosts Files

Problem

You want to set up name resolution on your LAN. Because you are not running any public services, you don't want to mess with registered domain names; you want to use whatever domain name you feel like inventing. You know that your invented domain name will not be valid outside your LAN, and that's okay, because you are not running any public services. Your network is stable and rarely changes, so it isn't worth setting up a DNS server; you just want to use nice, friendly hostnames on your LAN.

Or you are running public services, such as a mail or web server, and you are using a third-party DNS manager for your public services. Your LAN is small, so you don't want to hassle with setting up a DNS server just for your LAN.

Or you have a registered domain name, and you are already running a DNS server, but you want to enter important machines in *hosts* files as a backup in case the DNS server goes down.

Solution

Use *hosts* files. *hosts* files are the same on both Linux and Windows.

On most Linuxes, you need to edit two files: */etc/hostname* and */etc/hosts*. In */etc/ hostname*, enter only the hostname of the machine:

```
windbag
```

On Red Hat and Fedora, you must edit */etc/sysconfig/network* instead of */etc/ hostname*:

```
HOSTNAME=windbag
```

/etc/hosts sets the domain name. You must always have a *localhost* entry, then add the IP address and the fully qualified domain name on a separate line:

```
127.0.0.1 localhost.localdomain localhost
192.168.1.5 windbag.test.net windbag
```

Check your configurations:

```
$ hostname
windbag
$ hostname --fqdn
windbag.test.net
$ dnsdomainname
test.net
```

You must reboot for hostname changes to take effect.

On Windows, set the hostname by right-clicking My Computer, left-clicking Properties, and entering the name. The location of the *hosts* file varies; the quickest way to find it is Start → Search.

Every machine on the LAN must have an identical copy of the *hosts* file. When this is done, everyone can ping each other by hostname, and applications like Samba that rely on hostnames can be used.

Discussion

hosts files are the original method for mapping hostnames to IP addresses. DNS was invented because managing more than a few hosts in *hosts* files quickly becomes difficult.

Using *hosts* files still has a number of advantages:

- You're not dependent on a single server.
- You can invent any old domain name you like, as long as you only need it for your local network, so you don't have to hassle with having a registered domain name.
- You can change domain names whenever you feel like it, which is handy for testing virtual Postfix and Apache domains.

- If you use /etc/hosts only for servers, which need static IP addresses, you can put the rest of your LAN on a DHCP server and not even bother with *hosts* entries for them (see Recipe 24.3).

Here is a sample *hosts* file. They look just the same on both Linux and Windows:

```
127.0.0.1        localhost.localdomain localhost
192.168.1.5      windbag.test.net  windbag
192.168.1.6      powerpc.test.net  powerpc
192.168.1.10     stinkpad.test.net  stinkpad
```

See Also

- *hosts(5)*

24.3 Setting Up a DHCP Server

Problem

You don't want to hassle with configuring name resolution on workstations. They don't need static IP addresses, so you want to set up a DHCP server to take care of them automatically.

Solution

Install and configure *dhcp*. You can get the source tarball from *http://www.isc.org*. RPMs and Debian packages are also available; just look for packages named "dhcp." Configure client PCs to point to your *dhcp* server, and you're done.

Discussion

A *dhcp* server can feed all network configuration data to the clients. The configuration file is */etc/dhcpd.conf*. Here is a sample configuration:

```
# /etc/dhcpd.conf
default-lease-time 259200;
max-lease-time 518400;

subnet 192.168.1.0 netmask 255.255.255.0 {
    option subnet-mask 255.255.255.0;
    option broadcast-address 192.168.1.255;
    option routers 192.168.1.1;
    option domain-name "test.net";
    range 192.168.1.50 192.168.1.100;
    option domain-name-servers 152.163.199.56, 198.83.210.28;
}
```

This is pretty straightforward. The lease times are in seconds, so the minimum and maximum in this example are three days and six days. "Option routers" points to your Internet gateway, or the gateway to the subnet. A pool of 50 addresses is made available in the "range." The name servers are either your own private caching server or servers, or the name servers at your ISP.

This example uses private, nonroutable IPv4 (Internet Protocol Version 4) addresses. Here are the private IPv4 address classes, in both dotted-quad and Classless Inter-Domain Routing (CIDR) notation:

```
10.0.0.0      - 10.255.255.255  (10/8)
172.16.0.0    - 172.31.255.255  (172.16/12)
192.168.0.0   - 192.168.255.255 (192.168/16)
```

These are for use on private networks, so you'll select your subnet ranges from these. See Section 2.2 of *TCP/IP Network Administration*, Third Edition, by Craig Hunt (O'Reilly) to learn more about IP addressing.

You've probably heard about IPv6, which is the next generation of IP addressing. IPv6 is not covered in this book; IPv4 is going to be with us for quite a while yet. To learn more about IPv6, start at *http://www.iana.org/ipaddress/ip-addresses.htm*.

See the next recipe to learn how to configure both Linux and Windows *dhcp* clients.

See Also

- *dhcp-options(5), dhcpd.conf(5), dhcpd(8)*
- RFC 1918 Address Allocation for Private Internets
- *TCP/IP Network Administration*, Third Edition

24.4 Configuring dhcp Clients

Problem

You need to know how to connect both your Linux and Windows client PCs to your nice new *dhcp* server, so that they will pick up their network assignments without your lifting a finger.

Solution

In Windows, open Control Panel → Networking, then open the Properties box for TCP/IP. Check "Obtain an IP address automatically."

It's just as easy in Linux; the only hard part is that every distribution puts the configuration file in a different place. In Red Hat and Fedora, edit */etc/sysconfig/network-scripts/ifcfg-eth0* as follows:

```
TYPE=Ethernet
DEVICE=eth0
BOOTPROTO=dhcp
ONBOOT=yes
DHCP_HOSTNAME=stinkpad
```

On Debian, edit */etc/network/interfaces* as follows:

```
auto lo
iface lo inet loopback
auto eth0
iface eth0 inet dhcp
```

Discussion

You may wish to use a graphical configuration tool. On Red Hat and Fedora, use *system-config-network*. KDE and Gnome have their own GUI configuration tools (as does practically every Linux distribution), so you won't be short of choices. Another option is *netGo*, a system-independent network configuration utility that lets you create profiles for easily connecting to different networks

See Also

- Documentation for your Linux distribution or your favorite window manager/ graphical enviroment

24.5   Adding Static Hosts to dhcp

Problem

You have some servers or other machines to which you want to assign static IP addresses. You can use */etc/hosts*, but it's a bit of bother to edit */etc/hosts* on each of the zillion PCs you're responsible for. Can you do it in *dhcpd.conf*?

Solution

Yes, you surely can. You'll need the MAC address of your network card, which you can find with *ifconfig*:

```
$ /sbin/ifconfig
eth0      Link encap:Ethernet  HWaddr 00:03:6D:00:83:CF
          inet addr:192.168.1.5  Bcast:192.168.1.255  Mask:255.255.255.0
          UP BROADCAST RUNNING MULTICAST  MTU:1500  Metric:1
.....
```

You want the *HWaddr* value.

On Windows 95/98/ME, open a DOS prompt and run *winipcfg*. On NT/2000/XP, run *ipconfig*.

Make an entry in *dhcpd.conf* like this:

```
host mail1 {
    hardware ethernet 00:03:6D:00:83:CF;
    fixed-address 192.168.1.100;
    }
```

Note that multiple-line directives must be enclosed in curly braces.

Name servers have their own directive in *dhcpd.conf*, so they don't need MAC addresses:

```
option domain-name-servers 192.168.1.10, 192.168.1.11
```

That's all there is to it. Use this for any machine you wish to have a static IP address.

Discussion

You can still use */etc/hosts* for important servers, as a fallback for local users. Remember, with */etc/hosts* the network does not break when a single server goes down.

Every network card ever made has a unique 48-bit Media Access Control (MAC address). The Institute of Electrical and Electronics Engineers, Inc. (IEEE) assigns the first 24 bits, then the manufacturer assigns the remaining 24 bits.

See Also

- *dhcp-options(5)*, *dhcpd.conf(5)*, *dhcpd(8)*

24.6 Running a Public DNS Server

Problem

You're running mail, web, or other public servers, and you want to control your DNS server yourself. You're tired of waiting on third-party service providers, and why should you pay them for something you can do yourself? You want the flexibility to set up your network however you please—maybe you want to own only a single public routable IP address and put all your servers behind a NAT firewall, or maybe you want to put workstations and internal servers behind NAT and put your public servers outside the firewall. However you elect to set up your network, you want control of the name services.

So you're ready to take the plunge and set up your own public DNS server.

Solution

You need five things:

- A static, public, routable IP address
- A registered name server
- A permanent Internet connection
- An ISP account that permits running servers
- Your actual server

After these items are in place, see the recipes in the rest of this chapter for configuring either a BIND or *djbdns* server.

Discussion

A static, routable IP address comes from your Internet service provider.

Your name server needs to be registered with your domain name registrar. If you have not already registered a domain name, visit *http://icann.org/registrars/accredited-list.html* for a list of ICANN-accredited domain name registrars. (This doesn't guarantee that you'll get good service, but they are official.) Figure 24-1 shows what the registration form looks like at Dotster.

Figure 24-1. Dotster's domain name registration form

A DNS server doesn't need much in the way of hardware or bandwidth. DNS requests are very low-bandwidth; after all, a single UDP packet is all it takes to satisfy a request. Ideally, you'll have enough RAM to keep all zone and cache data in memory. If you run your DNS server on a Linux server without X, and without any other services, something like an old P300 with 128 MB of RAM will handle a couple hundred BIND zones just fine, and many hundreds of *djbdns* hosts. So, if you were only managing the DNS for the little *windbag.net* network in this chapter, you could easily piggyback onto a machine running other services.

See Also

- *djbdns* documentation (*http://cr.yp.to/djbdns.html*)
- BIND 9 Administrator Reference Manual (*http://www.bind9.net/Bv9ARM.html*)

24.7   Installing djbdns

Problem

You want to use *djbdns* to build a DNS server, and you need to know what to install and how to install it. There seem to be a lot of different pieces, and it's a bit confusing.

Solution

You need three source tarballs: *daemontools*, *uscpi-tcp*, and *djbdns*. Get these from the *djbdns* home page at *http://cr.yp.to/djbdns.html*.

After installation, you're ready to start configuration, which is covered in the following recipes.

To install *daemontools*, follow these steps:

```
# mkdir -m 1755 /package
# cd /package
```

Download and unpack the latest *daemontools* tarball into */package*, as follows:

```
# tar xzvpf daemontools-0.76.tar.gz
# cd admin/daemontools-0.76
```

To compile and set up the *daemontools* programs, use:

```
# package/install
```

Next, fetch the latest *uspci-tcp* tarball and install it:

```
# cd /usr/sources
# tar xzvf ucspi-tcp-0.88.tar
# cd ucspi-tcp-0.88
# make
# make setup check
```

It puts itself into */usr/local/bin*.

Finally, fetch and install *djbdns*:

```
# tar xzvf djbdns-1.05.tar.gz
# cd  djbdns-1.05
# make
# make setup check
```

It puts itself into */usr/local/bin*.

Now read the following recipes to learn how to use *djbdns*.

Discussion

daemontools is a suite of utilities for managing services. In these recipes, you'll see *supervise, multilog,* and *svstat. supervise* automatically restarts services if they die unexpectedly. *multilog* is a nice log manager that automatically rotates log data, so that logs don't consume your disk space and you always have fresh data. *svstat* tells you the status of a service.

uspci-tcp takes the place of *inetd* and *xinetd*, for running *djbdns* and other Dan Bernstein programs. You don't have to do anything other than install it.

djbdns is a suite of DNS programs. This chapter contains recipes for *dnscache*, the caching/resolving DNS server, and *tinydns*, the authoritative DNS server.

See Also

- Life with Djbnds (*http://www.lifewithdjbdns.com*)
- *daemontools* (*http://cr.yp.to/daemontools.html*)
- *uspci-tcp* (*http://cr.yp.to/ucspi-tcp.html*)

24.8 Moving tinydns's and dnscache's Logfiles

Problem

By default, *tinydns-conf* and *dnscache-conf* put the logfiles in */etc/tinydns/log/main* and */etc/dnscache/log/main*, which are not the usual places for logfiles. You would rather move them to */var/log*, where they belong.

Solution

To put the logfiles for *tinydns* in */var/log/tinydns*, edit */etc/tinydns/log/run*, as follows:

```
#!/bin/sh
exec setuidgid dnslog multilog t /var/log/tinydns
```

Do the same for *dnscache*, editing */etc/dnscache/log/run*, as follows:

```
#!/bin/sh
exec setuidgid dnslog multilog t /var/log/dnscache
```

See Also

• How to install *djbdns* (*http://cr.yp.to/djbdns/install.html*)

24.9   Running a Local Caching Name Server with djbdns

Problem

You want to set up a local *djbdns* caching name server just to serve your LAN. This will speed up DNS lookups, which in turn will speed up web surfing, email, and all Internet services.

Solution

The caching component of *djbdns* is *dnscache*. First, prepare your system by installing *daemontools*, *uspci-tcp*, and *djbdns* (see Recipe 24.7).

After installing everything, run a *dnsip* query to confirm that *djbdns* installed correctly:

```
$ dnsip www.oreillynet.com
208.201.239.37 208.201.239.36
```

Now create two system users to own *dnscache* and *dnslog*. Call them anything you want. In this example, they are simply "dnscache" and "dnslog":

```
# useradd -d /dev/null -s /bin/false dnscache
# useradd -d /dev/null -s /bin/false dnslog
```

Then configure the IP address and service directory for *dnscache*. This also assigns the appropriate file ownerships:

```
# dnscache-conf dnscache dnslog /etc/dnscache 192.168.1.5
```

Create your "allow" list; this example permits your local subnet to use your *dnscache*:

```
# touch /etc/dnscache/root/ip/192.168.1
```

Now start it up:

```
# ln -s /etc/dnscache /service
```

To verify that it's running, use *svstat*:

```
# svstat /service/dnscache
/service/dnscache: up (pid 6776) 30 seconds
```

To verify that it's working, run *dnsqr* to query the local cache:

```
# env DNSCACHEIP=192.168.1.5 dnsqr a www.yahoo.com
1 www.yahoo.com:
193 bytes, 1+9+0+0 records, response, noerror
query: 1 www.yahoo.com
answer: www.yahoo.com 286 CNAME www.yahoo.akadns.net
answer: www.yahoo.akadns.net 60 A 66.94.230.52
answer: www.yahoo.akadns.net 60 A 66.94.230.48
```

Configure clients to point to your *dnscache* server (see Recipe 24.10), and you're finished.

Discussion

A caching server, or caching DNS resolver, does two things: it answers DNS requests by getting the information from other servers, and then it stores the results so that it can answer future requests for the same information directly. The cache lives only in memory, so restarting the cache's process or rebooting wipes it all out.

A caching server and an authoritative DNS server should always be strictly separated. This means the IP address of your caching server should never match any IP addresses listed in NS records. A few bad things can happen when you put them together:

- If an attacker seizes control of your DNS cache, the attacker can control not only your incoming DNS data, but also your outgoing DNS data—which means he can hijack your web sites, email, FTP, and any "secure" web-based applications.
- If your DNS cache suffers a Distributed Denial of Service (DDoS) attack, your authoritative server will also be pummeled, and you will have no DNS service.

RFC 2010 also advises keeping caching servers separate from authoritative servers:

> Recursion is a major source of cache pollution, and can be a major drain on name server performance. An organization's recursive DNS needs should be served by some other host than its root name server(s).

With BIND, you cannot separate the two. But you can with *djbdns,* as you will see in the following recipes.

When you're testing *dnscache*, and making changes and generally futzing around, sometimes you'll find it won't stay up:

```
# svstat /service/dnscache
/service/dnscache: up (pid 6776) 1 seconds
# svstat /service/dnscache
/service/dnscache: up (pid 6781) 0 seconds
```

You probably have too many instances of it running. Try this:

```
# netstat -nap | grep ":53"
tcp  0  0 127.0.0.1:53   0.0.0.0:*   LISTEN   6327/dnscache
tcp  0  0 192.168.1.5:53 0.0.0.0:*   LISTEN   6129/dnscache
```

```
udp  0  0 127.0.0.1:53    0.0.0.0:*              6327/dnscache
udp  0  0 192.168.1.5:53  0.0.0.0:*              6129/dnscache
```

Yep, that's too many. You should have two instances only: listening on TCP port 53 and UDP port 53. Do a *killall supervise dnscache*, give it a few seconds, then try again:

```
# svstat /service/dnscache
/service/dnscache: up (pid 6776) 21 seconds
# netstat -nap | grep ":53"
tcp  0  0 192.168.1.5:53  0.0.0.0:*    LISTEN    6776/dnscache
udp  0  0 192.168.1.5:53  0.0.0.0:*              6776/dnscache
```

That's what you want to see.

Another common problem is having an old BIND server still running. There Can Be Only One.

djbdns comes with a number of network querying and diagnostic utilities: *dnsqr*, *dnstrace*, *dnsip*, *tinydns-get*, *dnsipq*, *dnsmx*, and *dnsname*. See the links below to learn more about them.

See Also

- Command-line tools to look up DNS information (*http://cr.yp.to/djbdns/tools.html*)
- Command-line tools to debug DNS configuration (*http://cr.yp.to/djbdns/debugging.html*)
- There are several different ways to set up dnscache (*http://cr.yp.to/djbdns.html*)
- Life With *djbdns*, Simple Setup (*http://www.lifewithdjbdns.com/#Simple%20setup*)

24.10 Configuring Linux and Windows Clients to Use Your Caching DNS Server

Problem

Your caching server is ready to go to work—how you do tell your Linux and Windows clients how to find it?

Solution

If your clients are served by DHCP, you need to edit your DHCP configuration file to point to your new name server (see Recipe 24.3).

Linux hosts with static IP addresses that are not served by DHCP configure their name servers in */etc/resolv.conf*. In this example, your name server is at 192.168.1.200, so all you do is edit */etc/resolv.conf*:

```
nameserver 192.168.1.200
```

The resolver queries the entries in order, so make this the first one if you have others. Typically, your ISP will list a primary and a secondary name server in your account information, so you can list these next:

```
nameserver 192.168.1.200
nameserver 12.188.166.2
nameserver 12.188.166.3
```

On Windows hosts with static IP addresses, find the menu for configuring Internet Protocol (TCP/IP) properties. In Windows 95/98/ME, go to Control Panel → Network → TCP/IP → Properties. Go to the DNS Configuration tab, and there you are.

In Windows NT/2000/XP, go to Control Panel → Network Connections. Right-click Local Area Connection, then select Internet Protocol (TCP/IP) → Properties.

Whatever flavor of Windows you are using, the menu you want looks like Figure 24-2.

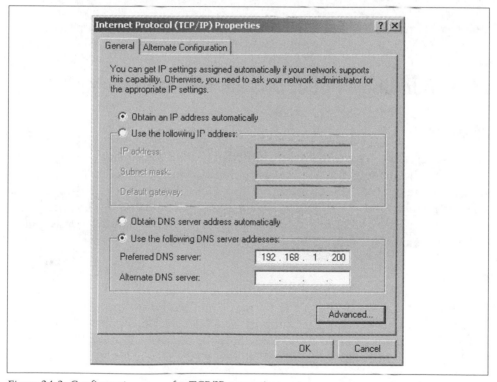

Figure 24-2. Configuration menu for TCP/IP properties

Discussion

That's pretty much all you have to do; a DNS cache is low-maintenance. You may enter up to three name servers on client machines.

Make sure you do not give the entire Internet access to your caching server! This is a big security hole; plus, there's no reason for you to provide caching for the masses. Recipes 24.9 tells how to avoid this.

Windows 2000/XP comes with its own built-in DNS cache. You didn't know it was there, did you. You can view the contents of the cache with this command:

```
C:\> ipconfig /displaydns
```

To flush the cache, use:

```
C:\> ipconfig /flushdns
```

Flushing the cache is a quick way to get rid of stale data, such as when you change a server's IP address.

See Also

- *resolv.conf(5)*
- "Get Started with Home Networking," a good reference for all aspects of networking Windows clients (search for it on Google or Microsoft.com)

24.11 Building a Public DNS Server with tinydns

Problem

You've set up some servers (mail, web, FTP) that need to be accessible to the outside world. They need domain names, like *www.oreilly.com*, since you don't want people using IP addresses. You want to run your own DNS server to provide those names. You tried BIND, and it was just too complicated. Or you heard some scary talk about BIND security problems. Whatever the reason, you've decided to use *djbdns*. So how do you make it go?

Solution

First, follow the preparatory steps in Recipe 24.6. Then follow these steps to install and set up *tinydns*, which is the authoritative DNS server component of *djbdns*. If you are also running *dnscache*, it must not have the same IP address as *tinydns*. This is a very important security measure. Both *dnscache* and *tinydns* will fail silently if you do it anyway.

Follow the steps in Recipe 24.7 for *djbdns* installation. Then, create two system users, using any names you like. They will own the *tinydns* server, and the *dnslog*:

```
# useradd -d /dev/null -s /bin/false tinydns
# useradd -d /dev/null -s /bin/false dnslog
```

Run *tinydns-conf* to create directories and set the IP address of the *tinydns* server. List your system users in the order shown here:

```
# tinydns-conf tinydns dnslog /etc/tinydns 208.201.239.36
```

Create a startup entry in *service*:

```
# ln -s /etc/tinydns /service
```

Wait a few seconds, then run *svstat* to verify that it started:

```
# svstat /service/tinydns
/service/tinydns: up (pid 6811) 14 seconds
```

If *tinydns* won't stay up continuously, check the logfile in */etc/tinydns/log/main/current*. That will tell you where the problem is.

Now it's time to create your host entries. This recipe shows how to create entries using the scripts that come with *tinydns*. In this example the domain name is *pixels.net*, which is duly registered with a domain name registrar. There are three hosts, shown in Table 24-1.

Table 24-1. pixels.net hosts

Address	Hostname	Role	Alias
208.201.239.36	parsley	DNS, mail	
208.201.239.37	sage	FTP	ftp
208.201.239.38	rosemary	Web server	www

Create the host entries as follows:

```
# cd /service/tinydns/root
# ./add-ns pixels.net 208.201.239.36
# ./add-ns .239.201.208.in-addr.arpa 208.201.239.36
# ./add-host parsley.pixels.net 208.201.239.36
# ./add-host sage.pixels.net 208.201.239.37
# ./add-host rosemary.pixels.net 208.201.239.38
# ./add-alias ftp.pixels.net 208.201.239.37
# ./add-alias www.pixels.net 208.201.239.38
# make
```

That's all it takes to build a *tinydns* server.

Discussion

The previous commands inserted data into */etc/tinydns/root/data*; here's what it looks like:

```
.pixels.net:208.201.239.36:a:259200
.239.201.208.in-addr.arpa:208.201.239.36:a:259200
=parsley.pixels.net:208.201.239.36:86400
=sage.pixels.net:208.201.239.37:86400
=rosemary.pixels.net:208.201.239.38:86400
```

```
+ftp.pixels.net:208.201.239.37:86400
+www.pixels.net:208.201.239.38:86400
```

You typically configure *djbdns* by running configuration scripts, not by editing the *data* file by hand. Here are the available configuration scripts:

add-host
> Creates both an A (alias) record and a PTR (reverse pointer)

add-mx
> Adds a mail server

add-ns
> Adds a name server

add-alias
> Creates an A record but not a matching PTR

add-childns
> Adds a child name server—use this when you want to act like an ISP and host other name servers

Here is a list of the leading symbols used by *tinydns*:

. *(leading dot)*
> Name server

=
> Both pointer (PTR) and A record

+
> A record

&
> NS and A records

@
> MX and A records

As you can see, *tinydns* thoughtfully calculates the time-to-live (TTL) values for you. The TTL tells caching servers, in seconds, how often they should come back to refresh their information. *tinydns* will continue to adjust these automatically; don't worry about tweaking them manually.

You can edit the *djbdns data* file manually, if you want. You can add comments, change the order of the entries, whatever you like. The scripts are for convenience, and to ensure that each entry is in the correct format. Just remember to run *make* every time you make a change, to convert the file to */etc/tinydns/root/data.cdb*.

The clear separation of functions is one of the strengths of *djbdns*. You do not want your caching server anywhere near your authoritative DNS server. In other words, the IP addresses listed in */etc/resolv.conf* should never match any IP addresses listed in NS records. If your caching server is compromised and is running on the same IP address as your DNS server, the attacker could misdirect all of your traffic, including "secure" web applications.

See Also

- How to run a DNS server (*http://cr.yp.to/djbdns/run-server.html*)

24.12 Building a Private tinydns Server

Problem

You've outgrown *hosts* files, so you want to use a DNS server for your LAN only. You won't be providing any public services. How do you do this with *tinydns*?

Solution

Set up a *dnscache* server for your LAN, as in Recipe 24.9. Set up a *tinydns* server as in Recipe 24.11, and enter your internal hosts in */etc/tinydns/root/data*.

Using the *pixels.net* domain to illustrate, the next step is to tell your local *dnscache* to query your local, private *tinydns* server for your domain information. Create these files using the IP address of your private *tinydns* server:

```
# echo 192.168.1.100 > /service/dnscache/root/servers/pixels.net
# echo 192.168.1.100 > /service/dnscache/root/servers/0.168.192.in-addr.arpa
```

The *dnscache* user should own these files:

```
# chown dnscache: /service/dnscache/root/servers/pixels.net
# chown dnscache: /service/dnscache/root/servers/0.168.192.in-addr.arpa
```

Next, restart *dnscache*:

```
# svc -t /service/dnscache
```

dnscache will now consult the local *tinydns* server for local addresses, and it will consult the */service/dnscache/root/servers/@* file for external addresses.

Discussion

You can easily do this for multiple domains; just add more domain files to */service/dnscache/root/servers/*.

You have to have officially registered domain names for this to work, even if you are not running any public services. If you want the ability to invent whatever domain names you want for your LAN, see Recipe 24.2.

Remember that *dnscache* and *tinydns* should be on separate machines. Always separate the caching/resolving server from the authoritative server. If you must put them on the same machine, give them separate IP addresses. *tinydns* can have 127.0.0.1, and *dnscache* can take the network IP address.

See Also

- How to run a DNS server (*http://cr.yp.to/djbdns/run-server.html*)

24.13 Enabling Simple Load Balancing with tinydns

Problem

You have redundant mail, FTP, or web servers, and you would like to configure them to automatically divide up the traffic load. For example, say you have a heavily trafficked web site that uses three separate redundant Apache servers. How do you make traffic automatically go to the least busy server?

Solution

DNS round-robin, or *load balancing*, is simple to implement. Just list all of your servers in */etc/tinydns/root/data*:

```
+www.pixels.net:208.201.239.37:86400
+www.pixels.net:208.201.239.38:86400
+www.pixels.net:208.201.239.39:86400
@mail.pixels.net:208.201.239.37:a::86400
@mail.pixels.net:208.201.239.37:b::86400
```

Discussion

tinydns returns a set of up to eight random addresses for any single request. If any single server becomes unavailable, the client attempting to connect to the server will go on to the next one in line.

See Also

- How to balance load among many web servers (*http://cr.yp.to/djbdns/balance.html*)

24.14 Synchronizing with a Second tinydns Server

Problem

You have a second *tinydns* server offsite, as a backup. How do you keep it synchronized with your main *tindydns* server?

Solution

Plain old *rsync-over-ssh* does the job just fine. This simple script copies your DNS *data* file to the backup, then runs *make* on the remote *data* file:

```
rsync -e ssh -az /etc/tinydns/root/data $backup-host:/etc/tinydns/root/data
ssh $backup-host "cd /etc/tinydns/root; make"
```

Replace *$backup-host* with the name or IP address of the remote server.

You can automate the entire process by adding these lines to */etc/tinydns/root/ Makefile*, so that when you run the *make* command on your primary server after updating */etc/tinydns/root/data*, the backup will automatically be updated as well:

```
data.cdb: data
        /usr/local/bin/tinydns-data
        rsync -e ssh -az /etc/tinydns/root/data $backup-host:/etc/tinydns/root/data
        ssh $backup-host "cd /etc/tinydns/root; make"
```

Discussion

Moving plain old text files doesn't require a lot of sophistication; *rsync* is a fine tool for the job. You may schedule regular updates via *cron,* or add transport security and authentication with encrypted *ssh* keys.

Your backup server can also function as your secondary DNS server. You can configure client PCs to use it, or register it just like your main DNS server for a public authoritative DNS server (see Recipe 24.6).

See Also

- Chapter 16, *Backup and Recovery*
- Chapter 17, *Remote Access*

24.15 Running a Local Caching Name Server with BIND

Problem

You want to set up a local BIND caching name server for your LAN to speed up DNS lookups, which in turn will speed up all of your Internet services.

Solution

Install BIND on a Linux machine with a static IP address. Be sure you get the latest version, which is currently BIND 9.2.3. Don't mess with older versions, as they are buggy and exploitable. After installation, you'll have four configuration files to edit or create:

- *named.conf*
- *named.root*
- *zone.localhost*
- *revp.127.0.0*

In this recipe, all of these files are in */var/named,* except for */etc/named.conf. named.conf* is the standard name for BIND's configuration file; all the others you can name to suit yourself. Here is a sample *named.conf*:

```
//BIND configuration file
//named.conf for caching server

options {
// where all zone files are
  directory "/var/named";
// accept queries only from local subnet
  listen-on {
            127.0.0.1;
            10.11.12.1;
    };
  allow-recursion {
            127.0.0.0/8;
            10.11.12.0/24;
    };
};

zone "." IN {
    type hint;
    file "named.root";
};

// location of the zone file for localhost
zone "localhost" IN {
```

```
    type master;
    file "zone.localhost";
    allow-update { none; };
};

// reverse pointer file for localhost
zone "0.0.127.in-addr.arpa" IN {
    type master;
    file "revp.127.0.0";
    allow-update { none; };
};
```

Now add *named.root*. This is the master list of the root name servers; simply fetch the current version from *ftp://ftp.internic.net/domain/named.root*, and put it in */var/named*.

Now create *zone.localhost*:

```
; zone.localhost
; loopback/localhost zone file
;
$TTL 1D
$ORIGIN localhost.
@               IN  SOA  @  root (
                             1   ; Serial
                             8H  ; Refresh
                             15M ; Retry
                             1W  ; Expire
                             1D) ; Minimum TTL
                IN  NS   @
                IN  A    127.0.0.1
```

Finally, create *revp.127.0.0*:

```
; revp.127.0.0
; reverse pointers for localhost
;
$TTL 1D
$ORIGIN 0.0.127.in-addr.arpa.
@   IN  SOA  localhost. root.localhost. (
                             1   ; serial
                             8H  ; refresh
                             15M ; retry
                             1W  ; expire
                             1D ) ; minimum
    IN  NS   localhost.
1   IN  PTR  localhost.
```

Then start up BIND:

```
# /etc/init.d/named start
```

You now have a local caching name server. See Recipe 24.10 to learn how to connect client PCs to your caching server.

Discussion

named is short for "name daemon."

BIND configuration files can grow and multiply like weeds, so using a naming convention like the one shown here will save your sanity. Zone files each start with "zone," and reverse pointer files start with "revp." You may call them anything you want, as long as you use a consistent naming scheme.

You can use each one of these sample files exactly as they are shown. The only change you might need to make is the *listen-on* directive in *named.conf*—be sure to use your own network IP addresses. Leave *localhost* exactly as it is shown, unless you're using some exotic networking voodoo, in which case you already know what to do. Do not allow traffic from outside your network! There is no reason for you to supply caching services to the world.

The *named.root* file does not change very often. Check it every few months just for kicks. You may call it anything you like, as long as you record the filename in *named.conf*.

zone.localhost tells *named* that the address of localhost is 127.0.0.1.

revp.127.0.0 does the opposite of *zone.localhost*—it tells *named* that the hostname associated with the IP address 127.0.0.1 is *localhost*.

Paul Heinlein wrote much of the gnarly BIND stuff for this chapter. Thank you, Paul! You can find Paul on *madboa.com*.

See Also

- *named(8)*, *named.conf(5)*
- Chapter 6 of the *Bind 9 Administrator's Reference Manual* (*http://www.bind9.net/Bv9ARM*)

24.16 Running a Private BIND DNS Server

Problem

You're tired of dinking around with */etc/hosts*; you're ready to implement some grown-up name resolution on your LAN by installing a BIND DNS server. You only want this server to be available to your local users, providing both name-resolution and caching services. It will not provide any public services.

Solution

Set up a caching name server according to Recipe 24.15. Then add zone blocks to *named.conf* to define the new zones for your LAN hosts, and construct the zone files.

Table 24-2 lists the five hosts on *windbag.net*.

Table 24-2. Five hosts

Address	Hostname	Role	Alias
10.11.12.1	parsley	DNS, mail	
10.11.12.2	sage	FTP	ftp
10.11.12.3	rosemary	Web server	www
10.11.12.4	thyme	Workstation	
10.11.12.5	cilantro	Workstation	

Add these zone blocks to *named.conf*:

```
zone "windbag.net" IN {
  type master;
  file "zone.net.windbag";
};

zone "12.11.10.in-addr.arpa" {
  type master;
  file "revp.10.11.12";
};
```

Here is the actual zone file for *windbag.net*:

```
// zone.net.windbag
// dns zone for for windbag.net
;
$ORIGIN windbag.net.
$TTL 1D
; any time you make a change to the domain, bump the
; "serial" setting below. the format is easy:
; YYYYMMDDI, with the I being an iterator in case you
; make more than one change during any one day
@      IN SOA    parsley hostmaster (
                      200405191 ; serial
                      8H        ; refresh
                      4H        ; retry
                      4W        ; expire
                      1D )      ; minimum
; parsley.windbag.net serves this domain as both the
; name server (NS) and mail exchange (MX)
               NS       parsley
               MX       10 parsley
; define domain functions with CNAMEs
ftp            CNAME    sage
www            CNAME    rosemary
```

```
; just in case someone asks for localhost.windbag.net
localhost          A       127.0.0.1
; our hostnames, in alphabetical order
rosemary           A       10.11.12.3
sage               A       10.11.12.2
parsley            A       10.11.12.1
thyme              A       10.11.12.4
cilantro           A       10.11.12.5
```

And finally, here are the reverse lookups for the domain in the *revp.10.11.12* file:

```
; revp.10.11.12
; reverse pointers for 10.11.12.0 subnet
;
$ORIGIN 12.11.10.in-addr.arpa.
$TTL 1D
@      IN SOA  parsley.windbag.net. hostmaster.windbag.net. (
                200405190  ; serial
                28800      ; refresh (8 hours)
                14400      ; retry (4 hours)
                2419200    ; expire (4 weeks)
                86400      ; minimum (1 day)
                )
; define the authoritative name server
                NS      parsley.windbag.net.
; our hosts, in numeric order
1               PTR     parsley.windbag.net.
2               PTR     sage.windbag.net.
3               PTR     rosemary.windbag.net.
4               PTR     thyme.windbag.net.
5               PTR     cilantro.windbag.net.
```

Save your changes and restart BIND:

 # /etc/init.d/named restart

And there you are—a shiny new fully functioning DNS server for your LAN.

Discussion

There's a whole lot happening in these three files. First of all, putting each zone into its own file is good organization. You may dump everything into a single zone file if you like, but you'll find that it's difficult to maintain.

In *named.conf*, the entries for *windbag.net* tell BIND that it is the authoritative server for *windbag.net*, and where to find the zone files.

The *$origin* directive is a nice timesaver. It lets you write:

```
$ORIGIN windbag.net.
www             CNAME   rosemary
```

instead of:

```
www.windbag.net    CNAME     rosemary.windbag.net
```

$TTL 1D sets a default time-to-live value. Values can be in this format:

w For week

d For day

h For hour

m For minute

s For second

Individual entries may have their own TTL values:

```
rosemary      72h    A      10.11.12.3
```

The TTL tells visitors how often to refresh their own caches. If your site is fairly static, set this to a higher value. If you're making frequent changes, use a lower value. The lower the TTL, the more hits there will be on your server.

@ IN SOA parsley hostmaster means:

@
> This holds the same value as *$ORIGIN*.

IN
> This defines the address class; IN = Internet.

SOA
> Start of Authority; the beginning of a zone file. Only A records can be used as the MNAME—don't use CNAMEs.

The SOA has 10 fields. These are the primary domain name, zone class, and SOA, plus the following:

MNAME
> The master name server for the zone.

RNAME
> The email address of the domain admin.

Serial number
> BIND converts zone files into a binary file format. When you make changes to the zone file, you must also change the serial number, or BIND will not recognize the changes.

Refresh
> This tells your slave, or secondary servers how often to check for updates.

Retry
> If the master DNS server for the zone fails to answer a slave server's request for an update, this tells the secondary server how often it should resend the request.

Expire
> If the master DNS server fails for a longer period of time, this tells the the secondary server how to continue to use its existing data. After the expire time has

passed, the data is considered stale and will not be used, at which time the domain will no longer resolve. Hopefully your master server will be back online before this happens.

Minimum, or Negative-caching TTL

Negative answers (such as when a requested record does not exist) should also be cached on nonauthoritative servers. Setting this value prevents your server from getting hammered by a bunch of repeated requests in a short time. A common use for this is when you are migrating to a new name server at a different IP address; setting a short value on the old server a few days before you take it offline assures that your change will propagate quickly.

The next section contains *resource records* (RRs).

NS parsley and *MX 10 parsley* define your name server and mail server. If you have more than one mail server for the domain, the number sets the priority. Lower numbers are higher priority. Because *$ORIGIN windbag.net.* defines the domain name for the whole record, these expand to *ns.windbag.net* and *mx.windbag.net*. Make note of the trailing dot—this is very important! That defines the qualified domain name. If you leave it off, BIND will think it needs to append the domain name, so you'll have silliness like *ns.windbag.net.windbag.net*.

CNAME (canonical name) is an alias to an A record. Thus, a single A record can have several aliases. You can use a CNAME to add subdomains for virtual web or mail hosting—for example, *programmers.only.domain.com* or *webmail.domain.com*.

Instead of using CNAMES, you may assign subdomains their own A records. This means one less hit on your server per CNAME request, but it also means more work when you need to make changes. Endless debates rage over the use of CNAMEs; use what suits you.

"Canonical" is one of those weirdo geek words that defies a precise, logical definition. In this context, "canonical name" means "an alias assigned to the true (canonical) name of the server."

And finally, we come to the A (alias) records. An A record is the primary address for each of your hosts, the direct match of hostname to IP address.

Reverse pointers (RPTs) are technically not required, but in the real world so many servers require them that you had better use them.

If things are not working right, chances are it's a syntax error or a typo—mind your dots and commas especially. There are two syntax checkers for BIND to help you; see the next recipe for details.

The other common error is not starting from A records. Every host must first have an A record. Then you can assign name servers, mail servers, and CNAMEs.

See Also

- *named(5), named(8)*
- Section 6.3 of *The Bind 9 Administrator's Reference Manual* (*http://www.bind9.net/Bv9ARM.html*)
- A named reference of *TCP/IP Network Administration*, by Craig Hunt (O'Reilly)

24.17 Checking Syntax

Problem

All those BIND files! All those commas, and dots, and semicolons! It's too easy to make typos—is there a syntax-checker to help?

Solution

Yes, in fact there are two. *named-checkconf* checks *named.conf*, and *named-checkzone* is for your zone files. Use them like this:

```
# named-checkconf named.conf
# named-checkzone windbag.net /var/named/db.zone.net.windbag
```

Discussion

Note that *named-checkzone* needs the zone name, as defined by the *$ORIGIN* directive, and also its corresponding binary database file.

See Also

- *named-checkconf(8)*, *named-checkzone(8)*

24.18 Configuring a Public BIND DNS Server

Problem

You've set up some servers (mail, web, FTP) that need to be accessible to the outside world. They need domain names, like *www.oreilly.com*, since you don't want people using IP addresses. You want to run your own DNS server to provide those names. Why? Perhaps you're not convinced your ISP is reliable, or perhaps you just like things under your own control. Or maybe you're just a glutton for punishment. Whatever the reason, you've decided to use BIND. So how do you make it go?

Solution

Follow the preparatory steps in Recipe 24.6. Table 24-3 shows the public servers for this recipe.

Table 24-3. Public servers

Address	Hostname	Role	Aliases
208.201.239.45	catmint	Public DNS	
208.201.239.46	henbane	Public FTP, WWW	FTP, www

First of all, BIND needs a *named.conf* file:

```
// named.conf for public services
// at windbag.net

options {
        directory "/var/named";
        allow-query { any; };
        recursion no;
};
zone "." IN {
        type hint;
        file "named.root";
};

zone "localhost" IN {
    type master;
    file "zone.localhost";
    allow-update { none; };
};

zone "0.0.127.in-addr.arpa" IN {
    type master;
    file "revp.127.0.0";
    allow-update { none; };
};
zone "windbag.net" IN {
    type master;
    file "zone.net.windbag";
};

zone "239.201.208.in-addr.arpa" {
    type master;
    file "revp.208.201.239";
};
```

Next, fetch a current copy of *named.root* from *ftp://ftp.internic.net/domain*, and put it in */var/named*.

Then create the zone files: *zone.localhost*, *revp.127.0.0*, *zone.net.windbag*, and *revp.208.201.239*. You can copy *zone.localhost* and *revp.127.0.0* from Recipe 24.15.

Here are sample *zone.net.windbag* and *revp.208.201.239* files:

```
// zone.net.windbag
// public dns zone for for windbag.net
;
$ORIGIN windbag.net.
$TTL 1D
; any time you make a change to the domain, bump the
; "serial" setting below. the format is easy:
; YYYYMMDDI, with the I being an iterator in case you
; make more than one change during any one day
@     IN SOA    catmint hostmaster (
                        200405191 ; serial
                        8H        ; refresh
                        4H        ; retry
                        4W        ; expire
                        1D )      ; minimum
; define the authoritative name server
              NS        catmint
; define domain functions with CNAMEs
ftp           CNAME     henbane
www           CNAME     henbane
; our hostnames, in alphabetical order
catmint           A         208.201.239.45
henbane           A         208.201.239.46
```

And finally, here are the reverse lookups for the domain in the *revp.208.201.239* file:

```
;   revp.208.201.239
; reverse pointers for 208.201.239 subnet
;
$ORIGIN 239.201.208.in-addr.arpa.
$TTL 1D
@     IN SOA  catmint.windbag.net. hostmaster.windbag.net. (
              200405190  ; serial
              28800      ; refresh (8 hours)
              14400      ; retry (4 hours)
              2419200    ; expire (4 weeks)
              86400      ; minimum (1 day)
              )
; define the authoritative name server
          NS       catmint.windbag.net.
; our hosts, in numeric order
45          PTR       catmint.windbag.net.
46          PTR       henbane.windbag.net.
```

Stuff all these files into */var/named* and restart BIND:

```
# /etc/init.d/named restart
```

Your new DNS server is now in business.

Discussion

Remember to use the syntax-checkers discussed in Recipe 24.17; the most common BIND problems are caused by typos.

Never use the same BIND authoritative server for both private, internal hosts and public, external hosts. The outside world does not need a direct pipeline to workstations, private servers, networked printers, or other internal resources.

Providing both private and public name services from the same DNS server is called "split horizon." With older versions of BIND, which no one should be using anyway, it's nearly impossible to implement a split horizon setup sanely. You're better off having two completely separate servers.

BIND 9 introduces "views," which are supposed to make it easier to implement a split horizon setup. In my opinion, it's still easier and more secure to use two separate BIND servers for private and public hosts. The easiest way of all is to use *djbdns* (see Recipes 24.11 and 24.12).

To learn more about BIND 9 views, see Chapter 10 of *DNS and BIND*, Fourth Edition, by those masters of BIND, Paul Albitz and Cricket Liu (O'Reilly).

See Also

- *named(5)*, *named.conf(8)*
- Chapter 3 of *The Bind 9 Administrator's Reference Manual* (*http://www.bind9.net/ Bv9ARM.html*)
- Chapter 10 of *DNS and BIND*, Fourth Edition
- Appendix C of *TCP/IP Network Administration*, Third Edition

24.19 Building a BIND Secondary Server

Problem

You have your public BIND server configured and running smoothly. Now you want to have a secondary BIND server in place.

Solution

There are four steps:

1. Configure the primary's *named.conf* so that it will transfer zone file changes to the secondary.
2. Configure the zone and reverse pointer files for the local domain so that the secondary is listed as one of the authoritative name servers for the domain.

3. Get a caching name server running on the host that will serve as secondary, and then configure it so that it is aware of its role as secondary.

4. Update client configurations.

The first step is accomplished by adding an *also-notify* directive to the zone blocks in *named.conf* on the primary. This example makes *henbane* the secondary to *catmint* (see Recipe 24.18):

```
zone "windbag.net" IN {
  type master;
  file "zone.net.windbag";
  // tell henbane when changes get made
  also-notify { 208.201.239.46; }
};

zone "239.201.208.in-addr.arpa" {
  type master;
  file "revp.208.201.239 ";
  also-notify { 208.201.239.46; }
};
```

Next, add *henbane* as a second name server in *zone.net.windbag*:

```
// zone.net.windbag
// public dns zone for for windbag.net
....
....
; define the authoritative name servers
                NS      catmint
                NS      henbane
```

Remember to advance your serial number after making changes to a zone file!

Don't forget to add *henbane* to *revp.208.201.239*, and mind your trailing dots:

```
;   revp.208.201.239
; reverse pointers for 208.201.239 subnet
....
....
; define the authoritative name servers
                NS      catmint.windbag.net.
                NS      henbane.windbag.net.
```

Remember to advance your serial number!

That takes care of steps 1 and 2. To complete step 3, set up a caching name server according to Recipe 24.15. Make it exactly the same. The only difference, other than being on a different machine, is in *named.conf* on the secondary. You'll add a *type slave* directive for both the zone blocks:

```
// serve as secondary for windbag.net domain
zone "windbag.net" IN {
  type slave;
  file "zone.net.windbag";
  // where the primary nameserver lives
```

```
    masters { 208.201.239.45; }
};

// serve as secondary for 208.201.239.45 net info
zone "239.201.208.in-addr.arpa" {
  type slave;
  file "revp.208.201.239 ";
  masters { 208.201.239.45; }
};
```

Restart BIND, add the second name server to your client PCs or DHCP server, and you're done.

Discussion

To really be useful as a secondary, the server should be at a different physical location and not right next to your primary, as in this recipe. Exchanging secondaries with friends is a good strategy, or you might get an account on a shared server in a data center; the cost is reasonable, and they have all the hardware and bandwidth headaches. All you have to do is make sure your configurations are correct.

The *also-notify* directive insures that when changes are made to zone files on the primary server, they will automatically be pushed out to the secondary. Remember to advance your serial number, or nothing will happen!

See Also

- *named(5)*, *named(8)*
- Chapter 6 of *The Bind 9 Administrator's Reference Manual* (*http://www.bind9.net/ Bv9ARM.html*)
- Appendix C of *TCP/IP Network Administration*, Third Edition

24.20 Simple Load Balancing with BIND

Problem

You have redundant mail, FTP, or web servers, and you would like to configure them to automatically share the load during times of heavy traffic.

Solution

Just give them all A records, using the same server alias for each IP address:

```
ftp   IN  A   192.168.0.4
      IN  A   192.168.0.5
      IN  A   192.168.0.6
www   IN  A   192.168.0.7
```

```
        IN   A    192.168.0.8
        IN   A    192.168.0.9
  mail  IN   A    192.168.0.10
        IN   A    192.168.0.11
        IN   A    192.168.0.12
```

An alternate trick with mail servers is to give them all the same priority:

```
IN   MX   10      mail.mydomain.com.
IN   MX   10      mail1.mydomain.com.
IN   MX   10      mail2.mydomain.com.


....

mail        IN      A      192.168.0.4
mail1       IN      A      192.168.0.5
mail2       IN      A      192.168.0.6
```

Discussion

Because of caching, you'll never get a perfect balance, but it's simple to set up, and works pretty well.

See Also

- Chapter 3 of *The BIND 9 Administrator Reference Manual* (*http://www.bind9.net/Bv9ARM.html*)

24.21 Testing Your tinydns Server

Problem

You want to check your *tinydns* configuration to see exactly what information *tinydns* will provide in response to queries.

Solution

djbdns comes with a number of useful querying utilities. Use *tinydns-get* to query your *tinydns* server. Run this command from the directory in which your *data.cdb* file is located. First tell what type of server it is, then give the domain name:

```
$ tinydns-get mx pixels.net
15 pixels.net:
80 bytes, 1+0+1+0 records, response, authoritative, noerror
query: 15 pixels.net
authority: pixels.net 2560 SOA a.ns.pixels.net hostmaster.pixels.net 1093229912 16384
2048 1048576 2560
```

Discussion

This is the quickest and easiest way to test your *tinydns* server. Run it every so often just to keep an eye on it. *tinydns* is very reliable and secure, so odds are any problems will be due to human error.

See Also

- Command-line tools to look up DNS information (*http://cr.yp.to/djbdns/tools.html*)
- Command-line tools to debug DNS configuration (*http://cr.yp.to/djbdns/debugging.html*)

24.22 Testing and Querying DNS Servers with dig and dnstrace

Problem

You want a utility for querying DNS servers; you want to be able to query specific servers for different record types, or make general queries that report all data for a domain. You are especially interested in what your servers are reporting to the world. You also want to trace all the upstream servers that affect the resolution of your domain name. And you are nosy about other people's networks.

Solution

dig, the Domain Information Groper, can do pretty much any kind of DNS query you want. *dnstrace* is the best tool for tracking down possible upstream troubles, such as misconfigured DNS servers that report your domain information incorrectly.

This is probably the most common *dig* query; it retrieves the complete resource record for a domain from the name servers specified in your *resolv.conf* file:

```
$ dig debian.org
; <<>> DiG 9.2.4rc5 <<>> debian.org
;; global options:  printcmd
;; Got answer:
;; ->>HEADER<<- opcode: QUERY, status: NOERROR, id: 43802
;; flags: qr rd ra; QUERY: 1, ANSWER: 1, AUTHORITY: 4, ADDITIONAL: 1

;; QUESTION SECTION:
;debian.org.                    IN      A

;; ANSWER SECTION:
debian.org.             3600    IN      A       192.25.206.10
```

```
;; AUTHORITY SECTION:
debian.org.          3600    IN      NS      saens.debian.org.
debian.org.          3600    IN      NS      spohr.debian.org.
debian.org.          3600    IN      NS      klecker.debian.org.
debian.org.          3600    IN      NS      newsamosa.debian.org.

;; ADDITIONAL SECTION:
newsamosa.debian.org.    3600    IN      A       208.185.25.35

;; Query time: 383 msec
;; SERVER: 12.169.174.2#53(12.169.174.2)
;; WHEN: Tue Aug 24 15:36:36 2004
;; MSG SIZE  rcvd: 146
```

It shows you three things:

- The *QUESTION SECTION* shows your inquiry.
- The *ANSWER SECTION* is your answer.
- The *AUTHORITY SECTION* lists the authoritative server(s) for the domain.

You can query the authoritative server for a domain directly. For example, to query your own authoritative server, you'd use:

```
$ dig @ns.pixels.net.  pixels.net
```

You can also specify a particular record type (*any, a, ns, mx, ptr, txt, cname, soa, hinfo, rp, sig, key, aaaa,* or *axfr*) like this:

```
$ dig cname @ns.pixels.net. pixels.net
```

dnstrace, which comes with *djbdns,* searches for all DNS servers that can affect the resolution of your selected domain name, starting from the specified root server. This can take a long time to run and may produce a lot of output, so the best thing to do is pipe it to a file, then run *dnstracesort* to format it nicely for reading:

```
$ dnstrace ptr www.bratgrrl.com a.root-servers.net > bratgrrl-trace.txt
$ dnstracesort < bratgrrl-trace.txt | less
```

Use this to see if any DNS servers are not resolving your domain correctly, or to hunt down mysterious errors and timeouts. You can quickly *grep* any error messages on the *ALERT* keyword:

```
$ cat bratgrrl-trace.txt | grep ALERT
1:1.gtld-servers.net:net:192.52.178.30:ALERT:took more than 1 second
1:h2.nstld.com:com:192.5.6.30:ALERT: query failed; connection refused
1 ns1.reno.bfp.net 209.160.7.3 ALERT: query failed; timed out
1 www.entero.net 192.216.155.10 ALERT: lame server; refers to  entero.net
```

Discussion

Lots of things can go wrong in the DNS world: timeouts, lame servers, even "martians." Timeouts are usually transient, caused by network problems or server downtime. Lame servers are a bigger problem. A *lame server*, or *lame delegation*, happens when an NS record points to an incorrect host. This means that DNS requests are being directed to a server that cannot answer them, so it wastes time and resources.

Because DNS is distributed, it may not matter if a server here or there is goofed up. But if you wish to contact the admin and correct the problem, you can run a *whois* on the domain to find out who to contact. The Internet is chock-full of misconfigured DNS servers. Use the *-H* option to turn off the deluge of legalese that accompanies a *whois* inquiry these days:

```
$ whois -H pixels.net
```

Sadly, most DNS troubles are local: a glitch in your network, or an error in the configuration.

You can use *dig* to query any DNS server—not just your local server and not just DNS servers. If a server can't answer a *dig* request, it's broken.

See Also

- Command-line tools to debug DNS configuration (*http://cr.yp.to/djbdns/debugging.html*)
- *dig(1)*, *whois(1)*

Finding Linux Documentation

Linux Documentation on the Web

Linux is truly a child of the Internet. Keeping up with advances, and finding documentation, means becoming acquainted with search engines, and relevant Web sites. The first stop is the Web site of your Linux distribution. Look for online manuals, howtos, FAQs, knowledge bases, mail lists, and list archives. Most Linux distributions are customized to some degree, so you'll need to know your distro-specific quirks.

Next, visit the Web sites of the individual programs you are using, and look for their mail lists, online documentation, and user communities.

Then there are a large number of general-interest Linux web sites, and online Linux publications. In this chapter are a number of resources I've found to be useful. Note that many of these welcome contributions from readers and ordinary Linux users. Don't be shy- share what you know.

As always, pay heed to proper netiquette. Search list archives before posting a question. If it's been answered recently, or often, you'll get yelled at. Mind your manners, and ignore trolls and rude people. Life is too short to waste in silly flame wars.

Linux Web Sites

The Linux Documentation Project
    http://www.tldp.org/

IBM developerWorks
    http://www-106.ibm.com/developerworks/linux/

Librenix
    http://librenix.com/

O'Reilly Network
    http://oreillynet.com/

TuxMobile
    http://www.tuxmobil.org/howtos.html

Wireless LAN resources for Linux
    http://www.hpl.hp.com/personal/Jean_Tourrilhes/Linux/

The Linux Kernel Archives
    http://www.kernel.org/

Linux Gazette
    http://linuxgazette.net/

This is, as far as I know, the only group devoted to supporting women Linux users, and an excellent group it is. There are several great mailing lists, including Newchix for newbies; courses on various subjects, such as programming, filesystems, and networking; and there are even Linuxchix chapters all over the world, where people can meet in the flesh. Yes, face-to-face, in person.

LinuxChix
    http://linuxchix.org/

O'Reilly's Safari Bookshelf deserves a special mention. It's an online, searchable library of over 1,300 computer books. It includes books from many good publishers. Subscriptions are quite affordable. Take it for a test-drive with their two-week free trial.

Safari Bookshelf
    http://safari.oreilly.com/

Usenet

There are dozens of Linux groups on Usenet. Try these for starters:

    comp.os.linux.announce
    comp.os.linux.hardware
    comp.os.linux.networking
    comp.os.linux.security

Google

How did we ever live without Google?

Google home page
    http://google.com

Google Groups, a great searchable front-end to Usenet
    http://groups.google.com/

Books and Magazines

First, check out any printed manuals for your Linux distribution. Red Hat and SuSE's manuals, for example, are very good.

These are my choices for an essential Linux library:

- *Linux in a Nutshell*, by Ellen Siever
- *Running Linux*, by Matt Welsh, Matthias Kalle Dalheimer, Terry Dawson, Lar Kaufman
- *Mastering Regular Expressions*, by By Jeffrey E. F. Friedl
- *Building Secure Servers with Linux*, by Mick Bauer
- *Linux Server Hacks*, by Rob Flickenger
- *Essential System Administration*, by Æleen Frisch
- *Linux Security Cookbook*, by Daniel J. Barrett, Richard Silverman,
- *Learning the bash Shell*, Second Edition, by Cameron Newham, Bill Rosenblatt
- *Linux Network Administrator's Guide*, by Olaf Kirch, Terry Dawson
- *TCP/IP Network Administration*, by Craig Hunt
- *PC Hardware in a Nutshell*, by Robert Bruce Thompson, Barbara Fritchman Thompson

Magazines:

- Linux Journal
- Linux Magazine
- SysAdmin Magazine
- Unix Review

You'll notice there are no distribution-specific publications, and nothing for dummies or idiots. Just good, well-written, thorough Linux materials.

Online References

Hardware Web Sites

Linux FAQ
 http://en.tldp.org/FAQ/Linux-FAQ/index.html

Linux Network Drivers at Scyld Computing Corporation
 http://www.scyld.com/network

Wireless LAN resources for Linux
 http://www.hpl.hp.com/personal/Jean_Tourrilhes/Linux

Linux On Mobile Computers
 http://tuxmobile.org/

Linux Devices
 http://www.linuxdevices.com/

Linux USB Project
 http://www.linux-usb.org/

Linux Firewire
 http://www.linux1394.org/

LinuxPrinting.org
 http://www.linuxprinting.org/

SANE - Scanner Access Now Easy
 http://www.sane-project.org/

Advanced Linux Sound Architecture
 http://www.alsa-project.org/

Open Sound System for Linux
 http://www.4front-tech.com/linux.htmlOSS/

XFree86
 http://www.xfree86.org/

Xouvert, a fork of XFree86, that aims for faster development, and better support of modern video cards
   http://www.xouvert.org/

KernelTrap
   http://kerneltrap.org/

Linux-Dell-laptops
   http://www.whacked.net/ldl/faq/

Debian-laptop mailing list
   http://lists.debian.org/debian-laptop/

Linmodems
   http://www.linmodems.org/

Hardware Guys
   http://www.hardwareguys.com

This is the companion site to the book *PC Hardware in a Nutshell*. It's not Linux-oriented, but it's a great resource all the same.

Usenet

comp.os.linux.hardware
comp.os.linux.portable
comp.os.linux.powerpc
comp.os.linux.x
comp.os.linux.alpha

Microsoft File Types

```
MS Access Database Wiz. Template  MDZ
MS Access Database/Template/Add.  MDB, MDT, MDA, MDW
MS Access Description File         DES
MS Access Menu File                MNU
MS Access Modem File               MDM
MS Archive                         MAR
MS Assembler Cross Reference       CRF, REF
MS Audio/Visual Interleave         AVI
MS Briefcase Database              BFC
MS Chat Animated Character         AVB
MS Clean Boot File                 CB
MS ClipArt Gallery                 CAG
MS Compatibility Database          CAT
MS Compiler Compiled Source Code   COD
MS Debug Information File           DBG
MS Developer Studio Project File   DSP
MS Developer Studio Workspace      DSW
MS DOS Code Page Information        CPI
MS DOS Help                        HLP
MS Draw Palette                    PAL
MS Excel Add-in File               XLL
MS Excel Backup                    XLK
MS Excel Chart                     XLC
MS Excel Dialogue                  XLD
MS Excel Macro                     XLM
MS Excel VBA Module                XLV
MS Excel Worksheet/Add-In/Templ.   XLS, XLA, XLT, XLB
MS Excel Workspace/Workbook        XLW
MS Find Saved Search               FND
MS HyperTerminal Shortcut          HT
MS IE Cascading Style Sheet        CSS
MS IExplorer Connection Wizard     ICW
MS Image Color Matching Profile    ICM
MS Internet Explorer Cache         DAT
MS Language Character Set          NLS
MS Linker Database                 ILK
MS Midi Music                      RMI
MS Money Data                      MNY
```

```
MS Multi-Media Movie            MMM
MS Multiplan Spreadsheet        COL
MS Network Shortcut             MCC
MS Office Assistant Actor       ACT
MS Office Assistant Preview     ACP
MS Office Binder Doc/Temp       OBD
MS Office Binder Template       OBT
MS Office Binder Wizard         OBZ
MS Outlook Message Store        PST
MS Outlook Express Email Folder MBX
MS Outlook Express Email Index  IDX
MS Outlook Express Email Tree   NCH
MS Outlook Express News Message NWS
MS Paint Bitmap                 MSP
MS Personal Address Book        PAB
MS Pictures                     PCS
MS PowerPoint Slides            PPT
MS PowerPoint Template          POT
MS Powerpoint Slideshow         PPS
MS Program Information          PNF
MS Project File                 MPP
MS Query Database               DBF
MS Query Database Index         MDX
MS Rich Text Format Document    RTF
MS ScanDisk/CHKDSK Fragment File CHK
MS Schedule+ Print File         FMT
MS Setup Wizard Dependency File DEP
MS Spell Checker Dictionary     DIC
MS Spelling Auto Correct List   ACL
MS Tip of the Day File          TIP
MS Visual BASIC Include File    BI
MS Visual C++ Compiled Resources RES, APS, RCT
MS Visual C++ Debug File        SBR
MS Visual C++ Definition File   DEF
MS Visual C++ DLL Exports File  EXP
MS Visual C++ Interface Des Lang IDL
MS Visual C++ Object Desc. Lang. ODL
MS Visual C++ Precompiled Header PCH
MS Visual C++ Program Database  PDB, BSC, NCB, IDB
MS Visual C++ Registry Source   RGS
MS Visual C++ Resource File     RC
MS Windows 3.1 True Type Font   TTF
MS Windows 3.x Logo             LGO
MS Windows 3.x Screen Grabber   2GR, 3GR
MS Windows 3.x Screen Saver     SCR
MS Windows 3.x System Font      FON, FOT
MS Windows 95 Password List File PWL
MS Windows 95 Plus! Palette     PAL
MS Windows Address Book         WAB
MS Windows Animated Cursor      ANI
MS Windows Audio Converter      ACM
MS Windows Bitmap               BMP
MS Windows Briefcase Document   BFC
MS Windows Cabinet Archive      CAB
```

```
MS Windows Calendar                CAL
MS Windows Card File               CRD
MS Windows Clipboard File          CLP
MS Windows Control Panel Applet    CPL
MS Windows Cue Cards               CUE
MS Windows Cursor                  CUR
MS Windows Desktop Theme           THEME
MS Windows Disk Map File           DMF
MS Windows Driver (16 bit)         DRV, DLL
MS Windows Driver (16 bit)         EXE, VXD, SYS, DRV
MS Windows Fax Cover               CPE, CPD
MS Windows Help Answer Wizard      AW
MS Windows Help Contents Table     CNT
MS Windows Help File               HLP
MS Windows Help Full Text Search   FTS
MS Windows Help Global Index       GID
MS Windows Help Module             CHM, CHI, CHQ
MS Windows Help Text Search        TSC
MS Windows Icon                    ICO
MS Windows Install Script          INS
MS Windows Library (16 bit)        DLL, DRV, VBX, EXE
MS Windows Library (32 bit)        DLL, TLS, OCX, CPL
MS Windows MetaFile (placeable)    WMF
MS Windows Office Toolbar Button   TBB
MS Windows Password List           PWL
MS Windows Printer Driver          WPD
MS Windows Program (16 bit)        EXE, MOD, BIN
MS Windows Program (32 bit)        EXE, SCR, MOD, SYS
MS Windows Program (WIN386)        EXE
MS Windows Program Group           GRP, GRB
MS Windows Program Information     PIF
MS Windows Registry                DAT, DAO
MS Windows Registry Import File    REG, DAT
MS Windows Resource                RES
MS Windows Shortcut/Link           LNK
MS Windows Sound Mix               MIX
MS Windows SQL Application         APP
MS Windows Swap File               SWP
MS Windows True Type Font          TTF
MS Windows Type Library            TLB, TWD
MS Windows Uninstall Script        ISU
MS Windows Wave Sound              WAV
MS Windows Welcome Bitmap          WBM
MS Word for DOS Document           DOC
MS Word for DOS Font               DAT
MS Word for DOS Printer Def.       PRD
MS Word for DOS Style Sheet        STY
MS Word for Macintosh Document     MCW
MS Word for Windows Document       DOC, DOT, WIZ, WZS, WRI
MS Word for Windows Template       DOT
MS Works Database                  WDB
MS Works Document                  WPS
MS Write Document                  WRI
```

Init Script for CVSD

```
#! /bin/sh
# /etc/init.d/cvsd script for starting cvsd
# copied from the Debian installation of CVSD
# Copyright (C) 2002, 2003, 2004 Arthur de Jong
#
# This program is free software; you can redistribute it and/or modify
# it under the terms of the GNU General Public License as published by
# the Free Software Foundation; either version 2 of the License, or
# (at your option) any later version.
#
# This program is distributed in the hope that it will be useful,
# but WITHOUT ANY WARRANTY; without even the implied warranty of
# MERCHANTABILITY or FITNESS FOR A PARTICULAR PURPOSE.  See the
# GNU General Public License for more details.
#
# You should have received a copy of the GNU General Public License
# along with this program; if not, write to the Free Software
# Foundation, Inc., 59 Temple Place, Suite 330, Boston, MA  02111-1307  USA

CVSD_BIN=/usr/sbin/cvsd
DESC="cvs pserver chroot wrapper"
CVSD_CFG=/etc/cvsd/cvsd.conf

[ -x "$CVSD_BIN" ] || exit 0
[ -f "$CVSD_CFG" ] || exit 0

PIDFILE=`sed -n 's/^ *PidFile *\([^ ]*\) *$/\1/p' < $CVSD_CFG`
[ -n "$PIDFILE" ] && PFO="--pidfile $PIDFILE"

case "$1" in
start)
   echo -n "Starting $DESC: cvsd"
   start-stop-daemon --start --quiet \
                     $PFO \
                     --exec $CVSD_BIN \
                     -- -f $CVSD_CFG \
     || echo -n " already running"
```

```
    echo "."
    ;;
stop)
  echo -n "Stopping $DESC: cvsd"
  start-stop-daemon --stop --quiet  \
                    $PFO \
                    --exec $CVSD_BIN \
    || echo -n " not running"
  echo "."
  [ -n "$PIDFILE" ] && rm -f $PIDFILE
  ;;
restart|force-reload)
  echo -n "Restarting $DESC: cvsd"
  start-stop-daemon --stop --quiet --retry 10 \
                    $PFO \
                    --exec $CVSD_BIN
  [ -n "$PIDFILE" ] && rm -f $PIDFILE
  start-stop-daemon --start --quiet \
                    $PFO \
                    --exec $CVSD_BIN \
                    -- -f $CVSD_CFG \
    || echo -n " not restarted"
  echo "."
  ;;
status)
  echo -n "Status of $DESC: "
  if [ -n "$PIDFILE" ]
  then
    if [ -f "$PIDFILE" ]
    then
      if kill -0 `cat $PIDFILE` > /dev/null 2>&1
      then
        echo "running."
        exit 0
      else
        echo "stopped."
        exit 1
      fi
    else
      echo "stopped."
      exit 3
    fi
  else
    if ps -ef | grep cvsd | grep -v grep > /dev/null 2>&1
    then
      echo "probably running. (no PidFile in cvsd.conf)"
    else
      echo "probably not running. (no PidFile in cvsd.conf)"
      exit 3
    fi
  fi
  ;;
*)
```

```
    echo "Usage: $0 {start|stop|restart|force-reload}" >&2
    exit 1
    ;;
esac

exit 0
```

Index

We'd like to hear your suggestions for improving our indexes. Send email to *index@oreilly.com*.

P

packages
  Apache web servers, documentation
    for, 425
  creating from source code, 56
  Debian (see Debian, packages)
  upgrades using apt-get install
    command, 41
  (see also RPM)
partitions, 200
  boot partition configuration, 210
  fdisk, creating with, 158–159
  filesystems, creating on, 159
  information, displaying, 65
passwd command, 113
  -e option, 107
passwd file, vulnerability, 103
passwords
  managing, 113
  mass changing of, 124
  password file integrity, checking, 117
patches for kernels, installing, 173
PCI bus, displaying connected devices, 59
PerChild MPM (Apache 2.0), 417
Pinfo, 2
ping, 50
  measuring timeserver distance with, 354
PLD (Polished Linux Distribution), 16
Polished Linux Distribution (PLD), 16
pool.ntp.org, 349
POP (Post Office Protocol), 361
POP3 mail servers, 362–370
  building, 362–368
    Courier-Imap, installing, 364
    on Debian, 366
    Postfix, installing, 363
    smtp daemon, verifying
      operation, 364
  common commands, 370
  testing, 368
    smtp with telnet and openssl s_
      client, 368
    TLS/SSL support, 369
    unencrypted POP3 with telnet, 368
Postfix mail servers, 361–394
  authentication to other servers with
    smtp-auth, 378
  Clam Anti-Virus scanner, 406–410
  configuration file, 363
    enabling SASL, 373

couriermlm mailing lists, 387–390
  administration, 389
  creating, 387–389
Cyrus-SASL installation, 372
  verifying support, 373
database file formats, 403
DNS blackhole lists, 403–405
installing, 363
Internet mail
  sending, 370
Internet mail, recieving, 371
log files, 399
messages with attachments, rejecting, 405
mime_header_checks, 405
POP3 mail servers (see POP3 mail servers)
root and postmaster alias files and
    database, 363
SASL libraries, 373
smtp daemon verification, 364
smtpd_sender_restriction directive, 402
SpamAssasin, setup, 410–414
  using amavisd-new, 410
starting, 364
UBE (unsolicited bulk email)
    controls, 398–402
  basic configurations, 399–402
user authentication with
    smtp-auth, 376–378
virtual mailbox domains, 385–387
(see also mail, servers)
(see also security)
/postfix/main.cf
  mail checks, 400–402
  managing unsolicited bulk email, 399
poweroff command, 100
ppid, 89
pre (pre-release candidate) patches, 174
Prefork MPM (Apache 1.3), 416
printers
  finding drivers for, 242
  installing, 243–245
  sharing over networks, 242, 246
    mixed LANS with Samba, 250
    serving Windows clients without
      Samba, 249
    troubleshooting, 253
    users, restricting, 252
    without name resolution, 247
  (see also CUPS)
private keys, 301
  changing, 305

About the Author

Carla Schroder is a Linux and Windows sysadmin who laid hands on her first computer on her 37th birthday. Her first PC was a Macintosh LC II. Next came an IBM clone, a 386sx running MS-DOS 5 and Windows 3.1, with a 14" color display, which was adequate for many pleasant hours of DOOM play. Then in 1997 she discovered Red Hat 5.0, and had a whole new world to explore. She liked the clear separation between the kernel, user-space, and graphical layers, the division of privileges, and found the Unix world to be sane and sensible.

Somewhere along the way she found herself doing freelance consulting for small businesses and home users, doing a little bit of everything: pulling cable, building and repairing computers, training on a number of software applications, networking, building servers, and generally making things go. Users tended to like mixed networks, throwing in Linux, Windows, and other platforms, so making these work together kept the work interesting.

Thanks to computers, the Internet, and DSL, Carla lives on a small horse ranch in the middle of nowhere and works from home writing Linux how-tos for several computer publications, consulting for small businesses, and teaching computer classes to quilting grannies and other fun folks. Nothing beats a brisk round of manure-shoveling for toning the muscles and stimulating the brain. She writes for IBM Developerworks, various Earthweb.com and Jupitermedia.com publications, and *Computer Bits* magazine. She also has an official O'Reilly weblog at *http://weblogs.oreilly.com*, where you may enjoy her deep thoughts and unfocused ramblings.

Carla has a theory that working with horses is great training for a system or network administrator, because just like users they can't be forced to do anything, even when it's good for them. One must employ a canny mix of affection, guile, persuasion, psychology, and Mrs. Pasture's horse cookies to train horses. She has not tried the cookies on human users, but food rewards are a proven training tool for all species.

Carla is living proof that you're never too old to try something new, computers are a heck of a lot of fun, and anyone can learn to do anything.

Colophon

Our look is the result of reader comments, our own experimentation, and feedback from distribution channels. Distinctive covers complement our distinctive approach to technical topics, breathing personality and life into potentially dry subjects.

The image on the cover of *Linux Cookbook* depicts armament workers. In World War I, women found opportunites in the workplace as skilled laborers in armament factories. A Women's Bureau was created to protect the women's jobs, but many returned to the home when the soldiers returned at the war's end. Women's contribution in the workplace was an important element in the growing support for women's suffrage, finally achieved in 1920 with the passing of the 20th Amendment.

During World War II, the number of women who found new jobs and responsibilities increased, with women filling the roles of journalist, nurse, and factory worker. The new wage laborers often found themselves working in poor conditions for low pay. They also encountered discrimination, harassment, and resentment, but they still made tremendous advances in the perception of women's abilities. The image of Rosie the Riveter evokes the attitude of many of the newly empowered women, who took a long-awaited opportunity to increase their strength and freedom.

Colleen Gorman was the production editor and proofreader, and Rachel Wheeler was the copyeditor for *Linux Cookbook*. Genevieve d'Entremont and Claire Cloutier provided quality control. Mary Agner and Meghan Lydon provided production support. John Bickelhaupt wrote the index.

Emma Colby designed the cover of this book, based on a series design by Hanna Dyer and Edie Freedman. The cover image is a 19th-century engraving from *Trades and Occupations*. Clay Fernald produced the cover layout with QuarkXPress 4.1 using Adobe's ITC Garamond font.

David Futato designed the interior layout. The chapter opening images are from *Marvels of the New West: A Vivid Portrayal of the Stupendous Marvels in the Vast Wonderland West of the Missouri River*, by William Thayer (The Henry Bill Publishing Co., 1888), and *The Pioneer History of America: A Popular Account of the Heroes and Adventures*, by Augustus Lynch Mason, A.M. (The Jones Brothers Publishing Company, 1884). This book was converted by Joe Wizda to FrameMaker 5.5.6 with a format conversion tool created by Erik Ray, Jason McIntosh, Neil Walls, and Mike Sierra that uses Perl and XML technologies. The text font is Linotype Birka; the heading font is Adobe Myriad Condensed; and the code font is Lucas-Font's TheSans Mono Condensed. The illustrations that appear in the book were produced by Robert Romano and Jessamyn Read using Macromedia FreeHand MX and Adobe Photoshop CS. The tip and warning icons were drawn by Christopher Bing. This colophon was written by Colleen Gorman.

Better than e-books

Search
inside electronic versions of thousands of books

Browse
books by category. With Safari researching any topic is a snap

Find
answers in an instant

Read books from cover to cover. Or, simply click to the page you need.

Search Safari! The premier electronic reference library for programmers and IT professionals

  Addison Wesley — AdobePress

   Sun microsystems — O'REILLY — SAMS

 A LPHA

  Java — New Riders — Cisco Press

  Microsoft Press — Que — macromedia PRESS

    Peachpit Press — PRENTICE HALL PTR

Related Titles Available from O'Reilly

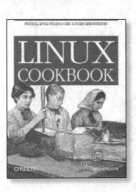

Linux

Building Embedded Linux Systems

Building Secure Servers with Linux

The Complete FreeBSD, *4th Edition*

Even Grues Get Full

Exploring the JDS Linux Desktop

Extreme Programming Pocket Guide

Knoppix Hacks

Learning Red Hat Enterprise Linux and Fedora, *4th Edition*

Linux Cookbook

Linux Device Drivers, *3rd Edition*

Linux in a Nutshell, *4th Edition*

Linux iptables Pocket Reference

Linux Network Administrator's Guide, *3rd Edition*

Linux Pocket Guide

Linux Security Cookbook

Linux Server Hacks

Linux Unwired

Linux Web Server CD Bookshelf, *Version 2.0*

LPI Linux Certification in a Nutshell, *2nd Edition*

Managing RAID on Linux

OpenOffice.org Writer

Programming with Qt, *2nd Edition*

Root of all Evil

Running Linux, *4th Edition*

Samba Pocket Reference, *2nd Edition*

Test Driving Linux

Understanding the Linux Kernel, *2nd Edition*

Understanding Open Source & Free Software Licensing

User Friendly

Using Samba, *3rd Edition*

O'REILLY®

Our books are available at most retail and online bookstores.
To order direct: 1-800-998-9938 • *order@oreilly.com* • *www.oreilly.com*
Online editions of most O'Reilly titles are available by subscription at *safari.oreilly.com*

Keep in touch with O'Reilly

1. Download examples from our books

To find example files for a book, go to:

www.oreilly.com/catalog

select the book, and follow the "Examples" link.

2. Register your O'Reilly books

Register your book at *register.oreilly.com*

Why register your books?
Once you've registered your O'Reilly books you can:

- Win O'Reilly books, T-shirts or discount coupons in our monthly drawing.
- Get special offers available only to registered O'Reilly customers.
- Get catalogs announcing new books (US and UK only).
- Get email notification of new editions of the O'Reilly books you own.

3. Join our email lists

Sign up to get topic-specific email announcements of new books and conferences, special offers, and O'Reilly Network technology newsletters at:

elists.oreilly.com

It's easy to customize your free elists subscription so you'll get exactly the O'Reilly news you want.

4. Get the latest news, tips, and tools

www.oreilly.com

- "Top 100 Sites on the Web"—PC Magazine
- CIO Magazine's Web Business 50 Awards

Our web site contains a library of comprehensive product information (including book excerpts and tables of contents), downloadable software, background articles, interviews with technology leaders, links to relevant sites, book cover art, and more.

5. Work for O'Reilly

Check out our web site for current employment opportunities:

jobs.oreilly.com

6. Contact us

O'Reilly & Associates
1005 Gravenstein Hwy North
Sebastopol, CA 95472 USA

TEL: 707-827-7000 or 800-998-9938
(6am to 5pm PST)

FAX: 707-829-0104

order@oreilly.com
For answers to problems regarding your order or our products. To place a book order online, visit:

www.oreilly.com/order_new

catalog@oreilly.com
To request a copy of our latest catalog.

booktech@oreilly.com
For book content technical questions or corrections.

corporate@oreilly.com
For educational, library, government, and corporate sales.

proposals@oreilly.com
To submit new book proposals to our editors and product managers.

international@oreilly.com
For information about our international distributors or translation queries. For a list of our distributors outside of North America check out:

international.oreilly.com/distributors.html

adoption@oreilly.com
For information about academic use of O'Reilly books, visit:

academic.oreilly.com